GOLD, SPORT, AND COFFEE PLANTING IN MYSORE

GOLD, SPORT, AND COFFEE
PLANTING IN MYSORE

WITH CHAPTERS ON
COFFEE PLANTING IN COORG, THE MYSORE REPRESEN-
TATIVE ASSEMBLY, THE INDIAN CON-
GRESS, CASTE AND THE INDIAN
SILVER QUESTION

BEING THE 38 YEARS' EXPERIENCES OF A MYSORE PLANTER

BY

ROBERT H. ELLIOT

GYAN

Published by

GYAN

Gyan Publishing House
5, Ansari Road
Daryaganj, New Delhi-110002
Phone: 011-47034999, 9811692060
E-mail: books@gyanbooks.com

Distribution Network
gyanbooks.com
India, USA, Canada, UK, Australia

ISBN: 978-93-6208-582-5 (PB)
First Published, 1894

2nd Impression 2024

Printed at: Gyan Press, Delhi.

GOLD, SPORT, AND COFFEE PLANTING IN MYSORE
Author: ROBERT H. ELLIOT

GOLD, SPORT, AND COFFEE PLANTING IN MYSORE.

GOLD, SPORT, AND COFFEE
PLANTING IN MYSORE

WITH CHAPTERS ON

COFFEE PLANTING IN COORG, THE MYSORE REPRESENTATIVE ASSEMBLY, THE INDIAN CONGRESS, CASTE, AND THE INDIAN SILVER QUESTION

BEING THE 38 YEARS' EXPERIENCES OF A MYSORE PLANTER

BY

ROBERT H. ELLIOT

AUTHOR OF "EXPERIENCES OF A PLANTER," "WRITTEN ON THEIR FOREHEADS," ETC.

WITH A MAP

WESTMINSTER

ARCHIBALD CONSTABLE AND CO.

14, PARLIAMENT STREET, S.W.

1894

PREFACE.

IN the year 1871 I published "The Experiences of a Planter in the Jungles of Mysore," and had intended to bring out a new edition of it, but, from various causes, the project was delayed, and when I at last took the matter in hand, I found that so many things had happened since 1871 that it was necessary to write a new book. In this, hardly anything of the "Experiences" has been reproduced, except a very few natural history notes and the chapter on Caste, a subject to which I would particularly call the attention of those interested in Indian missions.

I have been much assisted by informants too numerous for mention here, and can only allude to those who have most conspicuously aided me. Amongst these I am much indebted to my friend Sir K. Sheshadri Iyer, K.C.S.I., Dewan of Mysore, for access given me to information in the possession of the Government, and for returns specially prepared for the book. From my friends Mr. Graham Anderson and Mr. Brooke Mockett, two of the most able and experienced planters in Mysore, I have derived much information and assistance. I am particularly obliged to my friend Dr. Voelcker[1] for many valuable hints, and the

[1] Dr. Voelcker, Consulting Chemist to the Royal Agricultural Society of England, was, by the permission of the Society, employed for upwards of a year by the Government in India; and his "Report on the Improvement of Indian Agriculture" is an elaborate work, of upwards of 400 pages, and contains a large

chapter on manures has had the advantage of being read by him. For information as regards the history of coffee in Coorg I am much indebted to Mr. Meynell, who represents the large interests of Messrs. Matheson and Co. in that province, and indeed, without his aid, I could not at all have done full justice to the subject. To Mr. Grey, manager of the Nundydroog mine, I am indebted for information as regards the gold mines, and for the kind assistance he in many ways afforded me when I visited them last January. I am also obliged to Colonel Grant, Superintendent of the Mysore Revenue, Survey and Settlement Department, for information as regards game, and the proposed Game Act for Mysore.

I had intended to add a chapter on the cultivation of cardamoms and pepper, but have not done so, because, for the want of recent information from those specially engaged in these cultivations, I could not feel confident of doing full justice to the subject. I may, however, say that as regards cardamoms, I have good reason for supposing that there is not much to be added to the chapter on them which appeared in the "Experiences."

Though I have collected many experiences, I am of course aware that many more remain to be collected, and I should feel particularly obliged if planters and those who have any experiences to give me (natural history and sporting information would be very welcome) would be kind enough to do so. These I would propose to incorporate in an improved edition, which I look forward to bringing out when a sufficient amount of additional information has been collected. If those who have any information to give, suggestions to make, or criticisms to offer, would be kind enough to communicate with me, an im-

body of carefully digested information, remarks, and opinions which will be of great value to the Government, and of much practical value to planters, and all tropical agriculturists.

proved edition might be brought out which would be highly valuable to all tropical agriculturists, and all those interested in the various subjects on which I have written.

My Indian address is Bartchinhulla, Saklaspur, Mysore State, and home address, Clifton Park, Kelso, Roxburghshire.

ROBERT H. ELLIOT.

CONTENTS.

CHAPTER I.—INTRODUCTORY.

CHAPTER II.—THE SCENERY AND WATERFALLS OF MYSORE.

CHAPTER III.—MYSORE—ITS GOVERNMENT AND REPRESENTATIVE ASSEMBLY.

CHAPTER IV.—NATURAL HISTORY AND SPORT.

Chapter VI.—Bison Shooting.

CHAPTER VII.—GOLD.

CHAPTER IX.—COFFEE PLANTING IN COORG.

CHAPTER XI.—SHADE.

Chapter XII.—Manure.

CHAPTER XIII.—NURSERIES, TOPPING, HANDLING, PRUNING, ETC.

CHAPTER XIV.—THE DISEASES OF COFFEE.

CHAPTER I.

INTRODUCTORY.—PROGRESS IN MYSORE.

AS I now turn my thoughts back to the year 1855, when, being then in my eighteenth year, I sailed for India to seek my fortunes in the jungles of Mysore, it is difficult to believe that the journey is still the same, or that India is still the same country on the shores of which I landed so long ago. But after all, as a matter of fact, the journey is, practically speaking, not the same, and still less is India the same India which I knew in 1855. For the route across Egypt, which was then partly by rail, partly by water, and partly across the desert in transits, the bumping of which I even now distinctly remember, has been exchanged for the Suez Canal, and the frequent steamers with their accelerated rate of speed have altered all the relations of distances, and on landing at Bombay the traveller of 1855 would now find it difficult to recognize the place. For then there were the old fort walls and ditches, and narrow streets filled with a straggling throng of carts and people, while now the fort walls and ditches no longer exist, and the traveller drives into a city with public buildings, broad roads and beautiful squares and gardens, that would do credit to any capital in the world, and sees around him all the signs of advanced and advancing civilization. Then as, perhaps, he views the scene from the

Tower of the Elphinstone College, and looks down on the beautiful city, on the masts of the shipping lying in the splendid harbour, and on the moving throngs of people to whom we have given peace and order, what thoughts must fill his mind! And what thoughts further, as on turning to view the scene without the city he sees on one side of it the tall chimneys of the numerous mills which have sprung up in recent times, and which tell of the conjunction of English skill and capital with the cheap hand-labour of the East—a combination that is destined, and at no very distant period ahead, to produce remarkable effects. But I must not wander here into the consideration of matters to which I shall again have occasion to refer when I come to remark on the wonderful progress made in India in recent years owing to the introduction of English skill and capital, and shall now briefly describe my route to the western jungles of Mysore.

When I landed in Bombay, in 1855, the journey to the Native State of Mysore, now so easy and simple, was one requiring much time and no small degree of trouble, for the railway lines had then advanced but little—the first twenty miles in all India having been only opened near Bombay in 1853. A land journey then was not to be thought of, and as there were no coasting-steamers, I was compelled to take a passage in a Patama (native sailing craft) which was proceeding down the western coast with a cargo of salt which was stowed away in the after-part of the vessel. Over this was a low roofed and thatched house, the flooring of which was composed of strips of split bamboo laid upon the salt. On this I placed my mattress and bedding. My provisions for the voyage were very simple—a coop with some fowls, some tea, sugar, cooking utensils, and other small necessaries of life. A Portuguese servant I had hired in Bombay cooked my dinner and looked after me generally. We sailed along the sometimes bare, and occasionally palm-fringed, shores with that indifference to time and progress which is often the despair and not unfrequently the envy of Europeans. The hubble-bubble passed from mouth to mouth, and the crew whiled away the evening hours with their monotonous chants. We always anchored at night; sometimes we stopped for fishing, and once ran into a small bay—one of those charming scenic gems which can only be found in the eastern seas—to land some salt and take in cocoa-nuts and other items. As for the port of Mangalore, for which I was bound, it seemed to be, though only about 450 miles from Bombay, an immense distance away, and practically was nearly as far as Bombay is from Suez. At last, after a nine days' sail, we lay to off the mouth of the harbour into which, for reasons best known to himself, the captain of the craft did not choose to enter, and I was taken ashore in a canoe to be kindly received by the judge of the collectorate of South Kanara, to whom I had a letter of introduction.

After spending some pleasant days at Mangalore I set out for Manjarabad, the talook or county which borders on the South Kanara district—in what is called a manshiel—a kind of open-sided cot slung to a bamboo pole which projects far enough in front and rear to be placed with ease on the shoulders of the bearers. Four of these men are brought into play at once, while four others run along to relieve their fellows at intervals. I started in the afternoon, and was carried up the banks of a broad river by the side of which here and there the road wound pleasantly along. In the course of a few hours night fell, and then all nature seemed to come into active life with the hum of insects, the croaking of frogs, and various other indications of an abounding animal life. Presently I was lulled to sleep by the monotonous chant of the bearers—sleep only partially broken when changes of the whole set of bearers had to be made—and awoke the following morning to find myself some fifty miles from the coast, and amidst the gorges of the Ghauts, with vast heights towering upwards, and almost all around, while the river, which had now sunk to what in English ideas would still seem to be one of considerable size, appeared as if it had just emerged from the navel of a mountain-barrier some miles ahead. After a few miles more we passed the last hamlet of what was then called the Company's Country, and leaving the inhabited lands—if indeed in a European sense they may be called so—behind us, began to ascend the twenty miles of forest-clad gorges which lead up into the tableland of Mysore. The ascent was necessarily slow, and it was not till late in the afternoon that I saw, some 500 feet above me, and at a total elevation of about 3,200 feet above sea-level, the white walls of the only planter's bungalow in the southern part of Mysore. To this pioneer of our civilization—Mr. Frederick Green, who had begun work in 1843—I had a letter of introduction, and was most kindly received, and put in the way of acquiring land which I started on and still hold. To the south, in the adjacent little province of Coorg—now, as we shall afterwards see, an extensive coffee-field—the first European plantation had been started the year before, *i.e.*, 1854, while to the north some fifty to seventy miles away the country was, in a European sense, occupied by only three English, or, to be exact, Scotch planters. In 1856 I started active life as a planter on my own account, about twelve miles away from the estate of Mr. Green, while in the same year two other planters—Scotchmen by the way—made their appearance. The southern part of Mysore was thus occupied by four planters, and we were all about twelve miles from each other. It is difficult to conceive the state of isolation in which we lived, and as we were all Europeanly speaking single handed, and could seldom leave home, we often had not for weeks together an opportunity of seeing a single white face, and so rare indeed was a visit from a neighbour that, when one was coming to see me, I used to sit on a hill watching for the first glimpse of him, like a shipwrecked mariner on a desert island watching for the glimpse of a sail on the horizon. As for the Indian mutinies, which broke out the year after I had started work, they might have been going on in Norway as far as we were concerned; none of us at all appreciated the importance and gravity of the events that were occurring, and one of my neighbours said that it was not worth while trying to understand the situation, and that we had better wait for the book that would be sure to come out when things had settled down. And the native population around us appeared to know as little of the mutinies as we did. They seemed to be aware that some disturbance was going on somewhere in the north, and that represented the whole extent of their knowledge of the subject.

I have described our life as having been one of great isolation so far as European society was concerned, but I never felt it to be a dull one, nor did my neighbours ever complain of it, though we only took a holiday of a few weeks in the year. But we had plenty of work, and big game shooting, and the occupation was an interesting one, and as I even now return with pleasure every winter to my planter's life, this proves that my earlier days must have left behind them many pleasant associations. And the occupation and sport were really all we had to depend on. We had few books, nor any means of getting them, for I need hardly say that pioneer planters, who have to keep themselves and their coffee till the latter comes into bearing, cannot afford to buy anything that can be dispensed with. But after all this perhaps was no disadvantage, for, as a great moral philosopher has pointed out, nothing tends to weaken the resources of the mind so much as a miscellaneous course of reading unaccompanied (as it usually is, I may remark) by reflection. The management of people, the business of an estate, the exercise of the inventive powers, the cultivation of method, the sharpening of the observing and combining faculties, which are so well developed by big game shooting, yield real education, or the leading out and development of the mental resources, while books provide the individual merely with instruction which has often a tendency to cramp and even to fossilize the mind.

I have said at the outset, that the journey to India is not the same as it was in 1855, and that still less is India the same India, and I may certainly say that still less is Western Mysore the Western Mysore of 1855, except that its beautiful scenery is as beautiful as ever. For our planting is not like that of Ceylon, where the planter, like the locust, finds a paradise in front to leave a desert in his rear—a desert of bare hill sides from which the beautiful forest has been entirely swept away, while the most valuable constituents of the soil have been washed down to the river beds. And when standing in 1893 on a hill in my district of Manjarabad, and looking around, I can see no sign of change in the landscape from the days of 1855, except that the woodland paths leading from village to village are much more distinctly marked, owing to the great increase of labourers employed in the numerous native and European plantations, which now stretch in an unbroken line along all the western border of Mysore. And no sign of change is apparent, because all the coffee is planted either under the shade of the original forest trees, or under the shade of trees which have been planted to take their place. But all else is practically and largely changed by the agency of a universal progress, which has been brought about by British government and the introduction of British capital, skill, and energy. And this progress, I am glad to be able to say, has benefited all classes of the community, and the labouring classes by far the most of all, and the results as regards these are so striking, so interesting, and so much more widely diffused than could at first sight be thought possible, and are, as I shall show, of such vast importance to the finances of the State, that they are well worthy of special attention. Had the Government been aware of the enormous financial value to the State of the introduction of English capital, I feel sure that much greater efforts would have been made to stimulate European enterprise, and that the progress of India would have been much accelerated all along the line.

When I started my plantation in 1856, the pay of a labourer was 2 rupees 4 annas (4*s.* 6*d.*) a month. It is now, throughout the numerous plantations in Mysore, from six to seven rupees a month, and a labourer can live on about two rupees a month. Such a statement made of any country would indicate a satisfactory degree of progress; but whereas in England it would simply mean a greater ability in the working classes to live in an improved condition, and perhaps some improvement in the condition of the shopkeepers with whom they dealt, in India it means the creation of a social and ever wide-spreading revolution. For when in India capital is introduced, and employment on a large scale is afforded to the people, the poorer of the peasant classes are at once able to free themselves from debt, and the labourers soon save enough money to enable them to start in agriculture, coffee culture, or any culture within their reach. The result of this, in my experience, has been most remarkable. When I started in Manjarabad, for instance, the planters relied solely on labour procured from the adjacent villages. But now the local labourer is almost a thing of the past, for he has taken to agriculture and coffee culture, and now only occasionally works for a short time to earn some money to pay his taxes. When this change began, the planters had of course to go further afield for labour, but merely to produce over again a similar result by enabling labourers from distant villages to do what the local labourers in the coffee districts had done, and thus for labour we have to operate on ever-widening circles, till at last I have heard it remarked that the Kanarese language is often of little use, and the native overseers on my estate have complained that they now often cannot make the labourers understand them. And this of course is not surprising, as at one moment the overseer may have to deal with labourers from any one of the villages between Mysore and the Western Sea, and at another with people from villages in the Madras Presidency, far away on the route to the Bay of Bengal. Field after field, and village after village, has thus been irrigated by that capital for which India thirsts, and which, as we have seen, produces such wide-spreading social effects on the welfare of the people, and, consequently, on the resources of the State—enabling land to be more largely and fully developed, wells to be dug, gardens to be made, and the people to pay with greater ease the demands of the Government. But there is yet another point of great importance to notice as regards the introduction into India of European capital, with its accompanying effects—effects which largely enhance its value—namely, those arising from setting the natives practical examples of both method, skill, and energetic action. I allude to the bearing of these forces upon famine—a subject well worthy of some passing remarks, more especially because in Mysore we can furnish proofs of the value in times of famine of having Europeans settled in the country.

The actual money value of the infuse of English capitalists, and its bearing on the resources of the State, and in enabling the people the better to contest with famine and scarcity, is sufficiently apparent, but it was only when the terrible famine of 1876-77 (which cost Mysore the loss of about a fifth of its population, an immense sum of money, and crippled its resources for years) broke out that the value of having a European agency ready at hand to grapple with famine, and honestly administer the funds available, was absolutely proved. It would be tedious to go into this subject at any length, indeed I have not space to do so, and I can only say that, as far as I could learn, the only satisfactory treatment of the great famine was that initiated and carried out by the planters, or, to be at once just and exact, I should rather say that the system adopted was initiated by one of our leading planters —Mr. Graham Anderson—who, and entirely at his own cost, was the first to start and maintain on his estate a nursery for children. He saw that if the parents could only be relieved of their children the former could work and be able to maintain themselves, while all their efforts would be insufficient to maintain at once themselves and their children. The nursery system that was then initiated by Mr. Anderson, was adopted by other planters who were subsequently aided by the assistance of money from the Mansion House Fund, and Mr. Anderson was formally appointed by the Government as President of the relief operations in the Southern Mysore coffee district, and, owing to his energy, example, and administrative skill, most satisfactory results were obtained. I have before me, and written by Mr. Anderson, a full account of all the famine relief operations he had charge of, showing the assistance afforded by the planters in employing labour from which, owing to the weakness of the people, very little return could be got; and moreover by sheltering in their lines the wandering starvelings who were moving about the country. I can only regret that want of space prevents my going into the subject more in detail. I must, however, at least find room for his concluding remarks, in order to deliver for him a message he has long been desirous of sending to those of the English public who subscribed to the Mansion House Fund.

"If there is one thing," writes Mr. Anderson, "I am certain of it is this, that although some people think that natives have no gratitude, there has never been anything concerning which the natives have been so loud in their praise as the unbounded generosity of the London public, who in time of fearful distress came forward with money to feed and clothe hundreds and thousands of starving poor. Many a poor woman and man have asked me to express blessings to 'the people of my village' who rescued them in their dire distress. Perhaps you can give this message, which, as an outsider, I have never had an opportunity of doing." I only wish I could add that the gratitude of the Government was equal to that of the natives. Yes, Mr. Graham Anderson was an outsider, and the Government (Mysore was under British rule at the time) was evidently determined that he should remain so in the fullest sense of the word, for he never even received a letter of thanks for his valuable and gratuitous services, or the smallest notice of any kind. I have no hesitation in praising most highly the action of the planters, because, though one of them, I was not in India at the time, and, though my estate manager took an early and active part in relief operations, I had nothing personally to do with the famine relief work.

The subject of famines is of such vast importance to the people, the Government, and all who have any stake in India, that I think it well to offer here some remarks on them, and also suggest some measures for their prevention, or perhaps I should rather say for their mitigation.

The causes that would lead to an increase of famines in India were fully pointed out by me in 1871 in the "Experiences of a Planter," in letters to the "Times," and in the evidence I gave when examined by the India Finance Committee of the House of Commons in 1872. There were two principal causes—the spread of the use of money instead of grain as a medium of exchange, and such a restricted development of communications that, while these were sufficient to drain the countries in the interior of their grain, they were not sufficiently developed to enable the grain to be brought back again in sufficient quantities when it was necessary to do so in times of famine. Till, then, communications were developed to an adequate extent, it was quite clear that India would be much more exposed to risk from famines than she was in the days when grain was largely used as a medium of exchange, and when, besides, grain, from the want of communication, was largely kept in the country. The people, in short, in the olden days, and even for some time after I landed in India, hoarded grain, and in times of scarcity they encroached upon their supplies of buried grain, whereas now they hoard money, which in time of famine can go but a very short way in buying grain. The statement that an increase of famines would be sure to ensue from the causes above indicated is amply corroborated by the facts. There is no evidence to show that droughts have increased, but there can be no doubt that in comparatively recent times famines and scarcities have. And in looking over the list of famines from 1769 to 1877, I find that, comparing the first 84 years of the period in question with the years from then up to 1877, famines have more than doubled in number, and scarcities, causing great anxiety to the State, seem certainly to be increasing. That the latter are so we have strong evidence in Mysore, and in looking over the annual addresses of the Dewan at the meeting of the Representative Assembly of Mysore, I am struck with the frequent allusion to scarcities and grave apprehensions of famine. In his address of 1881, only four years after the great famine of 1876-77, the

Dewan refers to "the period of intense anxiety through which the Government and the people have passed owing to the recent failure of the rains. But," he adds, "such occasional failure of rains is almost a normal condition of the Province, and the Government must always remain in constant anxiety as to the fearful results which must follow from them." In his address of 1884 the Dewan says that "the condition of the Province is again causing grave anxiety." In the address of 1886 the Dewan says "this is the first year since the rendition of the Province (in 1881) in which the prospects of the season have caused no anxiety to the Government." But in the address of 1891 lamentations again occur, and we find the Dewan congratulating the members on the narrow escape, owing to rain having fallen just in time, they had had from famine. But our able Dewan—Sir K. Sheshadri Iyer, K.C.I.E.—has taken measures which must ultimately place the Province in a safe position, or at least in as safe a position as it can be placed. He has seen, and it has been amply proved by our experience in the Madras Presidency during the famine of 1876-77, that the only irrigation work that can withstand a serious drought is a deep well, and he has brought out a most admirable measure for encouraging the making of them by the ryots. The principal features of this are that money, to be repaid gradually over a long series of years, is to be advanced by the State on the most easy terms, and that, in the event of a ryot taking a loan, and water not being found, or found in inadequate quantity, the Government takes upon itself the entire loss. But the results from this highly liberal and valuable measure cannot be adequately arrived at for many years to come, and in the meanwhile the risks from famine go on, and as the Dewan has seen that these can only be immediately grappled with by an extension of the railway system, he has always been anxious to make a line to the western frontier of Mysore, if the Madras Government would agree to carry it on to Mangalore on the western coast. But the Madras Government felt itself unable to find funds to carry out the project, and hence Mysore, all along its western frontier, was, from a railway point of view, completely imprisoned, and there seemed to be no prospect of anything being done to connect the Province with the western seaboard for many years to come. However, a Mysore planter last year sought a personal interview with Viscount Cross, the Secretary of State for India, who has always taken a great interest in railway extensions, and the result of this was that Lord Cross initiated action which resulted in prompt steps being taken. Early this year a preliminary survey of the route from a point on the line in the interior of Mysore, *viâ* the Manjarabad Ghaut, to Mangalore was made, and I am in a position to state that the completion of this much and long-wanted line may be regarded as a thing of the near future. After this line has been made a line will be constructed from Hassan to Mysore, *viâ* Holî Nursipur, and Yedatora, and from Mysore a line will be run, *viâ* Nunjengode[1] to Erode, the junction of the Madras and South Indian Railways. I may mention here that Sir Andrew Clarke, in his able Minute of 1879 on Indian Harbours, says that "Mangalore undoubtedly admits of being converted into a useful harbour," though he adds that "the project may lie over until the prospects of a railway connecting it with the interior are better than at present." As the immediate prospects of a line being made are quite secure, it is of great importance to call attention to this matter now, as it is to the manifest interest of both Governments that the harbour of Mangalore should be improved as soon as possible.

[1] When this line is finished the planters of Mysore will have an easy and very direct route by rail to the Nilgiri Hills, and this will be of immense advantage to themselves, and especially to their families.

After having done so much to contend against famine-producing causes, it may seem that the Dewan might rest and be thankful; but it must be considered that, though railways will undoubtedly enable the State to save life, it will have to pay a ruinously heavy charge whenever a widespread and serious drought occurs, and, sooner or later, it seems inevitable that such a drought must occur. And it is therefore perfectly evident, that without the extension of deep wells the province cannot be placed in a thoroughly sound financial position. It is, then, of obvious importance to remove at once the great obstacle that stands in the way of the rapid addition to the number of deep wells. That obstacle, and a most formidable obstacle it is, as I shall fully show, lies in the fact that the present form of land tenure in Mysore (under which also about four-fifths of the land of British India are held) does not provide a sufficient security for investors in landed improvements. By the existing tenure the land is held by the occupier from the State at a rental which is fixed for thirty years, and after that it is liable to augmentation. The Government, it is true, has declared that it will not tax improvements, and that, for instance, if a man digs a well no augmentation of rent will be demanded for the productive power thus added to the land, but it has reserved to itself wide powers of enhancing the rent on general grounds, such as a rise in prices, improved communication, etc., and to what amount the enhancement may go the ryot cannot tell. And hence we find that the representatives in the Mysore Assembly have repeatedly argued that it is owing to the uncertainty as to what the rise of rent may be at the close of each thirty years' period that improvements are not more largely made, and have therefore prayed for a permanently fixed assessment. Now I am not prepared to say that, for the present at any rate, it would be wise to grant a fixed assessment on all lands, but I am quite sure that it would be wise to grant, for the irrigable area watered by a well dug at an occupier's expense, a permanent assessment at the rent now charged on the land. The Government, it is true, would sacrifice the rise it might obtain on the land at the close of each lease, but, as a compensation for this—and an ample compensation I feel sure it would be—the State would save in two ways, for it would never have to grant remissions of revenue on such lands, as it now often has to do in the case of dry lands, and with every well dug the expenditure in time of famine would be diminished. Such a measure, then, as I have proposed, would at once benefit the State and draw out for profitable investment much capital that is now lying idle. There is nothing new, I may add, in this proposal, for it was adopted by the old native rulers, who granted fixed tenures on favourable terms to those making irrigation works at their own expense. An English-speaking Mysore landholder once said to me, "I will not dig wells on my lands under my present tenure, but give me an assessment fixed for ever, and I will dig lots of wells." The present landed policy of the Indian Government[1] is as shallow as it is hidebound. It wants, like a child, to eat its cake and still remain in possession of the article. It is most anxious to see private capital invested in land, and it still wants to retain the power of every thirty years indefinitely augmenting the land revenue on general grounds. Surely it must be apparent to minds of even the humblest calibre that these two things are utterly incompatible!

I may mention that there is a strong party in India in favour of granting at once a permanent assessment at the existing rate of rent for all lands, and in reference to this point it may be interesting to give the following passage

[1] It has imposed this policy on Mysore, and by the terms of the deed of transfer to the Rajah, no alteration in the tenures can be made without the consent of the Supreme Government.

from a letter I once received from the late Prime Minister of Mysore, Mr. Rungacharlu, the minister who started the first Representative Assembly that ever sat in India:

"As you know," he wrote, "I hold decided views on the subject, and the withholding of the permanent assessment is a serious injury to the extensive petty landed interests in the country, and is no gain whatever to the Government. Nearly the whole population of the country are agriculturists, and live in one way or another upon the cultivation of the land. The effect of a permanent settlement will therefore create a greater feeling of security, and to encourage the outlay of capital and labour on land will be beneficial to the entire population. It will thus be quite a national measure reaching all, and not in the interests of a few, and is calculated to develop the capabilities of the land to the utmost. The prospect of the Government ever being benefited by the reservation of an increase of assessment on the unearned increment is a mere dream. Such increase is sure to be resisted or evaded, occasioning meanwhile great discontent. The Government may confidently look to the development of other sources of revenue from the increased prosperity of the people."

But whether the best remedy lies in granting, as I have proposed, a fixed assessment on land brought under well-irrigation at owners' expense, or in granting a permanent assessment for all lands, or, perhaps, in extending the period of lease from thirty to sixty years (and the last proposal would answer fairly well), one thing is certain, and that is, that under the thirty years' tenure system it is impossible to expect such a development of the landed resources of India as will secure the Government from the vast financial losses caused by famine, or at least reduce these losses to a moderate amount. And we have ample evidence to prove that, where adequate security exists, private enterprise will be sure to step in and carry out most extensive and important irrigation works. This has been particularly shown in the proceedings of the Government of the North-West Provinces and Oudh, where the condition of things in the permanently settled districts has been contrasted with that in the temporarily settled, or thirty year lease-hold districts. I have no space to go into the details. They would only weary the general reader, and it is sufficient to say that in the permanently settled districts there has been an immense progress in irrigation carried out by private enterprise; and that, to quote from the proceedings:—"Throughout the whole tract there have been occasional periods of agricultural distress, but it has always been in a mild form, and for a century famines such as have occurred in other parts of India have been unknown." In short, private enterprise, backed by a fair assessment fixed for ever, has driven famine from the tract in question, and this will occur in other parts of India if the Government will only grant tenures sufficiently safe to induce the people to invest their money in wells and permanent improvements. And if further proofs are needed, we have only to turn to Mr. Gribble's valuable memorandum on well irrigation, which is published in the proceedings of the Famine Commission.

In concluding my remarks on famines, I may say that the whole question regarding them is of the greatest practical importance to all employers of labour in India. Our labour market in Mysore was enormously injured by the great famine of 1876-77, when the loss of population amounted to about a million, and when, through the agency of railways, loss of life can be averted in the future, it will only be averted at such a cost as will cripple the resources of the State for years to come, and so lessen its powers for maintaining roads and other works in an efficient state, and developing the resources of the country. The whole of the evils arising from famine then can only be averted by a full development of well irrigation, and this and the development of the landed resources of the country in general can only be effected through the agency of improved tenures. This is a point which all individuals having a stake in India should continuously urge on the attention of the Government.

The reader will remember that when I started in Mysore in 1856, there were only seven European planters in the province. I have lately endeavoured to ascertain the number there are at present, and the Dewan, to whose kindness I have been much indebted for information when writing this book, has supplied me with a specially drawn up return, showing all the information available as regards coffee from the year 1831 up to 1890-91, and by this it seems that there were in 1890-91 662 plantations held by Europeans in Mysore, but there are no means of ascertaining the number of planters. I have referred the return to one of the oldest and most advanced planters, and in his reply he says, "It is impossible to say exactly how many landowners the 662 plantations represent, as several of the plantations in many cases go to make up what we call an estate, but I should not imagine that the number would be more than 300, and in that calculation I have allowed for there being partners in many of the properties." The area held by Europeans was 49,862 acres, and some increase has no doubt since been made to this.

The native plantations amounted to 27,180 in number in 1890-91, with an area of 96,814 acres, but many of these so-called plantations only consist of small patches of coffee. The total area of European and native holdings in 1890-91 was 146,676 acres. There are no means whatever of ascertaining from the returns at my command even approximately the amount of coffee produced. A reasonable calculation, however, based on a general knowledge of the circumstances, makes it probable that the European production of coffee may be put down at about an average of 120,000 cwts. a-year, and the native production at about 172,000 cwts., and if we put the average value of both as low as £3 a cwt. this would make the annual value of the coffee amount to £876,000. I now proceed to close this chapter with some remarks on manufactures in Mysore.

Many years ago I heard the late Mr. Hugh Mason (formerly President of the Manchester Chamber of Commerce) speak at a meeting of the Society of Arts on the manufacturing prospects of India, and, after reviewing the general situation, he said that it is difficult to see what other advantages India could require in order to raise itself into the position of a great manufacturing country. It is true, he said, that the operative there cannot do as much as the operative here, but, he continued, I can remember the time when the operative here could not do nearly as much as he can do now, and there is no reason to doubt but that a similar improvement would take place in the case of the Indian operative.. And when this improvement takes place, and India becomes more known and developed, her great manufacturing capabilities will become fully apparent. India has two very great advantages. She has an abundant, docile, and orderly population, and she obtains from the sun an ample supply of that heat which has to be paid largely for here. When, then, the Indian operative attains to an advanced degree of proficiency—and to this he undoubtedly will attain—the greatest labour competition that the world has ever seen will begin—a competition between the white labourer who requires to be expensively fed, warmly clothed, and well shod, and housed, and the black or brown skinned man who can live cheaply, and work naked, and who is as physically comfortable in a mere shelter as his rival is in a well built dwelling. The Indian peasant already, in the case of wheat, undersells the English farmer, and it seems merely a question of time as to when the Indian operative will undersell his Lancashire rival, and when perhaps calico will come to England, as it once did, from Calicut. And no doubt, some such thoughts were passing through Cobden's mind when he once said, "What ugly ruins our mills will make." We are, however, a considerable way from such remains as the reader will see if he consults the interesting paper on "The Manufactures of India," read by Sir Juland Danvers at a meeting of the Society of Arts on the 24th of April last, and by this it appears that the imports of cloths of English manufacture have increased in recent years. Still India is progressing, and there are now a total of 126 cotton mills in all India. Of these one is in Bangalore, and was opened in 1885. The Mysore Government took 250 shares in it, and to enable the Company to extend the buildings, subsequently lent it on easy terms two lakhs of rupees. There is also another company at work in Bangalore which started as a woollen factory, but which has now set up machines for spinning cotton. The efforts made to push forward industries of all kinds in Mysore are highly creditable to the administration, and I find numerous references in the annual addresses made by the Dewan at the meeting of the Representative Assembly to the desire of the Government to foster any kind of industry that is likely to afford increased employment to the people. A long reference is made in the Dewan's address of 1890, to the endeavours made by the Government to open up the iron wealth of the province, and it was then in correspondence with a native gentleman who had proposed to start iron works in the Malvalli Talook of the Mysore district. The Government, it appears, were prepared to grant most liberal concessions as regards the supply of fuel. But I regret that I have no information as to whether these proposed works have or have not been started. For the information of those who might be inclined to embark in this industry I may mention that a copy of the Dewan's annual addresses always appears in the "Mysore and Coorg Directory," which is a most valuable compilation on all points of importance relating to those provinces. These annual addresses are admirably drawn up and are most interesting to read. The attention shown to the many various points treated of is most remarkable. Nothing seems too great and nothing too small for notice by the Dewan, and it is this even attention all along the line that shows the fine administrator. As one instance to the point I may mention that when attending as a member of the Representative Assembly at Mysore in 1891, I happened to meet the Dewan and some of his officers in the veranda outside the great hall where our meetings were held, and his attention was attracted to a coffee peeler—the invention of a native who thought this a good opportunity for introducing his machines to the notice of the public, and had some cherry coffee at hand to show how they worked. The Dewan at once inspected the machine, saw the coffee put through, and himself turned the handle, and was so satisfied that he ordered some of the machines to be bought and sent for exhibition to the head-quarters of the coffee growing Talooks, or counties, and in his address of 1892 he reports that the machines had been found to be much in favour with the planters who had used them. The state of the box is the best evidence of the goodness of the gardener. But it is time now to draw this chapter to a close. I must, however, find room for a few remarks which will show those who might be inclined to settle in India that their interests are sure to be well attended to by the Government.

During my long Indian experience I have had occasion to represent grievances and wants to Government officers, from district officers to high Indian officials, to officials at the India office, and to more than one Secretary of State for India, and am therefore able to testify directly to their admirable courtesy, patience, and consideration. In the ordinary sense of the word, the planters in the various parts of India are not represented, but as a matter of fact their interests are most efficiently represented, for the officers of the Government, whether civilians or soldier-civilians (and when Mysore was under British rule I had practical experience of both), are distinguished by an amount of energy, industry, and ability, to which I believe it is impossible to find a parallel in the world, and combined with these qualities there is everywhere exhibited a conscientious zeal in promoting in every possible way the interests of the countries committed to their charge. And these officers know that they are at once the administrators and rulers of the land, and, as there is no representative system such as we have in England, freely admit that to them the people have a right to appeal in all matters affecting their interests. This right of personal appeal planters most freely exercise, and in this way are sure, sooner or later, and often with very little delay, to obtain the supply of wants or the redress of grievances. And here I may offer in conclusion one useful hint. The time of officials, and especially of high officials, is very valuable, and every effort should be made to avoid putting them to trouble that can be avoided. The subject to be brought forward should be carefully thought out, and put in the form of a memorandum. This in some cases it is advisable to forward by letter when asking for an interview, while in other cases I have thought it more advisable that the memorandum should be taken with one and read to the official, as this gives a good opportunity for discussing the points in regular order. In the latter case, at the close of the interview, the official will probably ask that the memorandum may be left with him for reference, but it is then better to ask to be allowed to send a well-written copy by post, as this gives an opportunity for making clearer any points that may have been discussed at the interview, and which may require further explanation. It is well always to bear in mind that all high officials, and the heads of districts, are representatives of the Crown, and as such are entitled to a due amount of deference and formality when being personally addressed, or addressed by letter. These are points which are sometimes not sufficiently taken into account by inexperienced persons.

I need hardly say that the remarks last made apply eually to native officials either in Mysore or elsewhere.

In conclusion, I may mention that I have always found the native officials to be most polite, considerate, and obliging, and such, I feel sure, is the general experience of those who have been brought in contact with them.

CHAPTER II.

THE SCENERY AND WATERFALLS OF MYSORE.

MYSORE is a tract of country in Southern India approximating in area to Scotland, and with a general elevation of from two to three thousand feet above the level of the sea. It is commonly spoken of as the Mysore tableland, but this is rather a misleading description if we adopt the dictionary definition of the word tableland as being "a tract of country at once elevated and level," for, though there are in the interior of the province considerable stretches of rolling plains, the so-called tableland presents to the view a country intersected at intervals, more or less remote, with mountain chains, while scattered here and there in the interior of the plateau are isolated rocky hills, or rather hills of rock, termed droogs (Sanscrit, durga, or difficult of access) which sometimes rise to a total height of 5,000 feet above sea level. The surface of the country, too, is often broken by groups, or clusters of rocks, either low or of moderate elevation, composed of immense boulders, the topmost ones of which are often so finely poised as to seem ready to topple over at the slightest touch. The highest point of the plateau is about 3,500 feet, and is crowned as it were by the fine bold range of the Bababooden mountains, which have an average elevation of about 6,000 feet. There are three mountains in Mysore which exceed this elevation, and the highest of them, Mulaìnagiri, is 6,317 feet above the level of the sea. The province, which is completely surrounded by British territory, is flanked on the west and east by the Ghauts, or ranges of hills up the passes through which the traveller ascends on to the tableland, and on the south it is, as it were, pointed off by the Nilgiri hills. The greatest breadth of Mysore from north to south is about 230 miles, and its greatest length from east to west is 290 miles. On the western side one part of the province runs to within ten miles of the sea, though the average distance from it is from thirty to fifty miles. The nearest point to the sea on the eastern side is about 120 miles, and the most southerly extremity of the tableland is 250 miles from the most southerly point of India.

As regards climate, cultivation, and the general appearance of the country, Mysore may be divided into two very distinctly marked tracts—the forest and woodland region which stretches from the foot of the Western Ghauts to distances varying from about twenty to as much as forty-five miles, and the rolling and comparatively speaking treeless plains of the central and eastern parts of the province, which are only occasionally broken by tracts which have some of the characteristics of both. In the western tract are numerous plantations of coffee and cardamoms, and the cereal cultivation consists mainly of rice fields irrigated from perennial streams; while in the central and eastern parts of the tableland, which by far exceed in area the woodland tracts of the west, the cultivation is mainly of the millets and other crops which do not depend on irrigation, though these are interspersed at intervals, more or less remote, with rice fields, the water for which is chiefly derived from tanks, or artificial reservoirs. The rainfall, temperature, and quality of the atmosphere in the western tract varies considerably from those of the open country of the interior. The rainfall of the first varies from sixty to one hundred inches, and, on the crests of the Ghauts, is probably often about 200 inches,[1] while in the interior of the province the rainfall is probably about thirty inches on the average. The temperature of the western tract too is naturally much damper and cooler than that of the rest of the tableland, and at my house within six miles of the crests of the Ghauts at an elevation of about 3,200 feet, the shade temperature at the hottest time of the year and of the day rarely exceeds eighty-five, and such a thing as a hot night is unknown, as the woodland tracts are within reach of the westerly sea breezes, while in the interior the climate is much hotter and drier, and the maximum day temperature of the hot weather is about ninety, and, in very hot seasons, about ninety-five. In the woodland tracts the cold weather and the monsoon months have a very pleasant temperature, and then flannel shirts and light tweeds—in short, English summer clothing—are used, and a blanket is always welcome at night. The climate of Mysore is considered to be a healthy one for Europeans of temperate habits, and who take reasonable care of themselves. As we are now hearing so much of cholera in Europe, it may not be uninteresting to mention that, though the province was under British administration from 1831 to 1881, and there have since been a considerable number of European officials in the employ of the now native government of Mysore, only one European official has died of cholera during that period, and that, though there are a considerable number of planters, only one has been reported to have died of the disease, though his, I am told, was a doubtful case.

I have said that there are marked differences between the western tracts and the remainder of the province, but

[1] No less than 291·53 inches fell this year, between April and the last day of September, at a Cardamom plantation on the crests of the Ghauts.

the most marked difference of course between the forest and woodland country of the west, and the country to the east, lies in the scenery of the two tracts, for, though in the latter case there are occasional bits of attractive landscape, and partially wooded hills, there is nothing at all to compare with the grand forest scenery of the Western Ghauts, or the charming park-like woodlands which stretch into the tableland at varying distances from the crests of the frontier mountains. Everyone who has seen the latter has been struck by their extraordinary and diversified beauty, and last year a friend of mine, who had for a considerable time been travelling all round the world, said to me, as he rode up to my house, "After all I have seen I have seen nothing to equal this." But this, I must add, was the very best of our Western Ghaut park scenery which is mostly contained in the talook or county of Manjarabad which stretches for about twenty-five miles along the western frontier of Mysore, a tract of country so beautiful that the laconic Colonel Wellesley (afterwards the great Duke of Wellington), who rarely put a superfluous word into his dispatches, could not refrain from remarking in one of them on the beautiful appearance of the country.[1] There are two things especially remarkable about this tract. The one is that throughout the best of it there is nothing distinctively Indian in the scenery. Bamboos are rare, and in much of the tract entirely absent, and as the palm trees are always concealed in the woods there is nothing to connect the country with the usual feature of Indian woodland scenery. Another point most worthy of notice is that the scenery which appears to one seeing it for the first time to be entirely natural, is in reality very largely the creation of man. And it has been much improved by his action for,

[1] After the fall of Seringapatam some further military operations were necessary in Manjarabad, and some of Colonel Wellesley's letters were written within a few miles of my bungalow.

as you leave Manjarabad to go northwards the jungle becomes too continuous, and it is the same if you go southwards into the adjacent district of Coorg, and when you compare the last mentioned tracts with Manjarabad you then begin to realize the fact that nature, if left to herself, is apt to become a trifle monotonous. But in Manjarabad man has invaded nature to beautify her and bring her to perfection—cutting down and turning eventually into stretches of grass much of the original forest—leaving blocks of from 50 to 200 acres of wood on the margin of each group of houses, clearing out the jungle in the bottoms for rice cultivation and thus forming what at some seasons appear to be bright green rivers winding through the forest-clad or wooded slopes, and here and there planting on the knolls trees of various widespreading kinds. And yet from the absence of fences, and of cultivation on the uplands, the whole scene appears to be one of Nature's creations, and all the more so because no houses nor farm-buildings are visible, as these are hidden amongst the trees on the margins of the forest lands. Then this long tract of beautifully wooded and watered country is fringed on its western border by the varied mountain crests of the Western Ghauts, while on the east it is traversed by the Hemavati river which is fed by the numerous streams, and brawling burns which descend from the frontier hills. But though Manjarabad has combinations of charms unrivalled in their kind, we must not forget that an examination of of them by no means exhausts the scenery of the Ghauts, for, on the north-western border of Mysore are the falls of Gairsoppa. Often had I read descriptions of them which I once thought must have been too highly coloured, but when I visited the falls some years ago I found that the accounts I had read were not only far below the reality, but that the most important parts of the wonderful combinations of the scenes had either never been noted, or been quite inadequately recorded. I do not now profess to give anything approaching an adequate account of them. Nor indeed do I think it would be possible to do so. But what follows will I think at least be of advantage in directing the attention of the traveller to the best way of observing the varied scenes, and noting the wonderful musical combinations, which are to be heard at these marvellously beautiful falls.

The falls of Gairsoppa are on the Sarawati, or Arrow-born[1] river, which, rising in the western woodland region of Northern Mysore, flows north-west for about sixty-two miles, and then, turning abruptly to the west, precipitates its waters over cliffs about 860 feet in height. When the river is at the full in the south-west monsoon an immense body of water rushes over the precipice, and from calculations made by some engineers, and which are recorded in the book at the Travellers' Bungalow, the volume and height of fall at that time, if taken together, would give a force of water about equal to that of Niagara. But, however that may be, a glance at the high water marks, and a knowledge of the immense rainfall on the crests of the Ghauts during the monsoon months, makes it certain that, at that time of year, the amount of water must be very large. At that season, though, the falls are almost invisible, as they are concealed by vast masses of mist and spray, and even were they visible, as the water then stretches from bank to bank, there would only be one vast monotonous fall. But after the heavy monsoon floods are over, the river above the falls shrinks back as it were into a long deep pool which lies at a distance of several hundred yards from the brink of the precipice, and from this pool the water of the river then escapes by four distinct rapids which have cut their way to the brink of the precipice, and fall over the cliffs in four

[1] So called from its flowing from a source which was supposed to have been formed by a stroke of Rama's arrow.

distinct falls, each one of widely different character from the others. The falls at this season are only 834 feet high, but when the river rises to the full the fall, as I before mentioned, must be about 860 feet, or approximating in height to the loftiest story of the Eiffel Tower. Across the rapids light bridges of bamboo are thrown, at the end of each monsoon. There are thus two ways of crossing the river—one by the pool above the falls where there is a ferry-boat which can take over horses as well as people—the other by the bridges of the rapids—and it is necessary to cross the river because the only bungalow is on the north, or Bombay side of the river, and the best point for seeing the falls is on the southern side. The only way too of reaching the bottom of the falls is by the southern side.

The only objection to these falls is the difficulty of getting at them, owing to their being quite out of the usual travellers' route, and that is why they have, if I may judge by the travellers' book at the bungalow,[1] been, comparatively speaking, rarely visited. Then there is no railway nearer than about ninety miles, and though the falls are only thirty-five miles from the western coast, steamers do not call at the nearest port to them. Nor is it at all even probable that any line will ever be brought nearer to the falls than about sixty miles. It is, too, rather discouraging to have the prospect of a ninety mile road journey to see the falls, and then return by the same route. But I would suggest that a traveller might make a very enjoyable trip by going from Bombay to Hoobli on the South Maharatta line, and, on the way to Gairsoppa visit the Lushington Falls which are about 400 feet in height, the Lalgali Fall which has a series of picturesque rapids and cascades, with a total fall of from 200 to 300 feet, and the Majod falls where the

[1] All travellers are obliged to record their names in these books, and state the time they have stayed, and the sums they have paid for the use of the bungalow.

Bedti-Gangaveli river forms a picturesque waterfall leaping in a series of cascades over cliffs varying in height from 100 to 200 feet in height, and together 800 feet high. I have not visited any of these last named falls. An account of them and other places of interest in the Kanara district is given in the "Bombay Gazetteer" for Kanara,[1] which gives a complete history of this interesting district, and is a book which the traveller should buy, as it is well worthy of a place in any library. I now proceed to give an account of my visit to the Gairsoppa Falls.

On the 12th of January, 1886 (I should not advise the traveller to visit the falls earlier than November 1st nor later than the middle of January, as the water lessens after the latter date), I arrived at the Travellers' Bungalow at the Falls, after having travelled there by the coast route from Bombay, which I found so troublesome that I cannot recommend its adoption. The bungalow, which is about thirty-five miles from the western coast, and on ground 1,800 feet above sea level, is situated in a truly romantic spot (in fact rather too romantic if we take the possibility of an earthquake into consideration), for it is close to the edge of a gorge 900 feet deep, and in full view of the face of the precipice over which the waters of the Arrowborn river precipitate themselves on their way to the western sea. To north, south, east, and west stretch hills and vales for the most part covered with the evergreen forest, and only here and there showing grassy slopes and summits. On the opposite side of the gorge as you peer down into it you can see emerging from the edge of the jungle about half way down from the top of the side of the gorge what looks like a long ladder of stone, but which really consists of the rough steps by which alone the bottom of the falls can be reached.

[1] "Gazetteer of the Bombay Presidency," vol. xv. Kanara, Bombay. Printed at the Government Central Press, 1883.

On the following morning I proceeded to cross the river by the bridges over the rapids. The first rapid is that of the Rajah Fall, the water of which shoots sheer from the cliff, and, without even touching a rock, falls 830 feet into a pool 132 feet deep. After crossing the bridge you sometimes walk through, and sometimes clamber over, the vast assemblage of rocks and huge boulders which form the bed of the river, and are deeply submerged when the river is full. The sight here is extremely curious and interesting as, after leaving the bridge of the Rajah rapid, there are about 1,000 feet of rock and boulders to pass through or over before you reach the next rapid, and, when half way, there would be nothing to show that you were not wandering through a mere wilderness of rocks were it not for the unceasing thunder, far below, from the bottom of the Rajah Fall. The next rapid to be crossed is that of the Roarer, which takes, before it goes over the precipice a most singular course—first flowing into a basin at the edge of the cliff, and then leaving this in a northerly direction, after which it rushes down a steep stony trough to fall into the same deep pool which receives the water of the Rajah Fall. After crossing the bridge of the Roarer rapid the bed of the river has again to be traversed and at a distance of about 700 feet you reach the rapid of the Rocket. This is a fall of wonderful beauty, for the water projects itself sheer from the cliff to fall about 100 feet on to a vast projecting piece, or rather buttress of rock, which causes the water to shoot out into a rocket-like course from which are thrown off wonderfully beautiful jets, and arrowy shoots of water, and spray, and foam, which seem to resemble falling stars or shooting meteors. You then pass over another section of the river bed for about 500 feet till you reach the rapid, or rather stream, of the la Dame Blanche Fall which glides gently over the precipice in a broad foaming silvery sheet. From the first rapid to the last the distance is about 733 yards. I have met with no estimate of the total width of the fall when the river is in full flood, but it can hardly be less than half a mile wide, and the depth of the water, as one can see from the high water mark, must be very great. It is interesting to note on the tops of the boulders here and there the circular stones that have, during each monsoon, been whirling round and round, each one in its own pothole.

After crossing the last bridge you then walk over the rocks into the forest beyond and strike the path which leads down through the forest on the Mysore side of the river, to a point called Watkin's platform—an open-sided shed about 100 feet below the top of the falls, and which commands a view of the gorge below the falls, and a fair, though rather distant view of the falls. When approaching the platform I was positively startled by a vast shrieking clang which suddenly burst on the ear and seemed to fill the air. This I afterwards found had come from the semi-cavernous gorge of rock about half a mile away, into which fall the waters of the Rajah and Roarer rapids, and though I afterwards heard somewhat similar sounds issuing from these falls, I never heard again anything approaching to this singular and startling burst of sound. These sounds have often been remarked upon, but no one seems to have attempted to trace their cause, but they most probably arise from the escape of air which has been driven by the falling waters into some deep fissures of the rock.

Having thus taken a general view of the situation, I then returned to the bungalow for breakfast, and in the afternoon at about two o'clock returned to Watkin's platform by the route of the ferry across the pool, and, with my companion, set out for the foot of the falls, first of all by a steep winding path, and then by a flight of very rough and uneven steps which had been formed by placing stones in places on and between the rocks. When descending, we often paused to view the constantly changing scene, for, as we got lower and lower, the rainbow hues across each fall, which were at first widely broken by the masses of cliff stretching between the falls, came closer and closer, till at last, when we reached the region where the spray of all the falls was mingled, the iris hues stretched across the gorge in an unbroken band of colour. At length, as we neared the foot of the fall, we reached a small open-sided shed, which had recently been erected on the occasion of the Maharajah of Mysore's visit. From this, which was probably fifty feet from the bottom of the gorge and about 100 yards from the falls, an admirable view was obtained of the entire situation, and we began to realize how impossible it is to form any adequate conception of the falls from the top, or from the higher sides of the gorge. We next descended to the bottom of the gorge, where the ground is strewn with vast boulders of rock, which had evidently fallen from the cliff as it had been eaten back by waters toiling through countless bygone ages. Many of these masses of rock lie at some distance from the foot of the falls, and on the partially decayed surfaces of some of them vegetation had evidently been flourishing for an indefinite period of time. Huge masses of rocks and boulders, as you look down the river, seem almost to block up its route towards the western sea, and indeed so completely seem to fill up the pass, that one seemed to be standing at the bottom of a rock-bound hollow which had been excavated by the agency of Nature, after a toil through periods of time far beyond the calculations of man.

As I found that the rocks at the foot of the falls were covered with a slimy mud, and as I was suffering slightly from a damaged foot, I presently returned to the shed, while my companion proceeded to explore the bed of the gorge further down the river. The floor of the shed had been strewed with straw, and I lay down at full length, partly to rest and partly to examine the situation more minutely, for the height is so great that it is impossible adequately to survey the scene in any other position. And then, when you have stillness and solitude, and when the body is in complete repose, there pour in on eye and ear floods of impressions so quickly varying that the mind feels quite unable to record them, and there is finally nothing left behind but a vague and indescribable sensation of all that is grand and beautiful and melodious in nature. For there are vast heights and gloomy depths and recesses, and varied forms of falling waters, and in the general surroundings everything to convey exalted ideas of grandeur to the mind, but grandeur accompanied by exquisite beauty, in colour, in the graceful movement of animal life, and in the varying sounds of falling waters—the charm of the iris hues which ever beautify the falling waters—beauty in the varied colours of the rocks, and in the plants and ferns growing in the fissures of the cliff—beauty in exquisite forms of motion—of water varied in countless ways as it descends from the four separate falls—beauty in the unceasing movements of countless swallows, mingled here and there with specimens of the Alpine swift and the pretty blue-hued rock pigeons, which build their nests on the ledges of the cliffs, and are constantly to be seen flying across the falls. Then there are the unceasing and ever varying sounds of falling waters, grand in their totality, grand and melodious in their separate cadences—the deep bass of the Rajah, sometimes like cannon thundering in the distance, and sometimes like the regular tolling of some vast Titanic bell; sounds of most varied and brilliant music from the Rocket; the jagged note of the Roarer, as its waters rush down their steep, stony trough; the eerie and mysterious sounds which, sometimes like a mingling of startling shrieks and clangs, and sometimes, to the active imagination, like the far-off lamentations of imprisoned spirits,[1] occasionally rise from the semi-cavernous chasm which has been hollowed out behind the great pool beneath the cliff; the gentle murmuring note of the White Lady Fall, tangled threads of sound from which fall in fitful cadences on the ear as the wind rises and falls athwart the falls; and lastly, but by no means leastly, the undulating and endless varieties of sounds which, having broken away from their original source, are ever wandering and echoing around the rock-bound gorge. Beautiful indeed and altogether indescribable are the elements of melody which are created by the falling waters of the Arrowborn river!

And the music, too, seemed to be for ever varying, for the choral odes which were sweetly chanted to the ear were not perpetually continuous, and at times, owing to some change in the direction of the wind as it swirled around the gorge, the choral element was subordinated to the deep thunder of the Rajah Fall, or the vague tumult of startling discords which arose at intervals from the semi-cavernous walls of the pool into which plunge the waters of the Rajah and Roarer Falls. And then these sounds would gradually lose their predominance, and the more uniform sounds in which all the four falls joined would once more fill the air and charm the ear. And thus the attention could never be lulled to sleep, for here monotony was not, and the mind was always kept in an attitude of expectancy for the variations in the music which were sure to come, and, so far as they reached the ear, were never the same combinations of sounds that had been heard before. All the elements of melody were here, indeed, in profuse abundance, and it seemed as if they only required to be caught by some master hand and strung into methodical musical combinations to yield to the mind and

[1] The native idea.

feelings those exquisite sensations which music alone can in any effective degree convey.

And besides the effects we have noticed, there is the motion of colour constantly, though gradually, shifting and altering, for, as the sun declines, the rainbow hues move steadily upwards on the face of the falls, and the colours of the rocks, which are of varying shades of purple and yellow, continually alter in character with the sinking day. But the finest combined effects of beauty and grandeur are, perhaps, most fully felt when, late in the afternoon, the eye wanders delighted over the vast combination of lofty cliffs and falling waters to rest finally far above on the iris tints of the Rajah and Roarer Falls, through the colours of which myriads of swallows incessantly wheel on lightsome wing, mingled with the quick, darting movement of the Alpine swifts, and the gentle flight of the blue rock pigeons, which occasionally wing their way through the mazy throng. For there the eye is ever delighted with the charm of colour and of those endless variations of graceful movement which continuously convey pleasurable sensations to the mind. But how could eye or ear ever tire of those rare combinations of form, colour, motion and rhythmic sounds which fill the mind with an exalted sense of feeling and of pleasure, and the conscious heart with exquisite sensations far beyond the power of language to describe?

Presently my companion returned and aroused me from my state of dreamy pleasure, and I turned reluctantly away from the scene as the rainbow colours were, with the sinking sun, beginning to disappear from the topmost heights of the falls.

Delightful indeed were the brilliant and varied scenes I have been attempting to describe, and after them the remainder was by comparison tame, but still I found that, as I took a canoe the following evening and rowed up the forest-margined pool from which the rapids emerge, that the minor scenes at the falls have exquisite charms of their own. And then it was that I realized that, varying though the scale may be, there is everywhere about the falls the same beauty of detail and beauty of combined effect, and that, too, unaccompanied by a single jarring note. For nowhere can you say, as you can often say in viewing scenes elsewhere, "leave out this, or alter that, and the scene would be perfect," and in none of the scenes about the falls does anything poor, or base, or mean, or uninteresting strike the eye, and as I rowed slowly up the pool I felt that the mind was both charmed and soothed by the exquisite repose of the scene, which is only broken, if indeed it can be said to be broken, by the beautiful birds and gaily painted kingfishers which occasionally wing their way across the water, or flit along the margin of the forest-clad shore. As you look towards the West the eye wanders over the wild assemblage of water-worn rocks and boulders which intervene between the pool and the head of the falls, to rest finally on the distant hills, covered mostly to their tips with the evergreen forest, while on looking up the river you see that it is flanked by woods on either hand, and as you lose sight of the water as it bends towards the south, the eye glances upwards to hills of moderate height, wooded in the hollows, and showing on the ridges grassy vistas dotted with occasional trees.

On returning, I went lower down in the pool than the point I had started at, and passed a number of rocks worn into all sorts of curious shapes, and one of these leaned, like some gigantic Saurian, over the flood. As we neared the rapids, one felt that one would by no means like to run any risk of being drawn into one of them, and I was by no means anxious to go nearer to them than the boatmen wished. One of them told me that the natives sometimes descended the cliffs between the Roarer and the Rocket

Falls in order to carry off the fledglings from the nests of the blue rock pigeons, and said that several lives had thus been lost. He said that there was no way of reaching the bottom of the cliff, and rather quaintly added, "Those who came up again came up, and those who did not, died." He said that some European had once put what was evidently dynamite into the pool. A great explosion followed, which killed a large number of fish, many of which were washed over the falls.

In the evening I sat for a long time in the bungalow veranda smoking my cigar, and looking dreamily out at the moonlit falls, and observing from time to time the scenic changes that were produced by the great masses of mist which drifted up the gorge below me to be dispersed as they touched the cliffs, and presenting, as they did so, most charming pictures. In the morning, too, beautiful effects were to be seen, as masses of mist arose from the chasm of the Rajah to flit in fleecy fragments across the face of the falls. But the scenes about this spot are of endless variety, and I must allow myself to mention only one more, which my companion saw one morning from Watkin's platform when the iris hues were on the pool below the falls, which, as the spray fell into it, seemed like a mass of golden water dotted all over, as if yellow tinted rain were falling into it. On some occasions visitors have illuminated the falls with fireworks, and by floating over the falls ignited bundles of straw soaked in paraffin, and I regret that I had not thought of following their example.

Next morning I set out on a drive of about 150 miles to my plantations in Manjarabad. As we left the falls, we passed, and close to the river pool above them, a tree covered with fruit which was being eaten by green pigeons and other birds, and on looking up into it I was surprised, as it is an animal of nocturnal habits, to see a large and beautiful flying squirrel peering at me with a quiet but by no means apprehensive eye. I was strongly tempted to shoot it for the sake of its skin, but my companion, who had been much affected by the beauties of the falls, said that it would be a sacrilege to shoot anything so near them. So I spared his feelings and the poor squirrel, and am now very glad to think that I did so. I may here mention that the traveller, though he sets out early in the morning and late in the afternoon, very rarely sees anything in the shape of big game, even though the jungles he may be driving through may abound with it, and the sole exception I can remember, after numerous journeys through them, occurred on the occasion of my drive home from the falls, when, early one morning, a tiger bounded across the road at a distance of about 100 yards ahead. It is also worthy of remark that you very seldom see a snake, and, though I landed on the Western coast at Carwar and travelled by easy stages by way of the falls to my estate, I did not see a single snake during the whole course of the journey.

As it is probable that this account of the Gairsoppa Falls may induce travellers to visit them, I think it may be useful to give an account of the Cauvery Falls on the southern frontier of Mysore, which are well worthy of a visit, and easily accessible. The best time for visiting them is generally said to be August, or not later than the middle of September, though when I visited them on the 25th of that month last year, the river, though not in full flood, had an ample supply of water in it, and, from Mr. Bowring's description of his visit to them on November 21st,[1] there must still, up to that date, be a considerable flow in the river. From my own experience, I feel sure that the best time to see these falls is after the great floods have subsided, as the water then is clear, or nearly

[1] "Eastern Experiences," by L. Bowring, C.S.I.; Henry S. King and Co., London, 1871. Before visiting Mysore the traveller should certainly buy or consult this book.

so, and the effects, as in the case of the Gairsoppa Falls, are far more varied and brilliant. There is one point I would here particularly impress on the traveller, and that is, that when visiting falls such as those of Gairsoppa and the Cauvery, which present a great variety of scenic effects, and are not merely monotonous single masses of water, he should devote at least two clear days to them, *i.e.*, he should arrive on one day, remain two days, and leave on the fourth day. He should also select a time when there is a sufficiency of moonlight. I was particularly impressed with the first point, because I most thoroughly enjoyed my visit to Gairsoppa as I had two clear days there, whereas my visit to the Cauvery Falls was attended with that sense of hurry which, if not destructive of all enjoyment, leaves behind on the mind a feeling that many points in the scenes must have been either missed or quite inadequately observed. The account of my visit to these falls, however, may at least be useful in showing a traveller short of time how to visit them with the least possible expenditure of it.

I left Bangalore, then, on the morning of Thursday, September 24th, 1891, by the 8.20 a.m. train, for the Mudoor Railway Station, on the line to Mysore city, and arrived there shortly after midday. I then had luncheon at the station, and left for the Malvalli Travellers' Bungalow at a little before three, in a carriage I had sent on from Bangalore with two pairs of horses (it is advisable to have an extra pair posted), and arrived at my destination shortly after five. To this bungalow, which is about fourteen miles from the falls, I had previously sent on with my native servants bedding and mosquito curtains, and the means necessary to prepare meals for the party. Reports had reached us of creeping things being abroad in this bungalow, and my servant had been particularly enjoined to look out for, and, as far as possible, guard against them. This he had done by putting the bedsteads in the sun and doing what further he could. But notwithstanding his assurances of safety, one of the ladies of the party insisted that, from all she had heard, there must be creeping things somewhere about. The servant listened with an air of respectful attention to all she had to say, and, when she had quite done, said with quiet persistence, and much to our amusement, " What Missus says is true, but there are no bugs," and I am glad to say that he was justified in making the assertion. We rose very early the following morning, started at 4.20, at 6.20 arrived at the bungalow near the falls, and, after a little delay to get a cup of tea, drove at once to the nearest fall. But I must here pause for a few moments to describe the general situation of the river, the islands formed by its splitting into two distinct branches, and the position of the fall—a total situation which is not easily comprehended without the aid of a map.

The Cauvery Falls are on the river of that name, which rises in Coorg, and, after a run of 646 miles to the south-east, falls into the Bay of Bengal about midway between Madras and Cape Comorin. Before reaching Seringapatam (which is on an island in the river) it is joined by the Hemavati which rises to the north of Manjarabad and, as we have seen, skirts the eastern border of that talook, or county. As the Hemavati sends down a large body of water the source of which is more distant from the sea than the spot in Coorg which is called the head of the Cauvery, I may remark in passing that it is singular that the latter should have been regarded as the source of this fine river, which really rises in Mysore. But, rise where it may, it at last arrives at a point on the southern frontier of Mysore where the bed of the Cauvery splits into two channels and forms the island of Hegora, which is about three miles long, and from a quarter of a mile to a mile wide, and, by a rather curious coincidence, almost exactly the size of the island on which the fortress of Seringapatam has been built. The northern branch of the river washes the Mysore frontier and this, after about two miles, again divides, or rather a small branch diverges to the north and, forming a loop, cuts away from the mainland the island of Ettikoor, and there falls into the northern branch of the river by various cascades, and just below the point where the falls on the main northern branch occur. This group of falls is called Gangana Chuckee.

The southern branch of the river on the Madras side flows as a single stream for about half a mile, and then splits off some of its water into various channels, but forming nothing worthy of the name of an island till it severs from the mainland the island of Hegora, a strip of land about two furlongs at the widest, and less than a mile in length. To the south of this the main body of the water goes to form lower down the fine series of cascades and falls called the Bar Chuckee, while a comparatively small body of water goes to the left to form the pretty series of cascades and steep runnels of water which fall, though at a different point of the compass from the main falls, into the wide pool at the foot of the Bar Chuckee Falls. After this necessary digression I now proceed to narrate what I saw and did.

I drove, then, after a short delay at the bungalow, to the Gangana Chuckee Falls, passing on the way the temple of Sivasamudrum, and various buildings connected with it, and leaving the carriage, walked down towards the falls, passing on the right Pir's Tomb, the grave of a Mahometan priest of that name, and went to a point just below it, from which a fine general view of these falls and the river can be obtained. Glancing upwards, the view of the river, as the waters race down their steep stony bed towards the falls amidst numerous projecting rocks, is extremely grand and picturesque. Then at a point just below the spot I was standing on, the water plunged down a nearly precipitous descent, from which it apparently (for the spray prevented one seeing exactly) fell perpendicularly into the pool below, sending up as it did so gossamer veils of spray full of fleeting, faint, and ever varying iris hues. This pool is flanked, and probably about 100 yards below the foot of the previously mentioned fall, on the northern side by a precipice about 250 feet high, down which, in four separate cascades, falls the water of the branch of the river which cuts off the small island of Ettikoor. On the side of the precipice next to the great fall of the main river stands a piece of tree-clad rocky ground, apparently about 50 feet higher than the precipice, and this is flanked by a rapid at the top, passing into a cascade lower down, which then held but little water, but which in floods must add much to the beauty of the scene. After viewing the scene for some time, I returned to the carriage, and drove across the island to visit the Bar Chuckee Falls, and left the carriage at a point where the road begins to descend into the valley into which the southern branch of the river precipitates itself. I then advanced to a point on the right of the road from which a fine general view can be obtained, though it is rather too distant as regards the main body of the falls, and, as I reached the point in question, came suddenly into view of such a number of separate falls and cascades that a description of them is extremely difficult. For, on the opposite side of the valley, I counted no less than thirteen, which leap partly over one side of a horseshoe shaped precipice which had evidently, from the huge boulders in the channel below, been eaten back into the side of the precipice, and partly shoot out through various hidden channels which the waters have deeply cut through a huge semi-circular platform of rock which overhangs the valley below. As they thus shoot out the effect is extremely striking and picturesque, and their resemblance to the spokes of light from a star no doubt caused the natives to give the very appropriate name of Chuckee (pronounced Chickee—Kanarese for star) to these beautiful falls. This semicircular platform of rock stands on one side of the river-bed, next to this we have the horseshoe-shaped precipice I have mentioned, and next to that again, as it were by way of quietly beautiful contrast, there is a vast sheet of steeply sloping rock, which is completely covered by a thin coating of white, and everywhere foaming water. When the river is at the full this fine series of falls and cascades vanishes, and is replaced, as in the case of the falls at Gairsoppa, by one great fall about half a mile wide.

After looking at this beautiful scene, the eye wanders next over some jungle-clad slopes on the western side of the main falls, to dwell on a series of cascades and racing waters which descend through channels flanked on either side by scrubby plants and trees—a series which arises from a branch which diverges about a mile higher up the river, and the cascades and runnels of water of which are scattered round precipitous slopes right up to, and immediately below, the point on which I was standing. All the falls and cascades unite in a pool below of great width, from which the water escapes through a narrow gorge, to join, further down, the river branch on which are the Gangana Chuckee Falls. The general effect here appears to be that you are looking at falls and cascades proceeding from two different rivers, the one flowing from the south and the other from the west, and the effect is the same at the first described falls. The general height of all the falls is said to be from 200 to 250 feet, and in Mr. Bowring's "Eastern Experiences" 300 feet, but I can find no account, and could hear of no particulars, as to when or how measurements were taken, as in the case of the falls at Gairsoppa, which were carefully surveyed by officers of the Indian Navy. I was particularly struck with the absence of bird life at these falls, and only saw two small birds, and one hawk, and a small flight of what in the distance appeared to be pigeons, which alit on a rock at the foot of one of the falls.

It is impossible to refrain from contrasting these falls with those at Gairsoppa. The Cauvery Falls have indeed much beauty and grandeur in river, and varied waterfall scenery, and had I not seen the Gairsoppa Falls I should have thought that it would have been difficult to find anywhere in the world scenes more varied and beautiful. But the beauties of the falls of Cauvery are set in comparatively speaking sterile surroundings of rock and scrubby jungle, trees and shrubs scattered over ground partly undulating, and partly over hills of moderate height and uninteresting form. Then the grandeur arising from their great height, and the charms of the varied sounds of the falls of Gairsoppa, and the marvellously beautiful effects of graceful bird life wheeling and darting amidst the iris hues of the falls, and the setting of the whole scene amidst the tropical wealth of the evergreen forest of the Western Ghauts, afford combinations which far exceed those of the Cauvery Falls. I have no hesitation in saying, as a traveller to the falls of Gairsoppa has said before, that they alone would repay one for all the trouble of the voyage to India. But, beautiful and grand as they undoubtedly are, I cannot quite say the same of the Cauvery falls, though I can with confidence say that if the traveller leaves India without seeing them he will certainly have missed one of the scenes best worth seeing in it.

After spending some time at the Bar Chuckee Falls I then drove back to the bungalow and, leaving the carriage there, walked rather more than half a mile to the bridge which connects the island with the Madras side of the river, and which I closely examined, as it is a most curious and interesting specimen of the work of native engineers, and as it has withstood the floods of about seventy years, one of which passed over the roadway of the bridge to a depth of three feet, is most highly creditable to native workmanship. A similar bridge connects the island with the Mysore side of the river, and both bridges were repaired at his own cost by a native in the employ of the Mysore Government, who in recognition of this important work, received from the British Government, for himself and his heirs (who are bound to keep up the bridges) land yielding an annual revenue of £800, and of £900 from the Mysore Government.

The bridge I now proceeded to examine. It is built entirely of stone without any mortar or cement, and is supported on two rows of single block stone pillars standing on slabs of stone placed on the river bed. Those pillars are about nine feet high and eight feet apart. On the top of each pillar is first of all a thick block of stone projecting about eighteen inches from the pillar on its upper and lower sides. Then on this was a rather thicker block of stone, and on the top of all cross beams of solid single stones had been laid, and from one cross beam to another were solid and closely put together slabs of stones, some of which were eighteen inches wide, and some rather wider, thus making a roadway above so narrow that two carriages cannot pass each other. In order to strengthen the pillars and keep them in position, a flat slab of stone had been laid on the bed of the river, from the base of the lower pillar to within about two feet of the upper one, and between the end of this slab and the pillar a thick, high block of stone had been wedged. In this bridge there were 109 pairs of pillars, giving a total length of about 1,000 feet. I was struck with the difference in the age of the pillars, and with the fact that, whereas some were plain, roughly hewn pillars, others, which had been dressed and chiselled into various forms, were evidently of great antiquity, and I was subsequently informed by the clerk of the proprietor of the island that the latter had been procured from ruined temples in the neighbourhood. These bridges at first sight seem to be curved in a slight loop up the stream, but a closer examination shows that they have been built in several lines, first slightly up the stream and then advancing by several straight lines to a blunt arrow-like point in the centre of the river, and this was evidently to enable the bridges the better to resist the heavy floods, one of which, as I have previously mentioned, went no less than three feet over the roadway. As you stand on the edge of the river and look along the centre of the rows of pillars the effect is very curious, as they then present the appearance of a long colonnade of pillars of various shapes, with a flat roof of solid slabs of stone overhead.

After thoroughly inspecting the bridge, I lay for some time in the shade of a tree which stood on the bank of the river about fifty yards below the bridge, and awaited the arrival of the carriage, which I had sent for as the day was getting hot, and as I thus lay languidly observing the long colonnade, and the water which rapidly flowed between the pillars, and looked up the river as it stretched away to the north-west, and enjoyed the cool air which gently moved along the water, I felt a quiet sense of enjoyment which gave me a greater, and certainly a more lasting, sense of pleasure than I had experienced when visiting the beautiful falls I have just endeavoured to describe. I mention this for the moral, which is, that to enjoy scenery the body must be comfortable and in complete repose. I would also add that you must be alone, or practically alone, by being out of sight or hearing of your companions. Presently I was aroused by the rumble of the carriage, and, collecting my party, returned to the bungalow for luncheon. At about half past four the carriage was brought round, and we drove to our temporary home to dinner, and on the following day reached Bangalore at two o'clock, the whole trip having thus occupied about sixty hours.

CHAPTER III.

MYSORE—ITS HISTORY, GOVERNMENT, AND REPRESENTATIVE ASSEMBLY.

IN my last chapter I gave a description of Mysore and its waterfalls. In the present chapter I purpose very briefly remarking on its history, government, and representative assembly, and shall conclude by contrasting the last with the so-called National Indian Congress.

In his Report of December, 1804, the Acting Resident of Mysore, Colonel Mark Wilks, observed that "the territories composing the present dominion of His Highness the Rajah of Mysore had, from the remotest periods of tradition, been held by a number of polygars and petty Rajahs, whose possessions were incessantly enlarged, diminished, or alienated, by a series of revolutions which it would perhaps be impossible to trace, and unprofitable to describe," and it is interesting to note how little, at that time, seems to have been known about the history of the kingdoms we conquered. But all doubts as to the early history of Mysore have now been removed, and the reader will find in Mr. Rice's admirable gazetteer of Mysore a minute history of the country accompanied by coloured maps which show at a glance the numerous transitions which the territories now comprised under the head of Mysore have undergone in former times, but as I think that it would certainly be unprofitable to describe these transitions here I shall content myself with a bare enumeration

E

of those leading facts which are necessary for a general comprehension of the situation. All, then, that the reader requires to know is, that a line of Hindoo Rajahs which once reigned over a very limited portion of Mysore gradually acquired about half of it; that a descendant of their line was set aside by the Mahometan usurper Hyder Ali (an able soldier of fortune, who had risen to the chief command of the army); that he conquered the remainder of the present territory and ruled it from 1761 to 1782; and that after his death he was succeeded by his son Sultan Tippoo, who on May 4th, 1799, lost his life at Seringapatam, and with it all the territories acquired by his father, thereby fulfilling what Hyder Ali said when he observed to his son one day, "I was born to win and you were born to lose an empire." The subsequent history of the province is soon told. After the fall of Seringapatam it was resolved to place a descendant of the old Hindoo line on the throne, and Krishna Rajah Woodeyar—then about five years old, became Maharajah of Mysore, with Purnaiya (formerly prime minister of Tippoo) as Dewan and Regent, and Colonel (afterwards Sir Barry) Close as Resident, while Colonel Arthur Wellesley (afterwards Duke of Wellington) commanded the division. Under the new Government all at first went well, and in 1804 the Governor-General declared that during the past five years "the affairs of the Government of Mysore had been conducted with a degree of regularity, wisdom, discretion and justice unparalleled in any native state in India." But, unfortunately for himself and his subjects, the Maharajah, in 1811, began to rule, and Purnaiya, the able prime minister, retired, and soon afterwards died. Then followed a long period of misgovernment, which culminated in the insurrection of 1830, to put down which the aid of British troops had to be called in. A formal inquiry was then made by the British Government, and the result of this was that it was determined to transfer the entire administration to British officers, and put the Maharajah on an allowance for his personal expenditure. At first two commissioners were appointed to administer the government, but this was found to be inconvenient, and in April, 1834, Colonel (afterwards Sir Mark) Cubbon was appointed as sole commissioner for the province. He occupied the post till February, 1861, when he retired, and when on his way home died at Suez at about seventy-seven years of age, having spent the whole of the previous years of the century in India. He was succeeded by other able commissioners, and nothing of any political importance happened in the province till June, 1865, when the Maharajah adopted as his heir a scion of one of the leading families of his house. It was for some time doubtful whether the Government would recognize the adoption, as, after the death of the Maharajah, it had been generally assumed that the province would be annexed, but in April, 1867, the Home Government decided that it should be recognized, and on September 23rd, 1868, six months after the death of Krishna Rajah, his adopted son, Chama Rajendra Wodeyar Bahadur, at that time between five and six years old, was duly installed at Mysore, and it was then decided that the country should remain under British administration till the Maharajah came of age. His Highness attained his majority at the age of eighteen, on the 5th of March, 1881, and was formally installed on the throne on the 25th of that month, and thus the province, after having been directly administered by the British for almost exactly fifty years, was handed over, not as we shall afterwards see, to native rule, but to native administration.

And here a rather interesting question naturally arises. How was such a change—one quite unique in the history of India—received by the inhabitants of the country? So far as the planters (of whom I am one of the oldest, having settled in the province in 1855) are concerned, I do not think they have been in the slightest degree affected. They were all well satisfied with the English administration, and I think they are equally well satisfied with the present native administration. In fact, there is no change perceptible, except that the criminal administration has somewhat fallen off, and it certainly has been occasionally found that an answer from a native official sometimes resembles death—you think it is never coming and then it comes when least expected. But I must confess that, as regards answers to communications, I have heard of similar complaints made by the former Mysore Government against the Supreme Government, and of a like complaint made by the latter against the Home Government. But, though the change was regarded with indifference by the settlers in the province, and was indeed of obvious advantage to them, as there is no income-tax, and the finances are flourishing, it was not at all acceptable to the native population in general, and the native officials were quite aware that the new administration was not popular. I made frequent inquiries as to the cause of this, not only from natives in my own neighbourhood, but from those I met when travelling by easy stages from the Gairsoppa Falls in the north-western corner of the province to my estates in Southern Mysore, and found that the universal complaint was that there was a want of Daryápti, or active inquiry into grievances, and one of my old native neighbours was loud in his praises of the palmy days of Sir Mark Cubbon. I confess, however, that though there may have been some grounds for complaint as regards "inquiry," owing to the greater zeal and personal activity of Englishmen, I do not think that there were any real grounds for dissatisfaction, and feel sure that the unpopularity of the new administration was owing partly to the fact of the country, at the time of the rendition, not being in a very prosperous condition, partly to the strong conservative instincts of the natives, and partly, perhaps, to their being under some apprehension that the abuses of the old native government might possibly be revived. But, however that may be, from inquiries made when last in India, and especially from the absence of any reference to the subject in the many conversations I had with natives of all classes, I believe that the unpopularity of the new administration, which at first undoubtedly existed, has now quite passed away.

It may be as well to mention here that, though the administration is now a native one, there are still, in the Mysore service, about thirty-five Englishmen in the various departments of the State, and that the most friendly relations exist between them and the native officials. I feel sure, too, that the value of an admixture of Englishmen in the administration is fully recognized by the native officials. As regards brain power they equal Englishmen, and indeed are often superior to them, but the classes from which the native officials are mainly drawn are, as a rule, deficient in that physical vigour which is required for executive work, as one of the native officials, who himself was an exception to the rule, once told me, "and therefore," he added, "we must have an admixture of natives and Europeans in the service." I must, however, observe that, though his remark is true as regards the Brahminical classes from which the officials are mainly taken, I think it probable that, when education spreads, there will ultimately be found amongst the hardy peasantry of Mysore a fair proportion of individuals who will have a sufficient degree of physical vigour for executive work. In confirmation of the remark I have made as to the want of executive vigour on the part of native officials, a defect which would be equally apparent in us were our energy not kept up by fresh importations from home, I may mention that, under the new régime, there has been a distinct falling off in the up-keep of roads, and in the detection of crime.

In connection with this subject I may make a passing remark on a point which has not hitherto been noticed, so far as I am aware, by previous writers. It has constantly been asserted by natives that we have not kept faith with them as regards opening to them many appointments in the public service which are at present reserved for Englishmen. I would call attention to the fact that one of the passages so often quoted contains really no general promise of employment. This passage—taken from a clause in the East India Act, passed in Parliament, 1833—merely says "That no native of the said territories, nor any natural born subject of his majesty resident therein, shall by reason *only* of his religion, place of birth, descent, colour, or any of them, be disabled from holding any place, office, or employment under the said company." "By reason *only*." Yes, but this does not bar disqualification for other reasons, as for instance the want of physical vigour to which I have alluded. Then mark the careful limitation contained in the often quoted passage from the Queen's proclamation of 1858, which sets forth that "It is our further will, that, *as far as may be*, our subjects, of whatever race or creed, be freely and impartially admitted to office in our service, the duties of which they may be qualified, by their education, *ability* and integrity, duly to discharge." But natives have not, generally speaking, the ability to discharge executive duties requiring much physical vigour, and no one is more ready to admit that than the best among the natives. But besides executive efficiency there is the fact that the mere sight of the zeal, energy, and general interest in progress exhibited by the English is to the natives around them an education worth all the book instruction we have imported into India. We cannot have too much of this leavening element, and the effects of it are everywhere apparent. It is extremely striking in the coffee districts, where many native planters have been much improved as regards go, and a desire to adopt improvements, since Europeans have settled more freely amongst them.

But it is time now to turn to the subject of the constitution of Mysore—a subject which, I need hardly say, is of the greatest practical importance to those who hold, or may think of acquiring, property in the province.

The Instrument of Transfer, then, as it is officially called, by which Mysore was made over to native administration on the 25th of March, 1881, begins by declaring the installation of the Maharajah and his power to rule under certain general conditions, which are—(1) That the Maharajah and those who are to succeed him in the manner hereinafter provided, are to hold possession of and administer the province as long as they fulfil the conditions laid down in the Instrument of Transfer; that (2) the succession should devolve on the Maharajah's lineal descendant, whether by blood or adoption, except in the case of disqualification through manifest unfitness to rule; and that (3) the Maharajah and his successors shall at all times remain faithful in allegiance and subordination to the British Crown, and perform all the duties which, in virtue of such allegiance and subordination, may be demanded of them. Then follow clauses with reference to the subsidy to be paid to the British Government for protecting and defending the province, military stipulations, foreign relations, coinage, railways and telegraphs, and extradition, and as regards the last, it is declared that plenary jurisdiction over European British subjects in Mysore shall continue to be invested in the Governor-General in Council, and that the Maharajah of Mysore shall only exercise such jurisdiction in respect to European British subjects as may from time to time be delegated to him by the Viceroy. Then with reference to "Laws and Settlements," it is declared that those in existence at the time of the transfer must be maintained, and that the Maharajah of Mysore "shall not repeal or modify such laws, or pass any laws or rules inconsistent therewith," and that no material change in the system of administration as established previous to the date of the transfer shall be made without the consent of the Viceroy. And finally, under this head, it is declared that all title-deeds granted, and all settlements of land revenues in force on March 25th, 1881 (the date of the transfer), shall be maintained, excepting so far as they may be rescinded or modified either by a competent court of law or with the consent of the Governor-General in Council. Lastly, under the heading of "British Relations," it is declared that "the Maharajah of Mysore shall at all times conform to such advice as the Governor-General in Council may offer him with a view to the management of the finances, the settlement and collection of the revenues, the imposition of taxes, the administration of justice, the extension of commerce, the encouragement of trade, agriculture, and industry, and any other objects connected with His Highness's interests, the happiness of his subjects, and his relations to the British Government." And, "In the event of the breach or non-observance of any of the foregoing conditions," the Governor-General may resume possession of Mysore and administer it as he thinks fit. Such, then, is a brief summary of the Constitution of Mysore; and it is most necessary to dwell on it with some degree of minuteness in order to show those Englishmen who are interested in Mysore, or who may be desirous of settling there, that they and their possessions in that country are as practically under British rule as they would be in any part of British India.

I have previously pointed out that there is no income-tax in Mysore. I have also alluded to the fact that, as the finances are in a flourishing condition, and, beyond the subsidy annually levied, are free from any obligation to contribute to the general expenditure of British India, there are ample and certain means available for developing the resources of the country. And that these means shall be devoted to that end exclusively, I would call particular attention to the fact that it has been laid down by the British Government that, after deducting the amount set apart annually for the personal expenses of the Maharajah, the remaining revenues of the province are to be spent on public purposes only, under a regular system of an annual budget appropriation, and the proper accounting for such expenditure. So that, taking all the circumstances into consideration, it is clear that the settlers in Mysore have advantages over any other settlers in India. The taxes they pay on their lands are fixed and most moderate in amount, they have every security that capital can enjoy, and they are living in a country which, after an ample expenditure on public works of all kinds, has an ample annual surplus. But, besides these circumstances, the settlers in the province, and the inhabitants as well, have another advantage which must by no means be lost sight of, for Mysore has a Representative Assembly, which sits once a year, and which affords a ready means for publicly ventilating any grievance, or making known any want which may be felt by the community; and as there is no institution exactly like it in the world, I propose to describe the constitution of the Assembly and its proceedings with some degree of minuteness.

The Mysore Representative Assembly, then, which was originated by Mr. Rungacharlu, the first Prime Minister of Mysore, was inaugurated on the 25th of August, 1881, or about five months after the accession of the Maharajah, by the following notification:

"His Highness the Maharajah is desirous that the views

and objects which his Government has in view in the measures adopted for the administration of the Province should be better known and appreciated by the people for whose benefit they are intended, and he is of opinion that a beginning towards the attainment of that object may be made by an annual meeting of the representative land-holders and merchants from all parts of the Province, before whom the Dewan will place the results of the past year's administration, and a programme of what is intended to be carried out in the coming year. Such an arrangement, by bringing the people into immediate connection with the Government, would serve to remove from their minds any misapprehension as regards the views and action of the Government, and would convince them that the interests of the Government are identical with those of the people.

"The annual meeting will be conveniently held at Mysore immediately after the close of the Dassara festival, which occasion will offer an additional inducement to those invited to attend the meeting. For the present the Local Fund Boards of the several districts will be asked to select from amongst themselves and others of the district the persons who are to be deputed to represent their respective districts at the meeting. In order to represent the landed interests of all the Talooks (counties), as well as the interests of trade, there should be sent one or two cultivating land-holders from each Talook, possessed of general influence and information amongst the people, and three or four leading merchants for the district generally. A list of them should be sent beforehand to this office, in order to arrange for their accommodation in Mysore. They may be allowed a small sum from the local funds to meet the actual expenses of their travelling."

The Assembly thus constituted was, as will have been perceived at a glance, a purely consultative body, and had no power whatever except (and a highly important exception it is) that of publicly stating to the rulers of the country all the grievances and wants of the people. The only institution that I can hear of that at all resembles it is the Egyptian General Assembly of the Legislative Council, but that, though a consultative, and not at all a law-making body, has the power of putting a veto on any new tax proposed by the Government. In constitution, too, it differs widely from the Mysore Assembly, as the ministers have seats in it, while in Mysore no Government official can be a member of the Assembly. I may mention here that the Egyptian Assembly was initiated by Lord Dufferin in May, 1883, and I would refer those interested in the creation of representative institutions to his Report, No. 6 (1883), and to the Report on Egypt, No. 3 (1892), by Sir Evelyn Baring (now Lord Cromer), both being Blue Books presented to the Houses of Parliament. It is interesting to note here that whereas Lord Dufferin took the first step in the direction of representative institutions by uniting, in the same assembly, Government officials, and members elected on the broad basis of manhood suffrage, the native statesman began by carefully excluding the officials, and allowing only the middle and upper classes to have anything to do with the Assembly.

The first meeting of the Mysore Representative Assembly took place on October 7th, 1881, when 144 members attended. The Dewan first of all read the annual report on the administration of the province, and after that the members were called up in succession and asked to state their grievances and wants. At the end of the session the Dewan's annual statement, or report, and an account of the proceedings of the Assembly, are printed in English and in Kanarese.

The Assembly, as we have seen, consisted of members partly appointed by the Local Fund Boards, and partly of members nominated through the agency of Government officials, but at the conclusion of the Dewan's address of October 28th, 1890, an important change in the constitution of the Assembly was announced, and a new body of rules was issued. By these all members were in future to be elected, and the qualifications entitling a man to vote for, or be elected a member for a county (talook), were (1) the payment of land revenues, a house and shop tax to the amount specified in the schedule[1] for each county; (2) the ownership of land to the value of 500 rupees a year, accompanied with residence in the county; and (3) any resident in a county who is a graduate of any Indian university is declared to be a duly qualified person. Those so qualified were to meet on a certain day, of which a month's notice was to be given, and elect members from amongst themselves. 212 members from the counties were to be thus elected. The cities of Bangalore and Mysore return four members each, and these must either pay a house or shop tax of twenty-four rupees, or be a graduate of any Indian university; the nine Local Fund Boards return two members each; the eighty-nine municipalities one for each municipality, and associations representing approved public interests, and of not less than 100 members, and also associations of smaller numbers, but recognized by Government—as for instance the Planters' Associations—may depute one member each, and the total of all the members is estimated at 351. By Rule 6 it is declared that "As the object of the Assembly is to elicit non-official public opinion, no person holding a salaried appointment under

[1] The landed qualification varies from 100 rupees to 300 rupees, and the house and shop qualification from 13 rupees to 18 rupees. This arrangement has evidently been made to suit the wealth or poverty of particular parts of the country. This seems to be rather an inconvenient system, and it is difficult to see why the lower rates of qualification should not be made universal.

Government shall vote for, or be returned as, a member of the Assembly." By Rule 7, each member is to prepare and forward to the deputy commissioner a memo describing seriatim the representations and suggestions he may desire to make at the meeting of the Assembly; and by Rule 9 the memoranda are to be forwarded, with the deputy-commissioner's remarks, to the Chief Secretary to Government. By Rule 10 all the members are to hold a formal meeting at Mysore not less than three days before the meeting of the Assembly, and should they decide at this preliminary meeting to bring forward at the Assembly any subjects not mentioned in the memoranda previously sent in by members, a supplemental list of such subjects must be sent in to the Chief Secretary.

When announcing the adoption of these new rules, the Dewan alluded to the fact that the constitution now given did not insure a full popular representation, and stated that numerous practical difficulties stood in the way of widening the representation. Finally he concluded by observing that, "It is His Highness' sincere hope that the privilege he has now been pleased to grant will be exercised to the fullest extent, and in the most beneficial manner possible, and that it will be so appreciated by all as to enable His Highness gradually to enlarge the circle of electors, so as to give wider effect to the principle of representation in the constitution of this Assembly."

To this, the first elected Assembly that ever sat in India, I was returned as representative of the South Mysore Planters' Association. On the 11th I proceeded to the city of Mysore, and on the 12th of October, 1891, attended the preliminary meeting of members, which was held in the Rungacharlu Memorial Hall—a fine building with a large hall, which has a wide daïs at one end, and a very wide gallery running along three sides of the hall.

The meeting was held at 8 a.m. in the body of the hall, where I found that a considerable body of people, who I presume were mostly representatives, were present. The hall was arranged with benches, very much as most modern churches are, and just below the daïs was a long table with chairs on one side of it. It was proposed that I, the only European present, should take the chair, and I accordingly did so, being supported on either hand by two members who had a fluent command of English, and what was of more importance to me, of Kanarese, for, though I had a colloquial knowledge of that language, I had not such a command of it as was necessary for satisfactory public speaking. I accordingly read out in English (which a certain number of the audience knew) each measure I proposed, and then informed the audience in Kanarese that one of the members would explain the subject in that language, and I found that this arrangement answered all practical purposes. The following measures had been drawn up by me previously in Bangalore after consultation with some leading members of the Assembly, and were printed and circulated amongst the members present, and it may not be uninteresting to give some of them here.

The first point taken up related to measures for the prevention of famine, and, after some discussion, four proposals were unanimously agreed to, all of them for the promotion of the digging of wells either by private enterprise or through the agency of the State. The next point related to fuel and fodder reserves, which it was agreed should be established on the lands of all villages, or near all villages, wherever land suitable for the purpose could be found. We then turned to a bill I had laid on the table with reference to advances to labourers—an important and difficult subject—when it was agreed that it should be referred to the Planters' Association for consideration. An amendment on the waste land rules for planting trees for timber and fuel was then considered and agreed to. After this it was resolved that a Government agricultural chemist ought to be appointed, who would be competent to advise on agricultural practice, cattle disease, etc., and give lectures on such subjects. We then took up the subject of British interference with proposed irrigation works in Mysore, and resolved that the Mysoreans should be allowed to have the full use of the water of Mysore for irrigation purposes, and be free from any interference as long as the water, or what is left of it, is returned to its original channel. The subject of extradition was next considered, when the representatives resolved that (1) complete reciprocity should be granted between British and Mysore territory as regards warrants, and (2) that British jurisdiction over railways in Mysore should be given up, or at least as regards all matters of theft. It was next decided that at the close of the session the representatives should continue in office till new members were elected. After this it was agreed that Government agricultural banks should be introduced. Then the representatives, having sat for about four hours, adjourned till the following day.

On the 13th we met again accordingly at 8 a.m., and on this occasion sat in the gallery, which was quite wide enough to accommodate the members. It was proposed that I should take the chair, and I did so, and opened the proceedings by introducing rules to regulate the discussion. These were that the introducer of a proposed measure should be allowed ten, and a discusser five minutes; that no one should interrupt or rise to speak before the previous speaker had sat down, and that a discusser could only be heard once. These rules were agreed to, and I found the last two of great advantage in managing the proceedings. The first two, I was glad to find, were hardly necessary, as anything in the shape of the

British, or, worse still, the Irish wind-bag, did not appear to exist amongst the members.

The next subject taken up was that of organization, and on the assumption that the Government would grant our prayer that the present members should not be dismissed at the end of the session, but should continue to be representatives till their successors were elected, it was resolved that there should be a standing central committee of the Assembly, and also district and county committees, and it was agreed that the first should consist of twenty-two members—for Bangalore and Mysore city six members each, one from each district, and one from each coffee planters' association. Seven members to constitute a quorum. The district committees were to consist of one from each county, and two from the head-quarters of the district, five being a quorum, and the county committees of three members. We then agreed to the members who were to form the central committee and district committees, and, after that, that the Maharajah should be formally thanked for his action on his part as regards the Assembly, and that it should be prayed that the measures now asked for might be granted. And finally, it was arranged that the standing central committee should draw up an address to the Maharajah, embodying the views and wishes of the representatives.

The meeting terminated at about 11 a.m., and immediately afterwards the central committee sat upstairs in a room at an angle of the building, when I was appointed chairman. We first took up the question of funds, and I suggested that each member of the Assembly should subscribe one rupee. This was agreed to, and I at once put a rupee on the table, and presently there were about fifteen added, and a list was made out of those who had paid. We then agreed that an address should be presented to the Maharajah after the termination of the meetings of the Assembly, and afterwards it was arranged that Mr. C. Rangiengar, B.A., Advocate, Mysore, should be secretary to the central committee, spend the funds at his discretion for printing and advertising, and render an account once a year.

The next day was a *dies non* as regards the Representative Assembly, but by no means so as regards the Rungacharlu Hall, which at eight in the morning presented a most interesting appearance, being filled with a large assemblage of native ladies who had met together to witness the giving of the prizes to the lady students of the Maharanee's College. The Maharajah presided on the occasion. Besides prizes for educational proficiency, there were others for music and singing, and the winners of these played and sang on a platform below, on one side of the daïs. One of the musicians, a tastefully-dressed young lady of thirteen, was a granddaughter of Mr. Rungacharlu, the first Prime Minister of Mysore. One of the prize-takers was a widow—plainly dressed as widows should be—and as she came forward there was a loud clapping of hands from the women spectators in the gallery. I found, on inquiry, that the reason of this demonstration was that she had lately given a lecture which had been much appreciated by the students. I have no space to give an account of the proceedings, though I hope to do so on some future occasion, and can only say that a more interesting and picturesque assemblage it would be difficult to imagine.

On the day following, October 15th, the Assembly was formally opened at twelve, when the Dewan presided at a table on the raised platform. He was backed and flanked by the principal European and native officers of State, while on his right sat Sir Harry Prendergast, V.C., the Resident at the Court of Mysore. The English representatives, five in all, one of them representing the gold mining interests of the province, had seats on the platform, and so had as many representatives as there was room for. The remainder occupied the body of the hall. The Dewan then opened the tenth annual meeting of the Representative Assembly of Mysore, by reading the already printed annual administration Report of the Province, and it may not be uninteresting to quote the opening sentences of it:

"Gentlemen,

"By command of His Highness the Maharajah, I have much pleasure in welcoming you to this Assembly, which meets here to-day for the first time under the election system sanctioned last year. You come here as the duly elected representatives of the agricultural, the industrial, and the commercial interests of the State. Last year, when His Highness was pleased to grant the valued privilege of election, he was not without some misgivings as to how the experiment would succeed, but it is most gratifying to His Highness that, though unused to the system, the electoral body has been able, in the very first year of its existence, to exercise the privilege with so much judgment and sense of responsibility as to send to this Assembly men in every way qualified to speak on their behalf. That men representing the industry and the intellect of the country should have already taken so much interest in the scheme augurs well for the future of the institution. His Highness asks me to take this opportunity publicly to acknowledge the expressions of warm gratitude which have reached him from all sides for the privilege of election granted last year."

The Dewan then proceeded to make his statement of the Revenue and Expenditure of 1890-91, by which it appeared that the Revenue for that period—the largest ever realized by the State—was 145 lakhs of rupees, or, at par,[1] £1,450,000, and the account showed a surplus of 23 lakhs,

[1] For all practical spending purposes in India the rupee may be reckoned at par. It is only when it requires to be turned into

or £230,000; but from this had to be deducted a sum for expenditure on new railways, which reduced the surplus, or rather, disposed of it to such an amount as to leave a balance of 12½ lakhs, or £125,000. The budget was then taken up in detail, and the Dewan showed in the most lucid manner the financial position as regards the various heads of receipts and expenditure, all of which I shall pass over except that relating to gold, which the reader will probably find interesting, for, as the Kanarese proverb says, "If gold is to be seen, even a corpse will open its mouth." There was, then, an increase in State receipts from gold mining dues to the extent of 37,000 rupees in the amount of royalty, while "Premia and deposits on leases" brought in 71,000 rupees. The mines in the Kolar gold field during 1890 extracted 106,903 ounces of gold. Three of them—the Mysore, Ooregum, and Nundydroog—showed a considerable increase in production over the previous year. The first increased from 49,238 oz. to 58,183 oz.; the second from 16,437 oz. to 27,351 oz., and the third from 6,129 oz. to 15,637 oz.

The Dewan then called the attention of the Assembly to the working of some of the principal departments of the State, beginning with the railways, and, after giving a very satisfactory account of the progress made, concluded this branch of his subject by observing that "As regards our main railway policy there will be no pause in the course of development, and should our financial condition continue to improve, the next decade will see the Province intersected with lines which, in the decade preceding the rendition, were only thought of as remote possibilities." He next remarked on other public works, and showed that in the last ten years no less than 471 miles of entirely new roads had been opened up, while 218 miles of incomplete

gold for the purchase of articles in England that its gold value must be taken into account.

roads, which had been inherited at the time of the rendition, had been brought up to standard. Then he turned to irrigation, and stated that the large irrigation works commenced in former years were advancing towards completion. And here the Dewan alluded to a matter of the greatest importance, and to which I shall again return further on. It appears that the Supreme Government had actually put a stop to certain irrigation works begun by the Mysore Government on the ground that these would lessen the supply of water from Mysore to British territory. As to this the Dewan now observed on "The difference which had arisen with the Madras authorities as to the rights of Mysore to the full use of its drainage areas." The case had been laid before the Government of India, and the Dewan said that "the basis for a solution of the difficulty has been arranged with the Madras Government in a way that is likely to remove to a considerable extent the check that the progress of our irrigation works had received in tracts bordering upon the Madras Presidency."

The subject of well irrigation too had not been neglected, and the Dewan pointed out that its protective value in times of drought is far superior to tank irrigation, and observed that, "During the last famine the only oases in the midst of the general desolate appearance of the country were, besides the tracts watered by our river channels, those special regions favoured with well irrigation." So important was well irrigation, that the Government had resolved to make advances to ryots willing to construct them, at a low rate of interest, and repayable by easy instalments in a long series of years. In the event of water not being found, or found in insufficient quantity, the Government had undertaken the risk of failure, so that the farmer was placed beyond all risk of loss. And, in order to facilitate the progress of such works, a special officer had been appointed to give the advances on the spot, so as to avoid the delay caused by the usual circuitous official correspondence.

I may here pause for one moment to remark on the great value of the Assembly as regards any new measure like the one just alluded to, for it often happens that from the scarcity of newspapers, and the inability of the poorer ryots to purchase them, measures of great value are not taken advantage of, or only are so after a long delay. Now an assembly like that of Mysore provides an excellent means for distributing information on all Government matters, and in one part of his address the Dewan particularly requested the representatives from two important districts to explain fully to the people certain matters, the particulars of which I cannot, for want of space, give here.

The Dewan then went into the interesting subject of Forests, and it was satisfactory to notice the progress that had been made in planting, and that sandal wood had year after year been yielding an increased revenue. The transition from forests to elephants was natural, and during the year 70 had been caught. Some died after capture and others were liberated. Of the 44 retained, 41, of which 14 were tuskers, were sold for 50,705 rupees. Having fully discussed the elephants, the Dewan turned next to education, and here he was able to record marked progress in every direction, and especially in female instruction. There were now 97 girls' schools in the province, and an important change had been made as regards their immediate supervision, which was now exercised by local committees. "The committees," said the Dewan, "have been given large powers of management, and the initiative rests, in almost all cases, with them, subject to the approval of Government." The object of this of course was to interest the people in the subject, and the Dewan observed that "Female education cannot become firmly established in the country until the people begin to look upon the education of their girls, whether children or adults, as necessary, and as obligatory as that of their boys. The Government have thought that the best way of securing this result in the infancy of female education is to leave as much as possible to the intelligent and sympathetic guidance of local committees."

After alluding to the results of the archæological survey, and dwelling on the fact that during the past year 1,500 inscriptions were secured, some of which were of great value and interest, the Dewan then took up the subject of excise, and went into the reforms he proposed to institute as regards that department. The census of Feb. 26th, 1891, was next alluded to, and by this it appeared that, including the civil and military station of Bangalore, the population returned was 4,943,079 as compared with 4,186,188 in 1881, and 5,055,412 in 1871. The increase during the last decade was thus very considerable, but Mysore has still some progress to make before it can bring up its numbers to the census return of 1871, nearly a million of persons having been swept away in the disastrous famine of 1876-77. The municipal elections were next alluded to, and it was announced that the cities of Bangalore and Mysore were to have an extension of the electoral system. The important subject of the reform of religious and charitable institutions (there had been several representations made as regards these in previous years by members of the Assembly) was next taken up, and it was announced that a specially qualified officer had been appointed to "inquire into the subject on the spot, and to carry out the needed reform in the case of each institution under the general and special orders of Government, and, when once all institutions are thoroughly reformed and placed upon a sound and efficient footing, the future management of them on the lines laid down will, as heretofore, have to be carried on by the local executive authorities." After alluding to some contemplated reforms in the Civil Service of the province, the

Dewan concluded his able address by alluding to the apprehensions of famine which had been consequent on the failure of the rains, and congratulating the members on the fact that owing to good rain having fallen only a fortnight ago, the threatened danger had now passed away.

After the conclusion of the Dewan's address I then rose, and, as chairman of the preliminary meetings of representatives, alluded to the subject of the organization of committees which we desired to carry into effect, and urged that, as far as possible, members should avoid going into petty local grievances, and devote their attention to those large general questions which affect the whole province. After I had sat down a translation of the Dewan's address was then delivered in Kanarese, for the benefit of the representatives who did not understand English, and the Assembly afterwards adjourned till the following morning.

After the Assembly had adjourned the members of the central committee met in a private room, and we agreed on the terms of the address to the Maharajah. Then we returned to the Hall, as it had been thought advisable to take up several matters which had not been discussed at our first preliminary meeting, and it was again proposed that I should take the chair. The first proposal made was that members, instead of being annually elected to the Assembly, should be elected for three years, and this was unanimously carried. A leading native member next rose and proposed that no girl under ten years of age should be given in marriage. Then ensued a scene of excitement that baffles description. The representatives who, the moment before, had been quite calm and collected, and who looked so passive that it seemed that nothing could have aroused them from a condition of profound composure, became suddenly electrified. A burst of tongues arose simultaneously all over the Assembly. Several members got up and tried to speak at once, and one of these (I think I see him now), a tall, stout, elderly man with a voice of thunder, and his appearance much accentuated by an enormous bamboo pen which he had thrust behind his ear, entered into an altercation with the proposer of the motion. I had no president's bell, and if I had had one I am sure I might have rung it in vain, and I thought it best to sit still for a little time, and let the representatives liberate their minds. Presently, and the moment I saw the first signs of an abatement of the excitement, I rose, and, with a slight signal of my hand quieted the audience, and observed that, as this was a subject as to which there was evidently much difference of opinion, and as it was very desirable that, as regards the measures proposed at our preliminary meetings,[1] there should be a complete unanimity of opinion, I begged leave to suggest to the meeting that the subject might be adjourned, and, if desired, brought up at the next day's meeting of the full Assembly. This was agreed to, and a member then proposed that two seers of grain (about equal to four lbs.) should be contributed yearly by each ryot, and stored up in a public granary against times of famine. This, I confess, I thought, and still think, a sensible proposal, as, in the first burst of a famine it is very desirable, till trade operations from a distance get under weigh, that local supplies should exist, but, after some discussion, I found that the proposal met with such small approval, that I did not think of putting it to the meeting. It was next proposed, and as can easily be imagined, carried unanimously, that where, from the failure of the rains, there was absolutely no crop whatever, a remission of the assessment should be granted. Finally it was agreed that, at the opening of the Assembly on the following morning, I should bring up and speak on all the points that had been agreed to at the

[1] The meeting now held was, I am aware, quite out of order, but as the Assembly had taken a new departure some laxness was permissible at first.

meetings over which I had presided, and the meeting broke up at three o'clock. After it was over several of the representatives expressed to me their gratitude for the interest I had shown in the affairs of Mysore, and from the numerous evidences I subsequently had of the appreciation of the natives, I felt most amply repaid for the trouble I had taken.

On the following morning, Friday, Oct. 16th, the Assembly met at eight o'clock, and I was called on to proceed with my address as chairman of the preliminary meetings, and though I spoke as briefly as possible on each of the points which had been agreed to, my speech lasted for one hour and twenty minutes. After it was over the Dewan asked if any member desired to speak on any of the points I had brought forward, but no one rose to do so, which was satisfactory evidence that complete unanimity had existed as regards the various points, and that I had correctly conveyed the opinions of the representatives. The Dewan then called upon each representative in turn to state any grievances, or make known any wants which his constituents had desired him to represent, and a great many local wants as regards roads, hospitals, telegraphs, etc., were brought forward. The subject that excited most interest, and afforded some amusement, was that of the age at which girls should be given in marriage, which had been brought forward at the meeting of the day previous. Some discussion ensued regarding it, when it appeared that the point as to which the representatives were really most concerned, was that of elderly men who had no children marrying again and again with the hope of getting them, regarding which one of the representatives said to me in conversation, "We object to old fogies marrying young girls." The point was especially urged by one member, who argued in the most serious manner that, if a man when in the prime of life had no family there was little likelihood of success when he was between sixty and seventy years of age. This remark was received with general laughter, and shortly afterwards the Dewan made a judicious reply on the whole question, and said that, in his opinion, the interference of the Government was inadvisable, and that the question was one that ought to be settled by the people consulting privately on the subject. Then the Assembly turned to other matters, and finally adjourned at midday.

I may here mention that I subsequently had some conversation with natives regarding the marriage question, especially as to the age for consummation, when I found that the pressure of public opinion, and the various discussions on the subject, which had appeared in the newspapers, had already produced a considerable effect in delaying the time for married girls leaving the paternal roof to join their husbands.

It may perhaps be not uninteresting to mention too that, on the afternoon of the day on which I made my speech I fell in with two native gentlemen who spoke to me about it. What I found had been particularly appreciated (and very naturally so as water is of such vital importance in India), was the firm protest I had made against the Supreme Government restricting the Mysoreans as to the use, for irrigation, of the waters of Mysore on the ground that a more extended use of them would lessen the supply to the adjacent British territory. In the course of my speech, I made a very telling point by supposing, for the sake of argument, that Mysore had, as had been originally proposed, been annexed, and made an integral part of the Madras Presidency. In that case, I asked, would the Government have limited the supply of the water to the Mysore part of the presidency in order to improve the more distant irrigated tracts in other parts of British territory? I then argued that the British Government would certainly not have done so, seeing that, to have so acted would have diminished the means available for contending with famine, for, as I fully urged, it is perfectly well known that the further the water travels the greater is the waste from percolation and evaporation, and the smaller the amount of land it can irrigate. If, then, the British Government would not have so acted had Mysore been annexed, what right, I asked, had it to interfere with Mysore regarding the use of its waters, and thereby to increase the risks of famine in that country? It was no wonder, I continued, that an English officer in the Mysore service had been heard to say that he supposed Mysore would not be allowed to plant a tree, in case it might precipitate some moisture that might otherwise pass over into British territory.

I may here mention another remark which the above mentioned native gentleman made as regards my speech. "It was not so much the speech as the sense of fairness, and frankness, and sincerity which you showed that impressed us." This remark showed, as I have often found, that the common idea of natives always having recourse to flattery is a mistaken one, and it was rather interesting to find the ideas of ancient times repeated by one who could have heard hardly anything in the way of public speaking. The reader may remember how Quinctilian in effect said that there is no instrument of persuasion more powerful than an opinion of probity and honour in the person who undertakes to persuade, and how it has been pointed out that the powerful effect caused by the speaking of Pericles really lay in the confidence which the people reposed in his integrity. But it is time now to turn to the proceedings of the Assembly, which had been adjourned to Saturday, October 17th.

On that day, then, we met at 8 a.m., and it was proposed by one of the representatives that the collection of the land revenues should in future be postponed till after the harvest, as the present times of collection were inconvenient to the cultivators and often compelled them to borrow money, or mortgage their crops in order to find money to meet the Government demands. The change asked for was warmly urged by the speaker, who gave very convincing reasons, which I have no space to repeat here, in favour of the proposed alteration. After this speech was over the Dewan turned to the head revenue officer and consulted him, and also two English officials of great experience. I did not look at my watch, but I am sure the consultation did not last five minutes. The Dewan then turned to the Assembly and said, "This proposal is granted," and the decision was received with loud applause. The chief revenue and settlement officer afterwards told me that this was the most important point ever gained by the Assembly.

I may pause here to remark that what I saw and heard at the Assembly, combined with what I previously knew of the Mysore Government, satisfied me that a more perfect form of government does not exist in the world. Here, as we have just seen, was a most important measure gained for the country after what was really a very short consultative meeting between the ruler and the ruled. The ruler—in other words the Dewan—was sitting like a judge on the bench, patiently listening to and taking notes of the various wants of the people as the representatives came forward—occasionally consulting with his officials—granting some things, absolutely refusing others, and announcing sometimes that the subject brought forward would be taken into consideration, while the representatives seemed to be perfectly satisfied that the ruler would willingly do, and was willingly doing, the best he could for the common interest. I may mention that I was particularly struck with the dignified, gentlemanly and friendly manner of the Dewan when consulting his English officials, and there was evidently a mutual appreciation existing, which I had afterwards distinct knowledge of when I subsequently heard some of these officials alluding, in private conversation, to the Dewan. I have a great dislike to the idea of being thought guilty of flattery, but I cannot refrain from recording the remarkable fact that (and how rarely can this be said of any public man), while I have heard much in favour of the Dewan, I have never heard a single deprecatory remark made concerning his administration of the province, either by natives or Europeans. Mysore is indeed extremely fortunate in having such a man as Mr. Sheshadri Iyer, since made Sir K. Sheshadri Iyer, K.C.I.E., at the head of affairs. He has already been granted an extension of the usual period of office (five years), and it is to be hoped that the very doubtful practice of selecting a new man for this important office, even though there may be a valuable one at the helm, may be put aside for at least some years more.

The Assembly sat on the two following days, and was concluded by the presentation of an address to the Maharajah, thanking His Highness for having instituted an elected Assembly, and praying that the various wants brought forward might meet with favourable consideration. In all, the Assembly, inclusive of the preliminary meetings of the representatives, sat for eight days, and though there was much earnestness in discussion, and much difference of opinion, not a single case of an exhibition of ill feeling occurred, with the exception, as we have seen, of the occasion when the marriage question was brought forward, though that may be called an exhibition of warm and excited feeling rather than ill feeling.

As the reader will remember, the representatives have no power whatever, except, and a very important exception it of course is, of ventilating in public, and in the presence of the Dewan and the leading officers of State, whatever grievances and wants they may desire to call attention to, and the machinery for this ventilation is now so complete that the requirements even of those inhabiting the most inaccessible corners of the province can be readily made known to the Government. And now this question naturally arises. When, if ever, is it probable that this Assembly will demand for itself some direct power of controlling, or directing the Government? As far as I could see at the time, or can see now, the Assembly is never likely to ask for any power whatever, and I confess that I was much struck with the fact that, though I had many private conversations relating to the Assembly, both with natives and Europeans, I never expressed myself, nor did I ever hear anyone express, a desire that the Assembly should have any power. But after a little reflection, the explanation of the absence of any such demand seems to be extremely obvious, for if we look into the history of all parliamentary institutions such as we have, we shall find that they have arisen primarily from misgovernment, and I say primarily because such institutions in the United States and in our colonies are merely inheritances from the forefathers of the English founders of these countries. The insuperable difficulty, then, in the way of those who desire to create parliamentary institutions in India is, that there is no misgovernment on which to start them, and that is why the Indian National (so called, for there is nothing really national about it) Congress have found it advisable, as a preliminary step, to try and persuade the people, with the aid of lying and seditious pamphlets, that they are misgoverned. If indeed I were the absolute monarch of Mysore I could certainly, I feel sure, create Parliamentary Institutions, but only in one way that I can think of. I should misgovern the country and worry and oppress the people, and at the same time keep the Assembly going, and after a time I should thus create a desire on the part of the representatives to have some means of keeping me in check. But at present there is no one to keep in check. The Government is really too good for the creation of any desire for change. For the ruler of Mysore is not only desirous of meeting the people half way, but even of anticipating their wants, and the people have a ready means of making their wants known. And, when making known these wants, their representatives are not only free from the expense and annoyances to which Members of Parliament are exposed, but have a most enjoyable time of it as well, for the Assembly is held at the time of the great annual festival of the Dassara, when there are wonderfully picturesque processions, illuminations, and displays of fireworks. In fact, were it not for these attractions, I feel sure that it would be a difficult matter to get the representatives together, because, though they are of course easily able to find many wants, there are no grievances so real as to make the people generally take much, or indeed any, interest in the proceedings of the Assembly, and in this connection I may mention the following confirmatory facts.

On the morning following the breaking up of the Assembly I left Mysore to make a tour in Coorg to visit the plantations in that district, and drove first of all sixteen miles to breakfast at a Travellers' Bungalow on the main road. While breakfast was being prepared I went for a stroll, and fell into conversation with the first native I met, who, I found, was, with the aid of a number of labourers, working a plantation of palms and fruit-trees at a short distance from the bungalow. I expressed a wish to see the plantation, and, when on our way there, told him that I had just been attending the Representative Assembly at Mysore. Just imagine my feelings, when he told me that he had never heard of it, nor indeed when he did hear of it did he ask me a single question about it. And yet we were only sixteen miles from the capital, and on one of the main roads of the province. He was, too, a man of fair intelligence and, though we conversed in Kanarese, he told me that he knew some English, which proved that he was a man of a certain degree of education. On my return to my estates I found that, though the natives had heard of the Assembly (probably because the native representative lived within a few miles of my house), no one seemed to take any interest in its proceedings, and I do not remember having been asked a single question with reference to it. The explanation, of course, of this state of things is that the people are perfectly contented, and satisfied with the steady progress they see going on around them. There is therefore no demand[1] for representative institutions, or the acquisition of power by the people, for while they see abundant signs of progress, there is no oppression, and therefore there are no real grievances. But, though there is no such demand, I must caution the reader against supposing that I do not attach much importance to the Assembly as a highly valuable means of bringing the people and their rulers into friendly touch with each other, and as a most useful means of inter-communication regarding every fact that it is important for the ruler and the ruled to know. Such an assembly is indeed of the highest value, and I have no doubt that a similar kind of assembly would be valuable in many parts of India. And such assemblies will in the future be far more necessary and valuable than such institutions would have been in the past, because, in former times, the rulers, not being nearly so much burdened with office and desk-work as they now are, had far more leisure time to mix with the people, and hear from them the expression of their wants or grievances.

[1] On looking at the Government Report of the proceedings of the Assembly for 1891 (which I may observe was not published till the year following), I find that, though 340 members were elected, only 262 attended. No less than seventy-eight members failed to put in an appearance, and the only probable explanation of this that I can give is that these members felt that they had nothing in particular to represent to the Government, and therefore thought that they might much better remain at home.

I have alluded previously to the lying and seditious pamphlets which have been circulated by the so-called Indian National Congress (and I say so-called because, as we shall see, there is really nothing national about it), and allude to them again partly in order to point out that they are a most cheering evidence of the universal good government in India, because, had it been really ill governed, there would have been no occasion to issue the pamphlets in question. The fact is, that the agitators of the Congress found it necessary to create a case as a ground-work for demanding representative institutions for India, and began by imitating the action of the Irish agitators. And here, for the benefit of those who have not had time to study Indian affairs, it may be as well to give a brief description of the Indian Congress, more especially as those who know but very little of India may confound it with the kind of assembly we have in Mysore, and which I have suggested for adoption in other parts of India.

When I was passing through Poona in the year 1879, I was called upon by seven leading members of the native community who knew of the interest I had taken in Indian affairs, and in the course of our conversation they made some remarks on the desire of the educated natives for some share of political power. I then explained to them that, as it was clear that India was entirely unfit for representative institutions, the only result would be that power would be transferred from a limited class of Englishmen to a very limited class of natives, which would be of no advantage to the country whatever. My remarks were followed by a dead silence which was broken by one of them saying, in a desponding tone, "you have educated us, and you have made us discontented accordingly," thus illustrating very forcibly what I suppose Solomon meant when he said, "He that increaseth knowledge increaseth sorrow." But, however that may be, the utterance of the native in question explains the origin of the Indian Congress which was started in 1885 by a small number of the educated classes who began to climb the political tree with considerable vigour, illustrating as they did so the native proverb which tells us that "The higher the monkey climbs the more he shows his tail." And, in fact, the members of the Congress showed theirs so completely when they climbed to the top of their political tree at Madras in 1887, that their proceedings would be hardly worth noticing were it not that they might be the means of prejudicing the proper claims of the natives to consultative assemblies like the one we have in Mysore. With people less advanced as regards common sense than the natives of India, and also less suspicious of the educated classes, the Congress wallahs, as they are sometimes called, might have done some mischief, but the only harm they have really done, and I consider it no small harm, is to lower the educated natives in general in the ideas of those who have not had an opportunity of knowing the best of them, and so appreciating their admirable abilities and calm common sense. For when the public knows, as all those who have paid any attention to the subject do know, that the members of the Congress are now selling pamphlets which are intended to bring the Queen's Government into hatred and contempt, its opinion of the educated natives of India is not likely to be a high one. And in order to make quite sure that the Congress is still selling the pamphlets in question, I suggested to the secretary of the Athenæum in June, 1892, to purchase for the library of that club (and he accordingly did so), from the Indian Congress office in London, a copy of the Congress proceedings with which the pamphlets in question are bound up. And it may not be uninteresting to note here that Mr. Dadabhai Naoroji, M.P., as a leading member of the Congress, is therefore one of the sellers of the pamphlets. It is, however, only fair to add, as an excuse for Mr. Dadabhai Naoroji and his misguided associates, that they have, after all, only followed on the track of the Irish agitators, and no doubt consider that the preaching of sedition against the Government to whom they owe so much is the proper course to pursue when aiming at political power. And as an extenuation of their action it should also be considered that the members of the Congress, who at first were acting in a perfectly legitimate manner, eventually fell under the guidance of a retired member of the Indian Civil Service —a certain Mr. Hume—who seems to have lodged some of his own extravagant ideas in the heads of the raw and inexperienced members of the Congress, and who is supposed to be the author of the seditious pamphlets. And now let me give a brief account of the Congress, and its aims and views.

The first Congress, which met in Bombay in December, 1885, consisted of seventy-eight persons, who came from twenty-five places. They were neither elected nor delegated, and how they came together does not appear in the published proceedings of the Congress. The principal resolution passed on the occasion related to the reforms of the various Indian Councils.

The second Congress, which was composed of 440 persons, who were partly elected and partly delegated, and of persons who could produce no evidence of being one or the other, met in Calcutta in December, 1886, and (p. 10 of Report of 1887) "passed a series of resolutions of the highest importance," which is undoubtedly true, as the result of them would, if carried into effect, practically be to substitute the rule of the Congress for that of the Queen. This change was proposed to be effected by reconstituting the Provincial, Legislative, and Governor-General's Council, enlarging them, and giving "not less than one half" (p. 217 of Report of 1887) of the seats to members elected through the agency of the Congress. This proposed measure was justly considered by the delegates to be the key of the position, as we shall more fully see when we come to the consideration of the proceedings of the next Congress.

This, the third Congress, met at Madras in December, 1887, when 604 delegates (a large number of whom were lawyers and newspaper editors), who "were appointed either at open public meetings or by a political or trade association," assembled and passed no less than eleven resolutions. The second, fifth and eighth of these are worthy of notice, as also are the seditious political pamphlets previously alluded to, which, for convenient reference, are bound up with the report of the proceedings.

The second resolution (p. 82 of Report of 1887) reaffirms the resolutions of the two previous Congresses, which demand the expansion and reforms of the various Indian Councils. Here the first speaker (p. 83) was a Mr. Bannerjee, a newspaper editor, who in his introductory remarks in support of the resolution assured the delegates that "the dream of ages is about to be realized." We are not the legislators of the country, he further on remarks, "though we hope to be so some day when the Councils are reconstituted," and eloquent was the language of the speaker when he subsequently dwelt on the fact that the power of making the laws would at once give them every reform they could desire. Mr. Bannerjee was succeeded by other native speakers, who dwelt warmly upon the advantages of representative institutions, and these were followed by Mr. Norton, Coroner of Madras, who most highly extolled the resolution. "That," he said, "is the key of all your future triumph" (p. 90), and further on in his speech he urges them to persevere up to the day "when you shall place your hand upon the purse strings of the country and the government," for, he continued, "once you control the finances, you will taste the true meaning of power and freedom."

And here, after all the talk about the value of representative institutions, and just as the Congress seemed to be on the verge of recommending parliamentary institutions such as we have, the members suddenly wheeled about and practically declared that India was unfit for them by deciding (p. 91) that, as the rural districts might not elect suitable members, the so-called representatives of the people were to be nominated by an electoral college, which was to be composed of members sent up from the various district and municipal boards, chambers of commerce, and universities. The power of election was thus to be conferred, to use Mr. Norton's words, on "a body of men who would practically represent the flower of the educated inhabitants." These views were much applauded by the delegates, who thus ratified the system of nominating the so-called representatives, and which system, I may add, is carefully laid down in Clause 2 of Resolution IV. of 1886 (p. 217). Having thus most practically declared that India is quite unfit for representative institutions in the ordinary sense of the word, Mr. Norton proceeded to point out that, as the desired power for reconstituting the government is not likely to be obtained in India, they must work on the people of England, who at present believe, he says (p. 92), that the Indian Government is "being beneficiently carried on." "You must disturb that belief," he continued. In other words, he might have said, you must do what the Parnellites did, or attempted to do, in England. And accordingly the Congress wirepullers have set up an agency in London, and have posted placards purporting to be an appeal from 200 millions of India to the people of England.

But after all, the desired majority in the Indian Councils, which the delegates rightly declared to be the key of the whole position, would be insufficiently supported without an army and an armed population at the back of it, and all in sympathy with the native soldiers in the English service. These wants, however, are carefully attended to in Resolutions 5 and 8, which we will now briefly glance at.

Read by itself, the Fifth Resolution seems to be harmless, and even laudable, for it expresses a desire (p. 123) for "A system of volunteering for the Indian inhabitants of the country such as may qualify them to support the Government in a crisis." But the writer of the introductory article to the Report (p. 48) shows the great value the force would be in bringing pressure to bear on the Government, and points out that, with 250,000 native volunteers, with many times that number trained in previous years, and backed by the whole country, and with all the native troops (p. 49) more in sympathy with their fellow-countrymen than with the English, the present system of government would be impossible. And it is further pointed out in the introductory article that "This means a revolution—a noiseless bloodless revolution—but none the less a complete revolution." Then the writer reckons that these volunteers "will be backed by the whole country," and this naturally leads to the consideration of the Eighth Resolution, for the backing would obviously be of much greater value were the whole population armed.

This Resolution (p. 147) demands the repeal of the Arms Act on account of the "hardship it causes, and the unmerited slur which it casts on the people of this country." Now as any respectable person can obtain a license to carry firearms for under 4*s.*, and as cultivators are granted licenses gratis in order that they may, free of all charge, defend themselves and their crops from wild animals, and as we know further from the great number of licenses granted that there can be no difficulty in obtaining them, it is evident that there can be no hardship in connection with this Act—a conclusion which is further confirmed by the fact that, in consequence of the number of guns in the hands of natives, wild animals are becoming rarer, and, as I can personally testify, have in many cases been almost completely exterminated. And if we consider further that the necessity for taking out a license in India can inflict no greater slur than is cast on the English in England by their having to take out gun licenses, it is evident that the vehemently expressed desire for the repeal of this Act is only explicable when read along with the previously quoted remarks with reference to the native volunteering and the armed population in sympathy with them at their back, and with the detonating matter which appears in those seditious pamphlets to which I shall now briefly refer.

These pamphlets, or rather translations of them, are printed at the close of the Report of 1887, and complete our view of the situation, which may be shortly described by saying that, while the delegates in the van deliver speeches for English consumption full of expressions of loyalty and praises of our rule, the wirepullers in the rear are distributing pamphlets amongst the people in which all expressions of loyalty are absent, while all the evils the people suffer from are attributed to our Government, and the Queen's English officials are held up to execration as types of everything that is at once brutal and tyrannical. The second pamphlet gives us a dialogue between a native barrister, and a farmer called Rambaksh, and between them as much evil is said of us and our rule as can well be packed into so short a space. As an instance of the way in which the English officials ill-treat the natives, Rambaksh declares that because on one occasion he had not furnished enough grass for the horses of the collector—Mr. Zabardust (literally a brutal and overbearing tyrant), he had been struck by the Sahib over the face and mouth, and that by his orders he (Rambaksh) had been "dragged away and flogged till he became insensible. It was months before he could walk" (p. 209 of Report). Then the India of the present is contrasted with what India would be if it were under the rule of the Congress, and an allegorical comparison is made between the village of Kambaktpur (the abode of misery) and that of Shamshpur (the abode of joy). The moral is that British rule, which is typified by the former, is making the people poorer and poorer, that through it land is going out of cultivation, that oxen for the plough are becoming scarce, that the villages are going to ruin, and that nothing flourishes except the liquor shops in which the Government encourages drinking, while the very irrigation works we are providing as a protection against famine are described as an evil, and a mere pretext for extorting more money from the people. The village of Shamshpur (the abode of joy), on the other hand, is described in glowing colours, and we need hardly say is the home of the institutions to be introduced by the Congress. The only conclusion to be drawn from all this by the masses of India is, that the sooner they rebel against the existing rule, and substitute for it the rule of the Congress, the sooner will they leave the abode of misery, and enter the abode of joy, where all the delights to be provided by the Congress will be theirs. The imaginary dialogue concludes (p. 214) with a demand for money to carry on the work, and the barrister suggests to the farmer various injurious means for the collection, which Rambaksh promises to carry out. He then tenders payment of some fees previously owing to the barrister, who indeed receives the money, but magnanimously declares his intention of enrolling Rambaksh as a member of the association, and paying in the fees as a contribution from Rambaksh. "Blessed are the earnings of the virtuous which go to the service of God," said the barrister, and with this pious utterance the dialogue closes.

With the aid of these pamphlets in dialogue form, it

appears, from the statement in the introductory article of the Report, that the emissaries of this Indian League have been gathering in money from the poorest classes in India, down even to coolies. No less than 5,500 rupees, it appears (p. 11), were collected from 8,000 persons, in sums varying from 1 anna to 1 rupee 8 annas, and some 8,000 rupees were contributed in sums of from 1 rupee 8 annas to 30 rupees. But it is unnecessary to pursue further the work of the Congress, and it is sufficient to say that its proceedings were lately brought before the House of Commons, and that the action of Mr. Hume, in writing and publishing a kind of proclamation of a most objectionable character in connection with the Congress, was denounced in the House of Commons in strong terms. It is time, however, to close these brief remarks on the Indian Congress. It still exists, but in a languishing form, and will probably gradually disappear. It has sought to bring the Queen's Government into hatred and contempt. The only effect it has had is to bring the educated classes of India into ridicule and contempt in the minds of those who are imperfectly acquainted with them, and perhaps to delay the extension of those Representative Assemblies which are so well suited to the requirements of the inhabitants of India, and the value of which I trust I have sufficiently shown.

Since this chapter was written I have met with a passage in one of the speeches of a member of the Congress which is highly creditable to the candour of the Congressionists, and which proves that we are quite right in keeping in our own hands all, or nearly all, important executive and governing power. The passage occurs in the Fourth Report of the Indian National Congress (p. 49), and one of the members said on this occasion:

"But it is a fact, which no one present will call in question, that what preponderates in the national character is quiescence or passivity, the active virtues being thrown into the background, or remaining in a state of dormancy." And further on the speaker says, "The virtues we are sadly deficient in are courage, enterprise, the will to do and the heart to do." (Cheers.)

These remarks, which were received with assenting cheers, should be read in connection with those made on the Queen's Proclamation in the earlier pages of this chapter.

I may observe finally that if the above-mentioned qualities are, as the native speaker complains, deficient, it is simply because the climate of India is not favourable to their production. As an Indian gentleman once said to me in London, "Here I am glad to go out for a walk. In Madras I find it an exertion to walk across a room." That explains our presence in India, and the necessity for keeping all important active work in our own hands. The natives are not at all to blame for being deficient in the active virtues. We ourselves, our bull-dogs, and our vegetables would alike decline without constant renewal by fresh importations from England.

CHAPTER IV.

NATURAL HISTORY AND SPORT.

AFTER the numerous books that have been written on Sport in India, a chapter on this subject might at first sight seem superfluous. So might, at first sight, another novel full of what has been written thousands of times before about love. And yet we never tire of hearing or reading of either, and naturally, for both appeal to the imagination, and carry the mind far away from business or carking cares, or, in other words, that proverbial smoky chimney with which every house is provided. And if the mere reading of love or sport makes men and women feel better because it takes them away from themselves (we should have no mirrors in our rooms), what must the reality of either be? For both dart through the system with electric and delight-yielding force, and produce effects which, to those who have not experienced them, are wellnigh incredible. And, as regards big game shooting in particular, the effects are so astonishing that one almost ceases to believe in them till another experience proves over again that sport, or even the prospect of sport, can effect miracles, or at least that it can cause an alteration in the system through the action of the mind. And, some eighteen months ago, I realized this most vividly when feeling much out of sorts, and indeed unfit for anything. For just at the time of my deepest depression, news came in that a tiger had killed two cattle in my plantation, and, what made the news much more acceptable, two trespassing cattle—animals which are the plague of a planter's life. The news acted like a charm. I at once felt slightly better, better still when I arrived at the spot and saw the traces of the cattle having been dragged along the ground, and the bodies of the slain—one more than half eaten and the other untouched—and almost well when I returned to the bungalow to make preparations for hunting up the tiger. There is no tonic half so good as news of a tiger, and I feel that even news of a bear would rival in a great many cases all that a doctor could do for me. But, though tiger shooting is a valuable and delightful sport, it is equalled if not eclipsed by stalking on the mountains amidst the beautiful and splendid scenery of the Western Ghauts, when you traverse the forest-margined open lands rifle in hand, feeling that everything depends upon yourself, and followed by a tried and experienced shikari on whose keen sight and coolness you can thoroughly rely. There are natives of course and natives, just as there are Europeans and Europeans, but there are natives who have been gifted with the greatest daring, coolness, and the promptest presence of mind, and who are capable of much personal devotion to those who know how to treat them. I was fortunate enough to have one of these in my service, and to no sporting scenes in life can I look back with greater pleasure than when I was able, with my trusted native follower, to spend delightful mornings and evenings, and at certain times whole days, in stalking bears, bison, and sambur in the Western Mysore mountains. Danger, too, there was at times, and quite sufficient to give a pleasing amount of adventurous feeling to the sport. Indeed, without this moderate degree of danger the sport would have been of quite a different kind, for is it not evident that all sport is to be divided into two widely different classes—sport in which you are liable to be attacked, and sport where the attack is all on one side? It is, in short, the danger, or the possibility of danger, which is the vital elixir of big game shooting, and which gives one, too, an opportunity of knowing oneself, and gauging one's presence of mind, or the want of it, as the case may be. But what, after all, is the amount of danger? That depends very much on the experience of the sportsman. You may make big game shooting as dangerous as you please, and by following up a wounded bear or bison in a careless manner meet with an accident, but if proper precautions are taken, the danger of following up these animals is by no means so great as is generally supposed. But, though that is so as regards bears and bisons, I must caution the reader against supposing that there is not considerable risk in following up wounded tigers on foot, and there can be no doubt that, as Sir Samuel Baker says, following a wounded tiger into the jungle on foot is a work of extreme danger. But even this may be largely diminished if proper precautions are taken, though it must be admitted that, from the great difficulty of distinguishing a tiger lying amongst dried forest leaves, there must be a considerable amount of risk, though the amount of it is rather difficult to determine, but I may mention that though I suppose upwards of forty tigers have been killed in the neighbourhood of my plantation, only two natives have been killed when out shooting. Besides these accidents, one man recovered from thirteen lacerated wounds, and another was deprived of his ear and cheek by the blow of a wounded tiger's paw. As regards the comparative risks to life of tigers, bears, and panthers, I have only been able to meet with one return which throws any light on the subject—a return which confirms the native view as to the bear being more dangerous than the tiger, and the panther much less dangerous than either. The return in question is to be found in the "North Kanara Gazetteer," and was supplied by the late Colonel W. Peyton, who wrote the section on Wild Animals. From this it appears that in North Kanara, during the twenty-two years ending 1877, 510 tigers were killed and 44 persons killed by them, one of whom was Lieutenant Power, of the 35th Madras Infantry. Between the years 1856 and 1882 51 bears were killed and 22 persons killed by them, one of whom was Lord Edward Percy St. Maur, second son of the Duke of Somerset. Between the years 1856 and 1877 805 panthers were killed and 22 persons killed by them. From these returns it would appear that the bear is about four times as dangerous as the tiger, that the tiger is about three times as dangerous as the panther, and that the bear is about fourteen times as dangerous to man as the panther. As regards comparative destructiveness to animal life, I may observe in passing that the tiger seems to be more troublesome than the panther, and that Colonel Peyton records between 1878 and 1882 4,041 deaths of cattle killed by tigers against 1,617 killed by panthers. The bison (*gavœus gaurus*) would appear to be very seldom dangerous to man, if I may judge by the fact that in his long experience Colonel Peyton does not record a single death from the gaur, though he observes that it frequently charges when attacked. In my part of Mysore I have heard of but one death, which occurred in the case of a native who was tracking a bull which had been wounded by one of my managers. The wild boars, I may here add, seem to be now, from being much hunted, no doubt, more dangerous than they were in former years. Within the last two years in my district five persons were severely wounded by them, of whom three died. But it is natural that all wild animals should become more dangerous the more they are hunted, and, rather to my amusement, my old shikari, to whom I have previously alluded, complained in a querulous and aggrieved tone that every animal—even the sambur deer—seemed to charge one nowadays. And this is a fact worth recording, and if wild animals are declining in numbers, it is some comfort to think that the sport to be had from the remainder will improve. But it is time to close these rather desultory remarks, and treat the subject in a systematic manner, and I now proceed to say (1) something as regards the natural history of Mysore, and (2) something as to the big game shooting of the Province. I may here mention that all the anecdotes given will either be interesting from a natural history point of view, or told with the view of illustrating points likely to be of use to the inexperienced sportsman.

As the author of the Gazetteer of the Province, in his opening sentence on the fauna of Mysore, says with much truth, that "Nothing less than a separate treatise, and that a voluminous one, could do justice to the marvellous wealth of the animal kingdom in a province under the tropics marked by so many varied natural features as Mysore," I need hardly say that I have only space to make a cursory allusion to the subject. The varieties of animals, reptiles, birds, fish, and insects are indeed very numerous, and though Mr. Rice informs us that he has only made an attempt to collect the names of the main representatives, he enumerates no less than 70 mammals, 332 birds, 35 reptiles, 42 fishes, and 49 insects, though only the leading families of the last are given, and many kinds of fish have not been identified. But, though I cannot, as I have said, go at any length into the subject, I can at least give the names of the animals and birds which are of more or less interest to sportsmen, and perhaps touch upon some which are mainly of interest to the naturalist. There are then to be found in Mysore, elephants, tigers, panthers, hunting leopards, bears, wolves, jungle-dogs, hyenas, and foxes. Amongst the graminivorous animals I may mention the *gavœus gaurus*, commonly called bison (a name to which I shall adhere as it is the one in common use), the sambur deer, the spotted deer, the hog deer, and the barking deer or jungle sheep. There are four kinds of antelopes, the nilgei, four-horned antelope, the antelope, and the gazelle. Of the birds, I may mention 12 varieties of pigeons, 2 of sandgrouse, 2 of partridges, 8 of quail, peafowl, jungle-fowl, spenfowl, bustard, floriken (a kind of bustard), woodcock, woodsnipe, common snipe, jacksnipe, painted snipe, widgeon, 4 kinds of teal, and 5 of wild ducks. I may mention that there are 9 kinds of eagles, 20 kinds of hawks, and 13 varieties of owls. As regards reptiles, crocodiles are the only ones that sportsmen take any interest in, and they are to be found in many of the rivers of Mysore. Fish of various kinds are to be found in the numerous large tanks in Mysore, though I may add, that some of these pieces of water would elsewhere be called lakes, as they are sometimes upwards of twelve miles in circumference. The well-known mahseer abounds in the rivers of the Western Ghauts of Mysore, and gives excellent sport, and in the opinion of some anglers, superior to salmon fishing. I have said in my first chapter on coffee, that the life of a planter to any one fond of nature and an open air life is an agreeable one, so agreeable that, though from accidents of fortune no longer dependeut on coffee, I still find it the most pleasant life in the world, and return to it annually with pleasure, and I think that the mere enumeration of the varied forms of animal life, which are so interesting both to the sportsman and the naturalist, will go far to justify my conclusions. Having thus glanced at a part of the fauna of the province, I now proceed to the big game shooting section of my chapter, but, before doing so, I may mention that it is stated in the "Mysore Gazetteer" (Vol. II., p. 13) that, according to old legends, the lion was once to be found in the Province.

Of elephants, and elephant shooting, I have had no experience. In Mysore and in British India they are reserved by the State which, from time to time, captures the elephants by driving them into large inclosures, and there is a record of one of the sales of captured elephants in my second chapter. But the reader need not regret my want of experience here, as it would be difficult for any one to add to the admirable and exhaustive account of elephants and their ways which is to be found in the late Mr. Sanderson's [1] admirable work. His death is really much to be lamented, for he was not merely a destructive sportsman, but an intelligent and sympathetic observer of the wild animals he lived amongst, and I think I am only repeating current opinion when I say that a more admirable and interesting work of its kind never was written. Mr. Sanderson, I may mention, was specially employed by Government to superintend the capture of herds of elephants, and also to hunt man-eating tigers, and tigers of obnoxious character.

Tigers, as to which I shall have, I am afraid, rather too long an account to give, are fairly numerous in the forests of the Western Ghauts, and some other parts of the country, if I may judge by the fact that rewards were paid for 68 in 1874, and for 100 in 1875, but in former times they were much more numerous in certain parts of the province, a fact which is testified to by General Dobbs, who when a young man was in civil employ in the Chittledroog division of Mysore in 1834. He mentions in his "Reminiscences of Life in Mysore" [2] that his division was infested with wild beasts and, to reduce their numbers, he obtained from one of the officials a plan of a pit 12 feet long,

[1] G. P. Sanderson's "Thirteen Years among the Wild Beasts of India," 1878.

[2] "Reminiscences of Life in Mysore, South Africa and Burmah." By Major-General R. S. Dobbs. London, Hatchards, Piccadilly, 1882.

12 feet deep, and $2\frac{1}{2}$ feet wide, closed with brushwood at both sides and one end. Wooden spikes were fixed at the bottom, and the top of the pit was covered over with light brushwood. A sheep or goat was then tied inside at the closed end, where there was standing place left for it. As tigers usually spring on their prey they are thus sure to fall through the light brushwood into the pit. "In a short time," writes the general, "48 royal tigers were thus destroyed, four of which were brought to me on one morning. Mr. Stokes, the superintendent of the Nuggur division, obtained from me the plan of these pits, and in an equally short time caught upwards of 70 tigers. Now comes a circumstance which I can vouch for, but cannot explain. In a short time the success in both divisions terminated, and never again did a tiger fall into one of these pits, though numbers of tigers continued to infest the country." One result of the success obtained is worth recording. The balance of nature had been destroyed; the tigers to a great extent lived on wild pigs, and these, after the destruction of the tigers, multiplied so rapidly that the general records that there was an increased destruction of extensive sugar plantations. And I may note in passing, that the balance of nature may equally be destroyed from the other end of the line, and tigers made much more destructive than they otherwise would be. This is remarkably so near the western passes of Mysore, for never were tigers more numerous or destructive than they have recently been in my neighbourhood, and this is clearly to be traced to the great destruction[1] of deer, pigs, and bison by the natives in the immediate vicinity of the great forests, a subject to which I shall afterwards have occasion to allude.

The sudden spread amongst the tigers of the news about these pits is really very remarkable. We know that animals and birds are taught by example and experience

[1] *Vide* Appendix C.

to avoid certain dangers—that birds, which are at first killed in considerable numbers by telegraph wires, gradually learn to avoid them, and that hares which are at first excluded by rabbit netting in the course of time take to jumping it, but it is certainly impossible to explain by anything we know as regards the spread of experience amongst animals as to how the news could spread amongst the tigers, over a tract of country about half as large as Scotland, for traps were set in two out of the four divisions into which Mysore was then divided.

It has often been a subject of remark that tigers, without any motive that we can even guess at, avoid certain parts of the country which, to us, seem to be equally favourable to them. This is remarkably so in my district in Mysore, parts of which, apparently quite as suitable for tigers as other parts, have never been known to hold one. It is also remarkable that they invariably cross from one range of hills to another by almost exactly the same route, at least such is my experience. These tiger passes as they are called by the natives are well known to them. There is one about a mile and a half to the north of my bungalow, and another at about the same distance to the south, and between these two points I have never heard of the track of a tiger being seen except on one occasion.

It seems singular that, as so much has been written about tigers, there should be any dispute as to the way in which the tiger usually seizes its prey, but I find that Mr. Sanderson differs widely from Captain Forsyth, and Captain Baldwin and others, and says that, though the tiger does occasionally seize by the nape of the neck in the case of his having to deal with very powerful animals, his usual method is to seize by the throat; and another sportsman of great experience tells me that, though he has seen hundreds of kills, the seizure was always by the throat. In my part of the country it is so much the usual method for the tiger to seize by the nape of the neck, that a native, when asked if he is sure that it was a tiger and not a panther, always puts his hand to the back of his neck, and if he says that the animal was seized by the throat, we invariably assume that the seizer is a panther. As Mr. Sanderson was a most careful observer, I cannot doubt the correctness of his experience, and as little can I doubt the experience in my neighbourhood. But this apparent discrepancy may easily be explained, and I regard it as probable, or even quite certain, that tigers may vary their method of attack in accordance as they live mainly on game or mainly on village cattle. In the case of a bison, a wild boar, or of a large and powerful village buffalo, Mr. Sanderson admits that the seizure is by the nape of the neck, and that no doubt is the rule with the forest tigers, such as those that have been killed near my estate, and which have lived mostly upon game, but I can easily conceive that tigers that have lived on village cattle would attack in a different way.

There is also another difference between Mr. Sanderson and other sportsmen as to the tiger killing animals with a blow of its paw. Mr. Sanderson does not in the least believe that the paw is so used, but Captain Williamson [1] considers the paw as "the invariable engine of destruction." "I have seen," he says, "many men and oxen that had been killed by tigers, in most of which no mark of a claw could be seen." I have not paid much attention to this subject, but I do recollect one instance of a bullock that had been killed by a blow of the paw, as I remember being struck by the fact that there was no apparent cause of death, but on a closer examination I found a wide bruise, evidently from the tiger's paw, on the side of the head. A friend of mine of great experience tells me that he has known of animals being killed by a blow

[1] "Oriental Field Sports." By Captain Thomas Williamson, London, 1807.

of the paw. That men are commonly killed by a blow of the paw on the head I have little doubt. Captain Williamson mentions a case that occurred in his presence, and I knew of a doctor who had examined seven bodies, and in each case the skull had been fractured by a blow of the paw. General Rice,[1] when giving an account of the seizure of Cornet Elliot, mentions that he had a narrow escape from a blow of the tigress's paw, which he guarded off with his uplifted rifle. The stock of the rifle was marked with the claws, while the trigger and guard were knocked completely flat on one side, so that the gun was useless until repaired. There is no doubt, then, that the tiger can, and does sometimes, use his paw with deadly effect, though I have little doubt that he prefers to use his teeth, as the shock of a blow to the paw must, in the case of a bullock at any rate, be very considerable.

The carrying power of tigers is very great, and has often been remarked on, but it has been doubted whether they often carry off an animal without some part of it dragging on the ground. Mr. Sanderson gives some instances of their doing so; and I have known of one instance in my neighbourhood where a tiger after killing a bullock took it into the jungle and carried the carcase along the trunk of a tree which had fallen across a ravine. But, considering its size, the dragging power of a panther is much more remarkable, and it seems to carry off a bullock as easily as a tiger does. On one occasion a panther killed a donkey close to my bungalow, and carried it off, and had even attempted to jump up the bank of an old ditch with it, which was five or six feet high, but had failed in the attempt and abandoned the carcase. But why the panther did not drag the donkey down to another part of the jungle, where it could easily have dragged the carcase into it, is

[1] "Tiger Shooting in India; Experiences 1850 to 1854," by William Rice, 1857.

difficult to conceive, unless we suppose that these animals have not, after the failure of one plan, mind enough to try another. Perhaps this is so, or that they take the pet in a case of failure and go off in disgust. I imagine that this kind of feeling must influence tigers, for I once found an uneaten carcase of a bullock wedged between two rocks. A tiger had killed, high up on a mountain side, and taken the carcase into the nearest ravine, evidently with the view of dragging it towards the water further down the hill. On his way he had to pass through a narrow passage between two rocks, and here the carcase stuck fast, and he had in vain tried to pull it through, but it had never occurred to him to pull it out backwards (which he might easily have done when the carcase was only slightly wedged) and try another route. But, after all, we must not be surprised at this, as even the human animal does not always readily find the solution of a fresh difficulty. Tigers, it is well known, are good swimmers, and seem to have no difficulty in taking the carcase of a bullock with them, if I may judge by the fact, which was told me by a friend, that a tiger once swam eighty yards across a river in the northern part of Mysore, taking with it the carcase of a newly killed bullock.

Tiger shooting in the Western Ghauts is always carried out without the aid of elephants, and it is seldom that one can obtain, even for the first shot, a fairly safe position. Colonel Peyton, whom I have previously quoted, says that a man is not safe under sixteen feet from the ground, but it is seldom that such an elevation can be obtained, as the country is so steep that, though you have a fair drop on the lower side of the tree, a tiger from the upper side may easily spring on to you, and is then generally on your level, or even higher. Of course you select a tree where, in theory, the tiger must come on the lower side, but tigers will often take most eccentric courses, and last year, after having taken up a position on a tree which had a drop of eight feet on the lower side, and where it was assumed by all of us as certain that the tiger would pass lower down the hill, it came on the upper side, on rather higher ground than the cleft I was sitting on, and so close that I could have touched it with a spear, and had I not fatally crippled it at the first shot, it might easily have jumped on to me. But I entirely agree with Colonel Peyton that it is always best for several reasons to get into a tree, even though it may not be a high one, or indeed into a scrubby tree so low that your feet are only some five feet from the ground. In the first place, you can command a wider view, then you are concealed, and can let the tiger pass your line, and as the tiger could pass under your feet you are not in his way, and there would be little chance, if you reserved your fire till he had passed, in his either attacking you or being driven back on the beaters. Colonel Peyton, whom I quote with great confidence, is in favour of a bamboo ladder with broad rungs to sit on, and which will enable you to have your feet eleven feet from the ground. To illustrate the risk of sitting on the ground, I may mention the following incident:

Many years ago news was brought that a tiger had killed cattle some six or seven miles off. The distance was considerable, the news came late, and it was, I think, about three in the afternoon when I reached the spot. The beaters were all ready and impatient, no doubt, owing to being kept waiting so long, and as I did not wish to delay them, and had no ladder, and there was no suitable tree, I took a seat on the ground behind a bush which lay on one side of, and about twenty yards from, a depression in the land through the bottom of which, by all the laws of tigers, the tiger ought to have passed to the main forest beyond. I had no sooner seated myself than I saw, from the lay of the ground, that if the tiger should happen to break at a point in a line with my bush he would probably gallop on to the top of me before it would be possible to make more than a snap shot. I at once left the spot and climbed a small tree on the opposite side of the depression, and this enabled me to have my feet some five feet from the ground. Presently the beat began, and with a roar, and an evident determination to charge anything in his way, a very large tiger broke cover at full speed and went exactly over the very spot of ground I had been sitting on. At the pace he was coming at I do not indeed think he could have stopped himself, and I hardly think I should have had time to fire, and I have often wondered what would have happened had he galloped on to myself and my man. However, as it was, I was all right, fired just as he passed the bush and knocked him over with one shot, and put another into him as he got half up and struggled into the jungle, apparently with his back broken, and lay down about a few yards aside of it. And now by a curious coincidence we just missed what must have been a very serious accident, and this is well worth mentioning, as it confirms what another writer has said as to the care that should be used in approaching a tiger supposed to be dead.

After the beat was over the beaters rushed up, and one of the natives, who had no doubt seen the tiger from a point on the hill above, said, "His back is broken, and he must be dead; let us go in and drag him out." Feeling that it would be better to wait a little longer to make quite sure, I said, just to quiet them, "Stand the people in line and count them for the division of the reward." I had not counted more than five when up got the tiger close to us with a startling roar, and I then experienced what Colonel Peyton has said, namely, that there are very few even of the stanchest sportsmen who will not draw back a pace or two at the sudden roar of a wounded tiger. On this occasion I removed more than that, for I at once seized a rifle and ran several yards up the hill to gain the advantage of the ground, and I need hardly say that there was a slight scatter amongst the unarmed natives. But as the tiger did not charge out, I saw that he was probably off, and at once ran down the side of the jungly ravine to head him, and at the first break in the jungle got up into a tree. The tiger almost immediately appeared on the opposite side of the ravine, going steadily along, and showing no signs of being wounded whatever, and I fired at, but missed him, partly on account of my awkward position in the tree and partly from excitement. Then I ran on to the next open break in the jungly ravine, and again got up into a tree. By this time the beaters came up in the rear of the tiger, who refused to go further down the ravine, or was unable to do so, and the natives sent to me to go up and attack the tiger in the jungle, to which I replied by requesting them to be good enough to forward the animal to me. However, as he refused to move, and it was getting late, I went up the ravine, and they pointed out the tiger, which was lying on its side. I fired a shot at it, when it got up, then I fired another at once, and it fell and died almost immediately. This was by far the largest tiger ever killed in our district, and an old sportsman who had seen much of shooting during a long residence in India told me that he was sure he had never seen a larger skin, and did not know that he had ever seen one as big. As evidence of size, he attached, I may mention, great importance to the width of the skin of the tail just at its junction with the body. The paws of this tiger, too, were remarkably larger than those of other tigers. I found that the first bullet had taken effect in the neck, which it had no doubt grazed with sufficient force to paralyze the tiger for a time, and Colonel Peyton records a similar case where great risk had been incurred from approaching a tiger apparently dead, but where the spine had been merely grazed.

What I have previously mentioned illustrates one danger from sitting on the ground, and I may give another instance which occurred to me in 1891. I had gone after a tiger, and my shikari had prepared an excellent seat on a tree at an absolutely safe height. The tiger, however, had shifted his ground, it appears, to an adjacent jungle. This consisted of one long and rather deep ravine, with several spurs at which the tiger might break. It had several times previously happened that tigers had come up the bottom of this ravine, and I had once killed one there from a tree in the jungle, but the trees so situated are difficult to ascend, and we did not wish to make a noise nor to waste time by making a ladder, so I determined on sitting on the ground in the jungle, about twenty yards from the bottom of the ravine, and made myself perfectly comfortable. While keeping an eye on the bottom of the ravine up which the tiger was expected to pass, I was suddenly startled by a roar from some little distance behind us. My old shikari at once saw the danger we were in, and looked extremely disturbed, and no wonder, for he saw at once that the tiger had been driven back by a stop at one of the spurs, and might come down on us from behind, so that we should have had no chance of seeing him till he was almost on the top of us, and as a matter of fact he did pass down into the ravine rather higher up and just out of our sight, and from this we failed to dislodge him. On the whole, for every reason, I am much against sitting on the ground. You are liable to be run into sometimes, as we have seen, and at others you are not high enough up to command the ground, and there is a greater chance of driving a tiger back on the beaters. There are, however, occasions when one must sit on the ground, and if you have occasion to do so, it is of course advisable always to try and get about twenty or thirty yards on one side of the course the tiger is likely to take, and always let him pass your line of fire before firing. It is also of great importance to have as your second man one who can remain absolutely motionless when a tiger is advancing towards him. To illustrate the importance of this I may mention the following incident:

I was posted one day in a tree, when the tiger charged back through the beaters with a roar, and I had at once to get down and run to another point of the jungle to cut him off. I then tried to get up a tree on the grass land near the edge of the jungle, and next tried another a little further off, but could not get up into it, and when the beat recommenced there was nothing for it but to sit down beside a bush about one hundred yards from the jungle, and on ground on almost exactly the same level as the tiger would have to traverse. But this bush was so small that it only partially concealed me, and the entire body of my native second gun-bearer was exposed to view. This man fortunately had a most remarkable power of sitting absolutely motionless under any circumstances which required stillness. I also was fully prepared to remain quite still, and arranged myself so as to fire at the tiger when he was exactly in front of me. It was interesting to observe what followed. The tiger was evidently an old hand. He had anticipated our plan, and charged back through the beaters, as we have seen. He had also evidently anticipated the alterations we should probably make, and when the beat recommenced he cautiously emerged from the jungle and looked up (it is a rare thing for a tiger to do this) into the tree near the edge of the jungle into which I had tried to climb. He seemed then to be quite satisfied that all danger was at an end, and strolled leisurely towards us. As he was passing the point which put the whole bush between me and him, I cautiously levelled my rifle, which I already had in almost exact position to fire, so that when he came into my full view I had the sight on the second stripe behind the shoulder. By a curious coincidence he stood quite still when he came into my full view, and, as he was only about twenty yards away, presented a very fine sight. But I reserved my fire till he had moved forward a pace or two, and then I fired, and on he bounded. Then followed one of those picturesque, exciting, and somewhat amusing scenes, which can only occur in tiger shooting on foot. For the leisurely proceedings of the tiger had given the beaters time to get to the end of the cover just as I was firing at the tiger, and as I ran round the hillside to the other side of a ravine which ran down the hill, they ran forward so rapidly and plunged so suddenly into the jungle, that the tiger came out just below me. I fired at him, and so did one or two of the natives who had run up to join me, and the tiger fell dead in the air in the middle of a long bound. But running and excitement are not favourable to accuracy of aim, and the tiger, on this occasion, was struck by only one ball, and, strange to say, in the sole of the foot, and the only bullet-mark on his body was from my first shot at him. My account of the incident may be valuable to an inexperienced sportsman, and illustrates also the peculiar disadvantage of sitting on the ground, because if the tiger had walked straight up to me, and I had fired at him in the face, which I should have been obliged to do, he would, if not killed outright, probably have either gone back amongst the beaters, or charged me.

I have alluded to my second gun-carrier on this occasion as being a man who had the greatest power of remaining still under all circumstances, out shooting, when it was necessary to do so, and I may also mention that he was a man who combined the greatest coolness with the greatest daring. He was of a Hindoo peasant family, entered my service as a workman, rose to be a duffadar or overseer, and for many years has been head overseer on my coffee estates, and he is as good as a planter as he is as a shikari. I could give many instances of his cool daring. On one occasion a wounded tigress—it was the cold weather season, when everything was still green about the edges of the jungle—went into a ravine which was flanked by a great bed of ferns about five feet high. The natives looked at this bed into which the tigress had disappeared with considerable doubt, and one of them said, "How is anyone to go in here?" "I will show you," said Rama Gouda quietly, and he picked up several large stones, threw them into the ferns, and then plunged into them. I afterwards killed the tiger on foot in the ravine, but of course he ran the risk of coming upon it in the ferns. But the coolest thing I ever knew him to do was when a manager of mine wanted to fire at a tiger as it was approaching him. It was in the days of the muzzle-loaders, and as Rama Gouda knew that to speak would be fatal, he quietly but firmly put both his fingers on the caps when my manager presented the gun at the tiger, and kept them there till the tiger had reached the proper point for action. Then he withdrew them, and my manager killed the tiger. It is contrary to all rule, on account of the beaters, to fire at a tiger till he has passed you, and as the manager and Rama Gouda were seated on the ground, if the tiger had been fired at face to face an accident might have occurred. On only one occasion did I ever see him disturbed, and that was when he took up a position at a beat for big game. Presently he heard a hiss, and on looking round found a reared-up cobra about to strike at his naked thigh. He saved himself by a jump on one side, but he showed by his eye when he mentioned the circumstance that he had been somewhat commoved.

The natives have an idea that a tiger will not attack a

group of from four to five people massed together, and in 1891 four or five unarmed natives proposed that I should sit on an absolutely bare piece of ground, and that they should sit round me, and that the tiger should be driven up to us. But this offer, and more especially as I had only one gun, I declined with thanks, unless they could find a small bush or piece of rock to sit behind, and as neither could be found, I took up a position on a steep hillside and on a scrubby tree, which I thought safe enough, as I assumed that the tiger would pass on the lower side of it, but it approached close on the upper side, and on rather higher ground, and could easily have sprung on to me, as it was not more than fifteen feet distant, thus again illustrating how difficult it is in a hilly country to get into a reasonably safe position. Altogether, the risks of tiger shooting in a hilly country where elephants cannot be used, and where you may have to run to cut off a wounded tiger or follow one into the jungle, is attended with risk even to the most experienced. The amount of that risk is difficult to determine, but I may say generally it is such that while bachelors, or married men of independent means whose families are well provided for, in short, people whose lives are of no cash value, may freely go into the jungle on foot after wounded tigers, and generally throw themselves in the way of the animals, I do not consider it right for a married man, whose family is dependent wholly or partially on his exertions, to go after tigers on foot, or without the aid of elephants, for though a man may resolve to stick to safe positions, they are often difficult and sometimes impossible to find, and the excitement soon does away with all feelings for one's personal safety.

Though I have no doubt that it is, generally speaking, true that a tiger will not attack a group of four or five people, I am not at all sure that this is correct as regards a wounded tiger, and a tiger I had wounded once sprang into a party of I should say at least twenty people, and killed one of them—at least the poor man died in the course of a few hours. I always regretted that I did not obtain and preserve his belt. At the back of it was the iron catch with which to hitch his wood-knife, and the tiger's tooth had grazed one side of the iron, and cut it as if one had worked at the iron with a steel file. Another instance too occurred of a tiger attacking a party, or at least one of a party which was approaching a tiger. Several tigers, it appeared, had been marked down, and the jungle in which they were was surrounded by nets. This was done in Mysore on the arrival of the Russian princes some years ago, but one of the tigers had managed to elude the shooters, and, as the native magistrate of the district was anxious to have it killed, a sporting photographer who was there undertook to look it up. As they approached the thicket in which the tiger was concealed the tiger rushed out with a sudden bound, aimed a blow with its paw at the leading native, tore his scalp right off and flung it on to a bush, bit the man in the arm, and retreated into the thicket with such suddenness that no one had time to fire. The poor man afterwards died.

The great danger from following up wounded tigers on foot in the jungle arises from the extraordinary difficulty of seeing the animal when it is lying amongst dry fallen leaves, into which the body partially sinks, and this is more particularly the case if there is a flickering sunlight coming though the branches of the jungle trees. In one case of this kind, though I could see the tiger when it half raised itself up—it had been wounded in the back—I failed to pick it up the moment it sank back into the leaves; and my shikari told me of another similar case he had seen when there was a similar flickering light. But even without that source of confusion to the sight a tiger is extremely difficult to see, as difficult as a hare in a ploughed field, or perhaps more so. On one occasion Rama Gouda said to me, when we were attacking a wounded tiger, or rather tigress in the jungle, "There is the tiger." "What!" I said, "that thing looking like a stone?" The light was bad. We both supposed it to be dead, but I said, "I suppose I had better take a shot at it," and did so, and, when the smoke cleared away, found that the tiger had removed. Then a native went forward and gently parted the reeds with his hands, and showed me the tigress—which had moved about twenty yards—lying on her side, and evidently in a dying condition. She was now only a few yards from me, and I fired at her, and she rolled over and died. As it happened, I do not think that I ran much risk, but one never can exactly tell how much vitality a dying tiger has, and in the case previously alluded to I have no doubt that the tiger must have died immediately after he made his fatal attack on the party.

It is owing obviously to their great power of concealment that tigers are so very rarely ever seen by accident, and Mr. Sanderson says that during some years of wandering in tigerish localities he has only come upon them accidentally about half a dozen times, and my own experience, and that of other sportsmen to whom I have spoken, quite confirms this. But I am persuaded that a native can see a tiger much more readily than a European, and the former have, I think, much better distinguishing power. For instance, a European has great difficulty in seeing a green pigeon in a green tree till the bird moves, while a native seems to have no such difficulty. My own sight is, or rather was, very good, but I found on one occasion, when I was stalked by a tiger, that it was most provokingly defective as compared with that of a native. The incident occurred in this way. In cloudy weather, during a break in the monsoon, I was beating a ravine for game, and had sent my second gun-carrier with the beaters. As the beat was drawing to a close, I heard a sambur deer belling at the head of a ravine, about a few hundred yards from the termination of the jungle we were beating. As I thought I might get a shot at it, I went across the grassland in the direction of the sound, and up to within about ten yards of the edge of the jungle, the fringe of which at that point projected a little. I could see nothing, but as the people were coming my way in any case, I remained where I was. The first person to arrive was a very plucky Hindoo peasant—a keen sportsman and splendid stalker—and when he almost touched me he at once pointed and said "There is a tiger." I put my rifle to my shoulder, and said to him "Where?" "There," he said, and as he put his hand on my shoulder I could feel it trembling with excitement. Alas, I could not make out the tiger; but, after all, that was not so very wonderful, as the day was dark, and the underwood fringe rather thick, but the tiger actually managed to back gradually away without my being able to see him. He had evidently been stalking the sambur, which had uttered the note of alarm I had heard, and no doubt seeing that there was something at the edge of the jungle, had crawled to the edge, and there lain down within ten or twelve yards of me.

Tigers seem to recover easily from wounds, and so completely, that no trace of a bullet having entered the body can be found. On one occasion I shot a tiger, and when the skin was being removed we perceived a lump on the inner side of it. This we opened, and found that it contained a bullet which a brother of mine had fired into the tiger about a year before. We had no difficulty in identifying the bullet, as no other rifle in the country had anything like it. The tiger was perfectly well and fat, and had not a mark on it of having been previously wounded, and yet the bullet had gone close to mine, which proved fatal to the tiger. In 1891 I killed a tiger, which had evidently, from his action, been hunted before. He was in unusually good condition, and yet had a piece of lead in him, which appeared to be a fragment of an express bullet. But a friend of mine tells me that he has often found old bullets in tigers. It is a surprising thing that tigers and panthers seem often to be little influenced by wounds, and I have heard of one case of a panther, for which a sportsman was sitting up, which returned to the kill after being wounded and fired at several times. A friend of mine was once out small game shooting on the Nilgiris when a tiger seized one of his dogs. He at once put a ball cartridge into his smooth bore, had a beat, and wounded the tiger. On the following day he returned to the spot with his rifle, and again beat the jungle, when he killed the tiger, which had returned and finished the dog, and then found that the bullet of the day before, which had struck the tiger in the chest, had travelled nearly the whole length of the body. I recollect once shooting a spotted deer which had a matchlock ball lying up against its liver, and pressing on it, but the deer, though it had good horns, was rather a stunted animal.

I have previously remarked that, in the opinion of Colonel Peyton, even the stanchest sportsman when on foot in the jungle, is liable to be startled by the sudden roar of a wounded tiger close at hand, and so much so as even to draw back for a pace or two, but he says that the effect is only momentary. In 1891 I again had an opportunity of observing the effects on myself and others of the roar of a wounded tiger in the jungle, but on this occasion, though I confess I was very considerably startled, and generally commoved for a moment, as I had expected to find the tiger dead, I did not step back a pace, nor did the stanchest of the natives who were with me, though a certain number climbed right up to the tops of trees. As it happened, there was, after all, no danger, for the tiger had been damaged in the back, and I soon dispatched it. The effect of the roar of a tiger is really very remarkable, and of this the animal itself seems to be well aware, for the tiger I have just alluded to—evidently an old hand, from the trouble he had given us and the cunning he had displayed—remained in the open, or came out into the open as the beaters approached, then roared at them and afterwards retreated into the jungle—a narrow ravine in which he seemed determined to remain, though shots were fired into it, and in which I think he would have remained had not the beaters charged into it in a body in the most plucky manner. A friend of mine also met with a similar instance, where a tiger came out—confronted the beaters and roared at them. The beaters may see the tiger, and quite close, and yet not be much disturbed, but a roar even a good way off has on them a disturbing effect, though it is difficult to see why the nerves should be affected more easily through the medium of the ears than the eyes. I may here mention that, when the sportsman has a damaged heart, the roar of a wounded tiger, at least if the shooter is on foot in the jungle, is apt to produce a slight flutter of that organ, though that, too, like the effect alluded to by Colonel Peyton, is momentary. Having had for some years a rather damaged heart, I was interested in experimenting as regards the effects of tigers on its action, but could come to no very distinct conclusion. I was once in an extremely insecure position on a conspicuous cleft of a bare tree, with my feet not more than seven or eight feet from the ground, when the tiger galloped into the arena as it were in the most sudden manner, and passed within fifteen feet of me. I knocked him over with a ball in the back at the second shot—the first, from the awkward position I was placed in, having either missed, or done him little harm.

The tiger then lay on his side, with his head turned backwards and resting on his shoulder. He kept his eye on me, and I kept mine on him, and I did not fire again, as my second gun native (we had never expected the tiger to be where we found him, and were on our way home) had seated himself on another tree. In a low tone he said to me "Load, load!" but the moment I took my eye off the tiger to do so he began to wriggle into the jungle, and I only got a snap shot at his hind leg. Now when the tiger roared, which he did as he approached me, and he lay watching me, I felt no sensation of the heart, though I felt a distinct flutter when loading and when the tiger was wriggling away. On the following day, however, I felt my heart to be rather the worse, but I attributed this to exposure to the sun. On another occasion, which occurred shortly afterwards, I shot a tigress so close that I could have touched her with a spear, and she was on rather higher ground than myself, but on this occasion neither when I fired, nor when she fell, and turned her head to me and showed me all her teeth, did I experience any heart effect whatever. I must say, though, that I had my attention strongly turned to the necessity of not allowing myself to be excited, in case it should be bad for my heart, and the power of the will must no doubt have much effect in controlling the action of the heart. Anyone who has anything the matter with his heart should take digitalis before going out, and also take a few doses of this tonic with him, as well as some very strong beef-tea. He should also endeavour to go after the tiger in the morning or late in the afternoon, and lie in a cool place in the jungle in the heat of the day, as I am quite sure, from my own experience, that exposure to much sun heat is bad for the heart. As heart disease, from the excitement of life, is becoming more common, these hints may be useful.

Since writing the preceding, I went out after a tiger near

my house, where I was placed on a tree quite out of the reach of a tiger—in fact it was too high, and showed me the great disadvantage of being more than say fifteen feet from the ground. The beat was a peculiar one, and I was posted just inside the jungle. The beaters were rather long at their work, and I had fallen into a reverie, from which I was aroused by three roars of a tiger just behind me, and the roars were not charging roars, but of a character which meant, in tiger language, that people had better look out. Now the tiger was below me, and I was as absolutely safe as a man at home in his armchair, and yet I felt my heart throb quickly. The explanation of this no doubt was that I had forgotten to take my dose of digitalis before starting. Being in the jungle I was under great disadvantages from having to shoot through the underwood, and, though I knocked over the tiger, and there was plenty of blood to prove it, we lost him.

This tiger is known as the lame tiger from being so in the right fore leg—the result of an old wound probably—and some ten days after my wounding him a curious coincidence happened. A young married lady, who was at the time on a visit to my bungalow, had expressed a great wish to see a tiger, and, when leaving for Bangalore in her bullock coach between nine and ten o'clock one night, very nearly saw the lame tiger. He was standing in the road some miles from my house, at a sharp bend where the road deflects abruptly to cross a Nullah, and waited till the coach got within ten or fifteen yards of him, whereupon, after delivering three moderate growls, he limped down off the road, and stood for a moment looking at the coach and bullocks.

All sportsmen must regret the necessity for tying out live bait for tigers, but this is really a fully justifiable proceeding, as thereby an immense amount of pain is saved to animal life in general, and an immense sum of money to the native population. The destruction of cattle by tigers is really enormous, and, I believe, far exceeding that reported to Government, and it is so mainly because the tiger is only allowed to eat a fraction of what he kills, as the moment that news of a bullock being killed reaches the village, the low class natives at once proceed to the spot, drive away the tiger, and carry off the beef. And this is only prevented when an English sportsman is within reach, in which case the cattle owners prevent the people from touching the carcase. It is often very annoying when tying out baits for tigers, to find them destroyed by panthers, as the panther, of course, from his habit of climbing trees, and concealing himself in the foliage, and from a kind of general facility that he seems to have for getting out of the way, is a difficult animal to find, in fact so much so, that I latterly would never go out after one, unless it had killed quite close at hand. In 1891 I was once much annoyed to find that a new kind of bait with an additional attraction had been quite ruined by a panther. This attraction consisted of a goat picketed in an open-topped (that was the mistake, it ought to have been closed) wooden cage which was placed in the branches of a tree, on the edge of the jungle, and about fifteen feet from the ground, while a bullock was picketed on the ground in the open land, about twenty yards away. The theory was that the, to a tiger, attractive aroma of the goat would be widely diffused, and that he might, too, further attract the tiger by his cries. News (false as it afterwards turned out to be) was brought in that a tiger had killed the bullock, and I toiled up on to the mountain some seven miles away from my bungalow, merely to find that a panther had killed the bullock and that my goat was hanging dead by the neck outside the cage just like a carcase in a butcher's shop. The panther had seized the goat, killed it, and jumped out of the cage with it, and had either not sense enough to cut the rope with his teeth, or had his suspicions aroused from finding the animal tied. To show that the suspicions of an animal can thus be aroused, I may mention the following incident, which is also especially interesting as showing the great skill of the tiger as a stalker and the singular power he has of stepping noiselessly on dry leaves, and his power to do mischief after being apparently shot dead. But before doing so I may mention rather an interesting circumstance. Besides the bait killed by the panther, I had two bullocks tied out in the neighbourhood, and as I did not care much for that part of the country, ordered them to be released and brought home with us. I was much struck with the earnest and business-like air with which these poor animals, which had spent some miserable nights in the jungle, expecting every moment to be killed by a tiger, trotted along, on a line often parallel with the party, and it somewhat reminded me of a picture I had seen in an illustrated paper, of the hunted deer amicably trotting home with the hounds and huntsmen. The fact was that they were determined to get home in good time, for fear, I suppose, of being shut out of the cattle shed, and though, just as they neared the shed, the remainder of the herd, which had been out grazing in the neighbourhood, appeared within twenty yards, the liberated baits got first into the shed. And now for my story showing how easily the suspicions of the tiger are excited.

A near neighbour of mine—at least he lived ten miles off—was much annoyed by tigers which, from the continuous nature of his large block of evergreen forest land, he could only get at by sitting over a bait. On one occasion he had tied out a bullock, in a piece of land of a few acres which he had cleared in the middle of the forest, and concealed himself on a tree. It was during the day, and the ground was covered with dried leaves which are so brittle in the hot weather that even the scratching, or walking of a bird can be heard some way off. Presently a large tiger—my friend knew that he was about —made his appearance and commenced a stalk so elaborate and careful that my friend declared it would have been worth 1,000 rupees to a young sportsman to have witnessed it. He put every paw down so carefully, gradually crushing the leaves under it, that my friend, though quite close to the tiger, could not hear a sound. Between the tiger and the bullock was the butt, about four feet high, of a felled tree, with long projecting surface roots, and this saved the tiger much trouble, for he got on to one of the roots, and carefully balanced himself on it, and so without noise was able to walk quickly along till he came to the butt which he seemed to wind round like a snake, and he then got on to a corresponding root on the other side, and walked along that. In short, he approached so gradually and noiselessly, and his colour against the brown dry leaves was so invisible, that he got quite close to the bullock before it perceived him. The moment it did so it charged, but the tiger, avoiding the horns, swung round the back of the bullock, and then sat up and put both its paws on its neck evidently to drag it down, but it then perceived that the animal was tied, and at once turned and sprang into the forest with such rapidity that my friend did not fire. He however sat patiently on, and after a considerable time the tiger reappeared, went through the whole stalking performance as carefully and exactly as before, and was seen and charged by the bullock as before. But this time the tiger was in earnest and seized the bullock. There was a struggle, the rope broke, and the bullock dropped dead, and then the tiger stood for a few seconds, a magnificent figure in the bright sunlight, looking all round as it were for signs of danger. Whether the tiger saw or smelt my friend is uncertain, but it suddenly lay down behind the bullock, interposing the carcase between itself and my friend, and resting its head on the body. As it is always more or less precarious to fire at the head of an animal where it may suddenly move my friend waited to get a body shot, but as the tiger had evidently no intention of moving he fired at the head and the tiger was apparently shot dead on the spot. But my friend, who was an experienced sportsman, waited a little, and in the end thought it safe to fire another shot before going up to the tiger. He did so, when the tiger sprang up and went off into the forest at full speed, and fell and died at some little distance away. The first bullet had struck the tiger below the eye, but had been deflected, and was found lodged in the jaw. My friend thinks that it would have proved fatal to the tiger, but that is doubtful, as tigers make such wonderful recoveries from wounds.

In tying out baits it is very important to use a chain instead of a rope, as the tiger will commonly cut the latter and carry off the carcase, and it is sometimes desirable, or even necessary in some cases, to sit over the carcase and await the return of the tiger. The latter is always the case where there are great continuous forests, where tigers cannot be isolated, or successfully pursued, unless one has an army of men and many guns. This form of sport, which Mr. Sanderson speaks highly of, I can imagine may be very interesting, but it is also very tiresome and tantalizing. A great many years ago I remember trying it for two nights, but without any success, and never again tried it till some years ago, when I made an attempt in one of the forests at the foot of one of the passes leading down to Mangalore. My people had no experience in the matter either, still we might have been successful had the carcase been chained. I took down a small herd of cattle from my plantations, and ordered some baits to be tied one evening, and early the following morning went round to look at them. In the first case we found that the rope had been cut and the bullock carried off and deposited in a depression in the ground about fifty yards away. The carcase was untouched. In the next case we found that the rope, which was a very strong jungle creeper as thick as a large-sized rope, had not been cut, but that the animal had been killed, and merely a few steaks as it were eaten from the rump. In the third case we found that the bullock, which had evidently been the first one seized, was about half eaten. In the fourth case the bullock, which was an old one, had not been touched. I think my people made a great mistake in tying out so many cattle so close together—they were not one hundred yards apart—still this certainly made matters more sure from one point of view, as a tiger crossing the country might have missed one bait, whereas he could hardly have missed four, but his having killed three baits made our proceedings a little mixed. I first ordered the surviving bullock to be taken home, and two of the carcases to be dragged away to a considerable distance, and resolved to sit over kill number two, as it was the best animal, and in the most convenient position, but unfortunately I ordered two of my people to take a seat on a tree near the place where number one had been killed and carried off, and the tiger, which went there first, looked up and saw them and growled. His suspicions of course were aroused, and the result was that he did not come at all to the kill I was sitting over—at least while I was there. After it was too dark to see to shoot I went home, and returned the following morning, when I found that the tiger had returned, cut the rope, and carried off the bullock to a distance of about two hundred yards, and eaten a good deal of it. I organized a small silent beat of a section of the forest, but nothing came of it. My head man then resolved to prepare a watching place in a tree near the carcase, and this time I resolved to follow Mr. Sanderson's advice, and begin to watch quite early in the afternoon. My man finished his arrangements by about midday, and, after breakfasting at home, I returned with him to the spot at about three o'clock. Horror of horrors, the carcase was gone again. My head shikari—the Rama Gouda, whom I have previously noticed as being such a cool and daring fellow—was enraged beyond measure. He at once, without saying a word, cut a creeper from the nearest tree, and without even a gun in his hand set off on the trail, but not, I observed, before gun-bearer number two, also a daring fellow, had looked at him with an inquiring eye, as much as to say, "are you not a trifle rash?" I followed Rama Gouda, though I was not quite sure of the prudence of our proceedings, and presently we perceived by the chattering of a squirrel that the tiger was moving along close to us. Then we came to the carcase, of which there was now only about half left, and from the tracks about it, and the quantity of flesh eaten, Rama Gouda was satisfied that the tiger must have watched him making his preparations and then carried off the carcase the moment he had left. Rama Gouda now lashed the creeper to the bullock's horns, and, with the aid of the second man, proceeded to drag it back to the watching place he had prepared, and which was about one hundred yards away. By this time the hinder part of the bullock had been eaten and only the fore part was intact and the carcase smelt horribly. There was something so ludicrous in the whole thing that I could not, and much to Rama Gouda's surprise, help laughing. The unfortunate animal had first been driven thirty miles from his home into these remote forests, then killed, then his remains were carried off as we have seen, and then again carried off, and now what was left was being dragged back again to the watching place. Rama Gouda soon arranged matters to his satisfaction by restoring the remains to their original position, but certainly not to mine, for there presently arose a most asphyxiating stench, which seemed to fill the entire air, and reminded one of what soldiers must often have experienced in our eastern campaigns. We waited till it was too dark to see to shoot and then went home, and early next morning I had to start for the coast, and thus ignominiously ended the only attempt of the kind I ever made. The tiger was evidently an old hand and was playing a regular game of hide and seek with us. The great error made was the neglect of Mr. Sanderson's advice as to chaining the bait in the first instance. Some tigers always carry off the carcase each time they visit it, and a friend of mine told me that when he was once sitting over a carcase, the tiger made a sudden rush, picked up the carcase in the course of it, and made off so suddenly that he had no time to fire.

I can easily understand that, as Mr. Sanderson says, there is a considerable charm and interest connected with this method (and in some cases it is the only method) of pursuing tigers, but I can see that it requires much experience, caution, and patience, and I would particularly advise those interested in this matter to consult Mr. Sanderson's valuable work.

I have often found in conversation that people are surprised to find that tigers eat tigers when a suitable opportunity for doing so presents itself, but considering that man still, in some parts of the world, eats his fellow man, it seems to me extremely natural that a tiger should eat a tiger. I have, however, only met with one instance which occurred in my neighbourhood, and in this case I am strongly inclined to think that the eaten tiger was first of all killed. The incident occurred in this way. Shortly before my arrival in India one winter, my manager wounded a tiger, but I do not think very severely, as the tiger not only travelled at least two miles, but ascended a mountain up to a considerable elevation. Along one side of the mountain is a rather long strip of forest, which is a favourite place for tigers either to pass through or lie up in, as it is quite out of any village-to-village route, and had the tiger been hard hit he would certainly have remained there. But not only did he not do so, but skirting the jungle, or passing through it, he climbed up a steep ascent, evidently with the view of going into the next valley, and near the top of the ascent his living history ends. Knowing from the direction taken by the wounded tiger that he would probably be in the jungle on the mountain side, my manager had it beaten on the day following, when a tiger came out which he took to be the wounded tiger, and which he killed. It then turned out that it was not the wounded tiger, but a fresh tiger with the wounded tiger, or nearly all the meat of it, inside him, and all that was recovered was the head and the skin of the chest, which I saw after my arrival, and which was sent in to Government for the reward, and by the size of the head it must have been a fine tiger. When I visited the jungle in 1891, I carefully cross-examined the natives in the matter, and they said that they could not say whether the tiger had died from wounds or whether he had been killed by the tiger that had carried off and eaten the body, but they were positive that it was a tiger that had eaten the body, from the tracks, for the body had been taken down to water, on the margin of which no other tracks but those of a tiger were visible, and these were clearly defined. They could also be distinctly traced from the place in the open grassland whence the body was carried. Taking all the circumstances into consideration—the distance travelled, the steepness of the ground, and the fact that the tiger passed a favourable jungle for lying in, I am strongly of opinion, in fact, I consider it almost certain, that the wounded tiger must have been dispatched by the other tiger, which was hungry and could not resist the smell of the blood. There is nothing remarkable in a tiger eating a tiger found dead, and I have read and heard of instances of this, and also of tigers fighting, and the vanquished tiger being eaten.

It is a common idea that tigers cannot climb trees, but this has arisen from the fact that they have seldom occasion to do so. Mr. Sanderson mentions the case of a tigress having been seen to climb a tree in a wood on the Nilgiri Hills, and though he has never seen a tiger in a tree himself, deprecates the idea of there being anything impossible in the matter, and if we come to consider that the large forest panther, which commonly ascends trees, is really often nearly as heavy as a small-sized tigress, there is nothing at all improbable in the tiger doing so. I myself have never seen a tiger in a tree, but one of my managers did, who once went out after a tiger which he had wounded. He then ran on to cut him off, and tried to get up into a tree, but not succeeding in the attempt, went and took a seat some way off on the hillside. The tiger presently emerged from the jungle, went to the tree and began roaring and scraping at the ground, and he must have either smelt traces of the manager or seen him trying to get up into it, and concluded he was there. However, he deliberately went up the tree paw over paw, and got into a cleft of it and looked about in the tree, and then came down backwards, and was shot in the act of descending. I sent and obtained measurements of this tree, the stem of which was 16½ feet up to the first branch. The tiger climbed up so far, and looked around in the tree. Another case was told me by Rama Gouda, to whom I have previously alluded, of a wounded tiger going up a tree to get at a beater, whom he nearly reached. In the case just mentioned, the tiger rose on its hind legs and deliberately went up paw over paw, but in the second, started with a spring up the stem of the tree, and then ascended in the same way as the first tiger did.

There is a common idea that jackals attach themselves to tigers, and are useful in warning them of danger, and I have been informed by an experienced sportsman that they always howl when they find a bait tied out for a tiger, and, it is supposed, with the view of informing any tiger within hearing that there is a bullock all ready for him. I have never heard but one confirmatory instance of the former, which was told me by a planter on the Nilgiri Hills, who was opening some new land in quarters occasionally visited by tigers. One evening, after the day's work was over, he went out accompanied by a kangaroo dog, and took a seat on the hillside to enjoy the view. Immediately below him ran a jungly ravine, and behind him the hill rose sharply. He had no gun with him, not expecting any game so close to his new abode, and now, to his dismay, a large tiger emerged from the shola at a point between him and his bungalow. As the grass was long at that season, the tiger did not perceive my friend (and, as I have previously shown, tigers, and I believe all animals, do not readily perceive any non-conspicuous object which is not in motion), who, as may be supposed, sat as close and still as possible, and beckoning to the dog, held him fast by the collar. The tiger lay down in the grass, and was presently followed by another tiger, which lay down in front of the first and rolled over on its back. This was pretty well for a beginning, but presently, one after the other, emerged three smaller tigers, which also took their seats in the grass. Here then was a nice family to have between one and one's dinner. The sun presently set, and the prospect of darkness was not encouraging. My friend naturally waited for the tigers to go, and no doubt devoutly hoped that they would not come his way, but time seemed to them to be of no importance, and they showed not the slightest disposition to move. Presently there came on to the ridge of the hill above a jackal, which looked down upon the party and then set up a most unearthly howl. The three smaller tigers, evidently young and inexperienced animals, took no notice of the protestations of the jackal, but the two larger tigers at once got up and took a long steady look at him, and the jackal moved restlessly about and seemed to redouble his efforts to attract the attention of the tigers. The larger tigers now seemed satisfied that some danger was at hand, and to the immense relief of my friend, walked down into the jungle, followed by the three smaller tigers. After waiting a little my friend got up and proceeded homewards, and, he said, "I am not ashamed to own that, after passing the place where the tigers had disappeared from view, I fairly ran for the house." The most interesting experiences one hears of tigers and other wild animals are, as may be supposed, not from sportsmen engaged on shooting expeditions, and who have killed much game, but from pioneer planters and others whose business lies in tigerish localities, and that is why Mr. Sanderson's book is so particularly interesting. My friend told me when I last met him that he had only killed two tigers, but that he had had occasionally some unexpected interviews with them. One of these was interesting as showing that a tiger does not like the rearing of a horse. My friend was riding across the country one morning when he came suddenly, at the edge of a shola, on a tiger, which at once crouched as if to spring. The horse, an Australian, wished to turn, but my friend, being afraid that the tiger might then spring on him, turned his horse's head towards the tiger and touched him with the spur. This caused the horse to rear, and the moment he did so the tiger turned tail and ran off. We have seen that man does not relish the roar of a tiger, and it may be interesting to record one instance where a single tiger was commoved and put to flight by the yell of a single man. He was a planter on the Nilgiris, and the brother of a friend of mine, and was in the habit of going out at the end of his day's work with a book and a gun, and seating himself on the hillside to look out for sambur deer. On one occasion he was thus sitting in the long grass when he heard something coming through it. This turned out to be a large tiger which came into view suddenly, and quite close, as may be supposed from the fact that the planter was sitting in long grass. The tiger at once crouched, and the planter was afraid to raise his gun, as it was probable that the animal might spring at him before he was ready to fire. Tiger and man thus looked at each other in silence. Mr. B. had heard of the effect of the human eye, and he threw into his the fiercest glare he could, but found that the tiger returned his glance quite unmoved. Then he thought he would try the effect of the human voice, and gathering himself together uttered the most awe-inspiring yell he could command. The tiger at once rose to his legs and turned his body half round. This was encouraging, and he emitted another yell, when the tiger went off.

There can be no doubt that tigers, like men, are often very undecided how to act, and it would be interesting if we could penetrate their state of mind. Shall I attack, or shall I do nothing? and in the end, after long deliberation, the tiger will determine on doing nothing, and walk off. Of his state of mind the following is an instance. On one occasion I left my pony on the side of a hill just outside the forest, and went for a stalk over the mountain above. I could see nothing, and thought it would be well to take a seat and wait in case any game might turn up. I had not been seated more than a few minutes when one of my people, pointing downward, said, "There is a tiger," and we could see him at the foot of the hill about a quarter of a mile away, walking steadily across a piece of open land to the forest beyond. Just as he disappeared my horsekeeper came up alone, and evidently in a most agitated state, and no wonder, for we had no sooner got out of his sight when a tiger appeared from the jungle and lay down on the ground just above the pony and crouched. The horsekeeper had another man with him, but he not unnaturally said that he was afraid to come and tell us, as he thought that there was safety in numbers, and that the tiger might attack the pony if it was left with only one man. The tiger must have thus remained in a state of low doubt for at least half an hour. Finally he got up and left them, and, from the direction he took, was evidently the identical tiger which we had seen from the hill top.

Tigers, like wolves and other animals, form plans, communicate them to their companions, and conjointly carry them out. A friend of mine was once the subject of an excellent instance of this. He was out stalking one day, and with his glass was scanning the country carefully, when he made out a long way off, in a piece of open grassland which was surrounded by forest, three tigers looking in his direction. They evidently saw that there was something on the hillside, but the distance was, for them, too great to make out what. After steadily looking at him some time the tigers evidently formed their plan of operations, and plunged into the forest towards him. The tigers had taken my friend and his man for game of some kind, and had determined on a united stalk and drive, and, when they appeared, two remained at the edge of the jungle, while the third made a circuit evidently with the view of coming upon the supposed game from above. But presently they discovered their mistake and went off.

These forest tigers are rarely dangerous to man unless

attacked, and in my part of the country they never are so. However, there is no rule without an exception, and when making this assertion to some natives in my neighbourhood many years ago, one of them said, "I am not so sure about that. A tiger ate an aunt of mine not far from here some years ago." But that is the only instance I ever heard of in my neighbourhood, and even by tradition there were no instances of deaths from tigers, and it is also remarkable how in some cases tigers, when there is plenty of game, live for years near cattle without touching them. I was particularly struck with this in the case of a family who lived quite isolated at the crests of the Ghauts, and the head of it told me that, though tigers were often about they never touched his cattle. There is an amusing story told in "My Indian Journal"[1] (a charming book which everyone should read who is interested in India) of a native who was ready enough it appears to track down tigers to be shot by others, but who by no means wished that any of his family should interfere. On one occasion Colonel Campbell found him belabouring his son with a stout bamboo, and on inquiry learned that the said son had killed a tiger. The father said it was all very well for people who lived in the open country, but with him the case was quite different, as he lived on sociable terms with the tigers in the jungle, had never injured them nor they him, and while there was peace between them he could go amongst them without fear, but now that his rascally son had picked a quarrel with them, there was no knowing where the feud might end.

I have mentioned a case of tigers not interfering with cattle when there was plenty of game, but I should add that this was many years ago, when the natives had not so many guns as they have now. The rice-fields have been

[1] "My Indian Journal." By Colonel Walter Campbell. Edinburgh, Edmonston and Douglas, 1864.

abandoned and the house of course deserted, and of recent years the tigers have changed their ways, for, ten years ago, I killed a tigress close to the site of the abandoned house, in the neighbourhood of which it had been killing cattle.

I have said that forest tigers are rarely dangerous to man, and by that I mean the tigers inhabiting the long range of forests stretching along the south-western side of India at varying distances from the sea, but in the interior of Mysore very dangerous man-eaters have existed, and I have been shown places which people made up parties to cross. One man-eater, at least—for it was assumed that the deaths were the work of one animal—killed, I am informed on good authority, about 500 people. Two tigers were killed at one time, and after that the slaughter of human beings ceased, though it was never ascertained which was the culprit. There is no man-eater at present in Mysore. Mr. Sanderson says that bold man-eaters have been known to enter a village and carry off a victim from the first open hut. The boldest attempt I ever knew of was mentioned to me by my Nilgiri planter friend, and it occurred in this way. In the middle of the night there were loud cries of "Tiger!" from a hut near his house which was occupied by some of his people. He always kept a loaded gun near him at night, and at once rushed out and fired, when two men came up to the bungalow and declared that a tiger had begun to claw the thatch off the roof of the hut in order to get at them. This was alarming to the planter, as, if proved, many of his people might have left the place, and he told the men to sleep in his veranda, and that he would see in the morning if their story was true. He then went to bed and rose very early the following morning, before anyone was about, and found that the story was quite true, and saw the tracks of the tiger. These he carefully obliterated, and then went back to bed. Then when he rose at his usual time he roused the men and asked to be shown the track of the tiger. This of course they could not do, and he laughed off the whole story, and treated it as a fanciful illusion. I find many stories in sporting books of the great courage and determination often shown by natives in connection with tigers, but my Nilgiri planter friend told me one which was really astonishing. A tiger one day had carried off a Toda cattle herd, and his friend or relative was determined to recover the body, and was about to proceed single-handed and unarmed into the jungle with this view. My friend saw that he could not prevent him, and as he did not like to let him to go in alone, went with him. They went in accordingly, and presently heard the tiger crunching the bones of his unfortunate victim, but when the tiger heard them approaching he retired, and the Toda recovered what was left of the body. There can be no doubt, however, that the death of one of a party does exercise a chilling effect on the zeal of the natives, or at least on a considerable proportion of them, but after all this is not surprising, as I have found a similar coldness coming over my own proceedings when a tiger has retorted with effect on his pursuers. On the occasion I am now alluding to an unfortunate report had spread that a tiger I had wounded had left the jungle in which we found him, and whither he had retreated. I had wounded the tiger in the evening, and we went to look him up next morning, and the beaters, influenced no doubt by the report in question, went into the jungle in a body in a careless manner, and without sending men up trees to keep a look out ahead.

The tiger waited till the whole party was within springing distance, and then with a tremendous roar which I clearly heard at my post some way off, charged, and buried his deadly fangs in the back of an unfortunate

Hindoo peasant who was leading the way. The poor fellow was carried out of the jungle in an evidently dying state, and a caste dispute arose over him, the particulars of which I have given in my chapter on caste. After doing what we could for him we placed him on a rough litter and he was carried to the rear. I confess that after such an exhibition of temper on the part of the tiger and the nature of the jungle I, being Europeanly speaking single-handed, was not so very comfortable at the idea of approaching him, but luckily a toddyman who had run up a tree (these men are wonderful climbers) when the tiger charged, and was afraid for some time to come down, now emerged from the jungle, and reported that he could see the tiger from the tree he had climbed into. This of course much simplified matters, and I at once proceeded into the jungle, but only about ten people, mostly my own followers, cared to accompany me. As it happened, we after all ran no risk whatever, as the tiger was dead, though he was lying with his head on his paws in such a life-like position that we fired a shot into him to make sure. When we were skinning him the poor man expired. In the same jungle, I think about a year afterwards, an English visitor at my house wounded a tiger, which went into one of those reedy and cactus-grown bottoms which make tiger shooting on foot so dangerous. I then declared that none of my people should go into this, and that they might return the next day and see if the tiger was dead (by no means an absolutely safe proceeding even then as we have seen). Much to my amusement a lean toddy drawer of mine, an excellent shikari, went a few yards into the swampy ground, got on to a small boulder of rock, squatted down, took out his betel bag, threw some betel into his mouth preparatory to chewing, and then held out his long skinny arm and forefinger and said, "Look! A tiger made a meal of a man close to this last year. Let everyone therefore be careful and get up into trees, and mind what they are about." The next day the tiger was found dead quite close to the rock he had been squatting on. A most remarkable instance of courage on the part of a native occurred when a brother planter of mine was out tiger shooting on the Ghauts to the north of my abode. A tiger flew at a Hindoo peasant —a first-rate plucky sportsman, and as the tiger charged, the man struck at it with his hacking knife (a formidable weapon in the hands of a man who knows how to use it, and used to cut underwood, and thick boughs of trees), with the result that the tiger's skull was split open and the animal killed on the spot. The native was thrown backwards with great force, and his head came in contact with a stone. He got up, and by this time was surrounded by the people, when, holding out his hand, he said, "Look here," and then paused. Everyone expected some remark about the tiger, but, amidst general laughter —for the natives have a keen sense of humour—he continued, "There will be a bump on my head to-morrow as big as a cocoanut." And now, as we have heard so much of the courage of man, it is time that the dogs should have their turn, and I will conclude these reminiscences with an account of how a dog saved the life of the brother planter to whom I have just alluded. I was so much interested in the story that I wrote down the particulars in my diary at the time and read them over to my informant to make sure they were right. I give the account verbatim as I took it down at the time.

Mr. A. told me that he once wounded a tiger which afterwards sprang on him, knocked him down, and seized him by the hand and arm. With Mr. A. was a large dog, half mastiff and half polygar (a savage and rare native breed), which at once attacked the tiger, and diverted its attention from Mr. A. After driving off the dog the tiger again returned to Mr. A. and commenced to worry him, but was again attacked by the dog. The dog was thus driven off about three or four times by the tiger. The tiger was all this time losing strength from his wounds, and the last time he returned to Mr. A., died on him. The dog was uninjured. Now comes the most curious and interesting part of the story.

The dog, which was not affectionate generally, and indifferent to being noticed, belonged to Mr. A.'s brother, and had previously taken no interest in anyone but his master, but after this event, he refused to go home with his master, and stuck closely to the wounded man, and when some carbolic was applied by Mr. A.'s brother which caused pain to the wound, the dog began to growl and showed signs of displeasure. The dog would not allow anyone to come near Mr. A. except his own special servant, and lay under the bed with his nose sticking out, and keeping close guard. When Mr. A. was carried to the doctor some thirty-five miles away the dog went too, and on the doctor applying carbolic, and setting the bones, which caused pain, the dog at once seized the doctor by the leg. (Evidently looking on him as tiger No. 2, I suppose.) In about three months Mr. A. was quite cured, and after that the dog lost all interest in him, and returned to his master; and if he met Mr. A. by chance, merely acknowledged him by the faintest wag of his tail. A year afterwards this dog, happening to meet the doctor, whom he had not met since, at once flew at him and seized him by the trousers.

One great danger attending the bite of a tiger is that of blood-poisoning from the frequently foul state of the animal's jaws, and it is, of course, of great consequence to cleanse wounds as soon as possible and apply carbolic. An engineer in the northern part of Mysore a good many years ago was bitten on the thigh by a tiger, and so little hurt that he walked home and went on with his business as usual, but a few days after he was suddenly taken ill and very soon died. Of course there may happen to be no foul matter about the tiger's mouth, and a Hindoo peasant wounded when I was out with no less than thirteen wounds in the arms—several of them double wounds as the man had thrust his locked arms into the tiger's mouth to keep him off—completely recovered. He goes by the nickname of Tiger Linga Gouda, and I always make a point of sending for him when I visit Mysore. On one occasion I was showing the marks of the wounds to a lady, and said that there were thirteen wounds. "Thirteen," echoed Linga Gouda, "There were fifteen, and you have forgotten those two on the head, and I slept on your bed too," he added with an air of great satisfaction—in fact he seemed to attach more importance to that than to anything connected with the transaction. I had given him up my bed because it was a broad one, and so most convenient for resting his lacerated arms. The natives were certain that he would die, and I felt a great triumph in bringing him round. The great thing with wounds of that kind is of course to cleanse them well, and apply carbolic if you have it (I had none on this occasion) and afterwards cover the wounds with damp lint, which should be kept constantly moist by frequent applications of water. This was done in the case I have alluded to. The arms, of course, swelled greatly, and the heat arising from them was very great, hence the need for the constant application of water. The flow of blood from the arms was checked by a tourniquet.

I never but once heard of a mad tiger. This animal was made over in an inoculated condition by a friend of mine to the Garden in Bangalore. He had caught it when out tiger shooting, and, when on the way to Bangalore, he had chained it outside his tent where it was attacked and bitten by what turned out to be a mad Pariah dog.

Before concluding this chapter I must say a few words,

which perhaps ought to have been said at an earlier period, as regards one of the most important points of tiger shooting—*i.e.*, that of taking up such a position as will enable you to fire to right or left without moving your body, or rather I should say without moving it more than in a most infinitesimal degree, for, as I have previously shown, it is movement of any kind which alone readily attracts the attention of an animal. It is evident that, if you sit facing the point from which the tiger is expected, though you can readily fire at him without moving if he passes to your left (and, as has been shown, you should not fire till he is just passing you) you cannot do so if he passes to your right without turning your whole body half round in that direction—a movement which might catch the eye of the tiger. To surmount this difficulty Sir Samuel Baker has invented a small stool with a revolving top, which is no doubt an excellent thing if there is time to erect a suitable platform on which to support the stool, but it often happens that positions have to be taken up in a hurry, and that you have to sit on the fork of a branch, or on the ground behind a bush or rock, where the tiger may pass on either side. In such cases the shooter should sit facing nearly full face to the right, as he can, with hardly any perceptible movement of his body fire readily to his left, and he should instruct his man with the second gun to point with his finger in order to indicate the side on which the tiger is approaching.

In all the books I have read about tigers I have never met with an allusion to tigers purring like cats from satisfaction, but a brother planter informs me that he heard a wounded tiger, that had killed one of the natives who was following him up, purr for several minutes, as he described it, "like a thousand cats." The evening was closing in when the accident occurred and as the jungle was thick nothing could be done. On the following morning the man and the tiger were found lying dead together.

Of all sports tiger shooting affords the most lasting satisfaction, and it is especially interesting when one lives in tigerish localities where one has more leisure and opportunity for going into all the details of this delightful sport, and where a knowledge of the people and their language makes the sport so much more agreeable, and one's acquaintance with the ground enables one to take an active and intelligent part in regulating the plan of operations when a tiger has killed. Then in the case of an animal so destructive it is seldom possible to feel any commiseration, though I have done so on certainly one, or perhaps two occasions. Against many sports something may be said, but that is impossible as regards tiger shooting. The tying out of live baits may be objected to, but after all the tooth of the tiger is to be preferred to the knife of the butcher.

CHAPTER V.

BEARS—PANTHERS—WILD BOARS—JUNGLE DOGS—SNAKES —JUNGLE PETS.

THE Indian black bear (*ursus labiatus*), we are informed by Jerdon, is found throughout India and Ceylon, from Cape Comorin to the Ganges, chiefly in the hilly and jungly districts. The bear, unlike the tiger, which has sometimes five cubs, appears never to have more than two cubs, and I have not been able to hear or read of their ever having more. We have no means of knowing how often they breed, but I imagine that they must seldom do so, and that that is why they are so soon almost exterminated. As I never kept a game diary on my estate (which I now much regret), I have no idea how many have been killed from it, but I am sure we have killed a smaller number of bears than of tigers, and yet the bear is now rarely seen or heard of in my neighbourhood, while we hear as much of tigers as ever, and indeed quite recently a great deal more, for last year they were apparently more numerous than they have ever been in the tiger range of my district; and I say apparently, because, from the destruction of game, the tigers have naturally been compelled to live more upon cattle. It is alleged by the natives that the tigers kill and eat the bears. Mr. Sanderson notices this in his work, and gives one reported instance of it, but I have never known of one in my part of the country. A friend of mine, formerly in the employ of the Mysore State, told me that he knew of two cases in the North-Eastern Division, of tigers killing bears, but in neither case did they eat them. In the first case the bear and tiger had met at a watering-place, and in the second in the jungle. Mr. Ball, in his "Jungle Life in India,"[1] tells us that he once came across the remains of a bear which the natives said had been killed by a tiger, and that a native shikari had sat over the carcase with the hope of getting a shot at the tiger. We have no returns as regards bears in Mysore, but in the adjacent Bombay districts—Kanara and Belgaum—Colonel Peyton tells us, in the "Kanara Gazetteer," they are fast becoming rare, except near the Sahyadris, and even there are no longer numerous. In Belgaum, between 1840 and 1880, he tells us that no fewer than 223 bears were killed. The steady decline of the numbers of the bears is shown by the fact that 137 were killed between 1840 and 1850, 51 between 1850 and 1860, 32 between 1860 and 1870, and 3 between 1870 and 1880. In Kanara 51 bears were killed between 1856 and 1882, so we have a total then of 274 bears for these two districts alone. As regards big game, the first comers obviously have the best of it.

Colonel Peyton tells us that the bear is, of all animals, most dreaded by the natives. There can be no doubt, he says, that an untouched bear will often charge, while a tiger will rarely do so, and there are numerous instances of people having been mauled and sometimes killed by them. I imagine, though—in fact, I am sure—that this must often occur from the bear constantly keeping his head down, evidently smelling and looking for things in or on the ground. All other game animals have some

[1] "Jungle Life in India, or the Journeys and Journals of an Indian Geologist," by V. Ball, M.A. London, Thos. De La Rue and Co., 1880.

motive for looking ahead and around—deer and bison for their enemies, and tigers for their prey. But the bear lives on insects and fruits, and flowers and honey, and as he is not apprehensive of being attacked by any animal, has no motive for keeping a lookout, and so does not do so. He may thus, and no doubt often does, run into a man, under the mistaken idea that the man is running into or attacking him, and then the bear, naturally, does the best he can. I can give a remarkable confirmation of this view.

One day, in a break in the monsoon, when the game lies much out of the forest, I was out in the mountains with my manager for a general stalk, when we saw, some way ahead of us, a bear walking along. We quickly formed a plan of operation, and it was arranged that I should make a circuit and get between the bear and a jungly ravine he appeared to be making for, and that my manager should follow on the track of the bear, which would thus be pretty certain to be overhauled. The bear was pottering along as bears do, and I had no difficulty in getting between him and the jungle he was approaching, and the moment I did so I advanced a little towards him. When the bear got within shooting distance—about fifty yards—I stooped down and moved a little on one side so as to get off his direct line, with the view of getting a side shot, but just as I did so he accidentally altered his route, thus bringing himself again head on to me. Then I manœuvred again to get out of his line, but the bear also altered his line, and as by this time he was getting rather too close—*i.e.*, about ten yards off—I stood up and took a steady shot at his head and dropped him dead. Now, strange to say, I do not believe that the bear ever saw me at all, and he could not wind me, as the south-westerly wind was blowing strongly from him to me, and yet, as the grass at that season was by no means long, he had no more difficulty in seeing me than I had in seeing him, and he probably would have walked right up to me. This instance is, I think, interesting, and goes far to explain the numerous accidents in connection with bears. Still there can be no doubt that, as Colonel Peyton says, an unwounded and untouched bear will deliberately attack people when there is no occasion for his doing so, and that too, under circumstances where no other animal would make an attack, and of this the following little incident will serve as an illustration.

On one occasion a bear was reported on a jungly hill about a mile from my bungalow, and as I was young and inexperienced then, I said that I would lie on the ground till I heard the beaters, and then stand behind a tree. I was alone, and had only a single barrelled rifle, which I laid on the ground beside me. As the cover was rather a large one, I had no reason to expect anything till I could at least hear the beaters in the distance, and I lay leaning on my elbow and thinking of I cannot now remember what, when on chancing to look up I saw a large bear standing at the edge of the jungle about twenty yards away. The moment I moved he charged, and I at once seized my rifle, sprang up and charged the bear at an angle (there was no time to fire), and made for the jungle from which he had emerged. I just missed his nose, and he followed me for a few paces as I ran towards the jungle from which he had come, which I did knowing that he would not be inclined to go in that direction. Then, having thus cleared me out of the way, he turned, and resumed his original route, and as he was disappearing into the next jungle I fired at him, but the charge must have had a discomposing effect on my shooting, for I missed the bear altogether. Now, as the beaters were far away and not within hearing, there was no occasion for the bear to have attacked me, and there was ample room for him to have altered his line. In fact, unless closely pressed by beaters, no other unwounded animal would have so acted. It will be observed that the bear, after having pursued me for a few yards, turned and went on his way, but had I not been nimble—in other words, had I been completely invested by the bear and thrown down—he might, as the natives would phrase it, have made my wife a widow. It is commonly supposed that, when making an attack, the bear stands on its hind legs, and thus gives the sportsman a good chance of killing him with a shot in the chest, but this is not my experience, and, though instances of the kind may have occurred, I should not advise the sportsman to count on any such delay in the proceedings of an attacking bear.

The preceding illustration, I may point out, affords a useful lesson. If so suddenly attacked by a wild animal that you have no time to fire, always rush towards it, and to one side, so that you may, as it were, dodge past it. This will enable you to gain ground on it, and room to turn round and fire.

I may observe that Mr. Ball, in his "Jungle Life in India," gives several instances of natives being wantonly attacked by bears, and Colonel Campbell[1] gives one remarkable instance of two bears attacking a party of his people, who were on the march through the jungle in Belgaum in charge of his horses, one of which was so severely wounded by one of the bears that the life of the horse was despaired of for some days. The Colonel was determined to be avenged on the bears, had them marked down, and, with the aid of his friends, bagged them both, but not before one of the bears had thrown down one of the party, who ran a great risk of being killed. The

[1] "My Indian Journal," by Colonel Walter Campbell. Edinburgh, Edmonston and Douglas, 1864.

determination of the bear in following up his assailant was in this instance very great.

I may here observe that some little caution is required in approaching, and looking into caves, and examining the entrances for tracks of bears, and the person doing so should be fully prepared for a sudden charge out of the cave, and be ready to jump on one side. No cave should be approached with the assumption that it is not at all likely that a bear will be at home, and especial care should be taken in the case of a cave with a drop in front of it over which a person might be hurled by a bear charging suddenly out. To get a bear out of a cave is often no easy matter, and different caves require, of course, different treatment. In some cases the bear may be poked out with the aid of a long pole, and when this is done the operation is both interesting and amusing, but care must be taken to see that you have a man who understands bears, and knows by the character of the growl when the bear really means to charge out into the open, and also that the man with the stick can readily get out of the way, which he cannot do in the case of every cave. The native with a long pole, or rather stick, usually commences with a quiet nervous sort of poke, which awakes the bear out of his midday slumbers and causes him to rush at the stick with a furious growl. But this is merely a demonstration, and the experienced native does not expect a charge, though I need hardly say that he is well prepared to get out of the way. Then the native commences to poke away in a more pronounced style, and at the same time excites himself by calling in question the purity of Bruin's mother, his female relations, and even those of his remote ancestors, to all of which the bear responds by growls and rushes at the stick. At last his growls and rushes at the stick become fierce and menacing, and all of a sudden the experienced

Hindoo, who by some instinctive knowledge is able to gauge the charging moment, drops the stick and scuttles out of the way, and the bear dashes headlong from the cave to be killed, or to make good his escape, as the case may be. Poking a bear out of a cave is rather a severe trial of one's nervous system, and if anyone doubts that he has only to try it for himself, as it will perhaps show the individual that we seldom rightly estimate the amount of nerve which we often expect natives to show. I think I was never more startled in my life than I was one day when I put my ramrod (it was of course in the muzzle loading days) into the very narrow mouth of a cave in which I thought there was little chance of Bruin being at home. A she-bear however was within, and all the fiercer as she had cubs, but luckily she did not charge out, and I need hardly say that I promptly drew back. Sometimes a cave may be so deep and tortuous that the bear cannot be got out with the aid of a pole, and to meet such cases I had stink balls made, as bears have very fine olfactory nerves and seem particularly to object to disagreeable smells. These balls were composed of asafœtida, pig dung, and any other offensive ingredient that suggested itself to me at the time, and made up into about the size of a cricket ball and then dried in the sun. The ball was, when required to drive a bear out of a cave, impaled on the end of a long pole and surrounded by dried grass, or any other inflammable material which was at hand, and this being ignited the pole was thrust as far as possible into the cave. This I found to be a highly successful plan, and I may mention in passing that I have met with no account in the many sporting books I have read of this being done previously. Sometimes large fires are lit in the mouth of a cave with the view of smoking a bear out, but this is rather a cruel process which I do not recommend. In some cases of peculiarly shaped and situated caves it is, however, the only practicable plan, but where adopted the bear should not be put to more inconvenience than is necessary to drive him out. A large fire should be lit at the entrance, and when the cave has got filled with smoke all the blazing fragments of wood should be removed from the entrance, and in doing this the people should talk loudly and make as much noise as possible, and afterwards retreat to a distance from the cave leaving the sportsman with his spare gun-carrier to sit just above the entrance to the cave. The bear finding that, as he erroneously supposes, every one has gone away, and being naturally desirous of quitting such uncomfortable quarters will, after a short time, come cautiously out and may thus be easily shot. It is very important to have a couple of bull-terriers when out bear shooting as they are most useful in bringing a wounded bear to bay.

In considering these remarks upon the various ways of getting bears out of caves it may be useful to show how not to attempt to get a bear out of a cave, and the connecting circumstances will also be useful to anyone who may be overtaken by a hill fire.

On one occasion many years ago news was brought in that a bear had been marked down into a small and very narrow mouthed cave on a bare hillside, and I accordingly proceeded to the spot. The whole mountain was at that time covered with long grass, and as the cave was closely surrounded by it, and the bear if poked out in the usual way would rush into the grass and thus give a bad chance to the shooter, I devised what I thought, and what at first appeared to be, an excellent plan for meeting the difficulty. This was to set fire to the whole hill just below the cave, and my theory was that, as the cave was a small one, the heat of the fire and the smoke would cause the bear to quit the cave after the fire had passed over it. The wind was, when we lit the fire, blowing from east to west and

I perched myself on a pile of rocks rather above, and to the east of the bear's cave as, when leaving it, he would naturally go in a direction opposite to that of the fire, in which case he would pass within easy shot of my position. With this distinctly original conception I was highly pleased and watched the progress of the terrific conflagration that ensued with interest and satisfaction. How it roared and leapt as it consumed the long dried grass, and how soon would the bear be likely to make its appearance! It reached the long grass around the cave and proceeded to sweep along the hill, away from me, and flying before the easterly wind. Presently there was a dead lull. A few seconds more and the whole position was reversed. I had quite forgotten that, at that season of the year, and that hour of the day, the east wind dies down, and the westerly sea breeze comes in, and in an instant I was caught in my own trap. First of all I thought I would screen myself behind one of the rocks and remain where I was, but I was of course speedily enveloped with masses of smoke, and then I thought I would get down and run; first of all, however, I peeped over the rock, but merely to perceive a terrifying mass of roaring red flames rushing towards me, and this finally determined me, and I stuffed my handkerchief into my mouth and held on. As I had of course leggings and was fully clothed I had much the best of it, but my shikari with his bare limbs got a pretty good roasting. But the fire seemed no sooner to have reached us than it was swept onwards quite away, and I was astonished at the pace it travelled, which one can have no idea of when one witnesses these conflagrations, as one usually does, from a distance. Beyond feeling as if my lungs were on fire for a day or two afterwards I experienced no ill effects from my temporary roasting, but the experience I had was quite sufficient to show me the amount of inconvenience a bear must suffer from being smoked out of his cave, and, as I have previously pointed out, no more fire should be lit at the entrance of a cave than is necessary to make it desirable for the bear to leave it, which, as I have shown, he will soon do, if the people retire to a distance. As for our bear, he probably knew far more about these hill fires and the sudden changes of wind than I did, and had not the slightest idea of coming out for some time, and I therefore had to introduce to his notice one of my stink balls, which had the effect of bringing him out. By way of a change I had intended fighting it out with the bear without firing, and told a native to attack the bear with my spear when he emerged, while I proposed, if he lodged his spear, to attack with the bayonet of my Enfield rifle. But the spear came into contact with a bone in the bear's back, and thus the point was broken off, and seeing that my man had not lodged his spear I fired and killed the bear. From my subsequent experience of the great power of the bear I am now glad that the spear was not lodged.

Bear shooting from caves I have found to be a most interesting and sometimes most entertaining and even amusing sport, while it is attended with a sufficient amount of danger for all practical purposes. You never get a laugh out of a tiger shikar, but you sometimes do in connection with bears, and the following is at once an instance in point, and will besides illustrate the danger of approaching a cave which is perhaps rarely inhabited by bears, as also the surprising promptness of the bear in action. And I say surprising, because from his shambling gait, general deliberation of movement, and the clothing of long black hair which hides the powerful form and limbs, his activity and quickness of movement when aroused is astonishing to those who have no experience of bears. But to proceed with my story.

One day, when returning from shooting in the mountains, we happened to pass a bear's cave which was rarely inhabited—at least on former occasions when we examined it we had found no traces of bears, nor had one ever been marked into it that I was able to hear of, though the cave had the reputation of being occasionally used by bears. The cave was in a beehive-shaped pile of rocks standing on, or rather projecting from, a steep hillside. From the upper side it is easily approached, but to get at the mouth of the cave you have to step down, as it were, from the roof of the beehive on to a ledge of rock about six feet wide, below which there is a drop of ten or twelve feet. From the absence of any signs of bears about the roof of the cave I assumed that the cave was as usual uninhabited, but I thought I would gratify my curiosity by looking into it, so I got down on to the ledge, and was imprudent enough to leave my guns with the people on the roof above. As there were no signs of bears on the ledge or at the entrance, I told one of the natives to go in and take a look at the cave, but he had only penetrated a few feet from the entrance, which was about five feet high, than with three furious growls a bear charged headlong, and drove the intruder out with such force that he was shot clean over the ledge, and alighting (luckily) on his side, rolled some way down the steep hillside at the bottom of the drop. Bruin then with wonderful readiness knocked down the other man, who had not presence of mind enough to get out of the way, and after inflicting a scalp wound on the back of his head, dropped over the ledge, and got off unharmed amidst several shots which were fired at him by the people above, who of course from their position could not see the bear till he had got to a considerable distance. In the confusion that had occurred amongst the people left on the roof of the cave, who were as much unprepared for a bear as I was, some one had jostled my principal shikari—a testy and at times rather troublesome old man, but a most keen sportsman—and, to the great delight of every one, his shins had in consequence been barked against a sharp piece of rock. All the sympathy that ought to have been devoted to the wounded man he diverted to himself by the tremendous fuss he made about his injured shins, and this, and the chaff he had to sustain in consequence, quite rounded off the affair, and we all went home in high good humour, and the wounded man for years afterwards used to show his ear-to-ear scar with considerable satisfaction. Some people might have objected to the escape of the bear, but I confess that I did not grudge him the victory he had earned so well, and we consoled ourselves further with the reflection that we would get the better of him next time. Before concluding the subject of bears, I may give another incident which was rather amusing, and the narration of which may be of use as illustrating one or two points which are worthy of notice, and especially the advantage of having a good dog with one.

On a mountain-side about five miles from my house is a rather large cave of considerable depth—so deep, at least, that the longest sticks would not reach to the end of it, and as we could get the bear out in no other way, I lit a large fire at the entrance, and, after some time, sent all the people away to a distance, and, with a single man to hold a second gun, sat over the mouth of the cave. The result that I anticipated soon followed, and, imagining that we had given up our project in despair, and being naturally desirous of leaving such uncomfortable quarters, Bruin presently appeared looking cautiously about. The smoke prevented my taking a very accurate shot. However, I fired, and wounded the bear somewhere in the throat, though not fatally, and he plunged into a jungly ravine close to the cave, pursued by my bull terrier, an admirable and very courageous animal, which attacked the bear, and detained him sufficiently long to give me time to run to the other side of the ravine, and so get in front of the bear. A hill-man accompanied me, armed with a general officer's sword which I had brought out—why I really forget now, for it was anything but sharp, which I now regret, as it would have been interesting to see the effect of a really sharp sword on a bear's back. The bull terrier now rejoined me, and, in company with two additional natives who had run after us, I got on a piece of rock about three feet high. The man with the sword stood on my right, and the two natives—who were unarmed—on my left, and in this order we awaited the arrival of the bear. Sore and angry, he presently emerged from the jungle at a distance of about twenty-five or thirty yards further down the slope of the hill. I fired at and hit him, and he then turned round, took a look at us, and charged. As he came on I fired my remaining shot. Then the man with the sword struck the bear a tremendous blow on the back (which I think would have stopped the bear had the sword been sharp), and in a second more old Bruin had thrown the whole of us off the rock on to the ground behind it. There we were then—four men, a wounded bear, and a bull terrier, all mixed up together. However, the man with the sword laid about him most manfully, and the bear, either not liking the situation, or being exhausted with his wounds and efforts (more likely the latter), retreated into the ravine out of which he had emerged. Into this we presently followed him, and after another shot or two he expired, and I have the skin at home with the mark of the sword-cut on the back. It had cut through the shaggy hair, and only penetrated the skin sufficiently to leave a scar. The man who had shown so much pluck was a young farmer from the adjacent village, and I at once offered him the sword with which he had defended me. But he seemed to think he had done nothing, and positively declined it, saying that his neighbours would be jealous of his having such a fine-looking thing. I had, however, a knife made after the native fashion, and afterwards gave it to him in commemoration of the event.

In Mysore there are two kinds of panthers. One, the largest of the two, is called by the natives the Male Kiraba, or forest panther, and confines itself generally to the forest regions, while the smaller kind haunts the neighbourhood of villages. The black panther, which is of rare occurrence, is merely an offshoot of the other varieties. The panther, in consequence of its tree-climbing habits, and general aptitude for suddenly disappearing, is of all animals the most disappointing to the sportsman, so much so, indeed, that I soon gave up going out after them. Though it has great strength, and from the amazing suddenness of its movements, great means at its disposal for making successful attacks on man, it seems, unlike the tiger, bear, and wild boar, to have no confidence in its own powers, and though in one sense showing great daring by attacking dogs even when they are in the house and quite close to people, is, when attacked itself, of all animals the most cowardly—a fact which the natives are well aware of, and which is proved by the small number of people killed by panthers in proportion to the number of them accounted for. The only way of insuring success when hunting panthers is to have a small pack of country-bred dogs of so little value that when one or two of them may chance to be killed by the panther the matter is of little or no consequence. The pack will soon find the panther, and perhaps run him up a tree, and thus give the sportsman a good, or rather certain chance of killing the animal. In this way a manager of mine was very successful in bagging panthers. I have some reason to suppose that the panther, when severely wounded, sometimes feigns death, and give the following incident with the view of eliciting further information on the subject.

Two natives in my neighbourhood once sat up over a kill, and apparently killed a panther—at least it lay as if dead. They then with the aid of some villagers, who afterwards arrived on the scene of action, began to skin the panther, and the man who had wounded it took hold of the tail to stretch the body out when the panther came suddenly to life, and bit the man in the leg. One of the people present then fired at the panther, apparently killing it outright. The man, who had been only slightly bitten, then again took the animal by the tail, a proceeding which it evidently could not stand, for this time it came to life in earnest, and inflicted a number of wounds on the man at the tail. The natives then attacked it with their hacking knives, and finally put an end to it. The dresser of my estate was sent to the village, which was about six miles away, to treat the wounds, but the unfortunate man died. I may add that this is the only instance I have known of a man being killed by a panther in my neighbourhood.

I now turn to an animal which is really dangerous, and I think more daring than any animal in the jungles—the wild boar—and whatever doubts the panther has of its own powers, I feel sure that the boar can have none—in fact its action is not only daring, but at times even insulting. To be threatened and attacked in the jungle one can understand, but to be growled at and menaced while on one's own premises is intolerable. I never but once heard the deep threatening don't-come-near-me growl of the wild boar (and in the many sporting books I have read I never met with any allusion to it), and that was some years ago, within about ten or fifteen yards of my bungalow, and the incident is worth mentioning as showing the great daring and coolness of the wild boar.

One evening at about seven o'clock, and on a clear but moonless night, I went into the garden in front of my house. This is flanked by a low retaining wall some three or four feet high—a wall built to retain the soil when the ground was levelled—and below this a few bushes and plants had sprung up close to the bottom of the wall. In these I heard what I supposed to be a pariah dog gnawing a bone, and, in order to frighten it away, I quietly approached within a few yards of the spot, and made a slight noise between my lips. I was at once answered by a low deep growl, which I at first took to be the growl of a panther, and I then walked back to the bungalow and told my manager to bring a gun, telling him that there was either a large dog (which on second thoughts appeared to me most probable), or some animal gnawing a bone. We then quietly approached the spot where we could hear the gnawing going on quite plainly about five yards off. By my direction he fired into the bushes, and we then stood still and listened, and presently heard what was evidently some heavy animal walk slowly away. On the following morning I sent my most experienced shikari to the spot, and he reported that the animal was a wild boar, which had been munching the root of some plant, and the soil being gravelly, the noise we had heard proceeded from the chewing of roots and gravel together. This boar then had not only refused to desist from his proceedings when I was within five yards of him, but had even warned me, by the low growl afore mentioned, that if I came any nearer serious consequences might ensue. On the following day I assembled some natives and beat a narrow jungly ravine below my house, at a distance of about fifty yards from it, and there came out, not the boar, but his wife with a family of five or six small pigs. She was shot by a native, and the young ones got away, but the boar either was not there, or, more probably, was too knowing to come out. He did not, however, neglect his family, but in some way best known to himself, collected them together, and went about with them, as, a day or two afterwards, he was seen with the young pigs by my manager, and their tracks were also to be seen on one of the paths in my compound, or the small inclosed park near my bungalow. This boar afterwards became very troublesome, ploughed up the beds in my rose garden at the foot of my veranda steps, and even injured a tree in the compound by tearing off the bark with his formidable tusks. But, daring though he was, he was once accidentally put to flight by a slash of an English hunting whip. The boar, it appears, was making his round one night when my manager, hearing something moving outside his bath-room, and imagining it to be a straying donkey—we keep some donkeys on the estate—rushed out with his hunting-whip, and made a tremendous slash at the animal, which turned out to be the boar, so startling him by this unexpected form of attack, that he charged up a steep bank near the house and disappeared. This boar was afterwards shot by one of my people in an adjacent jungle—at least a boar was shot, which we infer must have been the one in question, as since then my garden has not been disturbed. The boar is more dangerous to man than any animal in our jungles, and I have heard of three or four deaths caused by them in recent years in my district. The natives, however, say that, till he is wounded, the tiger is less dangerous than the boar, but that after a tiger is wounded, he is the more dangerous of the two; and I think that this is a correct view of the matter. The boar has a most remarkable power of starting at once into full speed, and that is why his attacks are so dangerous. In countries inhabited by wild boars it is very important to be always on the alert. As an illustration of this, and also of the great power of the boar, and of his sometimes attacking people without any provocation on their part, I may mention the following incident.

When I was walking round part of my plantation one morning with my manager, and we chanced to stand in a path for a few moments (I forget now for what reason), my dogs went down the hill into the coffee, and appear there to have disturbed a boar. Luckily for myself, I always keep a sharp look out, and my eye caught a glimpse of something black coming up amongst the coffee. In a single second a boar appeared in the path some twenty yards away. The path sloped downwards towards me, and at me he came, like an arrow from a bow. As there was no use in my attempting to arrest the progress of an animal of this kind, I stepped aside and let him into my manager, who, luckily for himself, was standing behind a broken off coffee tree, which stood at a sharp turn in the path some yards further on. The result was very remarkable. The boar's chest struck against the coffee tree and slightly bent it on one side. This threw the boar upwards, and, of course, broke the force of the charge, but there was still enough force left to toss my manager into an adjacent shallow pit with such violence that his ear was filled with earth. I was now seriously alarmed, as I had no weapon of any kind, but luckily the boar went on. His tusk, it appeared, had caught the manager—a man of about six feet, and thirteen stone in weight—under the armpit, but had merely torn his coat. We organized a beat the same afternoon, and killed the boar, which was suffering from an old wound, and this no doubt accounted, in some degree, for his sudden and gratuitous attack. Tigers often attack the wild boar, and there are often desperate battles between them, and well authenticated instances have been known of the boar killing the tiger. I have never met with one in my neighbourhood, though I once aided in killing a tiger which had been ripped in several places by a boar. As it is impossible in jungly districts to ride the wild boar, he is invariably shot, except when, in the monsoon rains, he is occasionally speared. At that season the wild pigs make houses, or rather shelters, for themselves by cutting with their teeth and bending over some of the underwood, and under these they repose. When such shelters are discovered, a man approaches them cautiously and drives his spear through the shelter into the boar's back. I have never seen this done, but have often heard of its being done where I lived in former days, during the rainy season.

Boar's head pickled in vinegar and garnished with onions makes a good dish, especially after harvest, when the pigs are in good condition, but, from what I have known of the habits of the wild boar, I do not think I should ever be inclined to partake of it again, and certainly not when cholera is about. A neighbour of mine told me that when he was once beating a jungle for game the natives backed out of it with great promptness, having come upon wild pigs in the act of devouring the dead bodies of some people who had died of cholera. I may mention that it was customary in former times, and doubtless is so still to some extent, to deposit the bodies of cholera victims anywhere in the jungle, instead of burying them in the ordinary way. An official of the Forest Department told me that, passing one day near the place where the carcase of an elephant lay, he had the curiosity to go and look at it. To his astonishment he found the flanks heaving as if the elephant were still alive, and while he was wondering what this could mean, two wild boars, which had tunnelled their way in, and were luxuriating on the contents of the carcase, suddenly rushed out. From what I have hitherto said it seems plain that wild boar is not a safe article of food, unless, perhaps, when it inhabits remote jungles where foul food can rarely be met with. I have never made any measurements of wild boars, but Colonel Peyton—a first-rate authority—writing in the "Kanara Gazetteer," says that some are to be found measuring forty inches high, and six feet long.

The jungle dog (*kuon rutilans*) is a wolfish-looking dog of a golden brown colour, with hair of moderate length, and a short and slightly bushy tail. It hunts in packs of seven and eight, and sometimes as many as twenty and even thirty have been reported. In my neighbourhood I have never actually known them to attack cattle or persons, but Colonel Peyton tells us, in the "Kanara Gazetteer," that they grew very bold in the 1876-77 famine, and killed great numbers of the half-starved cattle which were driven into the Kanara forests to graze, and since then a reward of 10 rupees has been paid for the destruction of each fully grown wild dog. Colonel Peyton alludes to the native idea that these dogs attack and kill tigers, but says that no instance of their having killed a tiger is known. At the same time it is, he says, a fact that the tiger will give up his kill to wild dogs, and will leave a place in which they are present in large numbers. Some years ago I beat a jungle in which a tiger had killed a bullock, and in which another tiger had on a former occasion lain up, but the tiger was not there, and a number of jungle dogs were beaten out. We afterwards found the tiger in a jungle about a mile away, and he had evidently abandoned his kill, for no other reason, apparently, than because of the presence of the dogs. An old Indian sportsman tells me of a very widespread native tradition as to the action of these dogs previous to attacking a tiger. Their belief is that the dogs first of all micturate on each others' bushy tails, and, when rushing past the tiger, whisk their tails into his eyes and thus blind him with the objectionable fluid, after which they can attack him with comparative impunity. A forest officer informs me that the Gonds have a somewhat similar tradition, and that they believe that the dogs first of all micturate on the ground around the tiger, and that the effluvium has the effect of blinding him.[1] The late Mr. Sanderson, in his "Thirteen Years amongst the Wild Beasts of India," mentions an instance reported to him by the natives of their finding a tiger sitting up with his back to a bamboo bush, so that nothing could pass behind him, while the wild dogs were walking up and down and passing quite close to him, evidently with the view of annoying the tiger, and the position then taken up by the tiger seemed to show that he was apprehensive of an attack. From his experience of the great power of the wild dog, Mr. Sanderson entertained no doubt that they could kill a tiger, though he knows of no instance of their having done so. The old Indian sportsman above alluded to told me of a case where a tiger had been marked down by native shikaris, and where they afterwards found wild dogs eating the carcase of the tiger, which they had presumably killed, but I cannot find any account of the dogs having been seen in the act of killing a tiger, though I can easily conceive that a hungry tiger, and an equally hungry pack of wild dogs may have come into collision over a newly killed animal, and that the dogs may then in desperation have killed the tiger.

[1] In Jerdon's "Mammals of India" it is stated that in Nepaul the wild dogs, whose urine is said to be peculiarly acrid, sprinkle it over bushes through which an animal will probably move with the view of blinding their victim. Jerdon certainly disbelieves the native story of their capturing their prey through the acridity of their urine. It seems to me not improbable that the wild dogs may have become aware of the offensive character of their urine, and in passing near a tiger might discharge some of it with the view of annoying the tiger and driving him away, and also perhaps as a mark of contempt, and that this probably was the origin of the widely spread story I have alluded to in the text.

A Coorg planter who has had opportunities of observing the habits of these dogs, tells me that when hunting a deer they do not run in a body, but spread out rather widely, so as to catch the deer on the turn if it moved to right or left. Some of the dogs hang behind to rest themselves, so as to take up the running when other dogs, which have pressed the deer hard, get tired. He once had a bitch the product of a cross between a Pariah and a jungle dog. When she had pups she concealed them in the jungle, and in order to find them she had to be carefully watched and followed up. She went through many manœuvres to prevent the discovery of her pups, and pottered about in the neighbourhood of the spot where she had concealed them, as if bent on nothing in particular. Then she made a sudden rush into the jungle and disappeared. After much search her pups were found in a hole about three feet deep, which she had dug on the side of a rising piece of ground. The bitch did not bark—the jungle dog does not—and the pups barked but slightly, but the next generation barked as domestic dogs do.

Many years ago I met with a very singular and puzzling circumstance in connection with jungle dogs. I had offered a reward of five rupees for a pup, and one day several natives from a village some three or four miles away, brought me a pup—apparently about six or eight months old. This, it appears, they had caught by placing some nets near the carcase of a tiger I had killed, and on which a pack of these dogs was feeding. They drove the dogs towards the nets, which they jumped, but the pup in question was caught in the net. My cook now appeared on the scene and declared that the pup belonged to him, and that he had brought it from Bangalore, and on hearing this I declined, of course, to pay the reward. As I had never, and have never, seen a jungle dog pup, I neither could then, nor can now, undertake to say whether the pup was a wild one or not, though it seemed to me that it might have been a kind of mongrel animal with a good deal of the pariah dog in it. The natives then requested the cook to take the pup and pay them five rupees for their trouble. This he declined to do, and they then said they would take it back to the carcase of the tiger and let it go. This they did, and the pup was never heard of again, and I assume that it must have rejoined the wild dogs. As my cook had no conceivable motive for falsely asserting that the dog was his, I can only assume that the animal had strayed away and joined the pack of wild dogs.

There is no reward for killing wild dogs in Mysore, as is the case in the Madras Presidency, and I should strongly advise that one should be given, as from the great destruction of the game, on which they at present live, these animals will soon become very destructive to cattle, and possibly, or even probably, dangerous to man. And it is the more important to attend to this matter at once, because I find, from Jerdon's "Mammals of India," that the bitch has at least six whelps at a birth, and he mentions that Mr. Elliot (the late Sir Walter) remarks that the wild dog was not known in the Southern Maharatta country until of late years, but that it was now very common; and he adds that he once captured a bitch and seven cubs, and had them alive for some time. No one has any interest in killing these jungle dogs, and until a reward is offered for their destruction, they will go on increasing at an alarming rate.

I now pass on to offer some remarks on snakes, and especially on the great number of deaths said to be caused by them, and I say said to be caused by them, because I have good reason to suppose that the immense number of deaths (sometimes returned at 17,000 or 18,000 for all India) reported as being caused by them, are really poisoning cases which are falsely returned as being due to snake bite. When mentioning this surmise on board of a P. and O. ship to two civilians, they demurred to the idea, and I then asked them if they had ever known within their own cognizance of a man being killed by a snake—*i.e.*, either seen a man fatally bitten, or who had been fatally bitten. They never had, and that too during a service of about twenty-four years. I then, out of curiosity, made inquiries through all the first-class passengers, and at last met with one lady who had a gardener who had been killed by a snake. I also got my English servant to make a similar inquiry in the second-class, and no passenger there had known of a case, though one of them had been engaged in surveying operations for ten years. My attention has been particularly called to this subject in consequence of my own long experience, which stretches back to the year 1855, and, though cobras have been killed in and around my house, and in the plantations, I have not only never known of a death from snake bite on my estates, but have, since the date mentioned, never heard of but one case in my neighbourhood, and that was of a boy who was killed by some deadly snake about four or five miles from my house. I made inquiries in Bangalore on this subject. Now Bangalore is a place which always had a bad reputation as regards cobras. The population is large, and there are, of course, numerous gardens, and many grass cutters are employed, and the occupations there of a large number of people are such as to make them liable to risk from snake bite; and yet, in the course of the year, there had only been three cases of snake bite. How is it then that such an infinitesimal number of the cases reported on occur within the cognizance of Europeans? And unless some competent observer is at hand to determine the cause of death, what can be easier than to poison a man, puncture his skin, and then point to the puncture as an evidence that the death was caused by snake bite?

Of one thing I feel certain, and that is, that the cobra is a timid snake, that it is not at all inclined to bite, and unless assailed and so infuriated, will not bite, even if trodden on by accident, as long as the snake is not hurt, which, of course, it would not be if trodden upon by the bare foot, and that is why, I feel sure, I have so rarely heard of a man being bitten by a snake during my long experience in India. I can give a remarkable confirmatory instance, which happened at my bungalow some years ago. My English servant had got his feet wet one morning, and had placed his shoes to dry on a ledge of the bungalow just above the place where the bath-room water runs out. At about three in the afternoon he went in his slippers round the end of the bungalow to get his shoes, and trod on a cobra which was lying in the soft and rather muddy ground created by the bath-room water. He had stepped on to about the middle of the snake's body, but probably rather nearer the tail than the head. The cobra then reared up its body, spread its hood, hissed, and struggled to get free, while my servant held up his hands to avoid the chance of being bitten, and he said that he could see that the afternoon sun was illuminating the interior of its throat, but he was afraid to let it go, thinking that it would then be more able to bite him. This, however, he is quite positive it never attempted to do, and after some moments of hesitation he jumped to one side, and the snake, so far from offering to bite when liberated, went off in the opposite direction with all speed. I am sure that wild animals perceive quite as readily as tame ones do the difference between what is purely accidental, and what results from malice prepense. The snake must have perceived that its being trodden upon was a pure accident, and, as it was not hurt, did not bite. A Brahmin once told me of a somewhat similar case, where his mother, seeing what she supposed was a kitten in a passage of the house, gave it a push on one side with her foot. It turned out to be a cobra, which spread its hood and hissed, but never offered to bite her. Colonel Barras, the author of some charming natural history books, told me that he quite agrees that the cobra is disinclined to bite, and gave me a practical illustration of this which had fallen within his own observation. On one occasion, when some of my coolies were crossing a log, which was lying on the ground, my overseer, just as they were doing so, observed that under a bent-up portion of the log there was a cobra. He waited till all the coolies had crossed over and moved on, and then stirred up the cobra and killed it. I mention these instances to show that it is probably owing to the fact of the cobra not being at all an aggressive snake, and not being given to bite unless attacked, or hurt, that no death has occurred on my estates, or in my neighbourhood during such a long period of time.

But there is probably another reason, which has not, that I am aware of, been taken into account by previous writers, and that is that snakes keep a much better look out, and perceive the approach of people from a much greater distance than is usually supposed. I was much struck with this fact on two occasions this year. In one case I was walking along a foot road in my compound, and on going round a bend of the road saw, about thirty yards away, a snake in the road with its body half raised, and evidently in an on-the-look-out attitude, and the moment it perceived me it lowered its body and went off through the long grass. In the other case I saw a snake on bare ground upwards of 100 yards away which had evidently seen me, for it made off in the way which a disturbed snake always does. I was this year surprised to hear tigers and snakes classed together as to running away by a toddy-drawer—a class of people who are often out in the jungle at dusk, and sometimes later. I had made a new four feet trace of about a mile long along a beautiful ridge which connects my estate with an outlying piece of the property, and unfortunately mentioned to my wife that at the end of the path tigers crossed over occasionally (it was a tiger pass as the natives call it), and she objected to go there late in the evening. Being desirous of going to the end of the path one evening, I called to a toddy-man in my employ and told him to accompany us, telling my wife that he was a timid creature and not likely to incur any risk he could avoid. I mentioned to him the apprehension of the lady, when he said, "Tigers and snakes run away," and he seemed to have no apprehension as regards either of them, though part of the land in which he cut toddy trees was on the tiger pass. And I may mention that I this year wounded a tiger within fifty yards of the pass, and on the following morning saw the tracks of a tiger and tigress (the track of the latter is easily to be distinguished as it is longer and narrower than that of the male) in the jungle adjoining the end of the foot road alluded to.

As many Europeans kill all snakes they meet with, it is well to mention that the tank snake—a large snake often from nine to ten feet long—is not only harmless but useful, as it lives so largely on rats and mice, and is in consequence sometimes called the rat snake. On one occasion a manager shot one of these snakes near my house, and it had a rat in its mouth when killed, and such snakes, so far from being killed, ought to be carefully protected. I was this year rather interested in observing the proceedings of one of these snakes when followed up by two dogs of mine in the open. First of all, it made for a clump of two or three scrubby trees, and, apparently first fastening itself by the neck to a stump, lashed out with its tail. Then when the dogs came closer it again made off through the grass, but on being overtaken by the dogs must have either bitten one of them, or lashed it with its tail, as the dog gave a sharp cry and retreated. On a previous occasion one of these snakes bit a dog of mine, and it was not in the slightest degree affected. These snakes travel at a fair pace, and I found by trotting along parallel to one that it can move at the rate of the moderate jog trot of a horse, and apparently keep up this pace with ease. But, though it would be easy for me to write more about snakes, the reader has probably heard enough of them, and I hope has learnt some facts of practical importance by the way, and I shall now offer a few remarks on jungle pets.

It is commonly supposed that wild animals naturally or instinctively dread man, but it seems to me that, though no doubt a certain degree of dread of man may have been, after having been acquired by experience, transmitted to the offspring, wild animals require to be taught to dread man by their parents, for we find that if animals are caught when very young and are not confined in any way, they not only do not dread man, but eventually prefer his society to that of their own species.

The first instance I have to notice of this is in the case of a spotted deer stag which belonged to a neighbour of mine. This animal, which had been caught when a fawn, used to accompany the coolies in the morning and remained with them all day, but in the evening it went into the jungle regularly and disappeared for the night, and again turned up at the morning muster with unfailing regularity. It thus roamed the jungle all night, and remained with man all day. At last it became dangerous to man, as tame stags often do, and had to be shot.

Another still more extraordinary instance was in the case of a pet of my own—what the natives call a flying cat, but in reality a flying squirrel (*Pteromys petaurista*)—an animal that sleeps all day and feeds at night (though on one occasion, mentioned in a previous chapter, I saw one feeding on fruit at about seven one morning), and is in habits somewhat like the bat, though clearly of the squirrel order. Its wings, if indeed they may be called such, consist merely of a flap of skin stretching from the fore to the hind legs. When at rest this flap, as it folds into the side, is not very noticeable, and the animal presents, when on the ground, or on the branch of a tree, the appearance of a very large, grey furred squirrel. It cannot, of course, rise from the ground, but, when travelling from tree to tree, it spreads its flap, or perhaps rather sets its sail, by the agency of osseous appendages attached to the feet, but which fold up against the leg when the animal is at rest, and starts like a man on the trapeze—descending from one point to rise again to about a similar level on the next tree, but when the flight is extended (Jerdon, in his "Mammals of India," says he has seen one traverse in the air a distance of sixty yards) the squirrel reaches the tree very low down. When clearing the forest these squirrels often emerged from their holes in the trees and gave me good opportunities of observing their movements, and I feel sure that I have seen them traverse distances of at least 100 yards. One of these squirrels was brought to me when it was about half grown, and came to consider my house as its natural home. It soon discovered a suitable retreat for the day in the shape of an empty clothes-bag hanging at the back of a door, and in this it slept all day. It came out at dusk, and used often to sit on the back of my high backed chair as I sat at dinner, and then I gave it fruit and bread. After dinner away it went to the jungle, and I seldom saw anything more of it till very early in the morning, when it used to enter the house by an open swing window, get on to my bed, and curl itself up at my feet. When I rose my pet did so too and betook itself to the clothes-bag, and there spent the day, to go through the same round the following night. This very pretty and interesting animal met with the common fate of defenceless pets, and was killed by a dog as it was making its way to the jungle one evening.

A third instance I may give as regards the way in which wild animals readily become domesticated, and eventually seem to prefer the society of man to that of their own species. In this case my pet was a hornbill, a bird of discordant note, and with a huge beak, and a box-like crowned head. This creature was also totally unrestrained, but showed a most decided preference for the society of man. One day it joined some of its species which made their appearance in the jungle near my house, but soon got tired of or disgusted with them, and speedily returned to the bungalow. It used to swallow its food like a man taking a pill, and it was surprising to observe the ease with which balls of rice of about the size of two large walnuts were dispatched. On one occasion it flew off with my bunch of keys, but was luckily seen by my servant, who gave the alarm. The bird threw back its head the moment it alighted on the first convenient branch, and it was only from the ring sticking in the front of its beak that it was prevented from swallowing the entire bunch. Finding my people close upon it, the bird flew away to a piece of forest some hundreds of yards away, where it seemed to take a most aggravating pleasure in dangling my keys from the tops of the loftiest trees, and it was some time before it let them drop, which I conclude it at last did merely because it could not swallow them.

Now, though none of the pets I have mentioned were made miserable by restraint, and evidently must have found themselves perfectly happy in the society of man, it is very remarkable that, though all of them must have had (and the bird certainly had) frequent opportunities of making the acquaintance of their species as they roamed the jungle at night, they regularly returned to the society of man. I can only conjecture that the force of habit must have, as it were, chained them to the place they had become accustomed to. It is difficult to guess at any other reason than the force of habit, but it is just possible that the following fact may have something to do with their neglect of their own species. It is well known that a great many animals and birds refuse to, or cannot, propagate their kind when in a state of confinement. Now these pets of mine, and the stag which belonged to my neighbour, were not indeed confined in any sense, but it is just possible that the altered conditions under which they lived may have acted on their animal desires, and so have rendered them indifferent to the society of their species. Or perhaps it is conceivable that, in consequence of their living in or about an inhabited dwelling, they may have contracted bodily impurities which may have been perceptible to their wild congeners.

I had here intended to close this chapter, but a few lines more must be devoted to guns, or rather to a gun, for the general opinion in India now seems to be that only one gun is necessary for shooting shot and ball—at least for all shot shooting and ball shooting in the jungly countries. That gun is the widely-known Paradox, which, up to 100 yards, is as accurate as a double rifle, and even at 150 yards makes very fair practice. This gun was a good many years ago recommended to me by Sir Samuel Baker, and I found it to be such an excellent weapon that I now use no other. The great advantage of the Paradox is that the gun is a good shot gun, and gives a pattern quite equal to the best of cylinder guns, and of course comes up to the shoulder so readily that the sportsman can take snap shots as well as with any other fowling-piece. The immense advantage of this in a jungly country, and in one with long grass, must be readily apparent to anyone accustomed to shoot in such regions, where you often require to be able to fire as sharply as you do at a snipe rising just within range.

I am informed by Messrs. Holland and Holland, of 98, New Bond Street (the makers of the Paradox guns), that the Paradox system of ball and shot guns was the invention of Colonel Fosbery, V.C. Originally it was intended for the ordinary 12-bore guns, but its principle has now been applied to smaller weapons, such as those of 20 bore, and also to heavy guns of 8 or 10 bore for attacking elephants, bison, and other very large game. Guns of the two last-named bores are from two to three pounds lighter than rifles of similar bores, and the increased handiness caused by the diminution of weight is of course of immense advantage. Messrs. Holland and Holland inform me that they have made many experiments with the 8-bore Paradox against the 8-bore rifle, and in every case have obtained higher velocity and greater penetration with the Paradox. The new 10-bore is almost a 9, and practically is big enough for any game. It shoots 8 drams of powder, and a fairly long conical bullet, and its weight is about 12½ lbs. Messrs. Holland and Holland have invented a new steel bullet for these guns, and with this the penetration is very great. The 20 and 16-bore Paradox guns weigh from 6½ lbs. to 7 lbs., and are largely used on the Continent for shooting wild boar, bears, and other large game. Nearly all these guns are made with hammers, because as a rule sportsmen travelling in wild countries prefer to have the old-fashioned hammer guns, which are so universally understood, instead of a hammerless gun, which cannot be so easily repaired should it break down in any part. Messrs. Holland and Holland inform me that for the ordinary 12-bore Paradox weighing 7 lbs. the usual charge of 3 drams is all that is necessary for soft-skinned animals such as tigers, leopards, and bears, but they also make a heavier 12-bore, weighing from 8 lbs. to

8½ lbs., and shooting 4 or 4½ drams of powder, but generally recommend the usual 7 lbs. Paradox, and, from my experience of the latter with tigers, I do not think one could desire a better gun for all jungle shooting, though I need hardly add that for antelope shooting on the plains a long range rifle is desirable.

CHAPTER VI.

THE INDIAN BISON.

THOUGH at the risk of being thought sentimental, I cannot say that I approach the subject of bison shooting with much satisfaction, except, perhaps, in the thought that what I am about to write may be the means of prolonging in some degree, however infinitesimal, the existence of the race of these splendid animals, for I am afraid that nothing that anyone could write would prevent their numbers from being steadily diminished, and diminished, too, in some cases even by people who call themselves sportsmen; for one rather well-known writer has not only killed cow bisons, but actually published the fact—a thing that he certainly would not have done had the custom of shooting them not been common in some parts of India. I am happy to say that I never saw a dead cow bison, and in my part of Mysore, in the course of upwards of thirty-seven years' experience, I have never heard of more than two or three cows having been killed. Anything more foolish and barbarous than the killing of cow bisons cannot be conceived, for there is not a more harmless and inoffensive animal in the jungle than the bison—harmless because it seldom attacks[1] crops (I have never known of

[1] In Jerdon's "Mammals of India," Roorkee, 1867, p. 304, however, I find that it is stated that the bison do ravage the fields of the ryots, but Mr. Sanderson has no mention of their doing so, and he had the best opportunities for observation.

more than one instance of their doing so), and inoffensive because, if not molested, it never attacks man; and Mr. Sanderson, in his admirable work entitled "Thirteen Years amongst the Wild Beasts of India," declares that even solitary bulls, which are supposed to be dangerous, even if not molested, are not really so, though in the event of a native coming suddenly on a bull in the long grass, he admits the bison may spring suddenly up and dash at the intruder to clear him from his path. He has a most sympathetic chapter on these noble animals, and has enjoyed from an elephant's back the best opportunities of observing them, as the bison does not fear the elephant, in whose company indeed it is often found to be, and after having thus observed a herd of bison grazing, he says that he has "often left the poor animals undisturbed." Latterly he never thought of attacking herd bison, as it is often difficult to get a shot at the bull of the herd, and confined his shooting to those old solitary bulls which have been turned out of the herds by younger and more vigorous animals. These ought alone, indeed, to be the object of pursuit, and it is one usually carried on under such circumstances and amidst such splendid scenes that the sport is very attractive, and the pursuit of the solitary bull, writes Mr. Sanderson, can never, he imagines, pall on the most successful hunter. Perhaps this is true, but after having killed, say six solitary bulls, I think that a sportsman ought to be content for the rest of his life. A young forest officer lately told me that, having killed about that number, he had announced to his friends his intention of not killing any more. Shortly afterwards he fell in with two bulls who were engaged in a fierce battle with each other, and he might easily have shot one or perhaps both of them, but he had strength of mind to resist the temptation, a fact which, if known, would certainly entitle him to advancement in the service.

I have said that the bison, unless molested, will never attack man, and I was so confident of this that I once sent a highly valued European in my employ, to photograph a solitary bull, merely sending with him a native with a gun, and with instructions to fire in the event of the photographer being attacked. I selected a small piece of open swampy grass ground in a detached piece of jungle through which solitary bulls often passed, and knowing the direction of the wind at that season of the year, had no difficulty in avoiding any chance of the bull winding the photographer. The camera was placed on the edge of the jungle, and presently a bull came slowly grazing along the swamp, when he unluckily looked up to find the photographer just taking the cap off, within about ten paces. Never was there anything more annoying, and the thing would have been a magnificent success had my man been provided with the instantaneous process. But he was not, and the bull turned and fled through the mud with a most tremendous rush, having, I suppose, taken the lens for the glare of the eye of some new kind of tiger. The sudden change in the appearance of the bull was described to me as being most remarkable, for as he grazed quietly along he appeared to be one of the most harmless and domestic of animals, while the moment the sight of the camera fell on his astonished vision he was at once transformed into the wildest looking animal conceivable.

It is difficult to believe that big game in remote spots can perceive whether a man means to harm them or not, but it is remarkable that when on his way to the jungle alluded to, the photographer passed two sambur deer in the long grass, and at no great distance away, and saw them still lying there on his return. A bear was also rolling and grunting in the jungle close to him as he was waiting for the bull. On his return to the hut (put up for the occasion about a mile away) he was amused to find the native servant I had sent with him seated between two roasting fires which he imagined, and perhaps not without reason, would prevent his being attacked by a tiger. During the absence of my amateur photographer either a tiger or panther had passed close to the hut.

The photographer returned to the swamp on the following morning, but no bull arrived, and I gave up the attempt to obtain a photograph of a bison. But it is time now to describe the bison.

The Indian bison (*Gavœus Gaurus*, sometimes called the Gaur) is the largest member in the world of the ox tribe. It is quite free from mane or shaggy hair of any kind. The cows are of a dark brown, while in mature and old bulls the colour approaches to black. The legs from the knee downwards are of a dirty white (I once saw two bison with apparently blue legs, the colour being caused by standing on ashes, and this gave them a very remarkable appearance), and so is the forehead. The bison has no hump. It has a marked peculiarity in the shape of the back from the dorsal ridge running with a slight upward slope to about the middle of the back and then dropping suddenly towards the rump. Mr. Sanderson has never shot a bull more than six feet in height at the shoulder (if measured at the top of the dorsal ridge the height would of course be more), but Jerdon the naturalist, quoting Elliot (the late Sir Walter, a very careful observer) mentions six feet one-and-a-half inch as the height of one. I have generally found that an average sized bull is six feet, but I once killed one that was seven feet, and a neighbour of mine who has seen a great deal of bison shooting has killed one of similar height, and he informs me that he is positive that he has seen a larger bull than either of these very exceptional animals.

Bison herds generally number about twelve or fourteen, and I have never seen one of more than twenty-three, but at certain seasons they congregate in considerable numbers and again separate into small herds. They lie at night in a compact circle so that if attacked by a tiger they are ready to oppose at once a good front to the enemy. They seem to be quite aware that if they were to lie scattered about a tiger might suddenly spring upon one of them.

The bison has never been kept long in captivity, and there is only one instance of its having been so, and that is in the case of a bull bison now in possession of His Highness the Maharajah of Mysore. The history of this animal, and more especially of the warm friendship that sprung up between it and a doe sambur deer, is extremely interesting. I took down the following from my neighbour Mr. Park, and read over to him the account I now give.

It appears then that Mr. Park when out shooting some years ago, caught a male calf bison which was supposed to be about three days old. About a week afterwards a young doe sambur, which was being pursued by jungle dogs, rushed into one of the labourer's huts and was secured. It was then resolved to keep the deer as a companion for the bison, and the two were kept together, though they were never shut up. They were first of all fed on milk, and then allowed to graze, and soon became quite inseparable companions. They were fed at twelve o'clock and at four in the afternoon, and seemed to know their feeding time exactly. When about two years old it was resolved to fit the bison with a nose rope, and for this the nose had of course to be bored. He was tied up to a tree to be operated on and, after the hole was bored, he was liberated, when he rushed all over the ground adjacent to the house bellowing with rage—the only time, I may add, Mr. Park ever heard him bellow. After this he was regularly led out to graze by a man who trained him, by pulling the nose rope, to go in one direction or another.

N

After this he was fed on gram (a kind of pea). When thus led out to graze the sambur sometimes remained behind, but seemed to have no difficulty in finding the bull even though it had been taken to a considerable distance. It would hold up its nose to catch the scent and then go off on the track. When the bison occasionally missed the doe he would wander about in search of her, but seemed to have no power of following her by scent—a power which she evidently possessed and practised. When the doe bathed in the river and splashed up the water with her fore feet the bull would stand upon the bank watching her proceedings with evident interest and curiosity, but did not himself bathe, nor appear to have any desire to go into the water. The bison, however, seemed to enjoy the cooling effect of the heavy monsoon rains, and no doubt thought that a shower bath of some hundreds of inches was quite enough for the rest of the year.

When the bull was about three years old it was presented to the Maharajah of Mysore, and sent off to the nearest railway station some sixty miles away. Some time after he had left, the doe discovered his absence, and then, in her usual way, went about holding up her nose in order to discover the direction in which he had gone. Presently she hit off the route and, setting off in pursuit, overtook her old companion after he gone about five or six miles, and, though the doe had not been given to the Maharajah, she was allowed to accompany the bull. When the doe overtook the bull he showed the greatest signs of pleasure at her arrival, and the two travelled happily along to Mysore.

I saw the bison at Mysore in 1891, when it looked remarkably well and happy, though the doe was not with it at the time. I was since glad to hear from a friend, who had seen them last October, that these strange and inseparable companions are in excellent health. It was very fortunate that the doe accompanied the bull, as I think it probable that the latter would have pined away and died, as the bison seems hitherto always to have done in captivity.

Bison are often attacked by tigers, and I once found the remains of one that had been killed by a tiger. It had been killed on the grass land between two and three hundred yards from the jungle, and I was much struck by the fact that the tiger had separated the head from the body and carried it into the forest, where I found the skull. It appeared to be that of a fair sized bull. But the largest bulls are sometimes killed by tigers, though I imagine that this must be rare, or we should not find very old bulls in a country where tigers are plentiful. A tiger I believe sometimes tires out a bull by inducing him to charge again and again till he is quite worn out, and sometimes, I am informed by an experienced sportsman, two tigers will join in attacking a bison, and have been known to hamstring it. I have been told by a toddyman who lived on the edge of the forest region, that in a valley near his house he had seen a tiger worrying a bison and inducing it to charge for nearly a whole day and ultimately killing it. But sometimes the bison succeeds in driving off the tiger, which then slinks away. About two years ago an interesting illustration took place of this, which was witnessed by a neighbour of mine, who found that when stalking a bull bison he had a fellow stalker in the shape of a tiger. The incident was at once rare and interesting—in fact, so far as I know, quite unique—and I asked my friend to write me an account of it for publication in my book.

"When I was returning," writes my friend Mr. Brooke Mockett, "one day in the beginning of the monsoon of 1891, from visiting a plantation of mine near the Ghauts, I deflected somewhat from my route to visit an adjacent range of minor hills, and presently entered a shallow valley, on the opposite side of which the forest land was fringed with some scrubby bushes mingled with ferns, outside of which was a stretch of open grass land. As I entered the valley I saw on the opposite side of it a solitary bull bison grazing along towards the open grass land. This, at the rate he was moving, he would soon reach. I therefore took up a position so as to get a shot at him when he got fairly into the open land, where he would be immediately below and opposite to me. Two Hindoo ryots—always called goudas in Manjarabad—from a neighbouring village were with me, and were keeping a sharp look out. We were all quite concealed in the long grass. Presently one of them whispered, 'Look, look, there is a tiger stalking the bison,' and, after peering into the bushes for a few seconds, I at last made out the tiger, which was about 200 yards further along the valley to the east of the bison, towards which it was stealthily creeping. I at once decided not to interfere at present, but to leave the animals alone and watch the result. The tiger struck me as being a small one, and the goudas thought so too. It was probably the same one that had some weeks before killed a three-parts-grown bison, the remains of which we saw when on the way to the spot. The bull was a magnificent animal, and just in his prime. It was a most exciting scene; the ponderous bull grazing quietly along the valley in utter ignorance of danger, and feeding so industriously that he never once lifted his head from the ground, while the tiger crawled towards him in a manner that was exquisite to see. Belly to the ground, its movements resembled rather those of a snake than an animal as it wound its way through the scrub, gliding through the ferns, and taking advantage of all the bushes. Occasionally it sat up to peer cautiously at the bull, and then sinking down it again glided on. Except now and then, when the bushes were low, I doubt if it could see the bull, nor could the latter scent the tiger, for the bull was feeding down the valley in the teeth of the strong monsoon winds, and the tiger was following in its tracks.

"As the two goudas sitting with me in the long grass observed the movements of the tiger, they could not contain their indignation. No doubt they thought of the many cattle they had recently lost, and, connecting the present revelation of the tiger's mode of proceeding with the slaughter of their buffaloes, they relieved their feelings by uttering *sotto voce* the most virulent abuse of the tiger, its wife, and its female relations in general, and every fresh movement of the tiger drew from them some extremely powerful and untranslatable epithets. The temptation to fire at the tiger was very great, but I refrained, as every moment brought them nearer to me, and it seemed certain that the fight must come off just below the ground I was seated on.

"The scene was now an extremely exciting one, for the animals were about 200 yards from us, the bull having fed to within fifty yards of the open grass, and the tiger having crept so close to him that every moment we expected something to happen. We saw the tiger crawl right up to the bull, and it seemed to get actually within a yard of it, and yet it did not spring. A few seconds more passed, and then the bull, suddenly becoming aware of the tiger's presence, made a rapid rush forward into the open grass land outside of the scrub. Then he pulled up at a distance from it of about sixty yards, and faced round in the direction of the tiger. Had he liked, he might have gone away altogether; but, far from showing fear, he was furious, and looked superb as he shook his head and snorted with rage. Then for about two minutes he stood as still as if carved of stone, evidently straining all his senses to discover the tiger, after which he made a terrific charge up to the edge of the scrub, where he pulled up and again snorted, and shook his head. If ever a bison meant business he did, and could he have seen the tiger he would have certainly tried to kill it, but it was hiding in the scrub and was invisible to him, though we could just make out its golden red skin.

"The sight of the infuriated bull within a few yards was altogether too much for the tiger, which now turned and commenced to sneak off with astonishing rapidity, keeping completely out of the bison's sight, and looking like the most abject wretch imaginable. My goudas became frantic at this, and seeing that there was now no chance of a fight between the bull and the tiger, I rushed along the hill with the view of trying to get a good shot at the latter, but this I found would be impossible, so I rested my rifle on a stump, and, as he moved through the scrub, took a long shot, which knocked him off his legs, and we saw him partly roll and partly scramble into the dense jungle below. A shout of 'The bull is going,' from the goudas, made me look back, and just as he was starting I hastily fired my second barrel into his shoulder and dropped him dead. We then went to look for the tiger, but, most unfortunately, the rain, which up to this time had kept off, descended in torrents, and the whole country became enveloped in dense mist. We found the spot where the tiger had been knocked over, and the goudas soon discovered cut hair (by the bullet), a sure proof of a hit. We could see where he had rolled down the slope to the thick forest, crushing the ferns, and tearing up the ground with his struggles, but the blood was of course washed away by the tropical rain torrents. Within the forest, which was almost impenetrable, all was dark as night, and as no track could be seen, and we were soon all drenched to the skin, it was impossible to do anything more, and I was compelled to give up the pursuit. Why the tiger, after getting so close to the bison did not attack, it is impossible to say, but the men who accompanied me were of opinion that, owing to the bison being partly hidden by the scrub, the tiger could not gauge its size till quite close to it, and then was afraid to attack such a large bull."

I think that their surmise is correct, and as I have before suggested, I think that these very large bulls are but rarely attacked by tigers, for my experience shows that solitary bulls are easily stalked, to within quite close distances, and, were the tigers easily able to kill them, I feel sure that a solitary bull would very seldom be found.

I have said that the bison is a harmless animal, but this of course is only when you keep away from it, and a wounded bison should be approached and tracked up with caution, and in no case should a single tracker follow up a wounded bull. He should always have a companion to keep a general look out in case of the bull suddenly charging the tracker when he is busy following the trail. On one occasion a manager of mine went out shooting, wounded a bull, and then went round to a point to cut him off, and sent in the only man he had to follow up the track and drive the bull on. He waited for some time and then shouted, but received no answer, for the poor tracker was dead. He had evidently been charged by the bull when he was busy tracking it, and was taken by surprise. By a curious coincidence my manager had dreamed the night before that he had gone out with this tracker, that he had been killed by a bull, and that the body was found extended in the position in which it was ultimately found on the following day.

Close to the place where the man was killed we had a capital illustration of the need for keeping a good look out when tracking. When out shooting one evening with a friend, we wounded a solitary bull (which I have reason to suppose was the same bull that killed the tracker), and on the following morning took up his track, which led down into a spot in the forest where, from some trees probably having been blown down in former years, there was a little thicket of small trees and underwood. Into this the bull had gone, and we soon found where he had been lying, and were proceeding to take up the track again, when one of our men, who stood a little way behind, and luckily, was looking about, said "There's the bull." He had evidently heard us coming, got up, gone ten yards away, and was waiting for a favourable moment to charge, and, had he done so when we were in the thicket, he probably would have killed one of the party. My friend, who was an old hand, and of course saw the danger at a glance, cleared out of the thicket with wonderful alertness, and the rest were not slow to follow his example. We then passed round the upper side of the thicket, and came down upon the bull in the more open forest, and soon killed him. Just as we had done so, news came that a herd of bison was grazing on a ridge about half or three-quarters of a mile or so away, and as our pursuit of them elucidates some points of practical importance, I give a short description of the stalk and its accompanying circumstances.

The herd of bison, it appears, were just outside a jungly ravine which ran up from the main forest through the grass land. The jungle terminated just below a ridge of hill, along which we approached the spot. Overhanging the hollow were some rocks which afforded us a convenient place to creep behind, and presently we lay down there, looking at the herd, which was below us, and about a hundred yards away. And then we found (as Mr. Sanderson so often did that he at last gave up attacking herd bison) that it was impossible to fire at the bull, as he was screened by the cows. How long we lay watching I cannot exactly tell, but as the day got hotter the bison began to move, and then we had a chance of firing at the big bull. The herd, bull included, then entered the jungly ravine, and presently reappeared a little further down and on the right of the ravine with a calf which had evidently been left in the ravine, and filed along the slope. The bull, however, had remained behind. Now comes a point of great importance in following up big game, and which, curiously enough, has never been noticed hitherto, at least I have not been able to meet with any reference to it in the many big game shooting books I have looked at. If an animal is wounded, it is a common practice to follow it up at once, the result of which is that it will often go off to a considerable distance (which is often highly inconvenient) and frequently be lost. But if, instead of following the startled animal at once, a perfect silence is maintained, and you remain where you are, the animal, the moment it is inside the jungle, will stand to listen, and if it can neither hear nor see anything, will probably lie down to recover from the shock, and if it does so, will very probably not rise from the spot for a considerable time. You have thus an opportunity of getting ahead of your quarry and coming back to the margin of the forest from a direction opposite to that from which it naturally expects danger, and it will thus have to pass you again in order to get further into the forest, and you will then, as I have known from experience, get another shot. On this occasion it was of great importance to get between the wounded bull and the main forest towards the foot of the Ghauts, and we accordingly resolved to go down the grass land on the outside of the jungly ravine, enter it a good way down, and lie up to rest for some time, and then look up the wounded bull.

And now I received a lesson that I shall never forget. We had taken our early toast and tea, and had intended returning to breakfast, but we had been decoyed by the sport so far from home, and the weather was so hot, that we could not face the task of toiling back in the heat of the sun, and besides, we had our wounded bull to look up. The prospect of remaining all day without food was not pleasant, but luckily I had a few small biscuits in my pocket. Then we were afraid to drink the water, as at that season it is not considered to be wholesome. "Ah," said my friend, after fumbling in his pocket, "we are all right. I have got one peppermint lozenge. We will divide it into four parts, and it will last the day." This was my first introduction to the great practical value of the peppermint lozenge in taking away the sensation of thirst, and in hot climates I now never go without them. But they should be made at a good chemist's, as the peppermint then has none of that nauseous, or, at any rate, very disagreeable, smell which accompanies ordinary peppermint lozenges. They are also very useful in travelling, and in India I always carry them, as, if kept out longer in the morning than usual, they at once banish hunger and thirst, and are, besides, very refreshing, and I feel sure would be invaluable in the case of troops marching in hot weather, and where good water is not to be had. They are also very useful when going out after a tiger, and when news of one is brought in my first order is to put up two peppermint lozenges. Another point of value I may here mention. Always, if there is a chance of your being kept out late, take a lantern and matches. We experienced the evil of the neglect of this precaution when returning home. You may have starlight outside the forest, but darkness within, and a lantern is, of course, a great aid, and it is so even when there is moonlight, as you may be either on the wrong side of a ridge or have to pass through dark bottoms. But now as to the pursuit of the bull.

After resting for several hours we took our way up the ravine in the direction of the point at which the bull entered it. And here we made a cardinal mistake, for we went together, whereas had one of us remained on the grass land outside, we should almost certainly have got the bull. We, however, omitted to take this precaution, and proceeded up the ravine to within about fifty yards of the spot where the bull entered, when up he got close to us, but without our being able to see him, and went out of the ravine on to the grass land and down into the main forest beyond, into which we had neither time, strength, nor inclination to follow him. The preceding will be a good lesson to any young sportsman, firstly, as to the value of not following up a wounded animal at once, and, secondly, as to taking every kind of precaution when you do. How often is sport spoiled from the want of appreciating the truism that a wall is no stronger than its weakest point. The importance of carefully guarding and refusing to be decoyed away from the pass into the main forest is of such consequence that I proceed to enforce it with another illustration.

One day I found a fine bull grazing on the margin of a piece of detached jungle some five or six acres in extent; I got between him and the main forest, to which he would of course fly, fired at him, and he went at once into the ravine, or rather jungle-clad hollow, in front of him. I then ran to the only pass from it into the main forest, and told the two people who were with me to follow on the track of the bull, at which I should thus have been able to get another shot in the event of his having strength enough to leave the five or six acres of jungle he had entered. I waited for a considerable time, and at last went up the hill with the view of seeing what my people were about, and called out, to be answered by one man on the top of a hill on the other side, and by another from the top of a tree, who said that the bison had attacked them, and that one of them had run out of the jungle and the other up a tree. I called out to the man on the grass land to go and fetch a dog and some people from the village, and again returned to my pass, for had the bull once got down into the main forest which led to the foot of the Ghauts, we should probably have lost him. After rather a long interval some natives appeared with a dog, and I told them to drive the ravine, and soon there ensued a series of charges, accompanied by the barking of the dog, and a general state of confusion, from which it was evident that the bison had lots of go in him. Still I clung to the pass. At last my patience was worn out, and I went to look up the bull in the jungle. Horror of horrors! he made off in the very direction of the pass into the main forest, and had it not been for the dog we should probably have lost him, but I at once set on the dog, and this had the desired effect of making the bull turn, when he came towards us, looking for some one to charge. When he was a few yards from me I gave him a shot which turned him aside, and as he deflected he presented a good shot, and was soon killed.

The jumping, or rather bounding power of the bison is wonderful, and I was accidentally caused to ascertain it in this way. One evening, just at sundown, I found a bull in a very unexpected place, high up on a mountain, with very precipitous sides. He was on the edge of a piece of jungly, swampy land, about half an acre in extent, and when I fired at him he went into this, and I sent my second gun man round to drive him out. He soon appeared, took one look at me at a distance of about fifty yards, and then charged with wonderful suddenness. I was young and active then, and ran sideways to the only tree—a small one on the open land—but I had just time to save myself, for the bull, having struck or grazed the tree with his shoulder, fell at my feet, and as he rose, his horn caught my coat about the armpit and tore a hole in it. He galloped towards me with his nose up, but lowered his head as he approached me, evidently to clear me away. He, of course, was up again in a second, and disappeared over the crest of the hill. The ground I was standing on sloped only slightly upward towards the point at which the bison emerged, there being at the spot a length of about eighty yards of comparatively flat land, which, of course, accounted for the swampy ground, which, by the way, had been partly created by the natives having at some remote time formed a small tank there. Well, the following morning I went to the spot with an English sporting companion, and said, "This is the place where I was charged." "But," he said, and so said the natives with him, "there has never been a bison here at all," and as there had been some rain the day before, the tracks would, of course, have been plainly visible. As it turned out, we happened to be standing between the tracks, and on measuring the distance between them, we found that the bull had covered twenty-one feet from hind-foot to hind-foot, and that, too, on ground which, as we have seen, sloped but very slightly.

I cannot conclude this chapter without urging sportsmen to use every means in their power which can aid in the preservation of these harmless and interesting animals; and I trust that every effort may be made not only to obtain a Game Preservation Act for India, but to have a special clause inserted in it with reference to cow bisons, and the imposition of a heavy fine for killing one of them. Is not the intelligent preservation of game one of the most prominent signs of advancing civilization?

CHAPTER VII.

GOLD.

GOLD mines are as uncertain as women, and yet from either it seems impossible to keep away. Perhaps it is this very uncertainty which constitutes the chief charm of both. But, however that may be, it is certain that about gold in general, whether visible or prospective, there is such a degree of attractiveness that, as the Kanarese proverb puts it, if gold is to be seen even a corpse will open its mouth; and I feel sure as I write, that in this chapter at least I can count not only on attention, but on a general attitude of expectancy in the mind of the reader. And from one point of view he will be fairly satisfied, for the history of gold mining in Mysore has quite a romantic cast, and in the hands of a skilful novelist, there might be extracted from it much literary capital. The foremost fact indeed which I have to give has almost a sensational flavour, and at first sight seems a mere dream. We often read of fields of golden grain, but that corn should ever, by any process of nature, have on its ears grains of gold, seems beyond belief. And yet the fact of grains of gold being found on the ears of the rice plants is probably the very earliest tradition connected with gold, and it is not improbable that the circumstance may have been one of the means of calling attention to the existence of gold in Mysore. An account of this tradition is to be found in the "Selections from the

Records of the Mysore Government,"[1] and from them it appears that Lieutenant John Warren, when he was employed in surveying the eastern boundary of Mysore in 1800, was told by a Brahman that "In prosperous years when the gods favoured the Zillah of Kadogi (a small village on the west bank of the Pennar river, Hoskote Talook, 15 miles from Bangalore) with an ample harvest now and then grains of gold were found on the ears of the paddy (rice plants) grown under the tank lying close to the north of that village." And in this connection I may mention that, when visiting the Kolar mines last January, I found, in the course of a conversation with the head man of the village of Ooregum, that he was aware of this tradition, and that grains of gold were said to have been seen on the rice plants at a village about fifteen miles distant from his own. The explanation of this is extremely simple, as the rice plants are usually grown in nurseries and transplanted in bunches of several plants, after which the fields are flooded, and in heavy floods (and this accounts for the gold having been found in the years which are prosperous from the abundant rain) the plants would often be quite submerged. With the water no doubt came grains of gold, which were deposited on the rice plants, and as these grew, the grains of gold would naturally rise with them, and thus often be found adhering to the roughly-coated grain.

After the attention of Lieutenant Warren was called to the subject, he seems to have taken some trouble in investigating it, and having heard a vague report that gold had been found in the earth somewhere near a small hill about nine miles east of Budiakote, offered a reward for information regarding this, and shortly afterwards a ryot of the village offered to show him the place, which was close to

[1] Printed for the use of the Government, and kindly lent to me by the Dewan of Mysore.

his village. He visited the spot in question on February 17th, 1802, "when the women of the village were assembled, and, each being provided with a small broom and vaning basket, and hollow board to receive the earth, they went to a jungle on the west of the village. Here they entered some small nullahs, or rather breaks in the ground, and removing the gravel with their hands, they swept the earth underneath into their vaning baskets, by the help of which they further cleared it of the smaller stones and threw it into the hollow board above mentioned. Having thus got enough earth together, they adjourned to a tank and placed the hollow boards containing the earth in the water, but just deep enough for it to overflow when resting on the ground, and no more. Then they stirred the earth with the hand, but keeping it over the centre of the board, so that the metal should fall into the depression by its own weight, and the earth wash over the edges. After a few minutes' stirring, they put the metallic matter thus freed of earth into a piece of broken pot, but only after examining it for gold, which they did by inclining the board and passing water over the metallic sediment which adhered to it. They thus drove the light particles before the water, leaving the heavier metal behind just at the edge where it could easily be seen, however small the quantity." Lieutenant Warren, having afterwards heard that gold was extracted from mines near Marikoppa, three miles from Ooregum, visited four of the mines, the descent into which was made by means of small foot holes which had been made in their sides. The first was two feet in breadth and four in length with a depth of about thirty feet, and in distance fifty feet (of galleries I presume), the others were from thirty to forty-five feet deep. "The miners extracted the stones (how we are not informed) and they were passed from hand to hand in baskets by the miners who were stationed at different points for the purpose of banking the stones. The women then took them to a large rock, and pounded them to dust. The latter was then taken to a well and washed by the same process as that used when washing the earth for gold, when about an equal quantity of gold was found to that procured from an equal quantity of the auriferous earth."

The only people, writes Lieutenant Warren, who devote their time to searching for gold are Pariahs, who work as follows. "When they resolve on sinking a mine, they assemble to the number of ten or twelve from different villages. Then they elect a Daffadar, or head man, to superintend the work, and sell the gold, and they subscribe money to buy lamp oil, and the necessary iron tools, then partly from knowledge of the ground, and partly from the idea they have, that the tract over which a peacock has been observed to fly and alight, is that of a vein of gold, they fix on a spot and begin to mine."

Such, then, was the condition of gold mining in Mysore about the end of the last and the beginning of this century, but in ancient times mining was carried on by the natives to very considerable depths, and I am informed by Mr. B. D. Plummer, who has had ten years' experience of mines at Kolar, and worked the Mysore and Nundydroog mines, that the old native workings went down to a depth of about 260 feet. These, which were all choked up, were followed down to the bottom, and valuable lodes were found at about 150 to 260 feet. Nothing was found in the old native workings, but remains of old chatties (earthenware pots) and the wooden props put in to secure the sides. The native workings, in the opinion of Captain Plummer, were evidently carried on with skill and efficiency, and appear to be of great antiquity. Large quantities of water were found, requiring pumping machinery working day and night for its removal. How the natives in olden times got rid of the water is not known. It is supposed that they must have done so by chatties, and by hand, with the aid of large numbers of people. As no native iron tools[1] were found in the cases of the two above-mentioned mines, it is evident that they were deliberately abandoned, either from excess of water in them, or some unknown cause. As the lodes they worked at the depths they reached were rich, it is probable that the miners could no longer contend with the difficulty of removing the large quantities of water. I am informed by Mr. Plummer that the main lodes where the natives have formerly worked have, in nearly every case, proved successful. Mr. Plummer has examined other districts in the province, extending more than 100 miles north of Mysore city, and thinks that there is a very large mining future for the Mysore country. I am informed by one of the mine managers that from the quantity of charcoal found in the old native workings, it is probable that the natives first of all burnt the rock so as to make it the more easy of extraction, just as they now burn granite rock in order the more easily to split off the stone.

As the facts connected with these mines were brought very fully to the notice of the Government at such an early date, it at first sight seems strange that we have to skip over a period of about seventy years till we again meet, in the "Selections" previously quoted from, any further notice of the mines; but the neglect of them was evidently owing to the similar neglect of coffee and other industries, which might have been pushed forward at a much earlier date, and most certainly would have been, had the Government taken pains to see that the information so frequently obtained was published in an available and readable form, instead of being buried in the

[1] Mr. Bosworth-Smith, *vide* p. 36 of his Report, says that, up to 1889, only three finds of iron tools had been met with in the old native workings.

various offices of the State. That more efforts were not made in this direction was probably owing to the fact that the Government officers did not perceive the widespread effect that the introduction of European capital would have on the agriculture of the country, and, consequently, on the finances of the State—a subject referred to in my introductory chapter, and to which I shall again allude in the chapter on Coorg—while they were under the erroneous impression that Europeans would probably be a cause of annoyance to the Government and the people. We find a characteristic survival of the last idea in the "Selections," and in Clause X. of the conditions under which, in 1873, the first leave to mine was granted by the Government of Mysore, it is declared that, "In the event of the grantee causing annoyance or obstruction to any class of the people, or to the officers of Government, the chief commissioner reserves the power of annulling the mining right thus granted." But such apprehensions, I need hardly say, have long since passed away, and certainly within my long experience they never existed in Southern India in the case of the planters who, as a body, have always been encouraged by the State, and have always got on well with it and the people, though, of course, as in all countries, there are occasionally individuals who cannot bring themselves into harmony with any person, or condition of things.

And now, before proceeding with my narrative of gold mining in Mysore, I pause for one moment to note the rather remarkable fact that it seems impossible to find in old records or inscriptions any reference to gold mining in Mysore.[1] As to this I have made diligent inquiry, from

[1] In Mr. Hyde Clarke's paper entitled "Gold in India," London, Effingham Wilson, Royal Exchange, 1881, it is stated that "Dr. Burnell brings direct proof as to the abundance of gold, by his successful decipherment of a remarkable inscription in the Tanjore temple. Dr. Burnell is thus enabled to state that

the librarian of H.H. the Maharajah, from a member of the Archæological Survey of Mysore, and in every quarter that occurred to me. I was informed by a European resident at Bangalore that, at the Eurasian settlement near that city, there is a stone pillar with an inscription said by tradition to relate to gold mining, but I can hardly suppose it possible that this could have escaped the notice of the officers of the Archæological Survey. One of the officers of this department informed me that, in consequence of the absence of traditions regarding gold mining, he inferred that mining in Mysore must have been carried on from very remote times. But it is time to proceed with the history of mining in Mysore.

It appears, then, from the "Selections," that a Mr. Lavelle on the 20th of August, 1873, applied for the right to carry on mining operations in Kolar. Two years previously he had examined portions of the Kolar district (without any grant it would seem, from no mention of one being made), and found three auriferous strata, in one of which he sunk a shaft to the depth of eighteen feet, and found gold increase in quality and size as he went downwards. In the event of a mining right being granted he proposed to begin work again in November. After some correspondence came a letter from the chief commissioner, dated September 16th, 1874, submitting conditions (which must be regarded as final) as the basis of an agreement (to be afterwards legally drawn up) to be entered into between the Government and Mr. Lavelle. It is unnecessary to recapitulate all the conditions; suffice it to say that the right to mine in Kolar

in the eleventh century gold was still the most common precious metal in India, and stupendous quantities of it are mentioned. He considers, too, that this gold was obtained from mines, and that the Moslem invasion interrupted their workings." It does not, however, appear, at least in Mr. Hyde Clarke's paper, that the inscription deciphered by Dr. Burnell makes any reference to gold mining.

was to extend over twenty years, and that a royalty of ten per cent. on all metals and metallic ores, and of twenty per cent. on all precious stones, was to be paid. On September 20th, 1874, Mr. Lavelle accepted the terms, but what he did or did not do as regards mining does not appear in the "Selections," and I find it merely stated therein that on March 28th, 1876, leave was given him to transfer his rights to other parties. It, however, appears from a statement made by Mr. Lavelle in 1885 to the special correspondent of the "Madras Mail,"[1] that a small syndicate was formed, and some work carried on in the native style, though little success seems to have been met with, and the work was abandoned. About a year afterwards it was again recommenced by Mr. Lavelle, who in the meanwhile had been prospecting in other parts of Southern India, and he succeeded in once more attracting attention to the Kolar field, and subsequently various companies were formed, but so disappointing were the results obtained that all were practically closed in 1882, except the Mysore mine, which was working to a small extent. In February, 1883, the Nundydroog mine was ordered to be closed, and almost every other mine was in a state of collapse. Caretakers were put in and only a little work done. Early in 1884, when only twelve or thirteen thousand pounds of their capital were left, the Mysore shareholders were convened. Some were for closing at once and dividing the remaining capital, but, acting on the advise of Messrs. John Taylor and Sons, of 6, Queen Street Place, London, it was, fortunately for the province of Mysore, determined to spend it on the mine. The shares were then as low as tenpence. The company began to get gold about the end of 1884, and the prospect improved so much that the Nundydroog

[1] "The Kolar Gold Field in the State of Mysore." Reprinted from the "Madras Mail," December, 1885; Madras, the Madras Mail Press. London, Messrs. H. S. King and Co., 1885.

mine in May, 1885, was enabled to raise money on debentures, and so to again carry on work. If the shareholders of the Mysore company had not persevered, it is almost absolutely certain that the whole of the Kolar gold field would have been permanently abandoned. This is just one of those cases which cheer the sinking hopes of shareholders, and attract vast sums of money to gold mines; and no wonder, when we find the chairman of the Mysore company apologizing lately because he could not declare a dividend of more than fifty per cent.; that up to the end of 1892 the gold sold by the company realized £1,149,430 2*s.* 1*d.*, and that the total sum paid in dividends amounted to £602,156 10*s.* 6*d.*

The Mysore mine had been sunk to a depth of about 200 feet when it was proposed that the project should be abandoned. Just below this depth the miners struck the Champion lode on which the Mysore, Ooregum, Nundydroog, Balaghaut, and Indian Consolidated Companies are working. The Mysore mine has now been sunk to a depth of over 1,200 feet, Ooregum 850 feet, and Nundydroog over 860 feet. The lode is not richer per ton, as is commonly supposed, on greater depths being reached. The yield per ton is probably about the same, though from larger quantities being taken out, and the use of the rock drill, which causes a large extraction of country rock, the product per ton of quartz is apparently smaller. The specimens now found are as good as ever.

The circumstances of the Champion lode are briefly these. In the interior of a surrounding of granite there is a great basin of hornblende rock of schistose character, and through this, at an angle of about forty-five degrees, runs the lode. This is not of continuous thickness. In some places it is four or five feet wide, in others runs down to an almost vanishing point, and then again thickens. In the case of the mines now working on this lode, the basin of hornblende is more than two miles in width, and is possibly many thousands of feet in depth, so there seems to be a reasonable prospect of there being a long future before the workers on the Champion lode.

The Kolar gold field is about seven miles in length, and averages about two to three miles in width. There are in all fourteen mines, but two of them are practically stopped. The general appearance of it is at present by no means attractive, as the land is rocky and sterile, and unfavourable to the growth of trees, but, from the appearance of some of the Baubul trees, I feel sure that if large pits for the trees were dug, and filled with soil from the low-lying ground, a great deal might be done to beautify the field, by planting here and there groups of Baubul and other hardy trees indigenous to the locality. As I thought it would be interesting, and perhaps useful, to give some idea of life on the fields, I asked one of the ladies resident there to supply me with some notes for publication, and her observations on the situation from a social and general point of view are as follows.

"You ask me for some notes on the field, and I may begin by telling you that we usually rise about half-past six, when the menkind go off to their offices, or underground, as the case may be. We have tiffin between twelve and one, and dinner at half-past seven. Breakfast is generally at about eight, and the managers commonly have theirs sent down to the office.

"In the afternoon, that is to say, when the five o'clock whistle blows, we play tennis, or else go down to the Gymkana ground to watch the cricket. Sometimes there is a gymkana in which we all take great interest, particularly in those races called ladies' events, when the winners present their prizes to the ladies who have nominated them. The great drawback to the gold fields at present is the absence of some general meeting-place or club, but it is hoped that by next year this want will be supplied, as the Ooregum, Nundydroog, and Champion Reefs Companies have combined to build a hall, which is to contain a billiard-room, card-room, library, etc., and there is to be a tennis court in the compound.

"One of the great pleasures is gardening. The plants that grow best are jalaps, sunflowers, roses, cornflowers, nasturtiums, verbenas, and geraniums, all of which, with the exception of the two first-named plants, require water constantly. The creepers that grow best are passion-flowers, and a small kind of green creeper with convolvulus flowers, the name of which I do not know. Honeysuckle also grows, though but slowly. Trees have recently been planted in the various compounds, and also along some parts of the road leading to the bungalows, but owing to the shallowness of the soil, and the roots so soon reaching the rock, they seldom grow to any size. Some casuarinas in the Mysore mine camp have grown to about twenty feet in height, but these have now struck the rock, and most of them are dying.

"We have occasional visitors, many of them being shareholders in the various mines, bringing with them introductions from England, and wishing to inspect all the works, stamps, etc., on the surface, and very often going underground. Several ladies have been taken down the mines lately, but they do not seem to care for it much, for though of course it is interesting, still the fatigue of going down so many feet on ladders is great. The mines, too, in many parts are dirty and wet, and amongst other disagreeables are the cockroaches, which are enormous, and the stinging ants. Ladies too, I find, are as a rule disappointed at not seeing more 'visible gold.' I believe they cherish generally some idea of picking up a nice little nugget to keep as a souvenir of their expedition.

"None of the mines have any 'cages,' as they are called,

so if one does not want to go down by the ladders, one can only go in the box in which the quartz comes up, and as this is only two feet square and four feet deep, the journey by it would be decidedly uncomfortable. At every eighty feet, I may mention, you come to a small wooden platform (or level) where you can rest, and from which branch off the cross cuts and drives, or narrow passages. The depths of the different mines vary a great deal, Mysore being as low as 1,400 feet, the greatest depth sunk at present, while the least depth sunk is about 300 feet. Ladies going underground have to wear suitable attire. Skirts would be quite useless. A long coat, or short skirt reaching to the knees, and knickerbockers, is the most comfortable dress for the occasion. Very strong boots should be worn.

"Many of the miners and people employed in the gold fields have joined the Volunteers. There is now quite a strong corps of about 100 men, some being Eurasians, but the majority are either English or Italians. Once a year some 'bigwig' comes from Bangalore to review them. There is a sergeant-instructor on the field, and the adjutant comes very frequently to see them drill, etc.

"Round the various large tanks about six or eight miles away from the mines excellent snipe shooting is to be had, and duck and teal are also to be found. Spotted deer and bears are sometimes shot by sportsmen from the mines, but for these one must go further away. The fishing is not considered to be very good, but perhaps those who fish do not know how to set to work. The natives sometimes bring very large tank fish round for sale.

"Driving and riding are not very enjoyable, owing to the terribly bad state of the roads. When the railway to the mines is opened, which it soon will be, I am happy to say, the roads will be better. At present the heavy machinery for the mines, boilers, etc.—sometimes taking sixty bullocks to draw them—cut up the roads dreadfully. These will of course come by rail directly the line is open for traffic. The supplies, vegetables, fruit, etc., come from Bangalore three times a week, each mine keeping a 'Supply boy' (servant), who goes in from Kolar Road (our railway station, seven miles from the mines), and returns the following day. We get mutton and beef from the local butcher, and also good bread from the bakery on the field. Our butter comes from Bangalore, and from there we obtain peas, potatoes, French beans, tomatoes, cauliflowers, vegetable marrow, and lettuces, and also fruit, such as apples, peaches, grapes, plantains, custard apples, melons, and sometimes pine-apples. Servants on the whole are good. Most of them come from Madras. Wages are much higher on the gold fields than in Bangalore—head butlers, 16 rupees; ayahs, 12 to 14 rupees; chokras, 10 to 11 rupees; cooks, 11 to 14 rupees; and gardeners, 10 to 16 rupees a month. Many of them leave domestic service and take work in the mines, where they get higher wages very often."

As the elevation of Kolar is about 2,700 feet above sea level, the climate is for many months of the year extremely agreeable, and it would, so far as my experience goes, be difficult to find a more exhilarating and more exquisitely-tempered atmosphere than that of Kolar in the month of January—at least such was my conclusion when I stayed with my friends at the field last January. Nor did I hear anyone there complain of the climate, which, from the appearance of my host (who looked as if he had never left England) and others on the mines, must be a very healthy one, and in proof of this I may mention that Mr. Plummer, whom I have previously quoted, told me that the European miners had as good health as miners have in England. Cholera has on several occasions broken out amongst the coolies, but this was rather a proof of the want of attention paid to sanitation and water supply, as none I believe has occurred since an improved water supply has been introduced by all the companies now pumping it up from depths of 200 feet from the bottoms of abandoned shafts. There was a remarkable confirmation of the connection between cholera and water supply and sanitation one year, and the first company which paid attention to these points had no cholera amongst its people, while most of the other mines had more or less of the disease. I may mention here a fact to which I have alluded in my chapter on coffee planting in Mysore—namely, that Europeans in Mysore have been so little liable to cholera that in sixty years there has only been one death from it amongst the European officials of the province, and one doubtful case amongst the planters.

As regards mining and the extraction of gold, there is little to be said. I inspected the works and the rock drills. These work through the agency of compressed air, and at a cost of 15 rupees a day for coal for each drill, the same tool which is used in drilling by hand. It is doubtful whether hand-drilling is not cheaper, but the latter is far slower, and hence does not pay as well, rapid progress being absolutely essential. When working with rock drills, a shaft can be sunk 10 to 20 feet a month, against 7 to 8 feet by hand, and a level may on the average be driven 45 to 50 feet a month by rock drills against 10 or 12 feet by hand. When, however, a large surface for operating on is exposed, hand-drilling may be profitably employed. This is interesting as illustrating the fact that where labour is cheap machines seldom pay, and this is particularly worth mentioning for the benefit of those who have thought that it would be useful to introduce agricultural machinery into India. After looking at the rock drills I inspected the gold extraction works. The processes here need not detain us long. The quartz is first broken by stone-breakers like those used in England. The broken stone is then placed in an iron trough (battery box), and is pounded by iron stampers, which of course are worked by machinery. In front of this trough is a fine sieve. Water is incessantly run into the trough, and as it overflows, carries with it all the quartz which has been pounded sufficiently to pass through the sieve. The water, mingled with this finely powdered quartz, then falls on to a sloping plate of copper coated with quicksilver, which amalgamates with, and so detains, the gold. The deposit thus formed is scraped off the sheets of copper at intervals of about eight hours, and formed into balls of various sizes, which consist of about one-half gold and one-half quicksilver. The latter is subsequently separated from the gold by processes which I need not describe, and the gold is afterwards formed into bars for export.

I inquired particularly as to the rates of wages. These are, for coolies working underground, from 7 to 8 annas a day (with the rupee at par one anna is equal to $1\frac{1}{2}d.$, and 8 annas would therefore amount to 1*s.*). Those who work rock drills in mines, 12 annas to a rupee a day; ordinary coolies working aboveground, 4 to 8 annas; and women, 2 to 4 annas a day. The working population on the field numbers about 10,000, while 20,000 more, who work for varying periods of the year, reside in the neighbouring villages.

I was much struck with the fact that no advances whatever are given to coolies by the companies, as is the case with men working on plantations, and I would particularly call the attention of planters to this, as it proves what I have elsewhere stated—namely, that where labour rises to a comparatively high rate no advances are necessary, and I feel sure that if planters would resolve to reduce gradually the amount of advances, they might ultimately be altogether dispensed with.

My next subject of inquiry relating to labour was as to the probable total amount paid for it, and, from an estimate made for me by a very competent authority residing on the mines, I believe that the following account is substantially correct. The amount of wages paid monthly to native labourers and the small number of Eurasians working on the mines is about 2 lakhs of rupees. To natives who fell and bring in timber for fuel about 80,000 rupees monthly are paid. On quarrying and carting granite, and in building, about 30,000 rupees a month are spent; on the carriage of materials from the railway about 15,000 rupees, and probably from 5,000 to 10,000 rupees on local products such as straw, grain, oil, mats, bamboos, tiles, etc. Now, if we take no account of the last two items, and deduct 10,000 rupees from the second and third, we shall have a fair estimate of three lakhs of rupees a month as the amount spent on the Kolar gold field in wages, which, taking the rupee at par (and I think I am justified in doing so, as for expenditure in India by labourers it goes about as far as it ever did), amounts to £360,000 a year. And this great sum is earned by people who either have land and work for occasional periods of the year on the mines, or by labourers, who, when they have saved enough money from their wages (which they could do with ease in a year), will acquire and cultivate a small holding. A large proportion of this sum of £360,000 a year—probably two-thirds of it—goes to improving the status and condition of the agricultural and labouring classes, and I need hardly add that this not only leads to an improvement of the resources of the State, but enables the people the better to contend with famine and times of scarcity, and thus still further improves the financial condition of the Government. And it is largely in consequence of the great sums brought into Mysore by the planters and the gold companies that the revenues of Mysore are in such a flourishing condition, and that year after year the annual budget presents an appearance more and more favourable.

And here this question naturally arises. What can the Government of Mysore do to stimulate the employment of labour in mining, and thus still further strengthen the financial position of the State? I am prepared to show that it can do much to stimulate the opening of new mines, and also to encourage many of those now in existence which have not as yet been able to pay dividends.

The reader will see by a glance at the map that the auriferous tracts of Mysore (to which I shall presently more particularly allude) are of great extent, and, judging from the report of the geological surveyor employed by the Government, and especially from the existence of numerous old native workings, there is no reason why prizes even greater than the best of those already obtained should not exist. Now one of the greatest obstacles in the way of rapid progress lies in the fact that before mining can be got fairly under weigh much preliminary work has to be done, and the shareholders have therefore a long time to wait before any paying return can be obtained. But if the preliminary work, such as the providing of water, the collection of building materials, and the making of roads, etc., were carried out before a company was formed, mining could be begun at once, and results rapidly arrived at, and the frittering away of money, both in England and India, that at present necessarily occurs, would be averted. Now the country has already been largely explored, and the Government is therefore in a position to know the places where favourable results will probably be obtained, and as the State, besides the other advantages I have previously pointed out, gets a royalty on the gold, it has a natural interest in doing its utmost to select the most favourable sites for new mining operations. Such sites then should, with the aid of experienced mining advisers, be selected by the Government, which itself should execute the preliminary works previously specified, and then advertise the blocks, so selected and prepared, for sale in the London market. For such prepared blocks purchasers could readily be found, and if the price they paid merely covered the bare cost of the preliminary works, the expenditure of capital that would thus be stimulated, with all its consequent direct and indirect advantages to the province, would amply repay the Government for its trouble and outlay.

But the State may give yet another stimulus to mining, which, I feel sure, would prove of great advantage to the State. The present royalty is five per cent. on the value of the gold produced, and from this source the Government last year received 5 lakhs and 18,000 rupees. Now the prosperous companies which are paying good dividends do not feel this to be a very serious burden, but it is a serious burden—every shilling of expenditure indeed is—to a company which has not begun to pay dividends, and I would suggest that, till a company is able to pay dividends, one-half of the royalty, or, better still, the whole of it, might be remitted. This sum would by no means be lost to the State, for does not the milk that is left in the cow go to the calf?

The measures I have proposed would be of such obvious advantage to the State that, were I a shareholder, or intending investor, in mines in Mysore, I should have no hesitation in suggesting their adoption, but it may be as well to mention that I am neither.

I drove one afternoon with my host to the court on the field, and had some conversation with the magistrate regarding thefts at the mines, and it certainly appears that a special Act is required to check the stealing of gold. Sponge-gold (*i.e.*, gold from which the quicksilver has been evaporated), quartz, or gold amalgam, if found in the possession of any person, renders the individual liable to prosecution, if the possession of gold in any of these forms cannot be satisfactorily accounted for. But the individual cannot be called to account for having ordinary pure gold in possession. Now in a man's possession at the mines there has been found all the means of separating the gold by quicksilver, and it is therefore quite clear that gold stolen in either of the first three mentioned forms may, after having been deprived of its concomitant impurities, be held by an individual to any amount, and even by a workman earning 6*d.* a day, without his being liable to be called upon to account for its possession. Some Act to meet this kind of case is then clearly required—an Act similar to our Mysore Coffee-stealing Prevention Act, which provides that any person not a planter is liable to be called upon to account for coffee in his possession.

A difficult point occurs where quartz is found in a hut occupied by several people, as it is impossible to charge any one person with being in illegal possession of the article. There are numerous evidences of gold stealing, and certainly some summary process ought to be established with the view of checking these thefts. I may add that the Government is much interested in this matter, as five per cent. of the gold belongs to it, and is handed over in the shape of royalty. Those who are most concerned should bring the matter annually before the members of the Representative Assembly. Even in England remedies for, or mitigations of, evils are not provided without much continuous parliamentary hammering.

After discussing the subject of gold stealing with the magistrate, I called on the manager of the Mysore mine, and afterwards went with my host to a lawn tennis party at the house of the doctor of the mines, who is employed by the various companies. He has a comfortable bungalow, which is at a considerable elevation above the level of the valley, and commands an extensive view of the surrounding country and of the distant hills. Above the house, and at some little distance on one side of it, stands the hospital, and on a knoll just below, the building of the new Roman Catholic church was in progress, and the walls were nearly finished. From the doctor's bungalow a good general view of the whole field can be obtained, and I was particularly struck with the number of buildings to be seen in all directions. I was told that from this point as many as thirty tall chimneys can be counted.

There is a great want of water in the field, for purposes connected with the separation of the gold from the quartz, and tanks are being provided to store it. I venture to suggest that a considerable distance of the catchment area on the sides, and especially at the back, of the tanks should be honeycombed with pits, as the water, which is often largely lost from falling in heavy deluges, would thus percolate into the ground, and so find its way into the bed of the tank by degrees. I may mention that a great effect has been produced in the case of a tank on one of my coffee estates by thus digging pits to catch water that would otherwise run directly down into the tank, to be largely lost by the overflow during heavy rains, and a similar effect has been produced on the property of a neighbour. In fact, the effect produced by such pits on the supply of water in tanks is far greater than one could have imagined to be possible, and I may therefore, in passing, call particular attention to the advisability of such pits being made near tanks used for agricultural purposes. On the margins of the tanks, and in parts of the bed where sufficient soil exists, trees should be planted, with the view of diminishing evaporation from the surface of the water.

When the railway is completed, soil might easily be

brought into the field on trucks, and the pits dug for trees should be filled with it. The planting of trees in and around the field would certainly be beneficial in many obvious ways, and would improve the climate and probably affect, not perhaps the amount, but the distribution of the rainfall. I would suggest that if earth closets were used by the people, and the used earth spread around the trees, there would be a great improvement in their growth. This would at once improve the sanitation of the field and beautify it at the same time.

The reader has now probably learned enough of this rising settlement,[1] and I have only to add that on the day following I returned to Bangalore, after having had a most pleasant and interesting time of it with my friends on the Kolar field.

I next pass to a brief mention of the other auriferous tracts in Mysore, which were surveyed in 1887 by Mr. R. Bruce Foote, Superintendent of the Geological Survey of India, who, in connection with his investigations between February 2nd and May 7th of that year, travelled no less than 1,300 miles in Mysore in marching and field work. A full report of his work appears in the "Selections,"[2] and this is accompanied by a map in which Mr. Foote has sketched out the distribution of the auriferous rocks. In the "Selections" alluded to there is also a "Report on the Auriferous Tracts in Mysore," by Mr. M. F. Lavelle, and "Notes on the Occurrence of Gold and other Minerals in Mysore," by Mr. Walter Marsh, Mining Engineer. But in

[1] Those who desire detailed information are referred to Mr. P. Bosworth-Smith's "Report on the Kolar Gold Field and its Southern Extension." Madras, Government Press, 1889. Mr. Bosworth-Smith writes as Government Mineralogist to the Madras Presidency.

[2] "Selections from the Records of the Mysore Government. Reports on Auriferous Tracts in Mysore." Bangalore. Printed at the Mysore Government Press, 1887.

the brief remarks I have to make I shall confine my attention to Mr. Foote's Report.

Mr. Foote informs us that the chief gold-yielding rocks of Southern India belong to one great geological system, to which, from the rocks forming it occurring very largely in the Dharwar country, he two years previously gave the name of the Dharwar System, as he saw the necessity of separating them from the great Gneissic System, with which they had formerly been grouped. In his long tour in Mysore he found that every important auriferous tract visited lies within one or other of the areas of the Dharwar rocks, or forms an outlying patch of the same. These Dharwar rocks, it appears, are the auriferous series in Mysore, the ceded districts, and the Southern Maharatta country.

Mr. Foote groups the auriferous rock series of Mysore into four groups—the central, west-central, western, and the eastern—the last group being formed by the Kolar gold field, which was not included in the tracts Mr. Foote was called upon to visit. He then gives a systematic account of his examination of the country, beginning with the central, and ending with the western group.

He examined ten auriferous tracts or localities in the central group, beginning with the Holgen workings near the southern border of the province, and ending with the Hale Kalgudda locality near the northern border, and reports more or less favourably on five out of the ten localities in question. For brevity I use the numbers into which he has divided the localities he regards as more or less promising. Of part of number three, he says that his examination, though but a cursory one, led him to regard it "very favourably," and of another part, he says that the whole outline indicated, which is seven miles long by about a mile wide, is deserving of very close examination, and the reefs of being prospected to some depth. As regards number five, he reports the existence of old native workings occupying a considerable area, and which showed evidence of much work being done. Fine reefs are to be seen pretty numerously, and he desires to draw attention to this promising tract. With reference to number eight, he says that "taking all things into consideration this tract is one of the most promising I have seen." Of number nine he says, "with regard to this gold-yielding locality, it is one of very great promise and worthy of all attention from mining capitalists," and as regards number ten, he reports that, though not so favourable as the two numbers previously mentioned, it is yet deserving of the closest investigation.

The west-central group was examined by Mr. Foote in the same order, *i.e.*, from south to north, and he tells us that the auriferous localities in this group occur all in small detached strips or patches of schistose rock scattered over the older gneissic series. They are really, he says, remnants of the once apparently continuous spread of schistose (Dharwar) rocks which covered great part of the southern half of the Peninsula. Mr. Foote examined in all fifteen localities, and they do not, from his account, seem to present appearances as favourable as those of the central group, and he only recommends that attention should be paid to six of them. As regards the first locality mentioned, he says that, though the results from washings and other indications were not very favourable, the field was deserving of further close prospecting, as the nature of the country is favourable. Of locality number five, he says that it contains a considerable number of large and well defined reefs, to which a great amount of attention has been paid by the old native miners, and thinks that they are deserving of the closest attention at the present time by deep prospecting on an ample scale. Of number seven he finds it impossible to form any positive opinion, though he adds that the size of the old workings show that the old miners found the place worth their attention for a long period. He advises that number eleven should be prospected and tested. Locality thirteen he considers to deserve close prospecting, and he makes much the same remark as to number fourteen.

The western group, Mr. Foote tells us, is far poorer in auriferous localities than either of the others, and they are scattered widely apart. He examined in all seven localities. Of the first locality examined, he says that the geological features are all favourable to the occurrence of gold, and that the locality is worthy of very careful prospecting. In locality number two, such a good show of coarse grained gold was got from the sands of a stream that he thought a portion of the land from which its water came ought to be closely tested in order to trace the source of the gold found in the stream. When writing on locality number three, Mr. Foote observes that the elevated tract of the auriferous rocks of which the Bababudan mountains form the centre is one well deserving great attention both from the geologist and the mining prospector, it being an area of great disturbance, the rocks being greatly contorted on a large scale and, the north and south sides at least of the area, much cut up by great faults. The whole of the auriferous areas here, he says, are deserving of close survey, for even the best of them are very imperfectly known, and much of what was known to the old miners in former generations has been forgotten. "From the fact," writes Mr. Foote, "that in my hurried tour I came upon no less than five sets of old workings that had not been brought under the notice of Messrs. Lavelle and Marsh (reports of whose investigations are given in the "Selections"), I quite expect to hear that many other old abandoned workings exist in wild and jungly tracts which bound in the hilly and mountainous parts of the country." In locality number five such fine shows of gold were obtained, and there was such a good looking old mine, and quartz reefs of great size, that Mr. Foote considered the place deserving of "very marked attention from earnest prospectors."

It is evident, from what Mr. Foote has said, that there is much to be done in the way of exploring and testing the Mysore province for gold, and I hope that what I have written may be the means of attracting further attention to the subject.

At the close of his report Mr. Foote mentions the fact that "a great dyke of beautiful porphyry traverses the hills east of the Karigatta temple overlooking Seringapatam. The porphyry, which is of warm brown or chocolate colour, includes many crystals of lighter coloured felspar, and dark crystals of hornblende. The stone would take a very high polish, and for decorative purposes of high class, such as vases, panels and bases for busts and tazzas, etc., it is unequalled in South India, and deserving of all attention. If well polished it fully equals many of the highly prized antique porphyries. The dyke is of great thickness and runs for fully a mile, so is practically inexhaustible. Blocks of very large size could be raised, and from the situation of the dyke on the side of two steep hills, it would be very easy to open up large quarries if needful." As this dyke is close to a railway it may be worthy of the attention of capitalists.

CHAPTER VIII.

CASTE.

IN Krilof's fable of "The Peasant and the Horse," the latter murmurs at the way his master throws oats broad-cast on the soil. "How much better," argues the horse, "it would have been to have kept them in his granary, or even to have given them to me to eat!" But the oats grow, and in due time are garnered, and from them the same horse is fed the year following. The horse, as we have seen, was unable to comprehend the working and the meaning of his master's acts; and, in the same way, we often see that man equally fails to comprehend the nature and effect of things around him. And thus it is, and for long has been, as regards the institution I am now about to consider. People in general have ignorantly murmured at the institution of caste; and, having ever looked at it with highly-civilized spectacles, and having seen especially a number of the inconveniences it has caused to the educated population of the towns, it has been argued that caste is the curse of all India. But it seems to me that an attentive, unprejudiced examination tends to prove that in former times it was exactly the reverse, and that at the present moment, as far as all the ignorant rural population is concerned, it may be considered, with reference to the state of the people, as a valuable and useful institution.

And here, at the outset, I wish it to be clearly understood that an immense divergence has taken place between the town and country populations of India. The former have advanced with rapid strides on the paths of enlightenment and progress, while the latter, it is hardly too much to say, have remained almost universally stationary. To argue, therefore, from one to the other is not only impossible, but absurd ; and it is merely a waste of time to point out, at any length, that what may be admirably suited to one set of people may be a positive nuisance to another. With reference, then, to this question of caste, instead of treating India as a whole, I shall divide it into town and country populations. In the first place, I shall treat of the effects of caste on the country populations, amongst whom I have lived; and, in the second place, I shall offer some considerations regarding the effects of the institution amongst the people of the towns.

And, first of all, as to its effects on the rural population.

In these observations on caste I shall not commence with any attempt to trace its origin, nor shall I endeavour to enumerate the countless forms it has assumed amongst the peoples of the great peninsula. My aim is to direct the attention of the reader not to the dry bones of its history so much as to the living effects of the institution. It is certainly a matter of interest to know something of the peculiar customs of the various tribes and races ; but it is to be regretted that people generally have rested content with information of that sort, and have seldom attempted to investigate those points which are, I conceive, mainly of use and interest. What Indians may or may not do—what they may eat, what they may drink, and what clothing they may put on—are not matters on which inquirers should bestow much time. The information most needed, and which has not yet, or only in the most imperfect sense, been acquired, is as to what caste has done for good or evil. It shall be my endeavour to solve that question; and I imagine the solution would be in a great measure effected if I could, in the first instance, answer the following questions:

1. How far has caste acted as a moral restraint amongst the Indians themselves?

2. How far advantageously or the reverse in segregating them socially from the conquerors who have overrun their country?

On the first of these points I may observe, without the slightest exaggeration, that very few of our countrymen indeed have had such opportunities as myself of forming a correct opinion; for very few Englishmen have been so entirely dependent on a native population for society. For the first four or five years of my residence in Manjarabad[1] there were only three Europeans besides myself, and we were all about twelve miles apart. The natural consequence was that the farmers of the country were my sole companions; and, as I joined in their sports and had some of them always about me, terms of intimacy sprang up which never could have existed under any other circumstances. And further, when it is taken into consideration that I have employed the poorer of the better castes in various capacities on my estates, and a large number of the Pariahs, or labourer caste, it seems pretty clear that I ought to be a tolerably competent judge as to whether caste did or did not exercise a favourable influence on the morals of the people. Now, as regards one department of morals, at least, I unhesitatingly affirm that it did, and that, as regards the connection of the sexes, it would be difficult to find in any part of the world a more moral people than the two higher castes of Manjarabad, who form about one-half of the population, and who may be termed the farming proprietors of the country. Amongst themselves, indeed,

[1] Manjarabad is a talook or county on the south-west frontier of Mysore.

it was not to be wondered at that their morality was extremely good, as, from the fact of nearly everyone being married at the age of puberty, and partly, perhaps, from the fact of their houses being more or less isolated, instead of being grouped in villages, the temptations to immorality were necessarily slight. Their temptations, though, as regards the Pariahs, who were, when I entered Manjarabad, merely hereditary serfs, were considerable; and there it was that the value of caste law came in. Caste said, "You shall not touch these women;" and so strong was this law, that I never knew of but one instance of one of the better classes offending with a Pariah woman.[1] Some aversion of race there might, no doubt, have been, but the police of caste and its penalties were so strong that he would be a bold man indeed who would venture to run any risk of detection. To give an idea of how the punishment for an offence of this kind would operate, it may be added that, if one of the farming classes in this country, on a case of seducing one of the lower, was fined by his neighbours £500, and cut by society till he paid the money, he would be in exactly the same position as a Manjarabad farmer would be who had violated the important caste law under consideration. Here, therefore, we have a moral police of tremendous power, and the very best proof we have of the regularity with which it has been enforced lies in the fact that the Pariahs and the farmers are distinguished by a form and physiognomy almost as distinct as those existing between an Englishman and a negro. Caste, then, as we have seen, protects the poor from the passions of the rich, and it equally protects the upper classes themselves, and enforcedly makes them more moral than, judging from our experience in other quarters of the globe, they would otherwise be.

[1] And that, I may observe, was a case in which a tody-drawer, the third caste in Manjarabad, was concerned.

Having thus briefly glanced at caste law, as controlling the connection of the sexes, let us now look at it from another point of view, which I venture to think is, as regards its ultimate consequences, of even still more importance. If there is one vice more than another which is productive of serious crime, it is the abuse of alcohol; and there is no doubt that, to use the words of an eminent statesman, "if we could subtract from the ignorance, the poverty, the suffering, the sickness, and the crime now witnessed among us, the ignorance, the poverty, the sickness, and the crime caused by the single vice of drinking, this country would be so changed for the better that we should hardly know it again." Regarding it, then, in all its consequences, whether physical or mental (and how many madmen and idiots are there not bred by drinking?[1]), it is difficult to estimate too highly the value of caste laws that utterly prohibit the use of those strong drinks that are injurious in any country, but are a thousand times more so under the rays of a tropical sun. And when we come to consider that a large proportion of the population of India are absolutely compelled to abstain from the use of alcohol, and that these being the very best, or at least equal to the very best, of the community, must always have exercised a large influence in discouraging the excessive use of intoxicating drinks, it is impossible to refrain from coming to the conclusion that this single fact is more than sufficient to counterbalance all the evils that have ever been said to arise from caste.

On two very important points, then—the connection of the sexes and the use of alcohol—it is evident that caste laws have produced some very favourable and valuable results; but I do not think we can accurately gauge their

[1] I observe in the Administration Report for Mysore, 1867-68, that nearly all the cases in the lunatic asylum were traced either to drinking or bhang-smoking.

value unless we compare the state of morality existing in Manjarabad with the state of morality existing in one of our home counties; and the comparison I have to make, if not very soothing, is, I am sure, very interesting. Take any one of our counties in Great Britain, for instance, and compare it with Manjarabad as regards the points I have particularly referred to, and it will be found that Manjarabad has an immense superiority. The crimes and misery arising from drinking are hardly to be found at all in Manjarabad, while the morality of the sexes, I should think, could hardly be surpassed. Now, there is nothing very surprising, considering that the people in this country are so heavily weighted, that this should be the case; on the contrary, it is the natural result of the circumstances of their worldly situation. But, supposing that the worldly situation as to the means of support and the opportunities of marrying were equal, it seems to me perfectly plain that the people who have a large proportion of the better classes total abstainers, and who have their society so controlled that the rich cannot gratify their passions at the expense of the poor, must be in the possession of a superior morality.

Before closing this branch of the subject, I may allude briefly to what has been so often attacked by the opponents of caste: I mean the prohibition of the marriage of widows. This rule exists in Manjarabad, but I am not aware that any great moral evil arises from it, as a widow can always contract to live with a man, the difference being that the ceremonies performed are of an inferior kind. This is not allowed to be a marriage, but, in fact, it is a marriage, though of a kind held in rather low estimation. On customs like these, which in a great measure neutralize the evils arising from the restrictions on re-marriage, it seems to me that our information is very scanty, and I am not aware how far the practice alluded to prevails in other parts of India.

Having taken into consideration the advantages of caste in acting as a moral restraint amongst the Indians themselves, I now purpose to inquire how far caste has acted advantageously, or the reverse, in segregating the people socially from the conquerors who have overrun their country.

If the advantages of caste are striking and plainly apparent as regards the moral points I have alluded to, they seem to me to be infinitely more so when we come to consider the happy influence this institution has had in segregating the Indians from the white races. And here I cannot help indulging in a vain regret that the blessings of caste have not been universally diffused amongst all inferior races. How many of these has our boasted civilization improved off the face of the earth? How much has that tide of civilization which the first conquerors invariably bring with them effected? How much, in other words, have their vice, rum, and gunpowder helped to exterminate those unhappy races which, unprotected by caste, have come in contact with the white man? Nor in India itself are we altogether without a well-marked instance of the value, for a time at least, of an entire social separation between the dark and white races; and the Todas, the lords of the soil on the Nilgiri Hills, furnish us with a lamentable example of what the absence of caste feeling is capable of producing. We found them a simple pastoral race, and the early visitors to the hills were struck with their inoffensive manners, and what was falsely considered to be their greatest advantage—freedom from caste associations. But what is their condition now? One of drunkenness, debauchery, and disease of the most fatal description. Had the much-reviled caste law been theirs, what a different result would have ensued from their contact with Europeans! Caste would have saved them from alcohol, and their women from contamination: they would thus have maintained their self-respect; and if, at first, separation brought no progress nor shadow of change, it would have at least induced no evil, and education and enlightenment would in time have modified these caste institutions, which, to a superficial observer, seem to be productive of nothing but evil.

We have now seen that social contact with whites, without any barrier between them and the inferior races, is not, in a moral point of view, a very desirable thing in any part of the world. But if there is a moral consequence, we may also point to a mental one, which exercises an immense influence: I mean the overwhelming sense of inferiority which is so apt to depress casteless races. I believe, then, for savages, or for people in a low state of civilization, it is of the greatest importance that they should have points of difference which may not only keep them socially apart, but which may enable them to maintain some feeling of superiority when coming in contact with highly-civilized races. Nor is it necessary that the feeling of superiority should be well founded. An imaginary superiority will, I believe, answer the purpose equally well. "We don't touch beef, nor would we touch food cooked by Englishmen or Pariahs," seem but poor matters for self-congratulation. But if these considerations prevent a man from forming a poor opinion of himself, they should be carefully cherished. On these points, at least, a feeling of superiority is sustained, and therefore the tendency to degradation is diminished. But if on all points the white man makes his superiority felt, the weaker people speedily acquire a thorough contempt for themselves, and soon become careless of what they do, or of what becomes of them. Their mental spring becomes fatally depressed, and this circumstance has probably more to do with the deterioration and extinction of inferior races than most people would be inclined to admit.[1] Nothing, then, I believe, chills the soul and checks the progress of man so much as a hopeless sense of inferiority; and, had I time, I might turn the attention of the reader to the universality of this law, and to the numerous instances that have been collected to prove the depressing and injurious effects that even nature, on a grand and overwhelming scale, seems to exercise on the mind and spirit of man—how it makes him timid, credulous, and superstitious, and produces effects which retard his progress. But to advance further on this point, however interesting it may be, would only tend to distract the attention of the reader from the subject with which we are mainly concerned.

If the remarks hitherto made are of any value, they undoubtedly tend to prove that all inferior races have a tendency, in the first instance, to adopt the vices rather than the virtues of the more civilized races they may come in contact with. Assuming, then, as I think we have every right to do, that this statement is universally true, it is evident that the social separation maintained by caste has been of incalculable advantage. On the other hand, however, a number of disadvantages have been indicated by various writers; but only one of them seems to me at all worthy of serious attention. It has been asserted that this segregation has impeded advancement, that it has prevented the Indians learning as much from us as they otherwise might, and that it has impeded the mainspring of all advancement—education. Here, I apprehend, the argument against caste, as far as rural populations are concerned, utterly fails, and, in a province contiguous to my own, a most signal instance to the contrary can be pointed

[1] *Vide* Sproat's "Studies of Savage Life."

to. Few people have more proudly segregated themselves than the Coorgs; nowhere is the chastity of women more jealously guarded; and yet they were the first people in India who desired and petitioned for female education. And how, then, can it be for one moment asserted that the tendency of caste is to check the progress of the people?

Having thus glanced at some of the effects of caste institutions as they affect the rural population, we will now consider caste as it affects the people of the towns. Following, then, the same order, and directing our attention to the same points selected for consideration when treating of the rural classes, let us ask how far caste has operated with the townspeople as regards the connection of the sexes and the use of alcohol. And here we shall find that the subject may be dismissed in almost a single sentence; for caste laws, as regards these points, can never act as a moral restraint, because the possibility of enforcing them cannot and does not exist. Nor need I waste time in proving that people in towns, whether in India, or any other part of the world, may readily do things which could never escape the prying eyes of a country society.

Then, as regards the segregation from foreigners, it is evident that we need employ little time, for such of the town populations as have maintained a fair state of morality amid the evils of large cities, are not likely to be materially affected by the bad habits and customs of the white races; and as for those who have never led a steady life, it would not much matter with whom they mixed. But caste not only brings with it no good as far as the town population is concerned, but its continuance is fraught with a multitude of painful and vexatious evils, which meet us at every turn, for it hampers the actions, and clogs those efforts at progress which are the natural result of intellectual advancement. And here I cannot do better than quote the words of a Parsee gentleman, whose unceasing efforts to aid the progress of India entitle him to be placed in the very highest rank of those who spend much time and labour to produce effects which they can never live to see the fruits of. These remarks of his, which I am now about to quote, were made at the close of a paper on caste, which I read at a meeting of the East India Association, and are quoted from the report published in the journal of the Association. After fully granting that, in the condition of society existing at the time the system of caste was established, it may have done a great deal of good, Mr. Dadabhai Naoroji proceeded to remark on the way the present system of caste interferes with progress among the higher classes, and then gave several instances to illustrate his observation. "The great struggle," he said, "which is now going on in Bombay about the widow-marriage question is an apt illustration of this; and, also, the fear of excommunication prevents a large body of natives from coming to this country, and profiting by their visit. It is often said, 'educated Hindoos ought not to care for this excommunication;' but those who say that, little think what excommunication means. A man who is excommunicated may not care for it for his own sake, but he has his family to consider. What is to be done with daughters? They cannot marry if their father is excommunicated, and the result is, therefore, most serious to them. I knew of one instance of a native gentleman who, being excommunicated from his caste for having visited England, had, on the death of his child, been put to the very painful necessity of having the body carried by his servant, without anyone accompanying him."

It would be impossible, I think, to furnish two better instances of the evils of caste to people desirous of shaking off in any way the habits of their forefathers; and a more melancholy picture than that of this unfortunate man setting out with his dead child without a single friend to accompany him it would indeed be difficult to find. Many other illustrations might, of course, be given; but enough has been said already, and we may safely consider it as a settled question that, as far as the people of the towns are concerned, the sooner caste is abolished the better.

I may here be permitted to remind the reader that we have considered the effects of caste, as regards the country population, in two very important particulars: first of all, as to the morality of the sexes, which is controlled to such a large extent by caste law; and secondly, we have looked at the effects of caste as controlling the use of alcohol, and consequently limiting the crimes and evils that can in most countries be traced to drinking. On both of these points we have compared an Indian county with any county in Great Britain, and saw reason to think that morality, as regards the points under consideration, is better in Manjarabad than in any British county. And, by facts which may be brought from many quarters of the globe, we have seen that it is a universal law that inferior races have a tendency to adopt the vices rather than the virtues of superior races, and that, therefore, caste laws which enjoin social separation are of the highest value. We have seen, too, the value of caste in keeping up feelings of superiority and self-respect. We have also seen that these caste laws can exist without retarding the progress of the people, or their desire for education. And, finally, taking all these points into consideration, we concluded that there were no drawbacks, and many striking advantages, connected with caste as far as the country populations are concerned.

In the next place, we looked at the circumstances of the people of the towns, inquired as to how caste has affected them for good or evil, and came to the conclusion that not only does no good arise from caste, but that it is plainly and unmistakably an unmitigated evil.

Keeping these conclusions firmly in mind, let us now advance to the consideration of a third question, which naturally arises out of those facts which I assume to have been established.

That question is—How far has caste acted beneficially, or the reverse, in helping to retard our interpretation of Christianity? Pursuing the same order as before, let us ask, in the first place, whether caste has, as regards the country populations, acted beneficially in this as well as in the other points we have looked at. But, before attempting to answer this question, it may be as well to offer a few general remarks which tend to show that, independently of any question of caste, it is hopeless to expect that any ignorant and generally unenlightened race can possibly derive any benefit from adopting the formulas and dogmas of a pure faith.

To illustrate this old and well-established truth, let us point to four of the many instances which may be adduced as decisively confirming it—the history of Christianity in Europe, of Islam amongst the Indian Mahomedans, and the history of Christianity in Abyssinia and India. As to the first, to use the words of Buckle, "after the new religion had received the homage of the best part of Europe, it was found that nothing had really been effected." Superstition was merely turned from one channel into another. The adoration of idols was succeeded by the adoration of saints, and for centuries after Christianity had become the established religion it entirely failed to produce its natural fruits, because ignorance imperatively demanded superstition in some shape or other. To some it may seem, at first sight, a curious circumstance that the same remarks may be applied to the history of Mahomedanism in India. The idols were broken and the one God declared. But how long was it before the people, like the Israelites of old, fell away from the grand central doctrine of Mahomedanism—the unity of God? How long was it before the adoration of idols was followed by the adoration of saints? The exact coincidence, however, is no more striking than that given causes produce fixed results with an Eastern as well as with a Western people. When we turn, thirdly, to Abyssinia, what do we find? How have the dogmas of Christianity fared there? The Abyssinians did not rise to the level of the dogmas and principles of Christianity—that we all know. They simply reduced it to their own level. Look, lastly, at our native Christians in India. I believe it is quite certain that, in the general opinion of Englishmen, they are, to say the least, very far from being the best class in India; in fact, I do not think it too much to say that most Europeans hold them to be about the worst class of people in India. I confess that I do not share this opinion altogether. The fact probably is that, in consequence of their extreme ignorance and generally debased state, they are, in the rural districts, neither better nor worse than the classes from which they are principally drawn. In our cantonments, however, and especially in those where European soldiery abounds, there is every probability of their being worse than the classes from which they have sprung; and I have little doubt that the low estimation in which the native Christians are held is owing to the fact that our countrymen have generally come in contact with the specimens that have been nurtured amidst the scum of our Indian towns. Were we to believe the assertions of our English missionaries, very different conclusions would, of course, be arrived at; but unless they can show that the lowest and most ignorant classes of natives, who from their habits, and from having nothing to lose, are under great temptations, form an exception to all specimens of humanity in other quarters of the globe, I am afraid there can be little reason to doubt that the opinions I have expressed are fairly correct. I doubt very much, in fact, from my intimate knowledge of the lower classes of natives—and it is from these, as I said before, that our converts are mainly derived—whether they are capable of comprehending our religion at all. Of one thing I think we may be quite certain, and that is, that the moment the missionary's back is turned, these people return to their devils in the event of any danger or sickness arising. This might be arrived at deductively with perfect accuracy, and arguing solely from our knowledge of humanity under certain conditions; but I may mention that in Ceylon instances of people reverting to their devil-worship are common amongst the native Christians, and instances might, no doubt, be soon collected in India, if anyone thought it worth the trouble. While alluding to missionary assertions, I may mention that the credulity of these gentlemen seems only to be equalled by the credulity of the British public. If they would only extend their belief in the goodness of natives a little further, one might be tempted to sympathize with this amiable weakness. But the peculiar part of their statements lies in the fact that their converts have got all the virtue and morality in India, while the respectable classes of the community seem, by their account, to be very badly off in these respects. The most curious instance, however, of missionary credulity that I have met with is to be found in the evidence of Mr. Underhill, given before the Committee on Colonization (India) in 1859. And it certainly is a surprising result of conversion to find that the wives of the converts become not only more beautiful, but also more fertile, than their heathen sisters. Two heathen natives had been heard to testify to these facts, and it is wonderful to observe the complacent air of satisfaction with which these statements are accepted by the witness, who added that "this difference evidently arises from the more chaste and regular modes of life in which they fall.[1]

I have said that the native Christians are probably neither better nor worse than the lower classes from which they are drawn, and the painfully truthful remarks given in the note below[2] seem to show that, whatever may be the case now (and I believe that the low-class converts are somewhat better than they were then), the converts to Christianity must have been originally a very indifferent set of people. Christianity, however, if it did not make

[1] It may be observed here that there are few who know so little as to the sexual morality of the people around them as clergymen. It does not become them, of course, to enter into the gossip of the village, nor does anyone care to broach such subjects in the first instance; and I may mention here that a relative of my own, a clergyman in a country parish, told me that if anything went wrong in these respects he was the very last person in the world to hear one word about it.

[2] The Abbé Dubois makes the following remarks: "During the long period I lived in India, in the capacity of a missionary, I have made, with the assistance of a native missionary, in all between two and three hundred converts of both sexes. Of this number two-thirds were Pariahs or beggars, and the rest were composed of Sudras, vagrants, and outcasts of several tribes, who, being without resources, turned Christians in order to form new connections, chiefly for the purpose of marriage, or with some other interested motive. Among them are also to be found some who believed themselves to be possessed with the devil, and who turned Christians after having been assured that on receiving baptism the unclean spirits would leave them and never return; and I will declare it with shame and confusion that I do not remember any one who may be said to have embraced Christianity from conviction and from quite disinterested motives. Among these new-comers many apostatized and relapsed into paganism, finding that the Christian religion did not afford them the temporal advantages they had looked for in embracing it; and I am very much ashamed that the resolution I have taken to tell the whole truth on this subject forces me to make the humiliating avowal that those who continued Christians are the very worst among my flock."—DR. ALLEN'S *India*, p. 522.

these classes much better, at any rate made them no worse. When we turn, however, to the middle-class farmers, it is evident that to have converted them, unless that conversion had been preceded by enlightenment, and a more advanced civilization than they had hitherto enjoyed, would have inflicted on them an incalculable injury, by depriving them of restraints which, as we have seen, are in some particulars of immense importance. To become a Christian, the first thing required of a man is that he should give up caste, and deliver himself to the sole guidance of his conscience; that he should give up a powerful and effective moral restraint; that he should abandon a position which carries with it feelings of self-respect and superiority, and resign himself to the degrading reflection that he may eat from the same platter and drink from the same vessel as the filthiest Pariah; and that this would be degrading there can be little doubt. Were he an educated and enlightened man, he would be sustained by feelings which would raise him above the influence of such considerations. But, in the absence of enlightenment, sad would be his fate, and melancholy the deterioration that would inevitably ensue. The way in which that deterioration would take place, the way in which he would become careless of what he did, or of what became of him, has been sufficiently indicated in the previous pages of this chapter; and to give in detail the principal reasons against a change of faith which involved the abolition of caste, would only be to repeat what I have already said as to the effect of the institution in controlling the morality of the sexes and the use of alcohol. Not only, then, I repeat, would a change of dogma be as unimproving and superficial as changes of that sort always are with unenlightened people, but a number of positive evils would follow from the necessary abandonment of the restrictions of caste; and we may therefore conclude that, as regards the whole population, the effect of caste in helping to prevent the adoption of our interpretation of Christianity is of incalculable advantage.

When we turn to the town populations the case is widely different. We have seen that for them the practical advantages of caste can hardly be said to exist at all, and therefore a change of religion which involved its abolition would, as regards any part of the society, at least produce no evil. Here, at least, we are on safe ground. But this is not all. We see that with the better classes education and enlightenment have borne their natural fruit, and demanded a pure faith, which has already sprung up in the shape of Deism. Enlightenment, then, will produce a pure faith, which will in time react on society, and push it forward with accelerated speed. Now, it cannot be denied that caste laws do retard the free and unfettered adoption of a pure faith; and if we assume that a pure faith will in turn become a cause, or even an accelerator, of progress, then it is certain that, as regards the peoples of the towns, caste, as retarding the adoption of the most advanced principles of religion, is an undoubted calamity.

We have now looked at the bearings of caste on three very important points—its moral bearing amongst the Indians themselves, its effects in maintaining a social separation between the white and dark races, and its effects in retarding the adoption of a religion which involves the entire abolition of caste laws. In the first place, we looked at the effects of caste laws on the rural populations, and came to the conclusion that on all these points caste has operated, and continues to operate, advantageously. In the second place, we looked at its effects on the peoples of the towns, and came to the conclusion that caste confers on them no advantages, while it is often productive of serious evil.

Let us now glance for one moment at the causes of the general outcry which you everywhere hear against caste institutions, and at the same time suggest the line of conduct that the people of the towns ought to adopt with reference to this question.

And here I need not occupy much space in indicating the causes of that abuse of caste which has always been so popular with my countrymen. In fact, if we admit the truth of the facts and arguments hitherto adduced, these causes are so apparent that the reader must have already anticipated the solution I have to give. Caste, as we have seen, is a serious evil to the peoples of the towns. Now, it is amongst towns and cantonments that our principal experiences of this institution have been acquired, and the educated natives of the Indian capitals, feeling all the evils and experiencing none of the advantages of caste, are naturally loud in its condemnation. Hence the cry arising from all Europeans and a trifling section of the Indians, that caste should be abolished from one end of India to the other. But how is it that no response comes from these country populations amongst whom I have lived? How is it that these shrewd-headed people[1] are so insensible to the evils of caste, and that you never hear one word about it? The answer is extremely simple. They have never felt these evils, because for them they do not exist. If they felt the pressure of caste laws as do the people of the towns, the outcry would be universal, and

[1] I may mention here that Sir Bartle Frere, in his paper on "Indian Public Works," said, with reference to opening up districts hitherto unpierced by roads, "And here let me observe, in passing, without any disparagement of my own countrymen, that I have generally found the agricultural and commercial classes of India quite as intelligent on points of this kind as the agricultural and commercial classes of our own old-fashioned country." But I have always found that the people who have had the best opportunities of judging have formed very favourable opinions as to the intelligence of the agricultural classes, who are generally painted as being entirely indifferent, and even hostile, to the best schemes undertaken for their benefit.

the institution speedily done away with. Need I add that when the people of the country are as advanced as the people of the towns, that then, and not till then, will the pressure, which is now confined to the latter, be universally felt; that then, and not till then, will this institution, being no longer suited to the requirements of the age, be universally discarded.

Let us now say a few words as to the line of conduct that should be adopted, as regards caste, by those who are desirous of freeing themselves from the restrictions of that institution.

In the first place, the opponents of caste should not weaken their case by talking nonsense; and, in the second place, they should remember, above all things, that, to use a common saying, "if you want a pig to go to Dublin, the best thing you can do is to start him off on the way to Cork." I shall now enlarge a little on both of these recommendations.

To illustrate my first suggestion—and to this suggestion I shall again have occasion to allude further on in this chapter—a few sentences may be devoted to glancing at some of those remarkable conclusions which sound so well in the observations one often hears when anything is said about India. The tendency of caste, you will hear it gravely urged, is to elevate the upper classes on the highest possible pinnacle, and keep the Pariah grovelling in the dust. "What," continues the speaker, "keeps the Brahmin at the top and the Pariah at the bottom?" Why, let me ask in turn, is a cow's tail long, and a fox's tail bushy? Is it in this nineteenth century that we are to try and din into people's ears that the upper classes in India were at the top of the social scale, and the Pariah at the bottom, centuries before caste, in its present shape, ever existed, and that the relative position of the two races would continue with little change if caste was to be abolished to-morrow morning? "What," gravely asks another, "has prevented the peoples of India uniting into one grand nation, and destroyed all hopes of political fusion?" Nor, to many, would the absurdity of the question be apparent till you asked them what has prevented all Europe becoming one nation; or, to take things on a smaller scale, till you asked what prevented the Highland clans forming themselves into a nation. In short, whenever a man is in difficulty, and at a loss to account for anything connected with the state of the people of India, he takes refuge in caste, combined, perhaps, with what is called native prejudice, though what that last means I do not pretend to explain. Now, it is not improbable that some of my readers may have heard of Holloway's pills, and we know, in fact, that thousands believe that medicine to be an efficacious remedy for every constitutional ailment. Only swallow Holloway, and you are a cured man. Well, the abolition of caste, with an incredible number of people, is, in like manner, confidently pronounced to be a universal remedy for all the political and social complaints of India. Remove that, and you will at one stroke secure social liberty, national unity, the removal of idolatry, and, some even are rash enough to affirm, the universal adoption of Christianity. Such, then, are a few examples of the nonsense you will hear commonly talked about caste, and I think I need not waste time in pointing out that the opponents of caste must take very different ground if they wish to obtain a hearing from the peoples of India.

In the second point to which I have called the attention of the reader I alluded to the general law of opposition, and used a common saying which exactly illustrates the probable result of violent and ill-judged attacks on caste. In fact, so apparent is this, that the reader must have already anticipated the line that, in my opinion, the opponents of caste should follow. What the opponents of caste should preach is, not the abolition of that institution, but toleration for the educated and advanced members of the community who, finding caste an impediment and a burden, wish to discard it. They should admit that this institution has been, and is at the present moment, of value amongst the rural populations, but they should, at the same time, point out that times are changing, and that the peoples of the towns ask for some toleration, not because caste is necessarily a universal evil in itself, but because it is, as far as they are concerned, highly inconvenient. This is the way—and, if this plan does not answer, I feel sure no other will—that the evils of caste are to be mitigated, and I urge these views accordingly on the serious attention of all enlightened Indians.

The reader will have observed that, when pointing out the advantages of caste in repelling our interpretation of Christianity, I have assumed that the adoption of Christianity necessarily involves the entire abolition of all those social distinctions that make up what we call caste. Such have been the terms on which Christianity has been offered to the peoples of India by our English missionaries; and I, for one, do most sincerely rejoice that their hide-bound interpretation of the Protestant faith has been as promptly as it has been decidedly rejected. But why should caste —which, as I have shown, can be proved to have produced such favourable results as regards drinking, and as regards the morality of the sexes—why should this institution, which in these respects can be proved to have produced better results than Christianity has ever done in Great Britain—why should this be swept away because you wish to introduce the religion of Christ? It has been alleged to be entirely incompatible with Christianity; and were this so, there would, of course, be no more to be said. But this I wholly deny. It is, of course, incompatible in some respects with exalted conceptions of the most advanced

Christianity; but there is no reason why Christianity should not be allowed to exist alongside of abnormal social growths, and why, in short, Christianity should not be stretched to tolerate caste, in the same way that it was allowed by the apostles to exist alongside of evils with which the institution of caste cannot, for iniquity or for general ill effects, be for one moment compared. Christianity was not held by the apostles to be an impossibility because the professors of that faith bought and sold slaves; it was not held so by their descendants for hundreds of years; and will those interpreters of Christianity whom we have sent to India venture to assert that the Americans had no right to the name of Christians until the close of the late war? Slavery was driven out at length, or at least in a great measure driven out, by Christianity; but Christianity, remember, had first of all to be introduced; and taking into consideration the acts of the apostles, the way in which they yielded to the customs and prejudices of their converts, and the resolution they came to "not to trouble those of the Gentiles who were turning to God," on what grounds do our missionaries rest their claim to debar from the advantages of Christianity those people who, wishing to retain their place in society, desire to become Christians? This is not the first time that these questions have been asked. They were asked at great length by Mr. Irving in his "Theory and Practice of Caste." Hitherto they have been asked in vain; and owing to the indifference of people in this country, and to the slavish submission of the laity to the opinion of the missionaries, a system of attempting to propagate Christianity has been allowed to exist which has been of incalculable mischief. But I think we may even go further than this. I think it may be asserted that the line taken up, as regards caste, by our missionaries has acted more prejudicially to the interests of Christianity than if we had deliberately dispatched emissaries to India with the view of preventing the people from adopting the religion of Christ. These may seem harsh, and I have no doubt they will prove to be unwelcome, expressions of opinion. They will hurt, and I am afraid will shock, the feelings of many a good and worthy man. I regret that this should be so, but I cannot help it. In any case good must arise. If I am right, as I firmly believe myself to be, the cause of enlightenment and Christianity will be advanced; and if I am wrong, and it can be proved that the missionaries are right, they will have as great, and it may even be a greater claim to public support than they ever had before. But it must be clearly understood that, as an individual desirous of propagating truth, I have a right to demand an answer. If that answer is satisfactory, well and good. If it is not satisfactory, or if no answer be supplied at all, I would then propose to ask the public here to consider whether it would not be better to withhold all their subscriptions from our English, or at least transfer them to such missions as will consent to attempt to propagate Christianity on the widest possible base.

In considering this important subject I shall, in the first place, glance at Bishop Heber's "Letter on Caste;" Bishop Wilson's "Circular;" the "Report" of the Madras Commissioners; and the "Statement" of the Tanjore German missionaries. This may seem a formidable list of documents to commence with, but it is my intention to make only the most cursory allusion to each, as to consider these papers at any length would occupy far too much space. Having thus stated the difference of opinions, as regards caste, between the Germans and the Protestant missionaries, I shall then proceed to inquire whether caste can or can not be traced to an idolatrous source; whether it was in any way necessarily wound up with religion; and whether, further, it is at all necessary that, supposing it to have been at any time wound up with religion, there should therefore be at the present day any necessary connection between the religions of the peoples and their caste customs.

In Bishop Heber's "Letter" of March 21st, 1826, he says that, "with regard to the distinctions of caste as yet maintained by professing Christians, it appears that they are manifested—(*a*) in desiring separate seats at church; (*b*) in going up at different times to receive the Holy Communion; (*c*) in insisting on their children having different sides of the school; (*d*) in refusing to eat, drink, or associate with those of a different caste."

On the first of these points the bishop observes, with great justice, that points of precedence have constantly been granted in Christian churches to people of noble birth and of great fortune, and that in the United States of America these distinctions were always maintained between the whites and the negroes. He also points out that a Christian gentleman conforms to those rules because, if he neglected them, he would lose influence with his own degree in society, and that a native of the better classes acts exactly on the same principle. And on this point he concludes that distinctions of caste in church may still be allowed, provided that due care is taken to teach the natives that in the sight of God they are all equal.

With reference to the second point the good bishop says nothing, because, I surmise, he concluded the going up at different times to receive the Sacrament was included in his remarks on precedence in church.

As regards the schools, and amongst the children, he observes that caste must, as to taking places, etc., not be taken into account, "but," he adds, "even here caution should be observed to disgust no man needlessly."

As to the fourth point, he was decidedly of opinion that, as regards private meals and social intercourse, we had no right to interfere whatever.

After alluding to the objections raised by some zealous missionaries to the processions in marriages and other matters, he intimates pretty plainly that he has some fears that recent missionaries have been more scrupulous in these matters than need requires. He then concludes by saying that "God forbid we should wink at sin; but God forbid, also, that we should make the narrow gate of life narrower than Christ has made it, or deal less favourably with the prejudices of this people than St. Paul and the primitive church dealt with the almost similar prejudices of the Jewish converts."

The bishop then framed a set of questions as regards caste observances, to which he required particular answers; but, in consequence of his untimely death, and of the short tenure of office held by his successors, Bishops James and Turner, no further official action was taken till the middle of 1833, when Bishop Wilson's "Circular"[1] dealt the most

[1] In this Circular of Bishop Wilson's, it is surprising to observe the contradictions that exist. At one part of the Circular we are told that the apostle's language is conclusive: and "Seeing ye have put off the old man, and have put on the new man, which is renewed in knowledge after the image of Him that created him, where there is neither Greek nor Jew, circumcision nor uncircumcision, barbarian, Scythian, bond nor free, but Christ is all, and in all," is quoted as evidence of the Divine wishes. "So overwhelming," continues the bishop, "is the flood by which all petty distinctions of nation, caste, privilege, rank, climate, position in civilization are effaced, and one grand distinction substituted." And yet, at another part of the Circular, we are told that the distinctions in civil society are acknowledged by the Gospel, when they are "the natural result of difference of talents, industry, piety, station, and success." Another decision of the apostle is quoted in the same Circular, and it is this—"There is neither Jew or Greek, there is neither bond nor free, there is neither male nor female, for we are all one in Christ Jesus;" and so, of course, we are all equal in his sight. And yet this is quoted as being a decision in favour of doing away with the civil institutions of caste, which are undoubtedly the marks of that "station" which the bishop tells us is acknowledged by the Gospel, and in

fatal blow to Christianity that it has ever received in India. For this "Circular" imperatively declared that the distinction of castes, as regards all the relations of life, must be abandoned, "decidedly, immediately, and finally." And in order that this mandate might be intensely galling to the upper class vegetarian Christian, it was especially ordered that "differences of food and dress" were to be included in those overt acts which were to mark out for condemnation the Christian who still clung to the habits of his fathers in these innocent and, as regards food, healthful restrictions. To cling to these differences of food and dress, and to abstain from alcohol, was to cling to caste; and it was especially ordered that the children of

no way different from the station that a member of the House of Lords inherits from his predecessors. And here, though I do not think that it is advisable to cling to isolated texts as evidence of the general conduct of the apostles regarding the prejudices of their converts, I may mention that Peter, in his first Epistle, says, "Submit yourself to every ordinance of man for the Lord's sake." And if we take Dean Alford's interpretation of this, and consider it as equivalent to a command, extending to every human institution (and I can see no reason why we should not), it is plain that our missionaries in India, if they wish to follow the examples of the apostles, should yield to the prejudices of caste as long as they do not involve idolatrous rites. But it is in the general action of the apostles, as illustrated in Acts xv. 19, that the safest guide may, I apprehend, be found; and when, with reference to difficulties as regarding the customs of their converts, St. James said (Dean Alford's edition), "Wherefore my sentence is, that we trouble not them which from the Gentiles are turned to God; but that we write to them, that they abstain from pollutions of idols, from fornication, and from things strangled, and from blood;" and again: "For it seemed good to the Holy Ghost, and to us, to lay upon you no greater burden than [these] necessary things; that ye abstain from meats offered unto idols, and from blood, and from things strangled, and from fornication; from which, if ye keep yourselves, ye shall do well;"—when the apostle said thus, I think we ought to feel little doubt as to the course we ought to pursue regarding the social customs of the peoples of India.

native Christians should not be admitted to the Holy Communion without a full renunciation of all those social differences which might distinguish them from other members of the society in which they lived. This was quite sufficient. "The 'Circular' was read in the churches of Tanjore. It was received by the native Christians with great displeasure, and they showed their views by seceding in a body."

Turning now to the Report of the Madras Commissioners, which was written in 1845, we shall at once see the cause and root of this violent attack on social usages. For the Commissioners commence their Report by stating that the institution of caste and the divisions of society were things of priestly invention, and that, in fact, the whole of Hindoo society, as we at present see it, originated in, and is maintained by, Hindoo idolatry. And they further allege that the tyranny of this institution is such as to be perfectly unaccountable on any other supposition. How any body of priests had the power to issue and enforce mandates regarding the extraordinary diversities as to food and dress that we see prevailing throughout India, where the council sat that issued these decrees, and where the members of this council came from, they give no account. They do not seem to have even thought of such questions, and, for evidence of these astounding assertions, they refer us to what they call "the laws of Manu,"[1] and

[1] "The name 'Laws of Manu,' somewhat resembles a pious fraud, for the 'laws' are merely the laws or customs of a school or association of Hindoos, called the Mânavas, who lived in the country rendered holy by the divine river Saraswati. In this district the Hindoos first felt themselves a settled people, and in this neighbourhood they established colleges and hermitages, or âsramas, from some of which we may suppose Brâhmanas, Upanishads, and other religious compositions may have issued; and under such influences we may imagine the Code of Manu to have been composed.

"The Mânavas were undoubtedly an active, energetic people,

to Halhed's "Gentoo Hindoo Code." Caste and idolatry, then, according to them, are not only inextricably wound up together, but caste itself was caused by, and is a part of, idolatry; and we are, therefore, plainly told that it is impossible that a man should abandon the one without abandoning the other, and that, in other words, the two institutions must stand or fall together. Leaving this part of these assertions to be commented on further on, I now pass on to the statement and arguments of the Tanjore German missionaries.

Shortly after Bishop Heber's "Letter," which I have referred to at the commencement of these remarks, he drew up a number of questions regarding caste practices amongst native Christians, to which he required special answers. These "Articles of Inquiry," as they are termed, were sent to the Tanjore missionaries, and by them a statement in reply was furnished. They were asked for their opinion in 1828, and though no date is affixed to these statements, I conclude that they probably replied towards the close of that year.

They commence by observing that the distinctions of caste had been observed since the establishment of the

who governed themselves, paid taxes to the king, established internal and external trade, and drew up an extensive system of laws and customs, to which they appended real and imaginary awards. This system appears to have worked so well, that it was adopted by other communities, and then the organizers announced it as laws given to them by their divine progenitor, the great Manu. They added passages, moreover, which assert the divine claims of Brâhmans and the inferiority of the rest of mankind. Such assertions are little more than rhetorical flourishes, for Brâhmans never were either so omnipotent or so unamiable as the Code would represent them; nor were the Sûdras ever so degraded. In Sanskrit plays and poems, weak and indigent Brâhmans are by no means unfrequent; and, on the other hand, we meet with Sûdras who had political rights, and even in the Code find the pedigrees of great men traced up to Sûdra ancestors." —MRS. MANNING'S *Ancient and Mediæval India*, v. i., p. 276.

mission by the Rev. Mr. Schwartz, soon after the year 1762, and that he himself had been guided, partly by his own discretion, and partly by the example of the clergy of the Tranquebar Mission, which was started in the year 1705, by those good and amiable men of whom I have given some account in another part of this work. These successors of Schwartz, then, observed that they had persistently imitated the conduct of that able and good man; but that, while they took care to imitate his caution and forbearance, they seized every opportunity of softening the mutual prejudices arising from distinctions of caste; and they also observe that, in consequence, those distinctions of caste have gradually lost a great deal of their importance.

Alluding, in the next place, to the assertion that castes had been invented and entirely originated by the Brahmins, the authors of the statement observe that, in the opinion of the most intelligent natives who were not of the Brahminical order, the social distinctions which constitute caste existed long before the Brahmins came into the country at all; and they assert, further, that though the Brahmin priests blended those social distinctions with their idolatry, and framed a convenient legend to account for their divine institution, the whole thing was a mere fiction, which had been invented with the view of adding to the power of an ambitious priesthood. But the missionaries of Tanjore asserted, further, that even if the legend of caste was a true one, and that caste had been a part of idolatry, still those who abandoned the worshipping of idols and superstitious rites were not therefore to be required to abandon such practices as had nothing of idolatry about them at all, and they distinctly declared that no rites of an idolatrous or even mixed nature were tolerated amongst their converts.

The missionaries then pointed out that their high-caste converts simply retained these privileges and social customs because they would lose the respect of their neighbours if they abandoned those marks of station which they had inherited, and which they looked upon entirely as a civil prerogative. It was also pointed out that high-caste priests gained ready access to the houses of the better classes, and had, therefore, better chances of spreading Christianity than Pariah priests, whom no good-caste native would allow to cross the threshold of his house.

At church those of the upper classes sat on one side, and those of the lower on the other, and the higher and lower castes went up at different times to the communion-table.

In the schools no difficulty was experienced, and high and low caste children sat quite indiscriminately.

As regards social intercourse, they observe that none of their converts have any objection to partake of food prepared by another caste, as long as that caste is of superior rank to them, but that no one would touch food prepared by a man of lower caste than himself. The distinction of caste was also preserved as regards marriages, though these, of course, were always solemnized in the church.

Finally, these good and sensible men regret the tendencies of caste, but seem to consider that more good was to be done by letting it alone, and, in short, letting it die a natural death, than by forcibly opposing the prejudices of the people. And they very justly observe, that to oblige a man of high caste to eat with the lowest is doing force to common delicacy and to natural feelings of sense, and may be sometimes of serious consequence to bodily health.

I may here mention that about thirty-five years ago, Dr. Graul, the head of the Leipsic Missionary Society, visited India, remained there three years at the various missionary stations, and was firmly convinced that to interfere with the social customs of the native Christians would be at once unjust and impolitic. As regards the exact action of the Roman Catholics at present, I have no information to lay before the reader, but I know that they always had the wisdom to interfere as little as possible with the prejudices of the people, as long as they did not involve idolatrous rites.

Having thus laid before the reader an outline of the views of the supporters and opponents of caste, I shall now offer the conclusions I have arrived at, partly from my own observations and partly from the writings of others. I shall

1. Inquire into the origin of caste.

2. I shall inquire into the sanitary uses of caste, more especially as it concerns the approaching the communion-table promiscuously, as to the sitting together in church or other places, and as to its effects as regards general social intercourse.

3. I shall inquire whether there are not some compensating advantages, as regards caste institutions, which tend in a great measure to neutralize the prejudicial effects that arise from people's sympathies and feelings being confined to the members of their own caste, instead of being evenly distributed over the human race, considered as a whole.

And, first of all, as to the origin of caste—a point which seems to have been thought of no little importance by our caste-condemning missionaries. I confess that I, for my part, do not attach much importance to this question of the origin of caste, and think it of far more importance to ascertain its present bearing and effect. But, as many have raised the question, and asserted that caste had an idolatrous origin, and was the invention of an idolatrous priesthood, it may be worth while to gather together such facts as we can lay our hands on regarding this somewhat obscure subject. And it seems to me that the first thing we have to do is to clear away the rubbish which has been piled upon it in common with most Indian institutions—to ask what is evidence, and what is not. Our missionaries have asserted that caste can be clearly traced to an idolatrous origin, and that the institution is entirely unaccountable on any other supposition, and they pointed to the Code of Manu in proof of that assertion. But, on referring to Mrs. Manning's valuable work on "Ancient and Mediæval India," we can find no evidence that caste originated in any special way whatever. And we are told, on the authority of Mr. Muir, that the sacred books of the Hindoos contain no uniform or consistent account of the origin of caste, and that the freest scope is given by the individual writers to fanciful and arbitrary conjecture. The story that the castes issued from the mouth, arms, thighs, and feet of Brahma was simply an allegory, which, in the course of time, hardened into a literal statement of fact. The Brahmins, of course, came out of the mouth of Brahma; and, considering that they were the authors and compilers of all the principal books relating to castes and customs, it would have been extremely odd if they had not exalted their own order, and indulged in a tone of Oriental exaggeration which was eminently calculated to deceive, not perhaps, their successors, but the Englishmen who went to India. But the most curious thing is, that it never seems to have occurred to our missionaries to suspect that what they took as evidence of facts, and of a state of things really existing, was, in reality, only evidence of what an order or set of people could write, with the view of exalting themselves, and depressing the rest of the society amongst which they lived. The Brahmins chose to assert that the castes were of divine origin. They wrote that down and handed it on. We came to India, and finding these statements ready to hand, have simply swallowed them down, and added them to the number of illusions existing as regards India. But the facts really are, that castes and orders of men sprang up, we don't exactly know how. Brahmin writers described the castes, or at least part of them, and, in the course of time, the writings were said to have caused the castes, instead of the castes having caused the writings.

But whatever may be the facts as regards caste, we know that caste can exist without idolatry, and idolatry without caste; and that though the Brahmins, with their usual desire to incorporate everything in life with religion, gathered caste into their garners, and endeavoured to increase and extend it, still there is fair evidence for asserting that these two institutions have no necessary connection, and that, as it was perfectly possible to wind them up together, so it is perfectly possible to unwind them and produce again an entire separation. In a word, it is perfectly possible for a man to retain caste, not as believing it to be part of his native idolatrous religion, but as believing it to be (what it really was till the Brahmins seized hold of it and attached it to their faith) a civil institution which had sprung up in remote times, and had been inherited by him, just as rank and station are inherited in this country.[1] And that caste can exist without religion, and alongside of a religion as opposite to Brahminism as Christianity is, we have the most indis-

[1] As an instance that a man can abandon all religious rites whatever, and retain his caste unimpaired and unaltered, I may mention that my native clerk told me that he had done nothing in the way of religion at all for years; but that, of course, made no difference to him in the eyes of his neighbours, who didn't care what he did, as long as he did not depart from the social customs of his caste. I once said to a native shopkeeper in Bangalore, "What religion are you of?" "Oh!" he answered with a smile, "no religion at all, sir." But I need not trouble the reader with further evidence to show that a man may drop his religion altogether without dropping his caste, and that therefore religion and caste have no necessary connection with one another whatever.

putable evidence supplied by the late Sir Emerson Tennent, in his "History of Christianity in Ceylon."

"Caste," he wrote, "as it exists at the present day amongst the Buddhists of Ceylon, is purely a social distinction, and entirely disconnected with any sanction or pretensions derivable from their system of religion. Nor is evidence wanting that, even at a comparatively modern period, such was equally its aspect amongst the natives throughout the continent of India, by whom caste was held not as a sacred, but as a secular discrimination of ranks. The earliest notice of India by the Greek historians and geographers enumerates the division of the people into Brahmins, Kistrayas, Vaisyas, and Sudras; but this was a classification which applied equally to the followers of Buddha" (who preached that, in the sight of God, all men were equal) "and of Brahma, nor were the members of either section held ineligible for the offices of the priesthood." And, in the note below, the reader will find additional evidence which will show him that caste in Ceylon, just as it originally was in India, can and does exist merely as a division of ranks, and that it need not at all be necessarily connected with any idolatrous rites or worship.[1]

[1] "Caste, though distinctly denounced by their sacred books, and ostensibly disavowed by the Singhalese themselves, still exists in their veneration for rank, whether hereditary or adventitious. Thus every district and every village has its little leader, a pre-eminence accorded to birth rather than property; and, by a descending scale, certain members of the community, in right of relationship or connection, assume an undefined superiority, and are tacitly admitted to the exercise of what is technically called an 'influence.' In the hamlets, so universal is this feeling amongst the natives, so habitual the impulse to classify themselves and to look up to some one as their superior in the scale of society, that the custom descends through every gradation of life and its occupations, and in some of the villages the missionaries found it necessary to appoint two schoolmasters, even where there was less

Having thus shown how caste did not originate, it may, perhaps, not be altogether superfluous if I hazard a few remarks as to the way in which it did probably originate.

The common idea of caste is that it is simply a combination of troublesome and fanciful restrictions, imposed upon the various peoples of India by those of the upper classes who desired to keep themselves above the jostling of the crowd. But this institution (if that be a correct term for it) arose naturally and regularly out of the circumstances of the times, and where these circumstances no longer exist, it will as naturally disappear; and that the last must happen we have seen from the fact that altered circumstances have already caused the commencement of its removal amongst the people of the towns. But the general circumstances which gave birth to caste require a few words of explanation, and the following solution seems not an unnatural one.

We know, as a certain fact, that peoples to whom we have given the names of Dravidians and Aryans entered

than occupation for one—'influence,' as well as ability to teach, being an essential qualification; and if the individual did not possess the former, it was most indispensable to associate with him some other who did.* Again, if a village could not furnish a master competent to teach, it was in vain to procure one from a distance; his 'influence' did not extend to that locality, and no pupils could be got to attend. Nor was caste itself without the open avowal of its force, the children of a Vellala or high-caste family being on no account permitted to enter the school-house of a lower-caste master. These are obstacles which prevail in all their original force even at the present day; and in the purely Singhalese districts, such as Matura, the prestige of caste is so despotic, that no amount of qualification in all other particulars can overcome the repugnance to intercourse with those who are deficient in the paramount requisite of rank."—SIR J. E. TENNENT'S *Christianity in Ceylon*, p. 286.

* MS. account of Baptist Mission.

India from the north and north-west; that they increased and multiplied, overspread the whole of India, and reduced the aborigines to serfdom. We also know that these tribes from the north, who were, comparatively speaking, fair, very naturally regarded the black, ugly, carrion-eating aborigines with disgust. Hence, naturally, must have arisen the opinions as regards Pariahs which all the superior castes hold to this day. Even to have food touched by people of such abominable habits must have been repulsive, and therefore the separation into men of caste and men of no caste, or, in other words, into browns and blacks (for the word for caste means colour), followed as a matter of course. Caste, then, seems naturally to have arisen from the idea that to associate in any way with people of bad habits and grovelling ideas is an intolerable degradation. The superior races, therefore must have considered it a matter of importance to retreat as far as possible from the habits of the aborigines; and when we take into consideration the influence of religion, the natural ambition of the priestly classes, the splitting up into sects, and the fondness of the Hindoo mind for subtle distinctions, the rest easily follows. But, though numerous castes arose amongst the invaders, the main line of demarcation, is still the original one of race—between the races of the north and the aborigines whom they found in possession of India. The base, then, of caste, we may rest assured, was simply the result of a people, or rather of peoples, wishing to keep themselves uncontaminated when coming in contact with a debased population.

This was exactly the case with the Jews. They were simply a very strongly guarded caste, with a number of regulations as to what they were and were not to eat, and with rules which prohibited them intermarrying or associating with peoples with whom they came in contact. Many of those rules may seem to us ridiculous and fanciful, but they were calculated to prevent the Jews from any chance of adopting the manners and customs of the peoples around them; and the Indians, having had similar views, naturally adopted similar means. Such then is a brief generalization of the causes which led to caste laws, which were, no doubt, carried in some instances to a ridiculous length, but which were founded in common sense, and were admirably adapted to carry into effect the opinions of the superior races.

We have now, in the second place, to consider caste with reference to the approach of native converts to the Lord's table, the sitting apart of the various castes in church, and the effects of caste as regards what is called social intercourse.

The whole difficulty of the caste question, as regards the Sacrament, lies in this, namely, that a high-caste vegetarian objects to drink wine at the same time and after a low-caste meat-eater. And here I find a great difficulty in finding words or illustrations that will at all convey the feelings of a high-caste vegetarian at the very idea of drinking after a low-caste carrion-eater. If from the lowest, filthiest, and most poisonous dens in London, you were to take a man, reeking with beer and tobacco, and with his clothes crawling with vermin, and presenting, in short, every appearence of foulness, dirt, and disease; if you were to take that man and place him between two ladies at the administration of the Holy Communion, I do not say that they would there and then refuse the Sacrament on these terms, but I think we may be pretty sure that, from sanitary motives, if from no others, they would in future take the Sacrament in a place where they would not be liable to such contact. Their feelings and senses would be shocked by such contact as I have imagined, but their sensations would merely bear the same proportion to the sensations of a high-caste vegetarian Hindoo who had to drink after a Pariah that a trifling cause of disgust would bear to the most intolerable and lasting degradation. Now, to people in this country, this may seem an extraordinary thing; but they will think it less extraordinary when I tell them that, if I could not take the Sacrament unless amongst Pariahs, I would never take it again, unless perhaps, I were to put myself bodily into one of Professor Tyndall's cotton-gauze air-cleansers, and drink the sacramental wine after it had been boiled at a temperature of 212 degrees, and passed through a filter. And when I talk of the lowest castes as carrion-eaters, I must tell the reader that I am not in the slightest degree guilty of exaggeration, and that they are carrion-eaters in exactly the same sense that vultures are carrion-eaters. In fact, these men never get any meat unless that of animals that have died of disease; and as in these climates decomposition is extremely rapid, the reader can imagine the result of coming in contact with a man who has, perhaps, a few hours before been eating a mass of diseased and half decomposed meat. And in case the reader should not be able to imagine what the result is, I may mention the following circumstance. A few days after I had killed a bison I had occasion to point out some pieces of sawn wood which I wished to be removed from the jungle to my house, and I accordingly took with me a native overseer, and two coolies to carry the timber. When I was pointing out the pieces to them, I smelt a strong smell of putrid meat, which seemed to fill the air so entirely that I at once concluded that a tiger must have killed some animal and left the carcase near the spot. My overseer and myself looked about everywhere, but at last happening to pass the coolies, I at once perceived that the smell arose from their breath, and on questioning them, I found that before coming to work they had been feasting on decayed bison flesh. In fact, after killing a bison, we could never go near our coolies for some days afterwards. But to see a party of these men sitting like vultures around the carcase of some animal that has just died of some abominable disease is quite enough to inspire even an unprejudiced European meat-eater with the most wholesome horror; and the reader need not, I think, be surprised at the feelings of disgust which these men's habits inspire amongst the respectable classes of the community. But independently of all feelings of disgust, there are sanitary considerations which are of infinitely more importance. For it so happens that, at a time when the weather is hottest and the season most unhealthy, a larger number of animals die; and I have very little doubt that this eating of rotten meat causes amongst the Pariahs a large quantity of disease, and especially of cholera, which they would not fail to disseminate with fatal certainty amongst all classes, were the native Christians compelled to take the Sacrament indiscriminately. And, in my own experience, I have observed that cholera has passed through districts, that the upper classes have been free from it, but that amongst the lower the victims were many. And the same sanitary reasons that apply to the Sacrament apply equally well to the mixing of castes indiscriminately in the churches; for it might so happen, as it frequently does, that fever and cholera may be prevalent amongst the lower castes, while the higher may be at that time comparatively free from such diseases. So that, when we take all these points into consideration, we shall find that the German missionaries were perfectly right in placing the men of the higher caste on one side of the church, and those of the lower on the other, and that they were equally right in allowing the higher castes to approach the Sacrament at a different time from the lower. I may here remark that I once mentioned this taking of the Sacrament in a sort of order of precedence to a clergyman in a country parish, when he told me that exactly the same sort of thing occurred in his parish, and that the lord of the manor invariably took the Sacrament first, and, if I recollect rightly, the parish clerk last; and a special instance of this in a Scotch parish was mentioned to me not long ago.

The same sanitary considerations will also naturally be of value when we come to consider that indiscriminate social intercourse which the missionaries so much insist upon as one of the necessary signs of grace. I do not, of course, say that it is not advisable, and that it would not be desirable to see a little more intercourse between class and class than exists at the present. But between all the better classes there is a much greater degree of intercourse than our missionaries would have us believe; and it is not true that one caste will eat only the food prepared by a person of his own caste. I cannot, of course, say what may be the case as regards other parts of India; but, as regards my own district, each caste will eat of the food prepared by any of the castes higher, or at least purer, than its own. For instance, a Gouda, who will not allow that the Lingayet caste is better than his own, will eat of food prepared by a Lingayet, while a Lingayet will not eat of food prepared by a Gouda. And the explanation of this is, that the Lingayet is a vegetarian, and meat might have been boiled in the Gouda's pots, while there would be nothing to offend the Gouda customs in the pots of a vegetarian host. But in these matters I entirely agree with the good Bishop Heber, who said that we had no right to interfere in their private life, or to meddle in any way with their social customs, as long as there was no idolatry in them.

Turning now to the third point I proposed to consider, I have a few remarks to make regarding the only (from a Christian point of view) solid objection that can, I conceive, be made to the institution of separate orders of men;

namely, that the tendency of caste is to shut up the bowels of compassion towards all the world outside of a man's particular class. And here I confess that I am very much in want of information, and can think of no unprejudiced individuals to whom to apply for the facts as really existing in other parts of India. As for books, when I look into them for any information, I am at once met by quantities of unlimited condemnations, or a host of contradictory statements. And, as an instance of the latter, I may mention that in Kerr's "Domestic Life of the Natives of India" we are informed, at page 31, that "alms are given to the poor without distinction of caste," while at page 343 of the same volume we are told that "to extend kindness and hospitality to one of a different caste is regarded as sinful." But in matters of this sort we want the experience of individuals who have actually lived amongst the people, as much as anyone can who is not actually one of them. As for my own part of the country, I can answer for it that caste has no such effect as has been alleged to arise from it regarding the extension of hospitality and kindness to people of various castes; and, as a confirmatory illustration, may mention that I have found members of every caste assembled at the house of a toddyman to inquire how he was, and to see whether they could do anything for him. These toddy-drawers rank at least third amongst the castes in Manjarabad, and though none of the members of the farmer castes above them would eat of food prepared in a toddy-drawer's house, yet there were numbers of both these castes present. This feeling would not, that I am aware of, go as far as one of the carrion-eating Pariahs, but I am quite certain that it would extend to any other caste but theirs in the country. But on this point I do not offer any decided opinion, as, for what I know to the contrary, acts of kindness and hospitality may, no doubt, often have been extended even to the lowest. And I may also mention here that I have slept in the veranda of a farmer's house, in which members of the family slept close to some of my people, who were of the toddy-drawer caste above alluded to, and who, I am sure, were quite as welcome as members of their own caste would have been. But as regards all these matters concerning the inner life of the people, we know nothing, unless we actually live amongst them, and sleep in their houses, and, in fact, see the people at home; and as it is extremely difficult to find anyone who has done anything of the kind, it naturally follows that it is almost impossible to find anything like reliable sources of information regarding native habits throughout India. You may, it is true, stuff your very soul with information of some sort or other, if you go about asking questions, but if you do you will find yourself much in the same predicament that Johnson found himself in his tour to the Hebrides; and the reader may recollect that the worthy doctor very soon found that nothing could be more vague, unsatisfactory, and uncertain than the answers of an unsophisticated simple people, who were not much in the habit of being asked questions of any sort. However, the reader may, in the meantime, reasonably infer that the conduct of the people in the rural districts of India, and situated under similar circumstances, would not materially differ, as regards matters of caste, from the practice as existing in Manjarabad. And should that turn out to be the case, it is plain that those notions, as regards the practice of caste, which have been so industriously circulated in England, are almost entirely false.

I have said that I proposed inquiring, further, whether there are not some compensating advantages in this division of the people into castes which tend, in a great measure, to neutralize the prejudicial effects that arise from people's sympathies and feelings being more or less confined to members of their own caste, instead of being distributed over the human race considered as a whole. Now, it is perfectly true that the tendency of caste is to weaken the claim that humanity in general has on an individual; but though the claim of society in general is weakened, it must be remembered that the claims of each caste on the members of it are strengthened. And though this fact may militate against an enlarged and Christian philanthropy, the aggregate force of claims will be found to amount to a much larger sum than if one part of a society had no more claim on a man than another. A man of one caste would not, for instance, perhaps feel that a man of another caste had much claim on him; but he would distinctly and strongly feel that a member of his own caste had. And every caste acting on the same principle of supporting and helping its members, I am convinced that the aggregate force of assistance rendered must be greater than in a country where there is little or no caste principle. This may seem a rash assertion, and of course it is one that it is impossible, as far as I am aware, to prove. But the fact that there is not a poor-house from one end of India to the other, seems to me a significant and satisfactory circumstance; and the only way I can account for there being no need of such a thing is,[1] that caste feeling must often come in where all other aids fail. Nor are we in this country without instances of the value of caste feelings, and both the Jews and the Scotch may still be pointed to as illustrations of what I mean. A Scotchman still has a sort of caste feeling for a Scotchman, and would do things for a man, as a Scotchman, that he would not do for people of either English or Irish descent. This principle may now have lessened, and is, no doubt, daily lessening. But when I started in India, I very soon experienced the benefit of this caste feeling; and, as one illustration to the

[1] In the large towns this remark might not, perhaps, be justifiable.

point, I may mention that, before my estates came into bearing, I was attended in a long and serious illness by two Scotch doctors (one of whom attended on me for six weeks incessantly), both of whom resolutely declined any remuneration whatever. I cannot, of course, positively assert that these gentlemen would not have attended me on the same terms had I been an Englishman, but, from my general experience with other doctors, I am sure that these gentlemen must have been not a little influenced by caste feeling. And I have no doubt whatever that the way the Scotch get on, wherever they go, is to be attributed, in no small measure, to the existence of the same feeling. It may seem to many of my readers that to use the term caste as a principle which impels one Scotchman to help another is not exactly correct; and I must admit to having some doubts on the subject myself. The case of the Jews, however, admits of none; and, if ever there was a caste of people in the world, in the strict Hindoo sense, they are certainly an unmistakable example. And what are the results of caste feeling with them? As to other parts of the world I have no precise information; but in England I have ascertained from the best authority that caste feeling has produced some extremely favourable results. In the first place, Jews are seldom or never found in our workhouses; and all cases of poverty are carefully investigated by a visiting committee, or board of guardians, and relief or employment is always afforded to every Jewish pauper. Then, again, no Jewish child ever was, and no Jewish child is now, without the means of obtaining elementary instruction; and it would be difficult to find an English Jew unable to read and write. Means are taken to secure the attendance of all poor children, and a sound middle-class education is afforded, while the study of the Hebrew language is compulsory. There were only, when I obtained my information on the point, about twenty

Jewish (principally foreigners) convicts in England, and no female convict was to be found.

Another of the principal complaints brought against caste is the fact that it has a tendency to keep one caste fixed below another; but even here we shall find some compensating considerations which are of great value. For, if caste in this respect has a keeping-down tendency, it has also a levelling one. It may keep one order above another, but within the limits of that caste order it has a levelling tendency, and in one respect the poorest of each class feel themselves on a level with the richest. Nor is a poor man of good caste made to experience the bitter sense of degradation which falls to the lot of a gentleman who, from poverty and misfortune, has fallen out of his original class into another far below him. The Indian may descend into the most humble spheres, but if he attends to the regulations of his caste he is always a member of it, and his feelings of self-respect are maintained by the fact that, however poor, it is quite possible that his daughter may be married by a man of wealth and position. But in this country, where a man has gone a long way down the hill, when he has descended—as many gentlemen especially do in our colonies—into the lower ranks of life, he loses all connection with people who are of his own rank by birth. I do not, of course, mean to allege that this want of caste feeling is to be lamented with us, but I am merely stating facts which seem to me to show the number of ways in which this much-reviled caste system can be proved to have compensating advantages which tend to counterbalance the drawbacks of the situation.

Before concluding this chapter, it may be useful to make a few remarks as to the way in which caste laws act as regards the social condition of people who have by wealth raised themselves above the general average of their order; and I shall at the same time notice a few instances that have fallen within my observation as to the way in which caste laws of the most stringent nature are occasionally set aside by universal consent.

The old idea we entertained of caste was that, to use the words of Tennent, "each class is stationed between certain walls of separation, which are impassable by the purest virtue or the most conspicuous merit;" or that, to come to more recent times, and to use the words of the late Mr. Wilson, in his speech before leaving for India, "in India you see people tied down by caste, and, whatever their talents or exertions may be, they cannot rise." Now the history of many families that have risen to eminence entirely belies this assertion, and the evidences are so numerous that I need not weary the reader by quoting them. But one instance I may perhaps mention, as the circumstances seem to me somewhat extraordinary, and a reference to them here may induce some one to make more particular inquiries in the locality alluded to. Buchanan notices that "in Bhagulpore there were certain families who, from having adopted a pure life, had within the memory of man risen from the lowest dregs of the people to the highest ranks of the nobility." In this instance, however, I cannot help suspecting that the families must have risen on something more substantial than their pure habits. But in matters of this sort we are very much in want (as indeed we are on almost every Indian subject) of more detailed and particularly substantiated evidence. As regards the subject of low castes raising themselves in the social scale, I know of no instances that have fallen within my own observation, but I have obtained information from other parts of Mysore, the truth of which I have no reason to doubt, although I would advise the reader to receive what I have to say on this point with the same caution that he should receive all information which is even in the smallest degree removed from the experience of personal observation. With this caution, I may then observe that, from information I have received, I have ample reason to believe that in the interior of Mysore there are many families of Pariahs who are as well off, in point of cattle, cash and land, as the average of the farmer caste, notwithstanding that the forefathers of these Pariahs were merely the servants of the farmer tribe. Nor is this all. Many instances, I believe, may be pointed out of members of the farmer tribe being the tenants of the once-despised Pariah. The Pariah, it is true, does not reap all the advantages from his altered circumstances that might be expected in other countries, but it is a mistake to suppose that wealth does not tell in India as it does elsewhere.[1] The well-to-do Pariah (and in the Nuggur division of Mysore I am told there are many such) receives that respect which is invariably paid to those who have much substance. He no longer stands respectfully without the veranda of a farmer of ordinary position, but takes his seat in the veranda itself, and on terms of perfect equality. But the farmer will not eat with his visitor, nor give him his daughter in marriage. This to us would be a disagreeable reflection, no doubt; but, in their present political state, I cannot see that the happiness or prosperity of the people is in any way affected by these facts, nor am I aware that any one has attempted to prove that the natural comforts of the people have been in any way lessened by these social separations.

Turning now to glance at the way in which caste laws are sometimes set aside, it is impossible to avoid suspecting that the instances given of caste feeling in these

[1] Since this chapter was written, I have received well authenticated information of a Pariah, who had acquired both wealth and position, having been adopted into a superior caste. The caste was not a rich one, and he no doubt paid heavily for his admission into it.

respects, though perhaps true in themselves, are not fair examples of what would universally occur in cases of emergency even with the most caste-observing people in India. From the instances given (and those most commonly given refer to natives preferring to die of thirst rather than take water from the hands of a person of inferior caste), people are led to believe that under no circumstances will a breach of caste take place, or be overlooked if it does take place, by members of the caste. But the illustration I have to give seem to point to a contrary conclusion, and if that is the case with people whom I know to be extremely strict, it seems very probable that we have adopted some very exaggerated notions as to the rigidity of caste laws. And what has contributed not a little to these delusions is, that tricky servants frequently make caste a most convenient pretence for avoiding to do this or that, or as an excuse wherever an excuse is for any purpose convenient. But however all this may be, the reader may form his opinions from the following cases.

The first I have to give of violation of caste law is certainly the most extraordinary that I ever heard of. The act was, indeed, a remarkable and touching tribute of regard, or I may even say of affection, on the part of a native overseer of the farmer caste in Manjarabad, and was a better monument than any that could have been erected to one of the best and most unselfish men I have ever met. When Mr. W——, my late manager, unhappily died on the estate, this overseer in question, understanding that it was considered by us as an honour to the deceased, volunteered to make one of the carrying party. This extraordinary determination was absolutely forbidden by the caste potail, or head man, who was present; but Rama Gouda[1] showed the same coolness and resolution

[1] The farmers in Manjarabad invariably tack on the word "Gouda" to their names, and it seems to answer for our Mr.

that he always did in the case of a bear or a tiger, and simply saying, "Let my caste go to-day," he made one of the carrying party in spite of every remonstrance. Hundreds of all castes were present, but so strong were their feelings of regard for Mr. W——, that no notice whatever was taken of the offence which was so publicly committed. The repugnance of all castes, except the very lowest, to touching the body of a European, is very well known to everyone who has been in India, and so fearful was the caste head man of sanctioning, even with his presence, this violation of caste law, that he immediately went home.

In the next instance I have to give, one of the Lingayet caste (vegetarians, and abstainers from intoxicating drinks) was wounded by a tiger, and there was a caste question raised, as to whether, under the circumstances, he should take wine. The occurrence came about in this way. Some miles from my house I once wounded a tiger, somewhat late in the day, and, owing to the broken nature of the ground, and a general confusion that seemed to take possession of the people, it seemed impossible to bring the affair to a satisfactory conclusion, so I went home. The following morning I returned to take up the track of the tiger, but it was unluckily reported that the animal had quitted the jungle we had left him in, so the party (I having been posted at a point where the tiger would probably break cover, in case the report should prove false), it appears, blundered carelessly into the place where the animal had been last seen the evening before. Now, this particular spot was full of a long sort of reed that grows in swampy ground, so that the people could not see far before them, and, to make a long story short, it seems that the tiger bided his time, sprang suddenly into the party, and gave one of them a fatal bite in the loins. The moment I heard the three roars, I expected that something disagreeable must have occurred, and, on arrival at the scene of events, I found a fine young fellow of the Lingayet caste lying bathed in blood, and my people vainly endeavouring to stanch the wounds. He was half swooning away from loss of blood, and I offered him some wine to keep up his strength. This, however, he refused to take, unless the head man of his village, who happened to be present, would consent. The head man, evidently wishing to shirk the responsibility, shook his head doubtfully; but the members of his caste all called out—"It's no matter; let him drink;" and he drank accordingly. While this was going on, I had a rough stretcher made, and, doing up his wounds as well as we could, sent him off on the way to his village. While we were attending to the wounded man, rather an amusing incident occurred. It appears that when the tiger charged, one of the party, a toddy-drawer, at once climbed up a tree, and when the party retreated, carrying off the wounded, he was afraid to come down. His absence had not been remarked, and when we were engaged in doing up the wounded man, the toddyman, who had taken heart and come down, slunk quietly out of the jungle, and startled some of the party not a little, as they thought that it was perhaps the tiger coming down on them again. However, this toddyman reported that the tiger was still almost in the same spot where he had been lying when he made his attack: and I then proposed we should go into the jungle, and see how we liked the look of him. But the tiger had given such indications of temper that the main body of the people seemed to have no desire to see him again, and I think that only ten (and those mostly my own people) accompanied me. As I was, Europeanly speaking, single-handed, this may have seemed an imprudent course, and no doubt it was not altogether unattended with danger; but it luckily turned out that the tiger was stone dead, though he was lying in such a natural position that we had some doubts as to whether he might not be shamming, even when we got within fifteen yards of him. As we were skinning the tiger, the wounded man (who had by that time only been carried a few hundred yards) expired: so, observing that it was "written on his forehead,"[1] we took up our man and our skin, and went home.

These instances of infringement of caste rules will show the reader the way in which they are sometimes abandoned; and I could mention other minor points where I have seen them occasionally abandoned. But not only are these rules thus, on urgent occasions, summarily set aside, but within a very short distance I have observed an alteration of custom. For instance, on our side of the river which separates our county from the next, neither the farmers nor the toddy-drawers will eat of an animal that has even been touched after death by a Pariah; whereas, on the other side of the river, the Pariahs who came out shooting not only touched, but carried a couple of wild boars we had killed. And yet the people on one side of the river are exactly of the same caste as those on the other. But the fact seems to be, that many of the minor points of what is called caste law have arisen from some accident, and in the course of time have hardened into local customs.

And here, before bringing this chapter to a close, I find it impossible to refrain from again alluding to the numerous instances where caste has been made the common scapegoat of every Indian difficulty. What is the meaning of this? What is the meaning of that? Why won't the natives do this, and why won't they do that? Caste—and caste is the common refuge; and with most of our countrymen who have tried to introduce new customs or a new religion, caste has ever been a handy and convenient peg

[1] The natives imagine that every man's fate is written in invisible characters on his forehead.

on which to hang any difficulties they may meet with, or any problem they cannot readily solve. In short, it is hard to say what difficulty has not been disposed of in this fashion. Let us glance at two instances to illustrate my meaning.

For the first instance, I cannot select, perhaps, a better example than that afforded by the Rev. G. U. Pope, in the notes he has made when editing a second edition of the valuable work of the Abbé Dubois. And, in alluding to these footnotes, it is impossible to repress some feeling of annoyance that the valuable work of the Abbé should, in an evil hour, have fallen into the hands of a writer who has thought fit often, in a few brief and contemptuous words, summarily to dismiss and overrule those conclusions which were the result of a life spent on more intimate terms with natives than any I have ever been able to hear of. And Mr. Pope's statements are the more calculated to impose on the general reader, as he speaks of having had "more than twenty years of a somewhat intimate intercourse with the Hindoos;" the fact being that he spent the greater part (in fact, all but a few years, as far as I have been able to ascertain) as head of the Grammar School on the Nilgiri Hills, where he had no more opportunity of having any intercourse with natives than a Hindoo would have of gaining experience of the natives of England, were he to take up his residence on the Grampians, and interchange a few words occasionally with the shepherds of those mountains. But as to what caste has done. "Caste," says Mr. Pope, "has prevented the Hindoos from availing themselves of the opportunities afforded them of acquiring the sciences, arts, and civilization of nations with whom they have come in contact." Caste, "the great petrifier," we are again told, is the real cause of the stagnation that everywhere abounds. Caste, again, "upholds immutable distinctions by arbitrary and absurd laws, which are enforced by irresponsible authority, and maintains a standard of right and wrong entirely independent of the essential principles of moral science;" and, in order that everything may be included at one blow, we are finally told, in a note appended to the remarks of the Abbé on the moral and social advantages of caste, that "caste, and its offspring custom, are among the hindrances to all good in India."

But it is still more curious to observe how men of intelligence and observation can be led, by the force of inherited opinion, into statements as to the effects of caste which are actually contradicted by their own experience. And in Mr. Raikes's interesting work, "Notes of the North-Western Provinces," we find an instance of how people will always attribute everything to this universal bugbear. Observing on the pride of high caste, "which withers whatever it touches," Mr. Raikes informs us that the Brahmins and Rajpoots of the rich province of Benares will not touch the plough owing to pride of caste. He next tells us that caste is little regarded to the north of Allahabad, where, from various causes, the demand for labour is greater. All of which, being traced to its true cause, simply amounts to this, namely, that where landed proprietors of good family are well off they naturally do not care to work, whereas in another part of the country where they are not well off, or cannot procure labourers, they do work. In the same way, the author, after telling us that infanticide has at one time or other been common all over the world, tells us that in India it is entirely caused by caste. Now, if we take caste to mean family pride solely, it certainly has influenced the matter, or at least tended to maintain the evil complained of; but I know of one instance, at least, in India where infanticide can be traced to satisfactory causes, and amongst a people who have always been observed to be remarkably free from what are called caste prejudices. The Toda tribe, on the Nilgiri Hills, are polyandrists, and, in order to keep down the number of the tribe, they naturally had recourse to female infanticide. This they have now abandoned, and my Toda guide very soon told me the reason. He said, "Formerly we used to kill the females, because we had little more than the produce of our buffaloes to depend on; but now that more people have flocked to the hills we can let our lands and get plenty to eat." He added, also, that the Government had ordered them not to kill their children; but, unless their means had improved, it is plain that a Government order would have had little effect. But, as regards this subject of infanticide, it seems to be a thing difficult to avoid, whenever conditions arise which are favourable to its extension; nor will repressive measures alone ever place any very complete check upon it. Like every other demand, it rises and falls with the necessities of the situation, and can never be originally caused by anything in the shape of caste feelings or regulations; and amongst these necessities I, of course, include the desire to avoid shame, or the prospect of shame in the family, or starvation, as well as the fact that women are an encumbrance to some tribes. Some people, I may add, are under the impression that polyandric habits, when once established, become necessarily a cause of infanticide. But we have no means of knowing that this was ever the case, while the Coorgs may be pointed to as a race who once were polyandrous, but who were never, that I am aware of, accused of infanticide. The explanation of this, I apprehend, is to be found in the fact that their circumstances were comfortable enough to preclude any necessity for keeping down the population.

It is time now that I should bring this chapter to a close, but, as it may be a convenience to the reader, I think it well, before doing so, to sum up those conclusions which I assume to have been established;

in doing so I shall, however, merely take notice of those points which seem to me to be of paramount importance.

In the first place, then, we compared the morality of our British counties, as regards the connection of the sexes and the use of alcohol, with the morality of the Indian county of Manjarabad; and having seen that, owing to caste laws, the morality of Manjarabad is superior, I think we are justified in concluding that these laws have acted more effectually than all the religious instruction that has for centuries been lavished on the people of this country; or, to put the case in shorter terms, we may assert that, as regards the branches of morality alluded to, caste has beaten Christian influences.

In the next place we took into consideration the action of our missionaries as regards caste, and having seen that they have always insisted on their converts entirely renouncing customs which can be proved to produce the most valuable results, we came to the conclusion that it has been a fortunate thing for India that its peoples have rejected our hide-bound interpretation of Christianity. We then inquired as to whether the missionaries had any right to debar from the advantages of Christianity those who, wishing to become Christians, yet desired to retain their social customs; and, having come to the conclusion that there is nothing idolatrous in these customs, we have distinctly asked those interpreters of Christianity whom we have in India to tell us by whose authority they have ventured to act in a way which, as has been shown, the Apostles never did as regards the prejudices of their Jewish converts. And generally, as regards the action of our missionaries in this matter, we have felt ourselves justified in asserting that our English missions have inflicted an incalculable injury on the cause of Christianity by presenting it to the people of India as something that must necessarily tear the whole framework of their society to pieces.

We then inquired more particularly into the origin of caste, and, having seen that it never could have originated in the way our missionaries suppose it to have done, we hazarded a conjecture as to the way in which it probably did originate, and saw grounds for supposing that the distinctions of caste came naturally about, and that they were in principle calculated to effect exactly the same ends that the Jewish lawgivers had in view when they framed that Levitical law which effectually prevented the Jews from mingling socially with the races they lived amongst. We then looked at caste from a sanitary point of view, and came to the conclusion that in consequence of the carrion-eating habits of the lowest castes, and of their liability to transmit the germs of disease, the rules which prevented them from coming into contact with the higher castes, either in the way of taking the Sacrament, or in any other way, are of the greatest value. We next inquired into the effects of caste as regards social intercourse, and especially as regards the exercise of hospitality amongst people of different castes, and saw reason to think that the restrictions of caste, with, perhaps, the exception of the very lowest, formed no bar whatever to the exercise of hospitality. Glancing subsequently at the action of caste feeling in confining the sympathies of individuals more especially to the members of their own caste, we came to the conclusion that, though caste had undoubtedly the effect of contracting the feelings within a narrow circle, there was to be found a compensating advantage in the fact that the claims of caste produced, in the aggregate, a greater amount of charity, and, in short, were calculated to produce a better general result than would be arrived at in the absence of caste feelings. And as illustrations of the advantages of this caste feeling, we pointed to the fact of there being no poor-houses in India, and especially to the Jews in England, as affording an example of the favourable effects of caste feeling. After this, we pointed to the fact that, though caste had the effect of keeping one caste or order of men above another, it had also a levelling tendency within each caste, and produced an important point of equality which no poverty can destroy. We then took into consideration some facts which seemed to show that families could raise themselves to a higher rank in society by adopting the purer habits of the classes above them; and we also saw that the influence of wealth does, to a very great degree, elevate a man of low caste in the social scale. We next saw reason to suppose that we have hitherto been labouring under very exaggerated notions as to the stringency of caste regulations, and two instances were given to illustrate the way in which caste laws are sometimes set summarily aside. And, finally, we pointed out, and gave some illustrations to prove, that with most of our countrymen who have either tried to introduce new customs or in any way to alter native habits of action, caste has ever been made, and very unjustly made, the common scapegoat.

One word more. The absolute good that caste has done may be briefly summed up. It has acted as a strong moral police, and as a preserver of order and decorum in the community,[1] and it has prevented the spread of bad habits and customs, more especially that of drinking, as far as large numbers of the people are concerned.[2] On the

[1] Abbé Dubois.

[2] It is satisfactory to learn that caste feelings and regulations have a favourable influence with natives, even when they go to a foreign country; and it is equally satisfactory to quote the evidence of a gentleman who laughs at caste as an absurd custom. Mr. W. Sabonadière, in his work of "The Coffee Planter in Ceylon" writes as follows: "The coolies who resort to Ceylon are of various castes. Those mostly preferred by planters are the

other hand, caste is said to have hindered the progress of the people taken as a whole. But in every instance where we have really tried the introduction of any art, the removal of any public crime (as suttee and human sacrifice, for instance), the improvement of any cultivation, the introduction of education, or of new means of moving from place to place, we have either found caste to be no impediment at all, or an impediment so slight as not to be worth mentioning.

NOTE.—With the view of obtaining information I briefly allude here to two points with reference to caste and its effects—the (1) curious custom of the Marasa Wokul tribe in Mysore, and (2) the influence of caste in developing improved aptitudes which afterwards descend by hereditary transmission.

As to the first, the mother of a girl is compelled to submit to the amputation of the terminal joints of the third and fourth fingers of the right hand on the occasion of the betrothal of her daughter, and in the event of a girl being motherless the mother of the bridegroom-elect must submit to the operation.

The custom is alluded to in the well-known work of the Abbé Dubois, and in the appendix the editor of the second edition confirms the account given, and quotes confirmatory evidence from Colonel Wilks' "Mysore," in which is published the legend which is reported to have given rise to the custom. Colonel Wilks, early in this century,

low castes, such as Pallans, shanars, and Pariahs, as being more accustomed to and fit for hard work; but, as a class, they are more given to drink, spend their money more freely, and are more quarrelsome than the higher classes, whom their caste forbids to drink arrack or spirits, and who are more cleanly in their habits, better behaved (as fearing to lose caste), who have land of their own on the coast, and are more interested in working regularly and gaining their wages to take away with them."

saw some of the women who had been operated on. The tribe in question lives in the north-east of Mysore, but after inquiry through the medium of natives in the interior of the country, I cannot now learn that the custom is continued. Perhaps, being a disagreeable one, it may have been given up. I should feel much obliged for any information as to the point in question.

As to the second point, I was informed in 1891 by Mr. Chatterton of the Engineering College at Madras, that he had many Brahmins under him in the workshops, and that, though more intelligent than other castes, they are less efficient, owing to their ancestors never having been practised in any mechanical work. The influence of caste was here most perceptible, and he could always pick out the work done by boys whose caste had been employed in that particular work, and he further informed me that boys showed poor proficiency in work out of the line of their particular caste.

CHAPTER IX.

COFFEE PLANTING IN COORG.

THE British Province of Coorg consists of a mountainous and jungly tract of country with elevations of from about 2,700 to 3,809 feet. The last is the elevation of the capital, Mercara, the tableland of which, for a stretch of about 26 miles, averages about 3,500 feet. This little province lies, as the reader will see by a glance at the map, on the south-west border of Mysore, with which, since its annexation, it has always been connected, and the Resident of Mysore invariably holds the post of Commissioner of Coorg. The population of Coorg is just over 170,000, and its area is 1,583 square miles, or about one-fourth of the size of Yorkshire. But, though small in extent and population, its Rajah and people played an important part as our allies in the war with Tippoo, and a full account of the facts is given in the history of Coorg which has been published in the "Mysore and Coorg Gazetteer." The history of the country, however, which has been gathered up by various European writers, is by no means of an alluring character, and indeed, after the beginning of this century, a more disgusting record of cruelty and oppression it would be difficult to find in the annals of any country. But three things at least the record most distinctly proves. The first is (though this hardly requires any additional proof) that man, though capable of being the best, is also capable of being by far the worst of animals; the second is that, Coorg being a sample of most of India in the times preceding ours, the Hindoos were perfectly right in leaving few annals behind them; and the third is that the blessings of British rule far exceed anything that anyone could imagine who had not read something of the condition of things in India before we took possession of it, for we have not only conferred on the people immeasurable positive benefits, but relieved them from the barbarous rule of cruel oppressors. In the case of Coorg there can be no doubt that we allowed the Rajahs of that country to carry on their work of cruelty and oppression towards their subjects for much too long a period of time, and our failure to act can only be partially excused by the fact that we were, in connection with the war with Tippoo, under great obligation to the ancestor of the Rajah we deposed. However, his vile oppression and cruel murders, which exceed anything the reader could believe to be possible, could no longer be tolerated, and in 1834 he was deposed, and his country absorbed into the British Dominions. Since that date the general welfare of the country was of course insured, and much of it is now a thriving coffee field which, as I shall afterwards show, has been of the greatest benefit to Mysore, and the adjacent British territory. Of the history and cultivation of coffee in Coorg, and my visits to the province, I now propose to give some account.

After the planting season of 1857 I went with a brother planter for a change of air to Mangalore, and from thence we went to Cannanore—a military station about 200 miles further down the coast—and, after a short stay there, rode up the Ghauts into Coorg, where we found the planters busy clearing the forest. Three years before our arrival Mr. Fowler had opened the Mercara Estate, and in 1855 Mr. H. Mann, and Mr. Donald Stewart had begun work on the Sumpaji Ghaut, while Dr. Maxwell opened up the Periambadi Ghaut Estates in 1856, and in 1857 Mr.

Kaundinya founded a plantation in the Bamboo district which lies on the eastern side of Coorg. The first European plantation was, as we have seen, started in 1854, but for many years previously coffee cultivation had been carried on by natives in the Nalknaad District, though it seems to be quite uncertain as to when or how it was first introduced, or where the first seeds were obtained.

At first all seemed to be going well with coffee in Coorg, and for a good many years the fatal mistake of the planters in clearing down the whole forest, and leaving no shade over the coffee, was not decisively apparent, and from the lands that were thus cleared down on the above-mentioned Ghauts, which lie on the western side of the province, from 700 to 1,000 tons were picked annually when the coffee was at its best. But what in "the seventies" represented about £100,000 of valuable property, gradually became more and more unprofitable, till at last the estates were abandoned, and the land has now become covered with masses of Lentana (a crawling, climbing, thorny plant which has become a perfect plague in Coorg), amidst which may occasionally be seen the white walls of unroofed bungalows, and dismantled pulping houses, which testify to the melancholy ending of the work of the planters whom I found so busily engaged when, in 1857, I first entered Coorg.

Some attributed the failure to the Bug, some to the Borer, and to leaf disease, while others blamed the heaviness of the tropical rains, which washed away the valuable surface soil, the flight of which towards the western sea was much expedited by weeding with the mamoty (a digging hoe), which loosened the soil, and so prepared the way for its more rapid disappearance. And these causes no doubt hastened the end, but they were mainly results arising from one great cause—the neglect to supply shade for the coffee, and this again arose from the circumstance that most of the pioneer planters came from Ceylon where the coffee is planted in the open, and where shade is not required. And this failure, owing to the neglect of shade, had a most unfortunate effect, for it was owing to this that Coorg naturally acquired such a doubtful coffee reputation in the eyes of the uninformed public—a reputation which, as I shall afterwards show, arose not from any fault of the country as a coffee field, but solely from the fatal mistake of attempting to plant without providing shade for the coffee. And this mistake the planters, as we shall see, had great difficulty in shaking off, for when they saw the inevitable end approaching, and hastened to take up land in the eastern part of Coorg in what is known as the Bamboo district (because the jungle lands there consist very largely of forest trees interspersed with clumps of bamboos), they persisted in carrying their fatal Ceylon system with them, and Mr. Donald Stewart, called the Coffee King in Mincing Lane, who was a warm supporter of planting in the open, even issued, it is said, an order to his managers saying that if he found a single forest tree standing (the coffee around even a single tree would have proved him to be wrong) dismissal would follow. But nature proved to be too strong for Mr. Stewart and those who followed his example, and whole estates in the Bamboo district were practically exterminated by the Borer insect. At last the planters, warned by a long and bitter experience, gave way all along the line, and began to imitate the shade planters of Mysore, and shade is now as universal in Coorg as in Mysore, and under its protection the coffee in both countries thrives equally well. I may mention here that the Rev. G. Richter, who is now the second oldest resident in Coorg, took an active part in opening up the Bamboo district, and was for some time a partner in one of the estates. He has shown great zeal in endeavouring to introduce new products, such as tea, cocoa, ceara rubber, and vanilla. His manual of Coorg, I may add, is most interesting and exhaustive.[1]

Besides the first mentioned, and now abandoned coffee district, and the Bamboo district, there is the important district of North Coorg, which, though it has a smaller number of estates, certainly contains coffee that, so far as I am able to judge, it would be impossible to surpass.

There are, in all, at present in Coorg 130 European estates, with a total area of 32,323 acres (of which 20,000 are in the Bamboo district), and 6,207 native estates and gardens, aggregating in all 70,669 acres. The average production of coffee from all these sources is estimated by competent authorities at from 4,000 to 5,000 tons of coffee per annum, or of a probable annual value of from £250,000 to £300,000. The yield from a well cultivated estate averages from 3 to 4 cwt. of clean coffee per acre. Exceptional properties there are, of course, which give higher returns than this, and some could be quoted which give 6 to 7 cwt. on the average, while sensational figures might be quoted as regards some remarkable estates. But to give an account of such exceptional estates might convey a misleading idea of the general return to be obtained from coffee in Coorg, though I think it well to allude to the fact that better returns than those first mentioned can be obtained, and have been obtained, as it is always of value to know what particular pieces of land can do under the most favourable circumstances, as this opens up the important question as to whether it would not pay better to confine cultivation on an estate to a narrow area of the best soils and situations on it—a subject to which I shall more particularly refer later on in this chapter.

In the case of well cultivated estates, an expenditure of

[1] "Manual of Coorg," compiled by Rev. G. Richter, Principal, Government Central College, Mercara. Mangalore, 1870.

eighty rupees per acre is incurred on superintendence and field labour, and fifty rupees an acre on manures and their application, but in many European, and most native estates, a total expenditure for superintendence, labour and manures of about eighty rupees only is incurred, and the results obtained are, of course, proportionately smaller. The native gardens and plantations are, as a rule, worked on the principle of taking everything that can be got out of the land, and putting nothing into it. Were these worked on European principles, it is hardly necessary to say that the export of coffee from Coorg would be largely increased.

Cattle manure, bones, oil-cake and fish constitute the manures mainly used in Coorg. The first is universally recognized as being the most valuable for coffee, but the supply available in the Bamboo district (which contains, I may remind the reader, 20,000 out of the 32,323 acres under cultivation by Europeans), where grazing is scarce, is so small that planters have to depend to a great extent on the three last-named manures. Messrs. Matheson & Co., the owners of about 7,000 acres of coffee in Coorg, kept for some years in their employ an analytical chemist,[1] whose time was devoted to the analysis of soil, and the making of experiments on their estates, with the view of ascertaining what was best adapted for maintaining and improving their fertility. Salts of various kinds were experimented with, but, though the results from them were generally favourable, they were found to be too rapidly soluble for a climate so subject to heavy falls of rain. In the end, after many experiments, he came to the conclusion that the four above-mentioned manures were the best for the climate, and that the proportion applied

[1] The late Mr. William Pringle, who, after leaving Coorg, wrote in 1891, for the "Madras Mail," some interesting and suggestive papers on the cultivation of coffee.

should vary with the condition of the coffee. To illustrate this point I may add that in Coorg, bones and oil-cake are usually applied in the proportion of two of the latter to one of the former. If, however, a field has suffered badly from leaf disease (which destroys many of the leaves), or is not making wood as rapidly as it ought, it is customary to apply a larger proportion of oil-cake, or in some cases, to put down that manure without adding any bones. On the other hand, if there is a superabundance of wood, and it is desirable to throw the whole energies of the tree into the production of berries, then the proportion of bone manure is increased and that of oil-cake diminished.

In former times all manures were applied immediately after the crop was picked, and on estates where labour is scarce, or comes in late in the season, this system is still carried on. But from results actually obtained on estates in Coorg, it has now been proved that it is more advantageous to apply part of the manure immediately after crop, in order to strengthen the tree when the blossom showers fall (which they usually do in March and April), and to aid it in perfecting and setting the blossom, and a second portion after the heavy monsoon rains are over, in order to assist the tree in growing fresh wood, and in maturing the crop. The bones, oil-cake, and fish are usually mixed with burnt earth—a cubic yard to every five cwt. of the manure—and then scattered on the surface of the land around the stems of the trees, and forked in. The burnt earth, or indeed almost any good earth, makes an admirable addition to bones, oil-cake, and fish, for, though the first two, or the last two, furnish complete manure for coffee, they of course cannot ameliorate the physical condition of the soil, which, as I have fully shown in the chapter on manures, is often of more importance than its strictly speaking chemical condition. The burnt earth, in short, takes the place of cattle manure as a physical agent, and, for that purpose, I think that the soil is to be preferred to cattle manure, as the former would certainly be cheaper and more lasting in its effects in keeping the soil in a loose and easily workable condition. On the other hand, it must be considered that cattle manure would be more moisture-holding than ordinary earth, though not more so than jungle top-soil, and when first applied, would be perhaps more opening to the land, than burnt or ordinary earth, but if the red earth (Kemmannu), to which I have alluded in my chapter on manures, can be obtained, that, I know from experience, would be more cooling, and moisture-absorbing than cattle manure.

I now turn to a point of great general interest, and one which furnishes another illustration of what I dwelt upon at some length in my introductory chapter, the wide-spreading value arising from the introduction into India of English capital which, as I have shown, develops the agricultural resources of the country in ever-widening circles. At first in Coorg the adjacent province of Mysore was the only source of labour supply, but the increased prosperity of the labourer consequent upon ample employment and enhanced rates of wages, enabled him to take up land for the cultivation of cereal crops in the neighbourhood of his own village, and hence the supply of labour declined, those who came to work in the plantations came later in the season, and altogether the labour supply from Mysore became more uncertain every year. Planters consequently, as they had in Mysore itself, had to go further afield, and now draw labour to a large extent from the Madras Presidency, the labourers from which in turn will now have the means of developing the agricultural resources of their native villages. This is a point to which the attention of the Government cannot be too often drawn with the view of encouraging the opening up, by it, of every means of stimulating the employment of labour in India.

Coorg is now fairly well off for labour, and the old labour difficulties which used to be experienced have to a great extent disappeared. The average cost of Mysore labour—men, women, and children, and including the commission of the Maistries (as the men who collect and bring the labourers to the estates are called), is from 3 annas 6 pie to 4 annas a day (or say *5d.* to *6d.* a day, calculating the rupee at par, or *2s.*). In quite recent times the maistries, who obtained large sums from the planters to make advances to the coolies, sometimes absconded with the money and thereby great losses ensued. But a better class of maistries have arisen, and Messrs. Matheson and Co. have now, with the aid of their permanent European labour agent, established a system of private registration by which the antecedents, status, and resources of the maistries are duly recorded. And though the services of doubtful maistries cannot as yet be altogether dispensed with, a preference is of course given to those of well established reputation, and the class of maistries generally is beginning to understand and appreciate the system of registration, which has every prospect of becoming general, and will, I need hardly add, be of great advantage to planters. But if maistries sometimes swindle their employers, the former are often liable to be swindled by the coolies to whom the advances have been made, and until a system of compulsory Government registration of advances to coolies is introduced, as recommended in one of my chapters on coffee planting in Mysore, it will be impossible to put our peculiar system of giving advances to coolies on a reasonably safe footing.

The plantations in Coorg have suffered, and still suffer considerably from leaf disease and Borer, to both of which I have, for practical purposes, sufficiently alluded in the chapter on the diseases of coffee. The effects of the former, though entailing much injury on coffee in Coorg, have not been so fatal as in Ceylon, as the long stretches of dry weather, often of four or five months' duration, seem to kill off large numbers of the spores, and so mitigate the damage arising from the disease. Messrs. Matheson and Co., at the instance of the chemist previously mentioned, sent out Strawsoniser spray engines for the purpose of treating afflicted trees with various solutions, but, though good effects were noticeable on individual trees, it was found that to treat whole estates in this way was quite impracticable, both from the cost and the immense amount of labour that would be required, and this fatal obstacle to the use of such remedies has been amply proved in Ceylon. But in Coorg the Borer is much more to be dreaded than leaf disease, and its ravages are such that even on the best estates fully twenty-five per cent.[1] of the acreage is under supplies (*i.e.*, young plants to take the place of the old ones which have died), and the late Mr. Pringle—the chemist—was of opinion that the loss of crop from Borer was not less than 2 cwt. per acre per annum. Before the introduction of shade the total extermination of an estate was far from uncommon, the estate in the Bamboo district opened by Rev. H. A. Kaundinya in 1857 being the first to perish, and though, as we have seen, owing to the introduction of shade, the Borer has been largely brought into subjection, considerable damage still takes place from it. Neither trouble nor expense has been spared in order to find an antidote to this pest. Rubbing the stems with the view of destroying the eggs of the insect, and applying thereto

[1] I make this statement on the authority of Mr. Meynell (*vide* preface), and it is, no doubt, the result of his experience in the Bamboo district, but his estimate could hardly, I should say, apply to the estates I visited in North Coorg.

chemical ingredients have both been tried, but with very limited results. The late Mr. Pringle's antidote consisted of the application of two washes of alkali vat waste, costing five rupees an acre each, but, when carried into practice, the results were far from what he anticipated. Taking out the bored trees and burning them has proved the most effectual way of dealing with the pest, and would be productive of still better results if native neighbours would adopt the same practice. But as they will not adopt this practice, their plantations become nursery grounds for the propagation of the insect. Many planters in the Bamboo district pay 1 rupee per hundred for the Borer fly, and this results in a large number being caught, but it is not supposed that any appreciable effect has been produced from this practice.

There can be no doubt, it seems to me, that the primary cause of the existence of so much Borer was owing to the planters having at first planted in the open. This must have created an enormous supply of the insect, which found a splendid breeding ground in the conditions furnished by the planters, as is evidenced by the fact of whole estates having been exterminated by it, and it will require many years of judicious shading before this insect can be reduced within comparatively harmless limits. The reader will observe that I say judicious shading, and I will more fully explain what I mean by that expression when, later on in the chapter, I give an account of my tour through Coorg in 1891, and make some observations on the proper shading of coffee.

Most of the European estates in Coorg and many of the larger native plantations are held under what are called "The Waste Land Rules," under which land is put up to auction by the State at an upset price of 2 rupees per acre (10 rupees is the upset price in Mysore), plus the value of the timber, which adds somewhat to the price.

As a rule there is now considerable competition for land, and as much as 100 to 150 rupees has frequently to be paid per acre. The land so purchased is subject to no assessment up to the fourth year, but from the fourth to the ninth year 1 rupee is charged, and after that 2 rupees in perpetuity. The bulk of the land suitable for coffee has been taken up, though large extents that might be utilized are included in the State forests, and thus are not available to the public. Hence there is little room for extension, and openings for young men with capital are few and far between, so far as obtaining fresh forest is concerned, though of course opportunities occasionally occur for purchasing estates, or acquiring shares in them on various terms.

And here I would particularly call the attention of the Government to the following remarks on the reservation of land in Coorg for State forests, much of which, as we have seen, might be utilized for coffee.

When, as in former times in Coorg, the planters used no shade, many good arguments existed in favour of making very large reserves of forest land in order to prevent denudation, and its injurious effects on climate, and on the water supply of the rivers and the country generally. But when you merely replace the underwood of the forest with an underwood of coffee which completely covers the ground, and again shield this from drying winds and the burning sun by a complete covering of trees, either those of the original forest or others planted to take their place, the case is entirely altered, and from the coffee land thus shaded there is no more loss of water and soil (perhaps not so much loss of water, as great pains are taken to avert wash) than there was in the original forest, and the climatic and conservative effects of forests are therefore entirely undisturbed. Wherever, then, lands exist which are suitable for coffee planting under shade, they should certainly, in the interests of the country generally, and especially of the rapidly increasing population, be taken up for coffee, and the State forests be confined to those tracts which, from over heavy rainfall, or other causes, are unsuitable for coffee planting.

Other products, and especially cinchona, have received a fair amount of attention in Coorg, and the land on the Ghauts to the westward, where, as we have seen, the coffee plantations have been abandoned, proved to be well suited for the production of the commoner kinds of bark, and large extents of abandoned or semi-abandoned lands were planted with cinchonas. But when the prices of bark fell (whoever takes to growing a drug will soon realize the meaning of the phrase "a drug in the market"), the cultivation was no longer worthy of attention, and has practically died out. Ceara rubber also met with the same fate.

I may here mention that Messrs. Matheson and Co., who held no less than 7,000 out of the 20,000 acres occupied by Europeans in the Bamboo district, went to great expense in introducing coffee seed from Brazil, Venezuela, Costa Rica, and Jamaica, with the view of ascertaining whether coffee grown from the seed thus imported would be less susceptible to attacks of leaf disease. But, though the plants raised from these seeds are doing exceedingly well, it was found that they were also liable to be attacked by leaf disease, often before they were even out of the nursery, and in this respect proved to be neither better nor worse than the Coorg variety of coffee. A clearing of fifty acres has been entirely planted with coffee raised from Blue Mountain seed, but there is nothing in the appearance of the trees to show that they are not indigenous to the country.

Liberian coffee has been tried experimentally in several parts of Coorg, but I cannot learn that any results have been obtained which would tend to encourage its adoption as a substitute for the variety at present grown.

It is estimated that the Coorg planters employ at least 30,000 Mysore labourers in addition to local labourers and those from the Madras Presidency, and of the 30,000 in question Messrs. Matheson and Co. employ no less than about 5,000 for six to eight months of the year. The 30,000 coolies, with their maistries, draw from 12 to 15 lakhs of rupees per annum (from £120,000 to £150,000, estimating the rupee at par, and for the purposes of a labourer it goes nearly as far in India as when it was so) in wages, very nearly the whole of which eventually reaches Mysore either in payment for grain or as a surplus income which the labourers annually take with them when they return to their homes in Mysore. And as this capital is largely employed in developing the agricultural resources of the Mysore State, it is evident that anything that its Government could do—in the way of railway extension or otherwise—that would stimulate the employment of labour in Coorg would be of great advantage to the finances of Mysore. It is extremely interesting to follow the labour-spent capital of the planters of Coorg to its ultimate destination—to the western coast, to various parts of the Madras Presidency, and far away into the interior of Mysore, and to observe its effects on the country and its financial results. I am not in a position to say exactly what should be done in the way of railways for Coorg, but I trust I have sufficiently shown that the British and Mysore Governments are equally interested in doing all they can, in the way of railway communication and new and improved roads, to develop and encourage the planting resources of Coorg.

The last visit I paid to Coorg was in October, 1891, immediately after the breaking up of the Representative Assembly at Mysore, a full account of which I have given in a previous chapter. I left Mysore on the morning of Tuesday, October 20th, and on the first day drove to Hunsur, a town of between four and five thousand inhabitants, which lies twenty-eight miles to the west of Mysore city. At this place are the extensive coffee works and manure preparing establishment of Messrs. Matheson and Co., by whose manager I was most hospitably and agreeably entertained. Rather an interesting incident in connection with a panther had once occurred at his house, and as this illustrates what I have previously mentioned as to the (to man) innocuous character of this animal, it may not be uninteresting to give an account of what occurred. The circumstances were these.

One night my hostess, some time after retiring to rest, heard a noise in the open veranda which runs round the side of the bungalow just outside her bedroom. She got up, and, taking a lamp in her hand, went round a corner of the building in the direction of the noise, and just as she turned the corner in question there fell upon her astonished vision the spectacle of a panther, which at the moment was busily engaged in devouring the family cat. When the panther saw the lady he tried to make off along the veranda (which at that point was shut in at the side by a trellis-work), but at the moment of his flight the cook, who had also heard the noise, appeared at the opposite end of the veranda with a lamp in his hand. The panther then turned back in the direction of the lady, who stood spell-bound with the lamp in her hand, and as the cook, apparently equally spell-bound, remained stationary with his lamp, the panther, being thus as it were between two fires, lay down under a table which was placed against the wall of the veranda. At last he got up, made a move in the direction of the cook, and then changing his mind, rushed past the lady, and thus made his escape. Panthers seem to be numerous about Hunsur, and I heard another interesting story of their boldness, which I have not space to give, from a neighbour of my host.

After staying for a day at Hunsur, I drove, on October 22nd, to Titimutty, a small village on the frontier of Coorg, where I was met by Mr. Rose, of Hill Grove Estate, who drove me to his plantation near Polibetta, which is in the Bamboo district previously alluded to as containing about two-thirds of the European plantations in Coorg. Shortly after leaving Titimutty we drove through coffee on both sides of the road, and, though I spent four days in the district, and was constantly on the move, I was never once out of sight of coffee, as the plantations lie in a continuous block, and, as they are all thoroughly shaded, sometimes by the original forest trees, and sometimes by trees planted for shade, the general effect is that you are travelling through a forest of which coffee is the underwood—a forest lying on gently undulating ground from which nothing can be seen of the surrounding country. As the bungalows of the planters are of course surrounded by coffee and shade trees, they have necessarily an extremely shut-in appearance. But this rather *triste* effect might be obviated (and I have with good effect obviated it in the case of a bungalow which lies in the centre of an estate of my own in Mysore) by cutting vistas here and there through the shade trees through which peeps may be had of distant hills. This may seem to be a point of little practical value, but, as I have shown in a previous chapter, the amenities of an estate are of value, and are likely to become more so when the desirable nature of shade coffee property is more widely known. The bungalows in the Bamboo district are very comfortable, most of them having tennis grounds, and if the vistas I have suggested were cut out, their attractiveness would be much enhanced. But if the Bamboo district has not the scenic advantages of plantations in other parts of Coorg and in Mysore, these are much compensated for by the close proximity of one plantation to another, and I was told that at certain seasons there was generally a well-attended lawn tennis party on every day of the week. There is besides, in the centre of the district, a comfortable club where balls and dances are occasionally given. In short, the Bamboo district has features of its own which make it entirely different from any planting district in India. From being so much shut in, it might, at first sight, be supposed to be not a very healthy district, but I heard no complaints on that score, nor, from the appearance of the planters, would it have occurred to me that the district was at all unhealthy. On the evening of my arrival there was a dinner-party, at which four ladies were present, and later on there was music and singing, and all the accompaniments of a pleasant social life. So much do coffee districts vary in India, that the party was to me a startling surprise, which the reader may easily understand when I mention that, after leaving the most northerly plantation in Coorg and entering my district of Manjarabad, there is only one resident lady to be found there, and it is not till you reach the northern district of Mysore, some sixty miles further, that ladies, in the plural, again commence, though even there they do not exist to a very serious extent.

On the afternoon of the day of my arrival I walked round my host's estate, which carried an excellent crop, and also visited a neighbouring property. On the following morning I drove to the Dubarri estate, and walked round part of it, and in the afternoon visited the club—a comfortable, and in every respect suitable, building which, as I mentioned, is occasionally used for dances. I also visited the co-operative store, which contained a large supply of various articles. The church, which was close to the club, had been recently built, at a cost of 5,000 rupees, but, when I saw it, the interior was not quite finished.

I may mention that in the Bamboo district there is a resident doctor who is employed by the various estates. Later on in the afternoon I rode from the club with Mr. William Davies to the Mattada Kadu estate (Messrs. Matheson and Co.'s property), of which he is manager, and rode through coffee all the way to the bungalow. I was most kindly entertained by Mr. Davies, who had a party of the neighbouring planters to meet me at dinner, after which we had much talk on the subject in which we were all mutually interested. On the following morning I awoke early, and was rather surprised, shortly after daylight, to hear the names of the coolies called over from the check-roll, as, though early hours were kept in the old days in Mysore, we have now become considerably later, owing, I surmise, to feeling that in these labour-competing days we are not as completely master as we once were. After a small breakfast I rode through the estate, guided by Mr. Davies, who was accompanied by two of his guests of the night before, and we then passed into the Nullagottay estate (all Messrs. Matheson's), after which we entered into Whust Nullagottay, and went to the bungalow from which (there is always an exception) there is a fine view of the Brahmagiri Hills. After a very short stay we again mounted, and presently passed into the Whoshully estate, and finally arrived, after riding through that property, at about midday at Mr. Robinson's bungalow, where we had breakfast. Mr. Rose came over in the afternoon, and we rode home to Hill Grove through Messrs. Matheson's estate which had been bought from Mr. Minchin, besides visiting the Hope estate. I thus rode through coffee for nearly the entire day. On the following day I went over another adjacent property, and on the day after, Monday, October 26th, started for Mercara, the capital of Coorg. I drove by way of Siddapur, paid a short visit to Cannon Kadu estate, and arrived at Abiel,

Mr. Martin's estate, at about midday, rode round his estate in the afternoon, and then drove on to Mr. E. Meynell's charming home—the Retreat—which is about a mile from the town of Mercara.

I was particularly struck with the arrangements of this house, as it was a thoroughly English-looking home in every respect, and I only wish I could give a plan of it as a model for a residence in the hill and planting districts of India. The front veranda was inclosed with glass, and lined with flowers in pots, and from the centre of this projected a conservatory, at the end of which was the front door. You thus, after driving up to the house, walked through a conservatory into the inclosed veranda, and this not only gave a very pretty effect, but was practically useful by keeping carriages, with their attendant dust and disagreeables, at a sufficient distance from the veranda. My hostess very kindly permitted me to see the kitchen arrangements. These, as well as the storerooms, were in a wing projecting from the back of the bungalow. The kitchen, which consisted of a separate room, with a single door, was furnished with a Wilson range, and there was no door between the kitchen and the scullery. The latter was at the outside edge of the wing, and was entered by its own door—an arrangement, by the way, that might be practised with advantage in this country, as a connecting door is liable to admit smells from the scullery into the kitchen. The reader will, I trust, excuse the mention of these apparently trivial matters, but as I strongly suspect that much of the ill-health in India is due to the dirt and horrors of the Indian cook-room, which is usually at a little distance from the bungalow, and turned into a general lounge for the servants, I think it well to show that, with a little contrivance and attention, as great a degree of order and cleanliness may exist in India as in any other portion of the globe.

On the following day I called on Mr. Mann, son of one of the pioneer planters of 1855, and inspected an interesting coffee garden of four acres which is close to his bungalow in Mercara. Some of the coffee trees were planted thirty and others forty years ago, and they have given for many years fifteen hundredweight an acre on the average, and though many of the trees were evidently suffering from the effects of overbearing, there seemed no reason why they should not continue to bear good crops for an indefinite period of time. Estimating the value of the coffee at 80*s*. a hundredweight, the produce of an acre would be worth £60, of 100 acres £6,000, and allowing one-half for expenses—a very liberal estimate—there would be a clear income of £3,000 a year from 100 acres of such coffee. As 100 acres of land so situated—it was flat, lay in a hollow, and was well sheltered—could not be obtained, it might seem that an account of this garden could be of no practical value. But the garden in question raises one very important point in the mind, and that is whether it would not be better to abandon all inferior soils and situations on an estate, and concentrate all the labour and manurial resources on a more limited area, every operation on which could be carried out exactly at the right moment. This is a highly important question which I state here for the consideration of planters.

After spending two pleasant days at the Retreat, I bade my kind host and hostess good-bye (I have thanked Mr. Meynell, who I may mention represents Messrs. Matheson's large interests in Coorg, in the preface for the valuable information he subsequently sent me as regards planting in Coorg), and went on my way towards my home in Mysore, and stayed first at the Hallery estate, which is about six miles from Mercara, and is the property of my friend Mr. Mangles. The approach to the bungalow through the coffee is very pretty; the building stands at the head of a slope, and commands a fine and extensive view of the country and the distant hills. The amenities here had been well attended to: below the front of the bungalow terraces edged with balustrades had been cut, and formed into flower gardens, and I was glad to see that, in parts of the plantation, from which good views could be had, there were seats. I may observe here that there is a great want in plantations of seats, which are now the more needed as all logs in the old plantations have of course disappeared. Near the bungalow is an excellent stable, well paved, and quite in English style. On the following morning I went with Mr. Sprott, who is in charge of Mr. Mangles's estate, to visit his Santigherry property, some seven miles distant, and on the way there went on the left of the road through a plantation belonging to Messrs. Macpherson and Ainslie. After this we re-entered the main road, passed the village of Santikoopa, and then entered and went round the estate we had come to visit. On the way home we diverged to the left and went through Mr. Murray Ainslie's estate, and round by an estate owned by Mr. Campbell, and finally arrived at Hallery at about half-past twelve. In the afternoon I went round part of the estate, which I had already seen something of on the day of my arrival.

Early the following morning, after bidding good-bye to the host and hostess who had so kindly entertained me, I started on my journey northwards, and after a troublesome and trying drive (for my horses), in which two rivers had to be crossed by ferry boats, and much deep unmetalled road struggled through, I arrived at 12.30 at Coovercolley—another estate of Mr. Mangles's—where I was kindly entertained by Mr. and Mrs. Trelawney (Mr. Trelawney manages this fine property). The bungalow here is particularly comfortable, and had the great advantage of a very wide open veranda. On the right of the approach to the bungalow was a neatly trimmed shoe flower hedge, which had a very pretty effect, and, as at Hallery, terraces had been cut in front for a flower garden. From the front of the bungalow there is an extensive view of much of the Coorg country, and I was particularly struck by its continuous jungly character, and with its great contrast to the Mysore country to the north, which is not so much a jungly country, as an open grass country studded with occasional wood, and park-like groups of trees. On the afternoon of my arrival I rode round part of this fine estate, and inspected other parts of it on the following morning and evening. On the next morning I started at a quarter to six, and after driving about twenty-four miles, crossed the frontier, and entered Manjarabad—the southernmost coffee district of Mysore. The northernmost part of Coorg consists of a long tongue of land which projects into Mysore, and the scenery, in its beautiful, open, and park-like character, naturally resembles that of Manjarabad.

On my visit to Coorg I look back with pleasure. It was, indeed, extremely enjoyable and instructive, and I cannot help regretting the fact that, owing to the nature of their duties, planters are obliged to remain so continuously at home; and then, of course, when they can get away, they naturally go for change of air and scene anywhere out of the coffee districts. The result of this is that the planters of the north of Mysore see little of those in the south, and that neither have any intercourse with Coorg, and that, in consequence, much valuable interchange of views and experiences that might otherwise take place cannot now do so. Had such intercourse existed, many of the mistakes made in Coorg as regards shade would probably have been avoided, and much loss of money averted.

The reader will have noticed that I have hitherto made no observations on the coffee I saw in Coorg, my reason for not doing so being that I thought they might be more conveniently reserved for the close of the chapter. I am glad that in the course of my observations I shall have much to say in praise of the state of coffee in Coorg, and if I should seem to be a little free in my remarks as to the management of shade, I trust that my Coorg readers will bear in mind that my experience of trees planted as shade to supply the place of original forest trees removed is the oldest in India, and stretches back to the year 1857, and that it requires a very long time, as they will see by consulting the chapter on shade, before all the points connected with shade trees can be proved with certainty. That mistakes as regards shade should have been made in Coorg, where shade experience is comparatively recent, is not at all surprising; in former times numerous mistakes were made in Mysore, and have only been rectified by long experience and observation.

My general impression on going through the Bamboo district of Coorg was that it contains a certain proportion of land of poor character (and this can be said of most coffee districts) which should never have been opened, but that there are many excellent and valuable estates, though it was plain to me that, from the more weakly, or perhaps I should rather say less robust, character of the shoots, and the appearance of the soil, it had, as a rule, much less growing power in it, and would consequently require more manure, than the deep and heavier soils of Mysore. But these soils in the Bamboo district, though lighter in character, are of course (and this is a fact of no small importance) more easily worked than those of Mysore. The next point that attracted my attention was the shade, and of the numerous estates that I saw in the Bamboo district there were only two that at all came up to my idea of what a well shaded property ought to be. I could see little signs of the shade being varied in kind and quantity to suit the various aspects, and many trees were preserved which were merely throwing shadow, not on to the coffee, but on to adjacent trees. Then I found that in one excellent piece of young coffee the shade had been planted in lines running from east to west, instead of being closely planted in lines from north to south (*vide* chapter on shade). The shade, too, generally speaking, was far too largely composed of one kind of tree,—the Attí-mara (*Ficus glomerata*)—and finally this tree, the defects of which I have remarked upon in my chapter on shade, was badly managed by being trimmed up to a considerable height above the ground. The result of this was that on land on which there was an enormous number of trees there was far too little shade, and a forester fresh from England would never have imagined that the planters had intended to grow umbrageous trees for the double purpose of lowering the temperature of the plantation and sheltering the coffee from sun and parching winds, but would have supposed that they were engaged in growing timber for sale. I saw land which, I feel sure, had at least three times the number of trees that would have been sufficient to shade it fully, had they been properly treated. Such a number of trees throw out, of course, a corresponding number of large roots, and one planter told me that in some instances coffee was being killed by the masses of Attí root in the land. As regards shade, then, there is much room for improvement in Coorg, and especial attention should be paid to this in the Bamboo district which has suffered so much from Borer. This pest, we know, thrives best under warm and dry conditions, and it is therefore of great importance that the kinds of shade most recommended in my chapter on shade should be freely planted, and other kinds gradually removed.

There was a very good crop on the trees when I passed through Coorg—one that, when picked, quite exceeded the expectations of the planters—and I saw two estates which had at once a good crop on the trees, leaves of good, well-fed looking colour, and a show of wood giving promise of an equally good crop for the following year; and it says well for cultivation in Coorg that any estate could show this, for the tendency of coffee, as of most fruit trees, is to give heavy and light crops alternately. As it is important to know the manures that were used to produce such results, I may mention that on one of these estates 6 cwt. of castor cake and 3 cwt. of bones had been applied the previous year, and for the four preceding years 2 cwt. of castor cake and 1 cwt. of bone had been used, but, in the opinion of the manager, the latter application had proved too small. On the other estate one-third of a bushel of cattle manure per tree, and from 7 cwt. to 10 cwt. of bones had been applied once in three years, and composts also had been used to a considerable extent. These were formed first of a layer of vegetable rubbish, then fresh pulp and lime, and lastly a layer of soil. The estate last referred to, on which the cattle manure, bones and compost had been used, belongs to Mr. Mangles—his Coovercolley estate—and is certainly the finest I ever saw, if we take into consideration the state of the soil, the colour of the foliage, and the evident prospect of continuously good crops. So well fed, indeed, was the land with nitrogen, that an application of nitrate of soda produced no perceptible effect on the trees. The land was probably over supplied with phosphoric acid, and an analysis of the soil would be of practical value, for if, as I have good reason to surmise, there is a very large supply of phosphoric acid in the soil, the use of bones might be suspended for some years, and a light application of lime used instead. Ten acres, at any rate, might be tried as an experiment. I was shown one piece of coffee which had been manured, when it was two years old, with cattle manure, and this piece had remained perceptibly superior ever since. On this estate 600 cattle are kept for the sake of their manure. I would suggest that the proprietor might, on say ten acres, discontinue the use of cattle manure, and, as an experiment, apply dressings of jungle top-soil instead, or the red earth alluded to in my chapter on manures, should that be available. The experiment might be valuable to the proprietor and to planters in general. Cattle manure is very expensive, and when 12 to 14 tons per acre—some fairly well rotted and some slightly so—were used in Coorg on one estate the cost was 72 rupees an acre, including cost of application.

In bringing these brief remarks to a close, I may observe that I formed a very high opinion of coffee in Coorg, and I feel confident that if the shade were remodelled on the system recommended in my chapter on that subject, the losses from Borer and leaf disease would be largely diminished, and a great general inprovement in the coffee take place. We have experienced such results from improved shade in Mysore, and there can be no doubt that similar results will follow in Coorg. In remodelling the shade system, all light and dry soils should be first attended to and planted up with trees which give an ample and cool shade. The treatment of other parts of plantations may be postponed.

As regards the profits that may reasonably be expected from well managed and well situated estates in Coorg, I am happy to say that I have obtained from a friend the returns from his estates for the last ten years, and as his properties are of large extent, the return may be regarded as a very reliable one, more especially as the prices for three years of the period were very low. The average yield per acre was 4 cwt. 1 qr. 7 lbs.; the expenses £9 4*s*. 2*d*., and the profits per acre £7 8*s*. 6*d*.

I only wish that, in conclusion, I could give as favourable an account of the prospects of sport in Coorg as I can of its coffee. Twenty-five years ago there was good big game shooting, but the absence of game laws, and the indiscriminate destruction of does, fawns, and cow bisons by the natives, at every season of the year, have changed all that, and it is with a melancholy smile that one reads in the "Coorg Gazetteer" that the Coorgs are such ardent sportsmen that they have hardly left a head of game in the country. But the first sign of advanced civilization—the intelligent preservation of wild animals—has begun, or will shortly be begun, in the enlightened state of Mysore, and I trust that its good example may soon be followed in Coorg, and all parts of India. With the aid of preservation game will soon increase in the more remote forests into which it has been driven back, and from thence spread into other parts of the country.

CHAPTER X.

COFFEE PLANTING IN MYSORE.

AFTER a long and attentive observation of the various occupations of life, I have no hesitation in saying that, for one who has to earn his bread somewhere, the life of a planter in Mysore, if not the very pleasantest and most interesting (and as far as my own experience goes it is both) in the world, is assuredly one of the most agreeable occupations that anyone of intelligence, industry, and active habits, and fond of sport and an independent and open-air life, could betake himself to. It will be observed that I place intelligence in the van, and I do so because, though there is some truth in the native proverb which declares that, "with plenty of manure even an idiot may be a successful agriculturist," I know of no occupation that calls for a greater degree of intelligence and steady application than that of a planter in Mysore, or any district where shade trees are required. For where the planter has only to deal, as he has in Ceylon, with the coffee on his land and nothing else, the business, though even then of course requiring considerable skill and intelligence, is comparatively speaking a simple one. But in Mysore the necessity of providing shade for the coffee gives us at once an additional and highly complicated business in the planting and management of the shade trees, and their selection and distribution to suit the various soils, aspects and gradients we have to deal with. Then the fact of having shade trees, which of course take up much of the manure intended for the coffee, makes the application of the manure, and especially the quantity to be put down at a time, a matter of constant doubt, for on the one hand, how much do the shade trees not rob us of, and on the other hand, how much do they not return to the land by their fallen leaves? Then should we not manure and cultivate in a different manner and degree the coffee under the direct shade of the trees, and the coffee in the open spaces between them? Such are some of the numerous points connected with coffee planting under shade, to which I briefly allude at the outset in order to show those who wish to plant coffee that a high degree of intelligence, and power of observation, are required to make a successful planter. Then it must be considered further that a colloquial knowledge of the Kanarese language must be acquired—a language which, from its admixture of ancient and modern Kanarese, the variation in the accent, and the words in common use in various parts of the country, is generally considered to be the most difficult in India. And, as will be seen further on, it requires no small amount of study and observation in order to determine how best to lay out money in the purchase or manufacture of manures. There is also occasion for much tact, firmness, and temper, in dealing with the labourers and overseers on the estates, and also the native population with which nearly all the estates in Mysore are surrounded. Then much tact and judgment is required in dealing with the Government officials. Other points might also be added, but I have probably said enough to caution those who may be inclined to embark in coffee planting in Mysore, against assuming, as has hitherto been too often done, that it is a business which may be managed by people of inferior capacity.

I have said that the occupation is an agreeable one,

and may add that, though the life of a planter involves much attention to his business, there is no really hard work in the sense that there is hard work in the colonies, and, from the coffee being in shade, there is no exposure to the sun, while as all the preparation of the crop is done by agents on the coast, there is none of that indoor factory work which tea planters have to undertake. Then the climate, taking it all the year round, is distinctly an agreeable one,—an exquisitely fine one in the winter, never disagreeably warm in the hot weather, owing to the coffee districts being under the influence of breezes from the western sea, only disagreeably wet in the monsoon, though then the climate is so fresh and healthy, that many find that season of the year to be by no means unpleasant. Besides, during the worst part of the wet season, there is comparatively little to do, and the owner of an estate can then leave home for change of air and scene. As regards the healthiness of Mysore, I can only say that everything depends on the discretion of the individual. If he chooses to take reasonable care of himself, experience shows that the climate is a decidedly healthy one, but if he chooses to expose himself unnecessarily, and fails to take those precautions as regards food, and against chills which all sensible people do, then he will be pretty sure to get fever. I may mention that the elevations of the coffee estates vary from 2,800 to about 4,000 feet above the level of the sea, which partly accounts for the temperate nature of the climate, though this of course is, as I have previously pointed out, very largely controlled and improved by the estates being under the influence of the charming sea-breezes of the Western Ghauts. And if the planter wishes to avoid the hot weather altogether, he has only to go to Ootacamund, 7,000 feet above sea-level, where he will not only come in for a delightful climate, but for the Ootacamund season. April and May may be pleasantly spent there, and when the monsoon begins in June, the planter who desires to avoid it can go to Bangalore, where he will be in time for the season there, and he can afterwards return to his estate in September. This is a change I can recommend from practical experience. Or should a change to England be preferred, the planter should leave India about the end of April, and return in October. Such changes as these of course are only to be thought of when the planter has made his way in the world; and I only allude to them here to show that he may personally see to the carrying out of all the important operations from October till April, and either spend the remainder of his time under most agreeable circumstances in India, or pass the summer and autumn in England. In former days such changes could not reasonably have been contemplated, owing partly to the time taken up in travelling, and partly to the cost, but we now have railways within thirty to sixty miles of the various plantations, and it is certain that at no very distant date these distances will be halved, and that we shall then be within seventeen to eighteen days of London—at present we may be said to be within eighteen to nineteen days of it. In expense the cost has been halved; a first-class return ticket from Bombay to London may now be had for £90, and on other lines of steamers the rates are lower. But it is now time to turn from matters of detail to consider the advantages of coffee in Mysore, as a good, safe, and permanent investment, and in order to show that the two last mentioned statements are well founded, I have obtained some details which will show the probable profits of coffee in Mysore. For obvious reasons I withhold the names of the estates. I have said that the investment is a permanent one, and by this I mean that, unless ruined by profound and incredible stupidity, a well shaded coffee estate in Mysore will last as long as the world will, or at any rate as long as the inhabitants of it choose to drink coffee, and in confirmation of this opinion, I may mention that one of the most flourishing pieces of coffee I have ever seen in Mysore was planted on land first opened about ninety-five years ago, and which was replanted about seventy years after it was first opened. I can also point to land opened in 1857, and which has in recent years been replanted with the new variety of coffee imported from Coorg, and, as the owner of it said to me last year when we were going round the property, "The estate is now looking better than you have ever seen it." But all the old estates in Mysore that were planted in the proper coffee zone are in existence now, and many of them look better than they ever did. The durability of coffee property in Mysore, then, is, as we have seen, not a subject of speculation, but an ascertained fact, and I now proceed to show that it is as profitable as it is durable.

The first case I have to give relates to coffee property purchased by a friend of mine with money borrowed at eight per cent. interest, and with his permission I publish an account of his investment, as it not only shows what has been done in Mysore in the face of great difficulties, but illustrates the profits that may be expected from a property that is well managed, and well situated as regards soil and climate. In 1876, then, he purchased a native estate of 240 acres of good coffee land, of which 180 acres had been very irregularly planted with "chick" coffee (the original Mysore plant). The total cost amounted to 98,000 rupees, which sum was borrowed at eight per cent. By 1880 the loan was reduced, from the profits of the coffee, by about 30,000 rupees, and my friend then purchased an adjoining native estate of 163 acres, sixty of which were also very irregularly planted with chick coffee. The price was 13,250 rupees, which he also borrowed at eight per cent. The total amount borrowed was thus 111,250 rupees, and the total coffee land was 403 acres. Up to about this time the chick coffee had done fairly well, and by 1880 the loan, as we have seen, was reduced by 30,000 rupees, but soon afterwards this variety of coffee plant began rapidly to deteriorate all over the district, and estates like my friend's, which had hitherto given satisfactory profits, did but little more than pay their working expenses. But, luckily for himself, my friend, directly after the purchase of each estate, began to plant them with the Coorg kind of coffee (afterwards fully alluded to in this chapter) which had been recently introduced, and, as the old chick trees were from six to seven feet high, and had no lower branches, they did not for some time interfere with the progress of the Coorg plants, and yielded enough to pay expenses. As the Coorg plants came into bearing the old chick plants were removed, and in 1887-88 nearly ninety tons of coffee were picked, and by that year the whole debt, principal and interest, was paid off, and a considerable balance was left over to my friend's credit. In 1889-90 the property gave him a clear profit of £3,350, and it has done well ever since. Thus with all these tremendous difficulties to contend with, and in the face of the loss of all the old coffee, and after having to replant the whole property at great expense, my friend found himself in the possession of an estate, free of all debt, capable of yielding good annual profits. And it must be remembered, further, that this result was obtained, not from virgin forest land exclusively, but from land the greater part of which consisted of old native plantations.

There are, I need hardly say, no means of ascertaining the profits that may be expected from coffee in Mysore, but the following analysis of a Manjarabad estate of 400 acres under cultivation, which has been supplied to me by a friend, will form a fair guide to what may be reasonably expected from a Mysore estate where the management is good. In the case in question, the average crop for the last five years, has been $3\frac{3}{4}$ cwt. an acre. The expenses were $111\frac{1}{2}$ rupees an acre, and the average profit $111\frac{1}{10}$ rupees per acre per annum, or rather over £7 2*s.* 6*d.* an acre. I may add that I consider this a fair average estimate of what may be expected in Mysore on a well managed estate, as a considerable proportion of the land in question is of decidedly inferior quality. I have no special details to give from the northern part of Mysore, but I am informed by a planter of experience, who resides in that part of the country that, from a good estate of 200 acres, a profit of from £1,500 to £2,000 a year may be counted on.

We have seen that the life is attractive, that coffee property is durable and profitable, and the reputation of the coffee is not exceeded by any coffee in the world, and, as I shall show further on, the plant is singularly free, when properly shaded and worked, from risk in any form, or pests of any kind. Nothing, in short, in the world would appear to be more desirable as a source of investment than coffee in Mysore, for those who are prepared to understand and look after it. And with all these alluring advantages, which I have, I believe, most accurately described, it might naturally be supposed that coffee property in Mysore could be readily disposed of on advantageous terms to the seller. As a matter of fact, it is quite unsalable at any price that would be at all satisfactory to the owners. The explanation of this is very simple. Those who are working their own estates on the spot seldom command enough capital to invest in new estates, or do not care to extend their property, while capitalists at a distance, have, from the absence of information, no means of judging as to whether coffee in Mysore is a good investment or not. Instead, then, of accurate, or fairly accurate, accounts to rely on, we have nothing but vague and misleading statements and reports, which often affect most injuriously industries of sound and thriving character, and, as an instance in point, I may mention that, from what I had heard of coffee in Coorg (to which I have devoted a chapter), I should have been fully prepared, had I not learnt to regard all such reports with suspicion, to find a district on the high road to ruin. As it was, I was certainly prepared, and, indeed, expected to find, coffee in Coorg in a doubtful position. That precisely the reverse proved to be the case was a most agreeable surprise to me. One of my informants dismissed the whole matter thus. Coffee in Ceylon, he said, has gone with leaf disease, Wynaad (the district in the Madras Presidency, south of Coorg) is following, Coorg will go next, and Mysore last. Ceylon certainly has gone, Wynaad I will not pronounce upon, as I have not visited the estates in that district, but that Coorg and Mysore with their shade grown coffee will go with leaf disease is a mere groundless assertion, as the reader will, I hope, admit when I come to treat, in its proper place, of leaf disease and the effect of shade in limiting its amount, and controlling its injurious effects. And so far had these reports gone, and so thoroughly do the public at home connect coffee with Ceylon, and Ceylon alone, that a most thriving Mysore planter told me that, when he visited England, he now took good care to conceal his occupation, as he found that when he mentioned he was a coffee planter, people concluded at once that he was ruined. It is, then, most necessary to lay all the facts connected with coffee in Mysore before the public, with the view of placing our industry in its legitimate position, and I therefore make no apology for having gone into this branch of my subject with considerable minuteness. But it is now time to address myself particularly to the history and cultivation of coffee in Mysore, and to other matters in which the planters are directly or indirectly interested, and first of all it may not be uninteresting if I say a few words as to the introduction of the plant into India, or at any rate as to the earliest notices I can find on the subject.

The earliest notice I can find of coffee in India is contained in a Dutch work entitled "Letters from Malabar," by Jacob Canter Visscher, chaplain at Cochin. This collection of letters has been translated by Major Drury, or rather at his instance, and as the date of the Dutch editor's preface is 1743, it is evident that the coffee plant must have at least been introduced five or six years earlier, but the date of its introduction is not mentioned, and we are merely informed, at page 160, that "the coffee shrub is planted in gardens for pleasure and yields plenty of fruit, which attains a proper degree of ripeness. But it has not the refined taste of the Mocha coffee. . . . An entire new plantation has been laid out in Ceylon." The plant, however, though introduced at that early period, does not seem to have met with much attention in India, and I can find no other allusion to coffee in Indian books till we come to Heyne's Tracts, which were published in 1800, and we are there merely told that coffee was sold in the bazaars of Bangalore and Seringapatam.

Turning next to the history of coffee in Mysore, we find that there is no official record of either plant or planting further back than the year 1822, which is not very surprising, as it was only placed under British rule in 1831; but tradition in these cases seldom fails to supply some story which is suitable enough, and it may after all be quite true that, as reported, a Mussulman pilgrim, about two hundred years ago, returned from Arabia with seven beans which he planted round his mutt (temple) on the Bababudan hills in the northern part of Mysore, near which some very old trees may still be seen, and that from these beans all the coffee in Mysore has descended. But, though the plant may have been introduced at this early period, I think it improbable that anything in the shape of plantations existed before about the close of the last century. And, though the plant has been known for such a number of years, it is not a little remarkable that coffee has only come into use by the natives who grow it in recent years, and when I first settled in Mysore, in 1856, I was repeatedly asked by the farmers of the country whether we ate the berry, and of what use it could possibly be. And even now, from all that I can learn, coffee is rarely used by the natives in the coffee growing districts, though I am informed that it is so to a considerable extent in the towns of the province.

I have alluded to the tradition of coffee being first introduced into Mysore by a Mussulman pilgrim about two hundred years ago, and the species of coffee that was introduced then, or at some subsequent period, was the only one known in Mysore when I entered the province in 1855. This plant was finally called the "Chick" variety of coffee, and the name was taken, I believe, from the town of Chickmaglur, which lies close to the original Mysore home of the coffee plant. This variety had thriven well and promised to do so for an indefinite period of time, but towards the end of 1866, and during the three succeeding years, we had dry hot seasons, which caused a general attack of the Borer insect, and at about the same time there occurred a general decline in the constitution of the trees, which, though no doubt greatly hastened in the majority of instances by the Borer, of which the reader will find a particular account in a subsequent chapter, has never been explained, and so serious was this decline that, had we been dependent wholly on the original Mysore variety, it is the opinion of one of our most experienced planters that, to use his own words, "there would have been an end of coffee planting in Mysore except in the case of a few elevated tracts on the Bababudan range of hills." But, most fortunately for the planters, the Government, and the people of Mysore, Mr. Stanley Jupp—a South Mysore planter—took in 1870 a trip into Coorg, which lies on the south-west of Mysore, and was so favourably impressed with the variety of coffee grown there that he recommended that experiments should be made with it in Mysore, and in 1871 experiments on a considerable scale were made with carefully selected seed which was obtained from Coorg by Messrs. R. A. and Graham Anderson, Mr. Brooke Mockett, and Mr. Arthur Jupp. The experiments turned out to be a remarkable success, the young plants raised from the imported seed grew with extraordinary vigour, and it was soon found that the new variety would grow and crop well, and even on land on which all attempts to reproduce the "Chick" variety had utterly failed. Then this sinking industry rose almost as suddenly as it had fallen; old and abandoned estates, and every available acre of forest, and even scrub, were planted up, and land which used to change hands at from 5 to 10 rupees an acre was eagerly bought in at twelve times these amounts. But there was still some anxiety felt as regards the new variety, or rather the produce of it, for when we took it to market the brokers at once objected and said, "We are not going to give you Mysore prices for Coorg coffee." But it was found, as had been anticipated by many experienced planters, that as the trees from Coorg seed aged the produce each year assimilated more and more in appearance and quality to that of the old Mysore plant, which is still grown on some estates in North Mysore, and some years ago I even obtained a slightly higher price for my coffee from the new variety than a friend had obtained for coffee of the old "Chick" kind. The coffee industry of Mysore is now established on a thoroughly sound basis. We have a plant which crops more regularly and heavily than the old variety, and which is in every respect satisfactory, and the produce of it has so improved under the influence of the soil and climate of Mysore, that, with the exception of the estates which produce the long-established brand of "Cannon's Mysore," and perhaps a few other estates on the Baba-budans which have retained the original "Chick" variety of coffee, there is little difference in value between the produce of Coorg plants which have been long established in Mysore and the coffee of the original and now generally discarded variety. I may here add that the coffee of Mysore has always had a high reputation. This high quality has been partly attributed to soil and climate and partly to the coffee being slowly ripened under shade. But, however that may be, a glance at the weekly lists in the "Economist" will show that Mysore coffee of the best quality is commonly valued at from 10*s.* to 15*s.* a cwt. above that of any other kind that reaches the London market.

I now propose to give a brief account of our coffee land tenures, and shall then address myself to the intricate question of coffee cultivation in Mysore, and the still more difficult question of the shade trees which shelter the coffee from sun and wind, and the soil from the wash of the tropical rains.

When I entered the province in 1855 anyone who desired to have a given tract of forest land for coffee planting sent an application to the Government for it. An inquiry was then made, and, if no objection existed to the land being made over to the intending settler, or applicant, a puttah or grant, free of any charge for the land or any fee even in connection with the grant, was made out in Kanarese, which mentioned the name of the land and the boundaries of it, and stated that the land was to be planted with coffee within three years' time, and that, if not so planted, it was liable to be resumed by the State. No survey was made of the land, nor was it of any importance to estimate the acreage, there being no land tax, but in its place a tax of 1 rupee per cwt. of clean coffee produced, which was only liable to be demanded when the coffee was exported from the country, and not before. This system may seem to many to have been an objectionable one, and, from one point of view, no doubt it was. because the more highly the planter cultivated, the more highly he paid on each acre of his holding, but, on the other hand, the system enabled the planter to start with a very small capital, as he paid nothing for his land, nor a single shilling to the State till he had produced his crop. For starting and stimulating the industry the system certainly had its merits; but after the industry had obtained a firm footing, it was evidently of advantage to institute a taxational system of a different character, and, after much discussion and correspondence on the subject, the existing forms of tenure were finally decided on, and the "Mysore Coffee Land Rules" were formally notified to the public in March, 1885. There are two forms of grant—Form A, with an assessment of one rupee and a half an acre, which rate is fixed permanently, and Form B, at one rupee per acre, with liability to revision at the end of each period of thirty years. The assessment for local purposes stands now at 1 anna an acre ($1\frac{1}{2}d.$ at 2*s.* exchange), and that is the only taxation we have. There is not, and never has been, an income-tax in Mysore, nor is it at all probable that there ever will be, as the finances are in a flourishing condition, and the revenues under several important heads are improving, as may be seen on referring to the chapter on the general history of the province.

Those who desire further and more detailed information regarding the rules in question, may be referred to the notification of March 24th, 1855, and I may mention that they are given in full in the "Mysore and Coorg Directory."[1]

I regret that I have no precise information to give as regards the unplanted coffee land in Mysore. With reference to the southern part of the province, I think I am quite safe in saying that all the land suitable for coffee has been taken up, but I am informed by a correspondent who resides in the northern part of the province, that in that part of the country there is much unplanted land both in the possession of the Government and in the hands of private individuals. All along the sides of the western passes there are indeed large blocks of forest, but these, from the excessive rainfall, are quite unsuitable for coffee, as I am able to testify from an unfortunate practical experience, as I once took up land for coffee on the crests of the Ghauts. After its failure had been completely proved I sold the land to a planter who has since cultivated cardamoms on it, and last year the rainfall registered there was no less than 340 inches, nearly all of which fell between May and the end of October.

From what has hitherto been written as regards our taxation, I need hardly say that the planters are well satisfied with the terms granted to them by the Government. With the roads, post, telegraphs, railways, dispensaries, and other facilities at their command, and the prospect of a further important development of communications, they have also every reason to be satisfied. In short, the progressive character of the Government would seem to leave nothing to be desired. There is, however, always a "but" in life, and in our case there are two "buts." The first of these relates to the state of the law as regards

[1] "Hayes' Mysore and Coorg Directory," Bangalore. This valuable compilation, which contains no less than 573 pages, gives a most complete account of almost everything relating to Mysore and Coorg.

advances given to labourers to be worked off by them, and to contractors to bring labourers; and the second to extradition. To these may be added three wants—I can hardly call them grievances—the want of a Wild Birds' Protection Act, a Game Act, and an agricultural chemist. On these five points I now propose briefly to remark.

The practice of giving money advances to labourers to be gradually worked off by them, and to contractors who undertake to supply labourers, has been productive of great loss and annoyance to employers, a great temptation to natives to commit fraud, and a source of constant worry to the officers of the Government. The Government sought by Act XIII. of 1859 to check these evils, not by preventive, but purely by punitive legislation. Since then there has been a constant demand by employers of labour for more punitive legislation in the shape of amendments to the Act of 1859, and from recent assurances made by the Viceroy when he visited Mysore in 1892, it seems probable that something further will be done on the same lines. And something may of course be done to insure that the defaulter shall be severely dealt with—when he is caught. When he is caught. Yes, therein lies the whole difficulty, one which seems to have been as completely ignored by the Government as it has been by the planters in the legislation adopted with a view to check the evils connected with advances. In order to prove the necessity for further legislation an old planter once printed an account of a case which he took up against a defaulting coolie. His description of the hunt, and the wiles of the defaulting labourer in moving from one part of the country to another, was positively amusing, and showed conclusively that it did not pay to attempt to catch a defaulting labourer. What, then, can be the use of an Act which after all only punishes the coolie when he is caught, if the trouble and expense involved in catching him be so great as to make the game not worth the candle? Is it not evident that the only thing which can help the planter is legislation which will make it very difficult for the labourer to obtain money from one employer and then run away and take an advance from another, and which will make it a comparatively easy matter to trace a defaulter? Now, after conferring with experienced planters and some leading native officials, I came to the conclusion that a system of registration could alone mitigate the serious evils of the advance system, and in conjunction with them I drew up a draft of a proposed Act which I laid on the table for the consideration of the Mysore Government when I attended the Representative Assembly in 1891, and I may mention that the draft in question has been printed in the Government Report of the Proceedings. It would be tedious to give an account of the provisions in the Bill, and it is sufficient to say that its two chief features were the registration of advances and the limitation of their amount. The registration was to be effected by its being made compulsory that when an advance was given three tickets on a Government form should be issued, one of which was to be held by the employer, the second by the labourer, and the third by the registrar of the talook. On each ticket was to be entered the name and address of the advancee, and the sum advanced, and as this was paid off the amounts so discharged were to be entered by the employer on the ticket retained by the labourer. When the whole amount was repaid, the ticket retained by the employer was to be handed to the registrar, who was then to erase the name of the labourer from the register of coolies under advances, and before any advance was handed to the labourer the registry was of course to be effected. The amount of advance was to be limited to ten rupees, and this was to be worked off in five months unless in the case of sickness.

The object of limiting advances is as much in the interest of the labourer as of the employer, as it has been found that native employers of labour often give large advances to labourers and charge heavy interest on them when the coolie does not come to work, and thus so effectually get him into debt that he is reduced to the position of a slave. This system of registration would no doubt be troublesome, but it is the only way of checking the present evil system of giving advances which, now that labour is so well paid, is not really necessary, and that it is not so is evidenced by the fact that the large bodies of labourers employed in the gold mines receive no advances whatever. I may here mention that a private system of registration with reference to labour contractors has been started by the firm of Messrs. Matheson and Co., in connection with their extensive estates in Coorg, and that it has been found most useful. The system I have proposed would be valuable to the contractors, who themselves are often swindled by labourers to whom they have advanced money.

I now turn to the subject of extradition, the law relating to which has much aggravated the evils connected with giving advances to labourers. The want of legislation on this subject has been brought to the notice of the Viceroy, and it is to be hoped that there may soon be complete reciprocity between native States and the British Government as regards warrants. At present a defaulter flying from Mysore to British territory can only be arrested by calling in the interposition of the Resident, a process so cumbrous that it is practically true, as alleged in the petition of the planters of Southern India, that "Planters or contractors residing in Mysore cannot obtain warrants against defaulters in British territory, though planters in British territory can obtain warrants against defaulters in Mysore." This is a grievance which requires redress, not only for the sake of the planters, but also of all other employers of labourers, or those who may have made contracts of any kind.

Cattle trespass, I may mention, is not here alluded to because, though it was at one time a great grievance, a Cattle Trespass Amendment Act received the assent of His Highness the Maharajah in December, 1892. By this, where it is proved to the satisfaction of Government that in any given local area cattle are habitually allowed to trespass on land and damage crops, the fines will be doubled, and the owner of the land has besides the right to bring an action for compensation for any damage done to his land or crops.

Having alluded to our grievances, I now pass on to consider lastly what may be called our wants as regards wild birds' protection, game preservation, and a Government agricultural chemist.

A Wild Birds' Protection Act exists in British India, but as its provisions have not as yet been extended to our province, I would suggest that Mysore, in consequence of its numerous plantations where coffee and other plants and trees are liable to be attacked by insects, probably requires such an Act even more than any other part of India, and I may at the same time take the opportunity of suggesting that all the native States should be communicated with so that an Act for the Protection of Wild Birds may be provided for every part of India. It would be superfluous to adduce here the numerous and evident advantages that would arise from the protection of wild birds, as their value is now so universally recognized, and I therefore pass on to offer a few brief remarks on game preservation, or, to speak more exactly, of the preservation of those wild birds and harmless animals which are useful as food.

The neglect of game preservation in India has not only been a cause of great loss to the country owing to the reckless waste of the sources of valuable supplies of food, but has severely injured the farmers in jungly tracts in a way that seems hitherto to have escaped notice. I allude to the fact that, in consequence of the wanton destruction of game in the western forests, tigers are compelled to inflict much greater losses on the herds of the natives. This is a fact to which I can personally testify, and which has since the middle of 1892 become steadily more apparent; for, when game was more plentiful in the forests along the crests, and at the foot of the Ghauts, the tigers lived largely upon game and rarely attacked cattle; indeed, so much was this the case that, about thirty years ago, a native who had the most outlying farm on the crests of the Ghauts told me that though tigers were constantly about they had never attacked his cattle. And as I was at the time living near his house, and clearing land for planting, and never got a shot at a tiger when residing there, I am sure that his statement was correct. But since that time English guns have become common, and the destruction of game of all kinds and of any age has gone on apace, and the result is that the tigers, which used to confine themselves mainly to preying on wild animals in the forests, have been forced to fall upon the village cattle, and I have never known tigers to be more destructive than they are now. On a single day this year no less than seven cattle were killed by tigers at one village, and an old planter of more than thirty years' standing, a near neighbour of mine, alluding to the subject in a recent letter, said, "Yes, there have been more tigers about this year than I have ever known." But it is not only on account of the supply of food from game, and for the sake of the cattle of the natives that a Game Preservation Act is urgently required, it is also urgently needed in order to check the abominable cruelties committed by the native hunters. Writing to me with reference to this subject,

Colonel J. P. Grant, the head of the Survey and Settlement Service, observes as follows:

"Gunning and especially netting, in the most reckless and improvident manner, are on the increase. Antelope are fast disappearing, and in the jungle tracts night shooting is clearing out spotted deer especially. As for cruelty nothing can exceed the indifference of net-workers to any pain they may cause their captures. Snipe are caught and their legs and wings broken, and in this condition they are kept alive and carried to market. The wounding, necessarily reckless during night shooting, is horribly cruel. Pea fowl, jungle fowl, or anything fairly big, have their eyes sewn up. I have often seen this. In the case of hares the tying is very cruel, the thong cutting down to the bone; and the same is the case with any deer they may catch alive."

The rapid destruction of game of all kinds has been as melancholy as it has been remarkable, and I confess I never could have believed how complete, especially as regards small game, the deadly work has been had I not had occasion in recent years to drive, by easy stages, and early in the morning, along the whole of the western frontier of Mysore, and also much of the adjacent district of Coorg. In the old days, when riding, we always went at a walk and took our guns with us for shots at pea fowl, jungle fowl, pigeons, and other small game. But now you can neither see nor hear anything to shoot. And yet one of the favourite accusations of the Indian Congress against the Indian Government is that in consequence of the Arms Act the natives are unable to obtain guns and ammunition in order to defend themselves and their crops from the attacks of wild animals, though the scarcity of large game, and, in many cases, its absolute extinction, is notorious to sportsmen all over India. But the Mysore Government, I am happy to say, has at last directed its attention to the subject, and I have every reason to believe that a Game Act will soon be introduced in Mysore.

The last want I have to allude to is that of a Government agricultural chemist, who should be empowered at a rate of fees, fixed by the State, to analyze soils and manures for private individuals, and to consult with planters and others as to the requirements of their soils and the best way of supplying them with manure. Such an officer would be very useful in searching for coprolites and new manurial resources. My life-long experience in agriculture on a large scale both in Scotland and Mysore has shown me more and more the great value of an agricultural chemist for discovering new manurial resources, and perhaps more especially economizing those that already exist; and the great want of such an officer was brought to the notice of Government by me when I was a member of the Representative Assembly in 1891.

I may conclude this chapter by alluding to a discovery, or rather, I should say, a probable discovery, of the greatest importance, of a new hybrid coffee plant—a cross between the Liberian and the coffea Arabica. This has occurred on the property of a friend of mine, but, at his request, I do not publish his name, as he would be inundated with applications for seed. This magnificent hybrid, of which there are only two trees in existence as yet, has enormous bearing powers, and leaves which are apparently absolutely impervious to leaf disease, for I could not discover a trace of it though the hybrid is standing next to a coffee plant which is covered with it. It is of course uncertain as yet whether the new plant can be established as a distinct variety, nor do we know anything of the flavour of the coffee, as the quantity produced is yet so small that berries are reserved exclusively for seed; but should it be possible to establish the new variety (and I know of no reason why it should not be established), quite a new departure will take place in coffee production in India, and the value of coffee land will be enormous, as, from calculations made, the hybrid can produce at the rate of eight or nine tons an acre, while as many hundredweights an acre would be considered an unusually heavy crop in Mysore.

CHAPTER XI.

SHADE.

I NOW turn to the greatest of all the points connected with coffee—the question of shade. And I call it the greatest point, because if good shade of the best kind is grown it is absolutely impossible to destroy a plantation in Mysore, even with the worst conceivable management or neglect, and I say this after ample experience, as had it not been for the abundant and excellent shade on a badly-managed property of my own it would have been permanently ruined. But with plenty of good kinds of shade trees on the land you might even close the plantation gates, and abandon the land, and, as long as cattle were kept out, return ten years afterwards, saw down the coffee, grow suckers from the stumps, plant up the land with young plants where vacancies had occurred, and in four or five years the plantation would be as good as ever, and the land even better, for it would not have been exhausted by crop, and the fallen leaves from the shade trees would have enriched the soil. And if the old trees were not in a condition, from old age, to grow suckers that would develop into good trees, the whole land could be advantageously replanted. But, as the reader will remember, I have said that the trees must be the best kinds of shade trees, a subject that requires great study and observation to master. Before beginning, however, it may be well to point out those general principles which govern the whole subject, and which at once show us the best kinds of trees to select, and what is nearly of as great importance, how to manage them after they have been selected or planted, and I would lay particular stress on the latter point, which has, I may observe, been largely if not entirely misunderstood, simply because the great governing principle has been neglected.

The governing principle, then, as regards shade for coffee is, that you should have on the land the smallest number of boles, because the more you multiply boles the more ground you waste; and the greater the number of large trees there are, the greater, of course, will be the number of large roots in the land, and the greater demand will there be on the resources of the soil; the greater, too, will be the waste of manure put down by the planter for the benefit of his coffee; and last, but by no means least, the smaller will be the amount of leaf deposit. I have seen much shade so managed as to give the greatest amount of boles with the smallest amount, and spread of branches, whereas the object of the planter ought to be to furnish the smallest number of boles with the greatest proportionate amount and spread of branches and foliage. And this unfortunate error, the evil of which will become more and more apparent as time advances, would never have been committed, had the primary principle I have pointed out been grasped at the outset.

Let us then keep firmly in mind that, (1) we require trees that will, from their wide-spreading branches, enable us to do with the smallest number possible on the land, and that (2) if we trim up the lower branches of these trees when the trees are young because we do not like to see them too closely over the coffee, we shall entirely defeat the main object we have in view, because we shall certainly produce a tall tree with a small head, and consequently small spread of branches; and the clear apprehension of the principle first named guides us at once to the selection of the right kind of trees, and their proper treatment. I will now proceed to state the names of the trees that are, in my experience, the most desirable, and, secondly, those which are good for coffee, but which for various reasons are undesirable. After much and close study of this important subject, and a very long experience, I have come to the conclusion that the only trees which are at once easily propagated; free from the risks of attacks from cattle owing to their being grown from long cuttings; little liable to attacks from parasites, and which afford a proper degree of shade, and also admit the largest relative supply of light; which afford a large supply of leaf deposit; and which lastly, but by no means leastly, have very wide spreading branches, are only five in number. I give first the Kanarese and then the botanical name of each. There are, then, Cub Busree (*Ficus tuberculata*), the Gonee (*Ficus Mysorensis*), the Kurry Busree (*Ficus infectoria*), Eelee Busree (a variety of the last named), and Mitlee.[1]

There are two kinds, Heb Mitlee, and Harl Mitlee—the second is a bad tree. The mitlee grows one fourth quicker than cub busree, and a recent close attention to this tree shows me that it is a much more desirable tree than either others or myself once supposed, for not only is it a quicker grower than the remainder of the most desirable kinds but its foliage lets in much light. It is, therefore, a most desirable tree for northern aspects.

I next turn to a class of trees which are undoubtedly good for coffee, but which, for various reasons to be hereafter given, are less desirable than the five trees first given.

[1] I regret that I am unable to give the botanical name of this tree, and of some others subsequently mentioned. I have drawn up a list of trees, some of which may be retained till better trees can be grown to supply their places, and also of other trees which are positively injurious to coffee, but do not publish them, partly in order to save space, and partly because I have not been able to ascertain the botanical names of all the trees in question.

The first of these less desirable trees is the Jack—Halsen-Mara (*Artocarpus integrifolia*), which was once a favourite tree, and there can be no doubt that coffee thrives well under it, but it is not a wide-spreading tree, the shade is too dense for every aspect, it is a slow grower, and it must be raised from young plants, which are very liable to be attacked by stray cattle. Then when old, and sometimes of medium age, it is very liable to be attacked by parasites; and it produces annually a heavy[1] crop of fruit which costs money and trouble to remove when immature, and which, if left to ripen, exhausts the soil. It is, too, liable to suffer much from wind, and, in situations which are at all windy, is not much to be relied on, as, when under the influence of wind, the foliage becomes poor and scanty, and the tree sometimes dies altogether. A study of the foliage will show, that in one important particular, the five first-named trees are superior to jack, for their leaves are attached to the twigs by long stalks, and much light is thus admitted through the spaces between the stalks, while the leaves of the jack are not only more numerous but are attached by short stalks, and the foliage thus throws a very dark shade. Then jack, as it is an evergreen, always affords a thick shade quite continuously, while the five first-named trees not only cast a chequered shade, but, at certain periods of the year, shed every leaf, leaving the tree quite bare for some time, which is an advantage to the coffee. And besides, I have some reason to suppose that the dense shade of the jack encourages rot (a disease remarked upon further on), as one of my managers reports that he has observed it under jack while it was not apparent on the coffee under other kinds of shade trees. But on hot westerly and southerly slopes,

[1] My manager last year weighed and counted the Jack fruits from a single tree. There were forty fruits which weighed 572 lbs. The largest fruit weighed 30 lbs.

and especially where the soil is a bad retainer of moisture, and where the gradient is rather steep, jack may be used with advantage, as in such situations the heat is great and the light strong. I am therefore taking steps to remove jack by degrees from all but southerly and westerly exposures. I may add here that I have found that plants grown from seed procured from the dry plains of the interior of Mysore, grow more than twice as fast as plants raised from local seed. In concluding my remarks on jack, I would particularly advise planters to remove the jack fruit when immature, and put it into the manure heap, or bury it, as, if left on the ground, it attracts cattle and village pigs into the plantation. The fruit is large and full of a great number of seeds which must be an exhaustive crop on the land. On the Nilgiri hills I am told by the planters that there is a ready sale for jack fruit, but this is not the case in coffee districts generally.

The Attí (*Ficus glomerata*) was with me once a favourite tree, and is generally considered to be a good one, as it affords a cool and desirable shade. As a young tree it is admirable, but as it ages the foliage becomes poor and scanty, and the tree has a tendency to run too much to thick bole, and thick branches, which are poorly supplied with smaller branches and foliage. When about thirty years old, I have generally found this tree to be a poor shader, but it can be much improved by severe pruning, or rather lopping. When thinning out shade on this estate about twenty years ago, a twelve year old tree had every branch removed preparatory to cutting down, but by some accident the tree was left standing, and the stumps of the branches threw out fresh shoots, and the tree is now flourishing, and has a comparatively wide spread of branches and fair amount of foliage. It is evident, then, that pruning heavily will cause the tree to throw out new and vigorous shoots, but as this is a troublesome and expensive work, and as attí is certainly liable to the defect above alluded to, and is, besides, not a wide-spreading tree, it is evidently not so desirable as any of the first five I have named. Attí can be grown from cuttings, but these must not be large ones, *i.e.*, they should be thinner than those commonly used when planting cuttings of the various fig trees recommended at the beginning of the section on shade.

The Noga (so called from its being much used to make bullock yokes from) or Nogurigay (*Cedrela Microcarpa*) is a favourite tree to plant for shade, as it is a quick grower, and cattle do not eat it, and it has been extensively planted in Mysore and Coorg. The shade is fairly good, but the tree is not a wide spreader. Then it has one very great objection owing to its being so peculiarly liable, when about thirty years old, to be severely attacked, and often killed, by parasites, and as it is so liable to be attacked, and therefore supplies a large quantity of parasite seed, the tree is the means of spreading these parasites to other shade trees. I have found that if you even remove every branch that is attacked, and quite below each parasite, the parasite will spring out again, and even more vigorously than before. In short, I found it impossible to contend with the parasites, and am ordering the removal of all Nogurigays from my plantations. I may add here that when jack is lopped in order to remove parasites, they do not spring out again in the same way. My head duffadar informs me that the reason why Nogurigays are so liable to parasites is on account of the rough, deeply-fissured bark, which retains the parasite seeds dropped by birds, whereas smooth-barked trees, like the first five named, of course do not retain them, and hence you rarely see parasites on smooth-barked trees. Another objection to this tree is that, from its shedding its leaves in the monsoon, and not growing them again till we are liable to have hot bursts of sun, you may have a thoroughly saturated soil exposed to a hot sun, which of course has the effect of rapidly hardening the soil. A neighbouring planter tells me that he finds the Noga tree liable to attacks from parasites at even ten years old, and that he therefore regards the tree as a temporary shade, *i.e.*, as a shade to be removed after other more desirable trees are ready to take their place.

Since writing this chapter I have again paid particular attention to this tree, and have been struck with the fact that, for some unknown reason, some trees of this variety seem to be much more liable to attacks of parasites than others, while some escape altogether. But it is quite clear to me that, generally speaking, this tree is not to be relied on, and I have, therefore, no hesitation in advising planters who have relied on it as a permanent shade to at once put down trees of the desirable kind first given with the view of gradually removing the Nogurigays.

Mullee Geruguttee. A very thick, tall tree with large buttresses. Coffee thrives well under this tree, but it is not a wide spreader, and, when old, the foliage becomes poor. It is evident that a tree of great thickness which is not a wide spreader, takes up an immense deal of room in proportion to the shade that it yields, and this tree is therefore not so desirable as any of the first five species I have given as being the most desirable trees.

Howligay (*Acrocarpus Flaxinifolia*). This tree has been largely planted in Mysore for shade, but no one speaks well of it now. We have some on my estate upwards of thirty years old, and the foliage is poor and scanty. The trees, too, shoot up to a great height, and spread but little. By topping at a certain height, this defect may be remedied to some extent, but in order to get an efficient shade from this tree you would require to plant it thickly, and would thus have a large proportion of stems and roots in the land. This tree, though not injurious to coffee, is certainly very undesirable as compared with the first-named kinds I have given. Some years ago two of these trees died on my property, and all the coffee died around them.

Hessan (*Artocarpus Hirsuta*). Though said to be injurious in poor and shallow soil, coffee thrives under it in good land, but it has a tendency everywhere to run to stem, and therefore affords poor shade. An occasional tree branches out, and affords fair, and in some cases, even good shade, but, as a rule, this is not a desirable tree. It spreads little and thus gives but a poor return for the space taken up by its stem and roots.

Nairul (*Eugenia Jambolana*). This is a good shade tree. Coffee thrives well under it, and wherever it exists, or may have sprung up accidentally in the plantation, it should be preserved, but it is not, I consider, a desirable tree to plant, as it is a slow grower and not a wide spreader.

Wartee. This is a tree we have always preserved, but it is a slow growing tree, not at all a wide spreader, and the leaf deposit from it is not of a valuable quality, and it is, therefore, not a desirable tree to plant.

Gwoddan (*Dolichos fabaeformis*). Coffee thrives well under this tree, but it has a great profusion of very hard fruits or seeds about the size of a small plum, and these, when falling from a high tree, injure the coffee berries, as may be readily supposed; the tree, too, is not a wide spreader. It is, therefore, not a desirable tree to plant.

I may mention here that I have recently obtained a supply of seed of *Albizzia Moluccana*, which is the tree most approved of for shading coffee in the Island of Java, and I am informed by the superintendent of the Agri-Horticultural Society's Gardens, Madras (from whom I obtained the seed), that one of their correspondents who tried it some years ago reports that, "It grows rapidly, and is of great utility in putting a field of coffee under a light shade such as coffee likes," and that, "in four years the *Albizzia Moluccana*, planted thirty feet apart, will cover the coffee trees." The leaves close during the night, thus giving the coffee plants the benefit of the moonlight and dew more freely. Each ounce of the seed contains roughly 1,200 seeds, which, with ordinary care, should give 1,000 plants, and which, when planted out thirty feet apart, should shade twenty acres.

I now proceed to consider the methods that are adopted for planting under shade in Mysore. The first is to clear down and burn the entire forest, and then plant shade trees along with the coffee. The second is to clear and burn the underwood, and a certain portion of the forest trees, leaving the remainder for shade, and the third is (a system which I have myself adopted in the case of land lying in ravines) to clear off and burn the entire underwood and trees of the lower part of the ravines, leaving the upper portions of them, and the remainder of the land to be cleared and planted, under the original forest trees, as in the second method mentioned.

There can be no doubt that the first-named method is the easiest. I am aware that it has been adopted by some very experienced planters, and it has been partially adopted by myself in the case of all my land in the lower part of ravines. I am well able to judge of the advantages and disadvantages of both systems, as I have them under observation and treatment side by side. On the whole, I think there can be no doubt that the balance of advantage lies much in favour of land that has not had the forest cleared wholly and burnt off. It is true that by a wholesale clearance you at once kill the vast mass of live forest tree roots in the land, but, on the other hand, you at the same time destroy a store of slowly-decaying vegetable matter, which is of vast importance, not only in feeding the coffee, but in maintaining the physical condition of the soil, and so making it more easily, and therefore cheaply, workable, and a better agent for preserving the health of the tree. And as a proof of the actual loss incurred, I may observe that Colonel C. I. Taylor, in his book on "The Borer in Coorg, Munzerabad and Nuggar," mentions that an iron peg driven into the ground so that not a part of it protruded, was found, after the cleared jungle had been burned, to be no less than six inches out of the ground. There seems to be a general opinion too that land that has not been burnt will last far longer, and one experienced planter, Mr. Brooke Mockett, attributes the circumstances of all the most ancient estates in Mysore being still in existence to the fact that the land has never been burnt. Mr. Mockett also informs me that in good land, where there has been no burn, he has never had Borer severely, though for a time there was no shade over it, as he cleared down ultimately all the old forest trees that had been left for shade, and planted fresh shade. I may mention, too, that I was lately shown an estate in Coorg which had been partially cleared down and burnt off, and partly planted under the shade of the old forest trees. In the latter case the plants had never suffered from Borer or leaf disease and were always healthy, while the coffee in the former case had suffered from both, and there was certainly a most marked difference perceptible in favour of the coffee planted in the unburnt land.

There is also a great difference in my own property in favour of the coffee planted under the original forest shade as compared with the coffee on the land that was cleared down and burnt off, notwithstanding that in the latter case the most approved kinds of shade trees were afterwards planted, and that the land is now admirably shaded. It is highly important to notice these facts, both as a guide to those who have land to open, and also as regards the value of any property that may be for sale, for, after what I have mentioned, it is clear that a property planted under original forest shade, where the land has not been burnt off (for it is quite possible gradually to remove all the old forest trees and replace them with newly planted shade), must be much more valuable than one where the entire forest has been cleared down and burnt off. I now proceed to remark (1) on the course that should be pursued in the case of clearing down and burning the whole jungle and planting fresh shade, and (2) when planting under the original shade.

After the land is ready for planting the coffee, and as early as possible in the monsoon, the young shade trees should be planted in lines or avenues running from east to west, and the trees should be planted so close that they may in five or six years touch each other, and thus form what looks like a series of hedges in parallel lines. The object of this formation is that as the declination of the sun is southerly during our non-cloudy or clear sky season, a close shadow may be cast from the south to the north, so that the spaces between the lines may have a lateral shade cast on them. When the trees begin to crowd each other every other one should of course be taken out, and this may be repeated a second time if necessary. But, besides the southerly, we have also to consider the hot westerly sun, which will strike down the avenues from, say, between two and four in the afternoon. This it is important to block out with occasional trees planted in the avenue, but it is only, of course, where the land is exposed to the afternoon sun that the avenues should be blocked with occasional trees. After fully considering the subject, I find it impossible to say even approximately at what distance the lines of trees should be planted, on account of the great variety in the gradients, and the planter must here use his own judgment; and I can only say generally that the lines of trees require to be much nearer each other on a southerly than on a northerly aspect; nearly as close on a westerly aspect as on a southerly; and on an easterly aspect, at a closer distance than on a northerly one. Some guide toward the nearness of these lines will afterwards be found in the remarks on the quantity of shade required for the various aspects.

After having planted the young shade trees, then, there comes the question of providing shade for them, for without it their growth will be very slow, and the planter would have to wait a great many years before obtaining such an amount of shade as would have an effect in lowering the temperature of the plantation. He requires then some quick-growing tree as a nurse for the good caste shade trees, and the only tree I know of that is suitable for this purpose is the quick-growing charcoal tree (*Sponia Wightii*)—Kanarese, *gorkul mara*—which springs up with the first rain after the forest has been cleared and burnt. Planters, I am aware, have, generally speaking, a great objection to this tree, and it is considered by Mr. Graham Anderson (*vide* his book previously quoted) as being "generally regarded as prejudicial and useless." This conclusion has probably arisen from the fact that it is certainly a bad thing to have a rapid grower, and therefore a greedy feeder on the land, and hence it has been found that the charcoal tree is bad when young. But when it has attained its full height, which in ordinary circumstances is about thirty feet (I have one specimen on my property about sixty feet high, the only one of such a size I ever saw), coffee thrives well under it. This I found to be the case on plantations on the slopes of the Nilgiri hills, where a very experienced planter told me that the tree was bad when young for coffee, but not so when old; and I there saw coffee thriving well under the shade of old charcoal trees. On my oldest plantation we only preserved one of the species (all the others having been cut down, as their good offices as nurses to better trees were no longer required), and the coffee always throve under it remarkably well. Where, too, the shade has subsequently become deficient we always plant charcoal as a nurse for the more desirable trees, and have never observed that it is injurious to coffee. On the whole, after a very long experience and observation of this tree, I have no hesitation in recommending it as a nurse to be thinly distributed amongst the newly-planted shade trees. It is, I may observe, too, a tree with very light branches, which, of course, can easily be removed without injury to the coffee, and its branches should be thinned away when they crowd the young shade trees, and when these have been sufficiently drawn up and expanded the charcoal tree should be entirely removed.

The subsequent treatment of the shade trees is of great importance. Their lower branches in the early years of their growth are commonly thin and weakly, and thus, of course, droop close over the coffee, and often touch it. Then the inexperienced shade tree grower begins to lop off the lower branches, with the result that he injures and bleeds the young tree, and deprives it of the nutriment it would otherwise derive from its full allowance of foliage. Some carry this trimming up to a very injurious extent, and the result is that they grow young trees with long stems and poor foliage, and a narrow spread of branches, and thus require many more trees in the land than they would if they exercised a little more patience at first. But if the tree is only left alone the evil of branches drooping downwards on to the coffee will soon disappear, as these branches will not only rise with the rising stem, but will thicken and grow upwards, instead of drooping as they did when young and weakly. And some planters, I observe, are by no means satisfied with lopping the lower boughs, but trim off branches fifteen feet from the ground. Under such a system the number of shade trees required is enormous, and the evils arising from the number of boles with their vast mass of large roots will only be the more severely apparent as time advances. By one shade planter in Coorg I have been told that coffee there has already been suffering much from the quantity of boles and tree roots in the land, in consequence of the trimming up system and the quantity of trees required in consequence. It should also be remembered that we require our shade not only to protect our coffee from the sun's rays, but to shield it from those parching winds which sweep across the arid plains of the interior of India, and to prevent the drying up of the land. And is it not perfectly obvious that if we trim up the trees so as to produce a long stem with a small crown, the parching winds will sweep unchecked over plants and soil? There is, however, the usual proverbial exception, and that is in the case of trees growing near the bottoms of ravines with steep sides to them, and where you often want a drawn up stem and crown to cast a shadow on to a hot western or southern bank, and in such cases, of course, trimming up is necessary. Having thus discussed the planting of coffee where the forest has been cut wholly down and burnt, we will now turn to planting under the shade of the original forest trees.

In opening, then, a plantation which is to be shaded by preserving a portion of the original forest trees, the first thing to be done is to clear a wide track through the underwood from one end of the block of forest to the other, and as many tracks at right angles to the line as may facilitate your getting about and thoroughly inspecting the land to be cleared. The next thing to be done is to cut a wide track round the entire portion to be cleared, leaving a belt of from fifteen to twenty yards as a margin between the land to be cleared and the grass-land lying outside the forest. This marginal belt will often be found useful for shelter in many cases, and it must be borne in mind, too, that the margins of jungles are generally composed of land into which the forest has more recently extended itself, and are therefore poorer than the interior portion of the forest, and consequently less adapted to the growth of the coffee. Another advantage of this marginal belt is that it will prevent fires spreading from the grass-lands, and that by planting thorny climbing plants on its outer edge a good fence may be formed. Another very great advantage I have found from such belts is that valuable top soil may be taken from them to manure the adjacent coffee, and especially to afford a supply of rich virgin soil when filling up vacancies in the old coffee. This last use of the marginal belt is particularly valuable, as it is both troublesome and expensive to lay down either cattle manure or top soil brought from a distance in those odd corners here and there in the plantations where vacancies are apt to occur.

After the above suggested preliminary tracks have been opened out, the whole underwood should be cleared and piled in heaps, and as far as possible, of course, from the trees which are most desirable for shade. Then the trees positively injurious to coffee should be cut down and their branches lopped and piled on the stumps of the objectionable trees, and after this a certain proportion of the less desirable kinds should be felled. All burning should be carried on in separate piles, as a running fire through the clearing would be fatal to the standing trees, and, when firing the piles they should be burnt off in detail at as great a distance from each other as possible, as the bark of many of the forest trees is easily injured by the heat arising from many blazing piles in their neighbourhood. The land having thus been thoroughly cleared, should be planted.

But by the process I have recommended much more shade will be left than will ultimately be required, and I have found that it is impossible to clear down at once all the trees you wish to get rid of, as, if you did, you would be sure to require such a number of piles as would, when they were burnt, be sure to injure the trees to be preserved. It is therefore necessary to complete the clearing during the season following. Such trees, then, as you may wish further to remove may be thrown down between the rows of coffee, and others which may be likely to do much damage, either to the coffee or to the shade trees to be preserved, may be lopped and barked, and they should be barked as high up as a man can reach, as we have found that trees barked close to the ground die slowly.

It sometimes, however, happens that the forest land is much cut up with narrow and deep ravines, and in that case the bottoms of such ravines should be cleared off entirely, and this can be done without injury to the standing trees above, as, when the wood in the bottom of the ravine is being burnt the flames will be too distant to inflict any injury to the trees left for shade higher up the slopes, but, as I have said, great care must be taken to prevent any running fire through the shaded land; and I can speak of the effect of such a fire from a melancholy experience. In the event of bottoms of ravines being thus cleared down, it may afterwards be found desirable to supply fresh shade on the southern and western slopes, and this can easily be done on the system recommended previously for lands which have been entirely cleared down.

It is time now to turn our attention to the extremely complicated question of the quantity of shade required for the various aspects, gradients, and soils we have to deal with, and let us in the first place begin with some remarks on the effects of aspect as regards heat.

In considering, then, aspect as regards sun and heat, I may observe that it is impossible to exaggerate the importance of taking into account the immense variation in temperature on the different exposures. For the effect that the sun's rays have on certain aspects in heating the soil and drying up the plant, are such as would be extremely difficult to believe, had the facts not been verified by competent observers, and with the aid of the thermometer. And as regards northern and southern slopes in particular, we shall find that the difference between one exposure and the other is just what constitutes the difference between green and dried grass, and between leaves luxuriantly green and leaves dry and withered. And that the first is literally true may be seen by anyone in the months of January and February, for in these months you will see grass on northern aspects green, and, comparatively speaking, fresh, while, even in a valley sheltered from drying winds, the grass on the southern slopes is completely withered. And you will see an equally striking difference in the coffee plants—those on the northern slopes full of health and life, while those on the southern ones are yellow, dried up, and sickly. Even in parts of the district where coffee will not thrive without a considerable amount of shade, you will always find the plants thrive well (with little or even none) on a northern bank, and look much better than on a moderately shaded southern bank. Nor in the nursery is the effect of aspect at all less striking. A nursery on a northern slope will require far less water, and far less shade over the plants, than one with a southern exposure. But the late Mr. MacIvor, superintendent of the Government Cinchona plantations on the Nilgiri hills, has tested the value of northern and southern aspects in a way which accurately judges their respective values. He accordingly tells us that, "The reason why a northern exposure in these latitudes is beneficial is from the fact that it is much more moist during the dry season than a southern aspect, because the sun's declension is southerly during the dry and cloudless season of the year, and thus, on the northern slopes, the rays of the sun do not penetrate and parch the soil. A northern aspect has also the advantage of preserving a much more uniform temperature than a southern aspect, because the excessive radiation and evaporation in the southern slopes greatly reduces the temperature at night, while in the day they are heated to excess by the action of the sun's rays striking the surface nearly at right angles. The practical effects of aspect on the plants are so great that they cannot be overlooked with impunity, and, in order to impress this on the minds of all those who may have the selection of localities for cinchona cultivation, I may mention that the difference of temperature is almost incredible; for example, at this elevation (probably about 7,000 feet) a thermometer laid on the surface of the southern face of a hill exposed to the sun at 3 p.m., will frequently indicate from 130° to 160° Fahr.; the same thermometer, if left in its position, and examined at 6 a.m., will generally be observed to indicate from 30° to 40°, while on a similar slope, if selected with a northern aspect, the thermometer, under the same circumstances, at 3 p.m., will generally indicate from 70° to 80°, and at 6 a.m. from 40° to 50°."

There is, then, about twice as much heat upon a southern as on a northern aspect, and, of course, a corresponding difference as regards the effect of sun and drought on plant and soil, and it is therefore obvious that our shade policy should be governed accordingly.

As regards the comparative heat on western and eastern exposures, Mr. MacIvor does not seem to have made any experiments with the thermometer, but where the slope is at all sharp the rays of the fierce western sun beat strongly into the soil, while it is quite off an easterly slope, of similar gradient, for the whole of the afternoon, and there is an enormous difference perceptible in the temperature. The effect, however, is in some degree counterbalanced by the fact that the soil and the plants on the easterly slope are swept by the withering and desiccating winds which sweep over the arid plains of the interior.

We have seen, then, that the heat is very largely affected by the aspect, but the relative amount of heat and coolness is of course controlled, to a very considerable degree, by the gradient of the land, and just as steep northern slopes will be very cool, and steep eastern slopes moderately so, so will steep southerly and steep westerly gradients be extremely hot. The heat and coolness of the land, then, is constantly varying, not only with the aspect, but with the steepness of the gradients, and both of these points must be taken into consideration in regulating the quantity of shade required; and the reader will therefore see how impossible it is to give more than a general guide towards the quantity of shade required, and all I can undertake to say is that about twice as much shade is required on a southerly as on a northerly slope, that rather more shade is required on a westerly than on an eastern aspect, and that the last named requires less than a southerly aspect.

But this question is further complicated by the varying quality of the soil.

For our soils vary much in the same plantation, and require a greater or less degree of shade accordingly. The lighter and drier soils, of course, require not only more shade, but different kinds of trees, and in the case of such soils jack and cub busree should be freely used, and especially the former.

The quantity and quality of the shade required is also complicated by considerations as regards wind, and, where the soil is exposed to drying east winds, more shade should be put down than would otherwise be necessary, had we only to deal with the drying caused by the sun's heat. And in the case of such lands the shade should consist very largely of jack and other thick foliaged trees, and these should be topped in order to keep them short and bushy, and thus the more able to shield the land from the effects of desiccating winds.

And the whole subject is further complicated by questions of elevation and the varying quantity of rainfall, as the planter is nearer to, or farther from the Western Ghauts, and here I can only say generally, that the nearer you go to the Ghauts the less shade you will require, and the further to the east the more is necessary, but the planter must be guided here by local experience, as it is impossible to write precisely on the subject.

Before quitting this branch of my subject, it may be well to show in a single sentence the overwhelming importance of having well regulated shade of the best kinds. If, then, the shade is excessive, the coffee will not bear well, and if it is deficient or composed of a bad class of trees, the coffee will be certain to suffer from Borer and leaf disease.

From what I have said in the previous sentence it is evident that the regulation of the shade is of great importance. And, as the plantation ages, this thinning of the shade, lopping sometimes lower boughs, removing others, and cutting down occasional trees, requires constant attention. As a rule the whole shade should be carefully re-regulated at the end of every second year, or at the beginning of the third, when it will generally be found that, in consequence of the spread of the trees, there will be much thinning to be done. To cut down trees without injury to the coffee is, I need hardly say, a very nice operation, though it is one that the natives of the wooded countries, and especially the labourers from the foot of the Ghauts, are very expert at. It should never be attempted with coolies from the plains, who, of course, are unused to climbing trees, and have no experience of woodland work. The branches and tops of the trees to be felled are first removed, after a stout rope has been attached to a fork, above the point to be cut, and the end of the rope is then run round the butt of an adjacent tree, and held by a man. A huge bough is cut and falls with a threatening crash, but so well is the end of the rope judged that the ends of the twigs just touch the tops of the coffee trees. Then a coolie proceeds to lop off the smaller twigs and branches of the bough, and as he does so, it is gradually lowered till all are removed, and the bough, bereft of its clothing, is laid on the ground. Then comes the difficult task of felling the trees between the rows of coffee, a work of great nicety, which is partly effected by the final stroke of the axe, and partly by hauling a rope attached to the top of the tree. When a tree cannot be felled between the rows, it may often be felled so as to fall into the fork of an adjacent tree, and there it may be either left till it decays or let gently down to the ground, if the stem is a thin one. Bamboo ladders should be used to ascend the tree up to the first branch, as, though coolies can readily ascend without them, their bare legs are apt to suffer, and it is for this reason that coolies often try to shirk joining the shade party. The branches lopped off should be cut up into short lengths, and piled between the coffee trees. Such branches and twigs, as they decay, form good manure.

I have said that the proper regulation of shade is a work of great importance. It is also one of great difficulty, for the person who marks the shade trees to be removed must have a thorough knowledge of the kinds most worthy of preservation, and at the same time bear in mind the aspects, the gradients, the relation of the earth to the sun during the hottest months, and the declination of the sun; and, as the planter will be usually marking shade trees in the morning, he must keep constantly in view the points where the sun will strike in during the hot afternoon hours.

Then as he looks at a shade tree that has shot up to a great height, he must consider whether its shade is thrown on the coffee it once shaded or on to the top of an adjacent shade tree, and, as regards such a tree, he will often find that he is keeping on his land a tree that is merely throwing a shade on to another shade tree. I was particularly struck with this lately when looking at some howligay trees that had shot up to a great height, and which I at once ordered to be removed, as I found that their shade was now simply thrown on to the surrounding shade trees. In short, the trees were now doing no good, and were therefore merely doing harm by occupying the land and robbing it of food. I have said that when marking shade the planters must bear in mind the relation of the earth to the sun during the hottest months, and this caution is very necessary, because if he should happen to be marking trees in January for removal after the crop season is over, and does not remember that the earth is daily shifting its position, he will find that he will have made many mistakes as to the trees which should be preserved, and that a tree that is very well placed for blocking out the hot afternoon sun in January, may be of very little use in March and April.

After a shade tree has been cut down it is necessary, in order to prevent the stump throwing up suckers, to remove the bark thoroughly from the stump, and also from any roots that project from the surface of the ground. If this is not done the stump and its roots will live on and take up manure intended for the coffee.

It is important to remember that, in many parts of an estate, as the shade trees become lofty the sun will come in, just as it would on a man's head if he carried his umbrella erect, and at the end of a long pole, and I have seen coffee trees so much exposed to the sun as to require fresh shade to be planted near them, notwithstanding that some of the coffee trees in question were almost touching the stem of a very tall shade tree. When the planter observes that the sun is thus likely to come in from the shooting up of the shade trees, he should plant fresh shade. Nor need he be afraid of putting down too much, for it is easily removed if this is done when the trees are small, and then it must also be remembered that, as the plantation ages, both coffee and soil call for more shade, as the growing power of the land, and its ability to keep the trees fresh and green, naturally diminishes with the advance of time. Whenever, then, the appearance of the coffee shows that it is needed, fresh shade should be at once supplied, for every yellow leaved patch of coffee in a plantation is a breeding ground for the Borer insects, which will gradually spread into the adjacent coffee, where their presence will never be detected till hot, dry seasons occur, which they are sure to do sooner or later. When spreading from such yellow patches the Borer insect may not attack strong trees. On the contrary, it will generally attack those which are in a dried up condition either from weakness of constitution or because they are suffering from the effects of an over heavy crop, but in such trees it will surely obtain a footing, and so be ready to spread further when hot, dry seasons arrive. When, then, the appearance of the coffee shows that more shade is required, charcoal trees should be planted, and on the northern side of them cuttings of the good caste shade trees should be put down; and I particularly emphasize the side for the nurse because it is thus interposed between the sun and the permanent shade trees to be sheltered.

When the permanent shade trees have grown to the required size, the charcoal trees should be removed. It must be remembered that the permanent shade trees will grow very slowly unless sheltered by such nurses from the sun, and further, that the older the land the slower is the growth of all trees. It is most necessary, then, in all old land to dig holes at least four feet deep, and fill them with some good top soil from the forest, or with ordinary soil and cattle manure and bones. In order fully to protect the young shade trees from cattle and the sun, I now erect a square of fencing composed of palm tree slabs, and so high that cattle cannot reach over it, and, in the dry season, place some toddy tree branches across the square so as to shade the plants put down. In each square I plant a cub busree cutting, or one of the five kinds of trees recommended; sow several jack seeds, and a charcoal tree as nurse. In the case of the tree cutting failing to thrive, the planter will then always have a jack tree to fall back on. Should the cutting succeed the jack plant may be removed. I may here add that the parts requiring more shade are naturally more apparent in the hot season, and the planter should then put down a short pole with a flag at the end of it, whenever more shade is required. This will greatly facilitate the work of shade planting in the monsoon, as at that time the places where more shade is required are not very readily apparent, as all the coffee then becomes more or less green.

I have alluded to the fact that parasites (Kanarese—*Bundlikay*) attack the shade trees, and especially the nogurigay and jack trees. They should, of course, be cut off along with the bough on which they may happen to be growing; and it is important to remember that this should be done before the seed ripens, which is usually at the beginning of the monsoon. The latter end of April is the best time to carry out this work, as, if deferred till rain begins, the trees become slippery, and so dangerous for the climbers.

I have pointed out that the five trees I have recommended as being the best for shade can all be grown from cuttings, and it is important to point out that these should be taken from young and vigorous trees, and not, as is often done, from trees which are declining from age. There are some useful remarks at pages 88 and 89 of Mr. Graham Anderson's "Jottings on Coffee," on the preparation and planting of cuttings. The holes should be two feet deep, and filled up to three-quarters of the depth with soil. The cuttings should be six feet long with a fork at the top. They should be made at the beginning of the monsoon, and left in a cool and shady place in order to thicken the sap, the lower extremity of the cutting should be cut off with a curved slope, like the mouth-piece of a flageolet. Put the cutting gently into the hole, so as not to fray the bark, and tread down firmly. Wounds should be smeared with a mixture of cowdung and mud. The attí (*Ficus glomerata*) may also be grown from cuttings, but these should be rather thinner than those taken from the five trees first mentioned as being the best to plant for shade.

It has been previously pointed out that charcoal trees are valuable as nurses. They may be raised by clearing and burning a small piece of jungle, or by putting some virgin jungle soil in a bed and watering it, when charcoal plants will spring up. When a few inches high, take the plants up carefully with a ball of earth and transplant into baskets filled with jungle top soil. Put out the plants with their baskets in holes about the size of those usually made for coffee plants, and early in the monsoon, and see that they are well protected from cattle.

In conclusion, I think it well to mention that we have on my property, so far as I am aware, by far the oldest artificial shading of coffee in India. For many years all the estates in Mysore relied on the original forest shade, but mine was partly destroyed by a running fire when the clearings were first made, and some of the land was cleared wholly down, burned off, and planted with the most desirable kinds of shade trees. Our experience on this property dates back to the year 1857, and is therefore particularly valuable, for the defects connected with some trees were not apparent for as much, in one important case, as thirty years.

CHAPTER XII.

MANURE.

THE question of shade is, as we have seen, a highly complicated one, and is also, as we shall see, a cause of complication in the subject we are now about to consider; for, were no shade required, the subject of manuring the land for coffee would, comparatively speaking, be a simple one. And it is very important to call attention to this point, because hitherto planters have not in any way allowed shade to disturb their manurial practices, but have applied their manures equally to land under the direct shade of the trees, and to the open spaces between them, which are only under the influence of lateral shade, or, in other words, have manured their land as if there were no shade trees on it whatever. A little consideration, however, will show that the kinds and qualities of the manures applied should be quite different under the shade of trees, from what they ought to be in the open spaces between them. For, close around the stems of the shade trees we have a large leaf deposit, which manures the soil and maintains its physical condition, and, at the same time, comparatively speaking, small crops of coffee, while in the open spaces between the shade trees we have a small amount of leaf deposit, and much heavier crops of coffee. If, then, we further take into consideration the fact that the soil between the shade trees is liable to be deteriorated by a greater exposure to wash and to baking from the sun after the soil has been thoroughly soaked, it is evident that manuring should be largely varied both in quality and quantity, if we are at once to manure efficiently and economically. And I desire the more particularly to call attention to this matter, because no planter, as far as I am aware, has at all studied the subject. And it is principally of very great importance because what we call bulk manures, *i.e.*, farmyard manures, pulp, composts, and top soil, are difficult to procure in large quantities, and cost much to apply, as they have to be carried on coolies' heads, and often for considerable distances, down the rows of coffee trees. The more, then, we can limit our applications of bulk manure to such lands as urgently require them, the better shall we be able to devote a full supply to the soil which most requires such manures. Now if we apply our bulk manures to the land directly under the shade trees, we shall certainly be injudiciously using our manurial resources, because the leaf deposit under the shade trees supplies exactly that kind of padding which gives its chief value to bulk manures, and, if these opinions are sound, it therefore follows that we should, as a rule, apply all our bulk manures to the spaces between the shade trees, and only apply them to the land under the shade trees, when, from the soil being of a clayey character, an occasional application of bulk manure may be required to improve the texture of the soil, or, in other words, make it more easily workable. And it also follows that we should only apply bones, lime, and ashes, fish and oil-cake to the coffee under the direct influence of the shade trees.

But there is another question as regards manuring under the shade trees that requires careful consideration, and that is, whether we can, by heavy manuring, produce in such situations a larger crop than we could by a small application of manure, and from an experiment made by the late Mr. Pringle, formerly chemist on Messrs. Matheson and Co.'s estates in Coorg, it would seem to be a waste of money to supply more than a very moderate amount to the coffee directly under the shade trees, for he found that a considerable increase in the quantity of manure gave no increase in the crop. But I do not, of course, accept this experiment as conclusive, as it was made with bones alone, and it is possible that a more favourable result might have been obtained had an application of foliage stimulating manure been used as well, for the growth of new wood under shade is extremely slow, and it is probable that this slow growth, by giving an insufficient supply of young wood, is really the main cause of the yield under the shade trees being so much less than that from the coffee in the spaces between them. But the whole of this branch of my subject requires further careful experiment and observation before we can arrive at any definite conclusion. In the meanwhile, and till it can be shown that, with the aid of foliage stimulating manures, we can increase the yield under the direct shade of the trees, it is evident that as coffee under direct shade produces less than coffee in the spaces between the shade trees, the coffee that produces more should have a larger supply of manure.

It is hardly necessary to add here that, in order to prevent confusion, the whole field of coffee to be operated on should first of all be manured evenly all over with the quantity and quality of manure which it is advisable to use under the shade trees. After that, additional manure should be applied to the spaces between the shade trees. It is quite clear to me that a great economy of manure would be effected by this practice, and that from not applying bulk manures to the coffee under the shade trees, the physical condition of the land in the spaces between them could be maintained in a much more satisfactory degree than it is at present.

Then there is another question which, I believe, has hitherto escaped notice, and that is, as to whether we should not make some alteration in the kinds of manure so as to suit them better to the various aspects we have to deal with, for even in land of the same quality, and treated in precisely the same way, there is a considerable difference in the appearance of the coffee when we pass from an eastern or southern aspect to a western one, and a very great and marked difference is at once perceptible when you enter the coffee on a northern aspect. In the last-named case the coffee is nearly always green, and steadily but slowly growing, while on the southern and eastern aspects the coffee in the hot weather is apt to present a dried-up and sickly appearance. Then on these two last-named aspects there is commonly an over supply of suddenly grown wood. We should therefore, I think, increase foliage-stimulating manures on northern aspects, and diminish them on the southern and eastern, while we should have a medium degree of such manure in the case of western aspects. It seems to me that the reasoning in favour of foliage-stimulating manures on northern aspects is the same as in the case of coffee trees under direct tree shade, which always prevents the rapid growth of new wood. But on this point, as well as on that in the previous section, experiments must be made before any definite conclusion can be arrived at.

The quantity of manure that should be annually supplied is evidently a matter of the greatest importance, and here the first thing to be borne in mind is that of the four manures we require, namely, lime, nitrogen, phosphoric acid, and potash, the first two are somewhat easily removed from the soil, while the last two are firmly retained by it. It is evident, then, that lime and nitrogen should be applied little and often, while phosphoric acid and potash may be applied either little and often, or in large quantities at longer intervals, whichever may be found most convenient. But in the opinion of an eminent agricultural chemist whom I have specially consulted on the subject, nitrogen, if applied in slowly decomposing form, as for instance, in the shape of oil-cake, would only be lost in an infinitesimal degree, but still he admits that there would be a loss, and as we cannot tell what that loss may amount to under the influence of our tropical climate and deluges of rain, it would be safe to assume that nitrogen, as well as lime, should be put down at short intervals and, in order to make up for the escape of these manures from the soil, in larger proportions than either phosphoric acid or potash.

I have pointed out that phosphoric acid is retained by the soil, and it is important to remember that it is only removed by the crops of coffee to the extent of from one-and-a-half to two pounds per acre per annum, and these are two facts that every planter should bear in mind when he contemplates following the common custom of manuring with bones. For if he remembers that about one-half of the bones consists of phosphate of lime, and that about one-half of the latter consists of phosphoric acid, he will at a glance see, when he estimates the amount of phosphoric acid removed by the crops, that if he puts down even 100 lbs. of bones per acre he will have put down enough phosphoric acid for about twelve crops of coffee. And yet for a planter to put down 3 cwt. of bones per annum regularly is quite a common thing, and a friend of mine, after having manured his land one year with bones to a moderate amount, put down each year, for the two following years, no less than three-quarters of a ton of bone-meal per acre. So that, making a large allowance for the phosphoric acid taken up by the shade trees, he had put down, in these last two years, enough phosphoric acid to last for the crops of 300 years. From the application of bones he had undoubtedly obtained a great benefit, but I feel sure that it was from the lime and the nitrogen of the bones, for the application of bones that preceded the two applications of three-quarters of a ton per annum must have left the soil amply supplied with phosphoric acid. Now assuming that the soil required lime, and a moderate degree of nitrogen, these could have been supplied far more cheaply, and just as efficiently had my friend applied a small dressing of ordinary lime, and some oil-cake, and I am the more convinced of the accuracy of this view after visiting Mr. Reilly's Hillgrove estate near Coonoor on the slopes of the Nilgiri hills, and hearing the result of his very long experience. Bones he had never used but once, and that on a small portion of the estate, but he had always applied lime once every three years at the rate of about 4 or 5 cwt. per acre; the other manures he had used were cattle manure, and town manure from Coonoor, and these added to the small quantity originally in the soil, had supplied his coffee amply with the 2 lbs. of phosphoric acid annually removed by the crops. After much consideration, and hearing Mr. Reilly's views, it seems quite clear to me that as but a small quantity of phosphoric acid is removed by the crops, and as that manure is firmly retained by the soil, bones need only be used at long intervals provided lime is regularly applied in small quantities.

And next, before we can approach, or attempt to determine, the quantity of manure required, we have to take into account the loss by wash, either from the surface or by downward percolation, and the absorption of manure by the roots of the shade trees. We have also to take into consideration the manure returned by the shade trees in the shape of fallen leaves, and the ammonia derived from the rainfall, so that it is impossible to state with any approach to accuracy the amount of manure that should be applied. We can only say then that, whatever the required amount may be it must be very considerable, for in addition to the above-mentioned losses of manure, we require a considerable amount for the demands of the coffee trees, and that, further, it must vary with the amount of the rainfall, and the retentive or non-retentive character of the soil. The crop, it is true, takes comparatively little from the soil, and Mr. John Hughes, Agricultural Chemist, 79, Mark Lane,—points out in his "Reports on Ceylon Soils and Coffee Manures," that 5 cwt. of parchment coffee an acre, which is an average crop over a long series of years, only removes from the soil—

	lbs.
Nitrogen	$8\frac{1}{4}$
Potash	$7\frac{1}{2}$
Phosphoric acid	$1\frac{1}{2}$
Lime	1
	$18\frac{1}{4}$.

Assuming then, he tells us, that the small quantity of potash required could be supplied by the soil, and that the pulp is returned to it, the loss by the crops could be fully supplied by 100 lbs. of castor cake and 10 lbs. of bones per acre. Then if we require much more from the plant than the production of crop (for we expect it, in addition, to grow wood for the succeeding crop, and during this process the plant grows much superfluous wood, besides suckers, which have to be removed), it must be remembered that all prunings and superfluous wood are left on the land. What there is actually carried off it is really very small in quantity. Why, then, it will naturally be asked, is it necessary that so much manure should be present in the soil if we wish to grow good coffee and have continuously good crops, and why is it that if manuring is neglected you will soon find that it is only the rich hollows that are able to maintain the coffee in good condition and produce good crops continuously? To such questions no distinct answer can be given, and we can only conjecture that coffee, when it wants its food, must, for some unknown reason, have a considerable supply at hand. There is, however, one test which, I think, always shows conclusively whether this food is present in the quantity required to supply the needs of the plant. Just before the hot weather the coffee trees throw out a small flush of young wood. Now if the trees have given a fair average crop, and at the same time have a good show of bearing wood for the next season's crop, and are also throwing out a good supply of vigorous young shoots, then you may be sure that your land is well fed. But if the trees throw out no young shoots at that time, or very few, then you will know that your land is not as well fed as it ought to be.

It might naturally be supposed that I could furnish some guide to the planter, from our experience in Mysore, as to the quantity of manure that should be put down, but I regret to say that I am unable to do so, as I know of no estate where a regular and continuous system of manuring has been carried out. But in North Coorg, and very close to the Mysore Border, the continuous practice on Mr. Mangles's Coovercolly Estate of 500 acres gives a fairly approximate idea of what can keep an estate in a well-fed condition. There the practice has been to put down every third year from 7 to 10 cwt. of bone-meal an acre, and one-third of a bushel of cattle manure, and, besides this, composts of pulp, mixed with top soil and lime. Now this is the finest estate I ever saw. The coffee was even and of a beautiful colour, and when I saw it towards the end of 1891 there was a fair crop of coffee on the trees, and an ample supply of young wood for the following crop, and the land was so well fed with nitrogen that an experimental application of nitrate of soda to a part of the land had produced no perceptible effect on the trees. From what I have previously said as to the application of bone-meal being overdone, I think it probable that the estate would have presented as good an appearance had the land, after once being well stored with phosphoric acid, been treated with small applications of lime instead of bones. Then another estate I saw in 1891 in Coorg, in the Bamboo district, furnished some guide as to the amount of manure required where cattle manure was not available, and on the estate in question, which had both a good crop on the trees and ample wood for the future, I was informed that, in the year previous, 6 cwt. of castor cake and 3 cwt. of bones had been applied per acre, and that for the four preceding years $4\frac{1}{3}$ cwt. of manure, containing 2 parts of castor to 1 of bones, had been applied, but that the last-named amount had been found to be too small. The reader will find in the chapter on Coorg some further information, which has since been supplied to me by Mr. Meynell, on this point.

The quantity of manure that should be put down at a time is evidently a matter of great importance, as if you begin by putting down a large application you are certain to have an over-heavy crop, followed by exhaustion, and a very poor crop the following year, while the object of all intelligent fruit cultivators is to work for moderate even crops. It seems quite clear, then, that we should manure little and often, as you thereby not only avoid the risk of over-heavy crops, but economize your manure. For is it not obvious that if you put down at once a supply of nitrogen and lime to last for three years, you increase the risk of loss from wash and downward percolation? And it must also be considered that an over-heavy crop leaves the trees in an exhausted and dried-up state to go through the hot weather, when they will be liable to be attacked by the Borer insect, which, as we shall afterwards more particularly see, delights in dry wood. So that when we further take into consideration the injury to the constitution of the trees which is caused by over-heavy crops, we need have no doubt that there is much reason to dread them. I would therefore strongly deprecate, for the preceding reasons, heavy manuring (even the mind may be over-manured in the eager desire to arrive at a cultured intellect), and would advise that a beginning be made with a moderate application, and, if this is found to be insufficient, that the amount be gradually increased till the trees show that they can with ease give regular average crops. If cattle manure or jungle top soil is available, a quarter of a bushel a tree may be annually applied of either, accompanied by 3 cwt. of bone-meal. And, if neither of the two former sources are available, then 3 cwt. of bone-meal and 2 cwt. of white castor cakes would be a reasonable application. After applying 3 cwt. of bone-meal per acre for three consecutive years the land ought to be amply stocked with phosphoric acid, and the bone-meal should be discontinued, and its place supplied with small applications of lime, either annually or at intervals of two or three years, should the latter course be more convenient. And subsequently, when there is reason to suppose that the land requires a fresh supply of phosphoric acid, an application of bone-meal may again be used. I would particularly warn the planter against over-manuring light dry soil, or south and south-western aspects, or the upper and drier portions of eastern aspects, as an over-heavy crop on these aspects is very perilous even with good shade, for we may not have a drop of rain from November till April, and should such a drought occur, and be preceded by a dry season (and such seasons occurred in 1865 and 1866, and caused the great attack of the Borer insect, which was so fatal to all insufficiently-shaded coffee, and from which even well-shaded coffee suffered to some extent), or should even a single dry, hot season follow immediately after the crop is picked, there would be sure to be a serious drying up of the plant, with but small chance of its bearing anything worth having the season following, and very great risk of a severe attack of Borer. But on northern and north-western aspects the land is not exposed to parching east winds, and, as we have seen, has a temperature about one-half cooler than that on a southern aspect, and the planter may therefore on such aspects manure with greater freedom. But even in these aspects I am sure that over-heavy manuring will lead ultimately to injury to the trees, and, in a series of years, to the production of a smaller amount of coffee.

I have indicated the amount of manure which in my opinion ought to be put down when manure is applied for the first time on a plantation, and if the plantation is of a flat character, or only on very moderate slopes, the manure should be evenly applied all over it. But if, as often happens, there are hollows and ridges on the land, then the ridges should be, as a rule, much more heavily manured than the hollows, for which a very little manure will suffice, as so much is washed into them, and they are, besides, much richer to start with. It is very important to note at the outset all those spots which, in the original forest, are very rich, so that the manure may be applied accordingly, and though, as I have said, the ridges as a rule are poor, there are many instances where the top of a ridge, from being pretty wide, is rich, though the sides of it for a little way down are nearly always poor. I have lately been minutely examining old forest land, with the view of removing top soil from it, and have been much struck with the variation in the depth of the rich surface soil.

We have next to consider the time of year at which manure should be applied to the land, and here we shall find that the planter, like the farmer, often has to do things when he can, and not when he should, and though, from the risk of loss by wash alone, there can be no doubt that all manures should be put down after the heavy rains of the monsoon are over, it is difficult to see how this can be carried out in the case of bulk manures, on account of the difficulty of getting enough labour to at once cope with the ordinary estate work, and apply a class of manure which absorbs so much hand labour. Then there is the difficulty of carting manure at that season when the roads, which are not macadamized, would be cut to pieces. But this difficulty could be overcome were a sufficient number of storage sheds provided to which the manure might be carted during the dry season. But the sheds would cost a good deal of money, and the cost of the manure would be increased by the cost of extra handling, or in other words putting the manure in the sheds and taking it out again. So that I am inclined to think that it would be better to apply, by direct cartage from the cattle sheds, as much bulk manure as can be applied in the month of September, and the remainder at any convenient time after crop. Another great objection to applying manure after crop, and before the monsoon, is, that you stimulate the growth of the weeds which spring up with the early rains, and also much growth of suckers, and superfluous wood in the coffee, all of which have to be handled off at considerable expense, whereas, it is hardly necessary to say, that the weed growth is smaller at the end of the monsoon, and the force of the plant directed rather to the maturing of the berry than the growth of surplus wood. But in the case of light manures such as bones and castor cake, there is no difficulty in applying them in September, and an effort should certainly be made to put them down then. Another advantage of manuring at the end of the monsoon would be that the planter could then clearly perceive what trees would be certain to give a good crop, and give them an extra quantity of manure, and also diminish his application of manure in the case of such parts of the plantation as might be yielding a small crop. I may here mention that, from reliable information received from Coorg, results there have shown that it is best to apply a portion of the manure after crop to strengthen the blossom, and a portion after the heavy monsoon rains are over to strengthen the trees and assist in maturing the crop.

But the most important point, perhaps, as regards the best time for manuring is the bearing that the time of manurial application has on leaf disease, and Mr. Marshall Ward in his third report on leaf disease (p. 15) has some most valuable remarks on this question. "The object of the planter should be," he says "to produce mature leaves as soon as possible and keep them on the branches as long as possible." Now if leaves are produced in April and May they become attacked by the fungus while still young, and in August and September the ripening crop is left bare on the branches. But the leaves which were in bud in December are matured and well hardened, and have already, by living longer, done much service to the tree. He then points out that when certain districts in Ceylon suffered from a bad attack of leaf disease in July, "a large surface of young and succulent leaves were ready to receive the spores of the Hemeleia." The germination of the spores was rapid, and the young leaves were soon destroyed. The planter then, he says, should manure and prune so as to grow matured leaves during those months when the least damp and wind may be expected. And the same remarks are evidently equally valuable as regards rot, and show us the necessity of modifying our manurial and pruning practices so as to enable the tree the better to contend against it as well as leaf disease. All manuring, then, which leads to the production of young succulent foliage just at the beginning of the rains should be avoided, and the same remark applies equally to pruning. But I shall again return to the subject when writing on pruning.

As to the best method of applying the manure, great differences of opinion and practice exist. At one time in Mysore it was customary to cut a shallow trench in the shape of a half moon around the upper sides of the trees about two feet from the stem, and deep enough to contain the manure, which was then covered in with the soil taken out. But this process was found to be expensive, and of course took much labour, which is sometimes extremely scarce, and on my property we have for some years past—excepting in the case of manuring with fish, which is liable to be carried off by birds, dogs, jackals, and village pigs—scattered all the manure on the surface, and close around the stem of the tree, with the idea that the manure would be less likely to be taken up by weeds, and by the roots of the shade trees. But in connection with this system there is a fact which I did not take into account, but which is well worthy of careful consideration, and that is, that the tendency of such a system of manuring is to keep the coffee roots close to the surface. Now it has been suggested by the late Mr. Pringle, whose opinion on another matter I have previously given, that this would have an unfavourable effect, if we had, as sometimes happens, deficient blossom showers; as in that case, and with many rootlets near the surface, a stimulus would be given to the plant which would induce it to throw out the blossom when there was not enough rain to bring it to perfection; whereas, if, by putting down the manure more deeply we attracted the roots downwards, the blossom buds could only be started after such an amount of rain as would give the soil such a soaking that a successful blossom would be insured. There certainly seems to me to be a great deal in this idea, but I am not aware that we have had any experiments made side by side as regards surface manuring, and manuring in pits, and therefore am not in a position to express a decided opinion on the subject, but theoretically there would seem to be much in favour of burying manure in pits, and it seems certain that the manure would be less likely to be taken up by weeds than in the case of surface manuring.

I need hardly add that in the case of all steep parts of a plantation all manure should be, if not buried deeply, at least covered with soil after the digging of a trench large enough to contain the manure. On the plantations on the Nilgiri Hills the manure is put into pits $2\frac{1}{2}$ feet long, 1 foot 6 inches wide, and 1 foot deep on the lower side of the pit, which of course would make the side of the pit on the upper side of them much more than one foot in depth. The trenches or pits are dug across the slope and in front of each coffee tree, and in the line (*i.e.*, not in the centre of each set of four plants). These pits are not filled up to the brim, but the manure is placed in the bottom of them, and is then covered with soil, so that the pit is about one-half filled up. The soil taken out is heaped in a curve above the pit so as to prevent heavy rain washing down into the pit. When more manure is required to be added—say bone-meal—it is scattered on the soil in the pit, or the top soil in it is scraped off and the manure scattered and then covered up.

I now propose to consider our manurial resources in detail, and shall begin with the first stay of all agriculture, farmyard manure, as to the value of which for coffee I have never met with any difference of opinion. But there are many objections to relying on farmyard manure, or, at least, to applying it on a large scale, as, if the planter keeps many cattle of his own, he runs great risk of his herd being invaded by disease, and the difficulty and expense of feeding a large number of cattle is very considerable. In some cases it is possible to hire cattle from the natives, and this is done occasionally, and at the rate of 15 rupees a month for 100 head, but here again risk from disease is often incurred, and if it broke out, the natives would withdraw their cattle. The question then naturally arises whether, considering the great cost and trouble attendant on manufacturing cattle manure on a large scale, we cannot find some substitute that would diminish the quantity now required. And here it is important to ask what farmyard manure consists of. It consists, then, of the excreta of animals, and the vegetable matter used as litter. From a chemical point of view it mainly provides, in addition to the organic matter, in a slowly-acting form, lime, nitrogen, potash, and phosphoric acid, and from a physical point of view it furnishes a padding to maintain the texture of the soil, or, in other words, to keep it in a loose and friable condition. And with reference to this last very important point, I may remind the reader that Sir John Lawes has well pointed out that "All our experiments tend to show that it is the physical condition of the soil, its capacity for absorbing and retaining moisture, its permeability to roots, and its capacity for absorbing and radiating heat, that is of more importance than its strictly-speaking chemical composition." Now as regards the chemical aspect of the manurial question, if we assume, as we have every reason to do from the small quantity of potash required, and its supply from decomposing stones in the land, that the potash does not require to be taken into account, we shall find that our nitrogen and phosphoric acid can be far more cheaply supplied by fish, or by a mixture of bone-meal and oil-cake than by farmyard manure, and should it be found that potash does require to be added, we could obtain it more cheaply from ashes or kainit. Then in order to provide the padding that farmyard manure supplies, and to furnish nitrogen in a slowly-acting form, we could collect dry leaves, twigs from jungle trees, ferns, and any other available vegetable matter, form them into a compost with some earth, or jungle top soil, and apply the mixture to the land. With such a compost as I have suggested, bone-meal or fish-manure in small quantity might be mixed, and we should then have a very good substitute for all the chemical and physical advantages to be derived from the very best kind of farmyard manure. But there is another way of arriving at the same end, which is open to many planters, and that it by collecting top soil from the fringe of jungle commonly left round the plantation, or from the uncultivated jungle of the estate, or from adjacent pieces of jungle land. And such pieces of land varying from ten to twenty acres can commonly be purchased, and can be used to supply top soil. This, of course, has in it much vegetable matter in various stages of decay, and a mixture of it with a small quantity of bone-meal would form a manure superior, as I shall afterwards show when I come to treat of top soil, to farmyard manure chemically, and superior to it from a physical point of view. To such local manurial resources I would call particular attention, as planters have hitherto relied far too exclusively on cattle manure, and imported manures, such as bones, fish, and oil-cake, and it is evident that we could dispense with much of all these manures if we made a full use of the resources I have recommended. In concluding my remarks on cattle manure I may observe that it is both costly to supply and to apply to the land. It is difficult, of course, to make exact calculations on the subject, as the facilities for supplying litter vary so much, but generally speaking it costs from 70 to 80 rupees an acre if we manure at about the rate of a third of a bushel per tree.

I now turn to a consideration of the value of jungle top soil, a manure to which I have only lately given particular attention, though I was, of course, well aware of its value in a general way, and may begin by stating that two samples of what we were using on my estates have been analyzed by Dr. Voelcker, the object being partly to ascertain the value of the soil and partly to compare its cost with the cost of cattle manure. After estimating the cost of making cattle manure, and calculating as closely as possible the cost of obtaining and applying jungle top soil from land adjacent to the plantation, it was found that in the case of the best sample of top soil, obtained by removing only four or five inches of the soil, it paid nearly twice as well to use it as a manurial agent as it would to use cattle manure, and I may add that three tons of the soil contain the same manurial matter as two tons of ordinary well-made English farmyard manure. In the case of the second sample analyzed, and which I was sure from the character of the land must be of inferior quality, it was found that 2¼ tons of the soil would contain as much manurial value as one ton of farmyard manure, and that the cost of using the two materials would be about the same.

I had also analyzed at the same time a sample of a kind of decayed pink-coloured rock, as I had found that coffee had thriven well in the pink soil which had evidently been formed from the rock in question, but the manurial value was so small that Dr. Voelcker thought that it might merely be of use in improving the physical condition of the soil. I however applied it to some backward coffee, and also applied some of the best top soil to a contiguous piece of backward coffee, and was much surprised to find that the pink soil, to which little direct manurial value was attached by Dr. Voelcker, showed results superior to the best top soil applied alongside of it, and I am now applying it on a large scale. This soil, I may mention, is applied by the natives to the surface of their vegetable beds. They do not attach any manurial value to it, but apply it to keep the vegetables cool, as the soil has quite a remarkable effect in keeping itself cool while the adjacent soil is quite hot, and I have now applied it to the flower beds near my house, and also to the walks around the bungalow. This pink decayed rock is sometimes streaked with a white decayed rock, which the natives call jadi mannu, and sometimes the latter so much preponderates that it looks nearly white. I am told by the natives that if you mix the red and white earth together and apply the mixture to the surface of the land it will never get dry.[1]

In concluding my remarks on soil applications, I may observe that if top soil costs the same price as cattle manure, the former is to be preferred for four reasons. It is much more easily handled and applied; it is a better substance for mixing with other manures, such as bonedust or ashes, for instance; it has a better physical effect on the soil; and is nearly free from weed seeds which abound in cattle manure.

I may add that I have since made a calculation with the object of seeing how, by the addition of manures to the kemmannu soil, I could make a mixture which would have

[1] I am now so satisfied with the capacity of these soils to keep themselves cool, that I am applying them as a top dressing to land deficient in shade and dry ridges. Since writing the above, I have ascertained from my manager the interesting fact that about seven weeks after putting down the red earth, newly grown white roots were found to be running all through this earth, though no rain had fallen from the time of the application of the soil up to the time the growth of the rootlets was observed. The adjacent land, to which virgin forest top soil had been applied, had no such growth of new rootlets, nor had any of the adjacent land, to which no top dressings had been applied. The red earth had evidently the power of taking in sufficient moisture from the atmosphere to stimulate a growth of young roots. The red earth was applied on February 20th, and no rain fell till April 7th. This growth of new rootlets, I may add, was also observed in another part of the plantation to which a top dressing of the red earth had been applied.

all the fertilizing ingredients of farmyard manure in addition to the advantages possessed by the soil, and which I have just enumerated. I find that if to 83 parts of the soil I added 1 part of bonedust, 12 parts of castor cake, 2 parts of potash salt, and 2 parts of lime, I should make up a compost equal to good English farmyard manure, and at but a slightly increased cost, which would be more than covered by the special physical and other advantages arising from the use of kemmannu.

The pulp of the coffee is very apt to be carelessly treated, and it is important to remember that Mr. Hughes, in his "Report on Ceylon Coffee, Soils, and Manures," estimates that, *if properly preserved*, two tons of pulp are equal to one ton of good farmyard manure. But it must not be washed, as it often is by being run into a pulp pit with water, or nearly all its valuable constituents would be lost. It should be mixed, he tells us, with cattle dung, or, if that is not procurable, with liberal supplies of lime, and he also suggests that it should be put under cover day by day. We have adopted on my property a plan which I think in these climates is the cheapest and best. A layer of top soil is placed in the road alongside of the coffee where we desire to use the manure; then each day's pulp is carted direct to the plantation and scattered over the top soil, and more top soil added, till we have a layer as thick as we find convenient, but of course not so thick as to prevent carts passing over it to other parts of the plantation. On these layers of pulp and top soil lime or bonedust may be sprinkled.

Dry fallen leaves is another local resource which should by no means be neglected, and they are commonly used for littering the cattle sheds. Such leaves are about equal to cattle dung. A sample of those we use was analyzed by Dr. Voelcker, and the result gave 1 per cent. of phosphate of lime, 1 per cent. of ammonia, and $\frac{3}{4}$ per cent. of potash.

Green twigs[1] cut from jungle trees are of considerable manurial value, and the natives seem well aware of the value of the different kinds. A sample of the following six kinds which are most approved of by the natives—namely, Japel, Nairal, Ubble, Gowl, Mutty and Hunchotee, was analyzed by Dr. Voelcker, and the result gave $\frac{1}{4}$ per cent. phosphate of lime, $\frac{3}{4}$ per cent. of potash, 1 per cent. of lime, and $\frac{3}{4}$ per cent. of nitrogen.

Ferns are of considerable manurial value, and are rich in potash, and they should be used to litter the cattle sheds.

Burnt earth has been formerly used in Ceylon, and has been recommended by Mr. Pringle for use in Coorg, but I have no experience of its use, but if it pays to use it in Coorg it would pay equally well to do so in Mysore.

Wood ashes are much valued in Ceylon, where they are applied at a cost of 1*s.* 3½*d.* a bushel. We buy ashes at 2 annas (less than 3*d.*) a bushel delivered on the estate. Though costing as much as 1*s.* 3½*d.* in Ceylon, Mr. Hughes says they are the cheapest form in which potash can be supplied there.

It should be remembered that the ashes of the stem wood and thick branches are not nearly so valuable as those of young branches and twigs. A good sample of the last-named contains 20½ per cent. of potash and more than 30 per cent. of lime. In many places in the vicinity of the estates much good manure might often be made by cutting down weeds and jungle plants of any kind, burning them, mixed with earth, slowly, and applying the mixture to the coffee.

[1] The full analyses of these leaves and twigs are given in the Appendix to Dr. Voelcker's work, "The Improvement of Indian Agriculture," which contains other analyses of interest to the planter. This important work should, I may repeat, be in the hands of all those interested in tropical cultivations.

I have only heard of one planter who used night soil. He had planks pierced with the necessary apertures, underneath which buckets with some soil in each were placed; these were removed daily and emptied into renovation pits in the coffee. Anybody depositing elsewhere was fined, and the fine given to the Toty, who had thus an interest in looking out for defaulters. There can be no doubt that this is an excellent system, and obviously advantageous from a sanitary point of view, and that it could with ease be carried out on an estate where all the coolies were of the lower castes, but it could not be carried out, and it would be very unwise to attempt it, in the case of an estate on which there are poor members of the better castes. It is even important on such a property to see that no pieces of ordinary paper find their way on to the farmyard manure heap, as, when such has been detected on my property, the women of the better castes refused to carry out the manure.

We have now examined what I may call the local manurial resources, and I propose to consider in detail those manures which have to be imported into the coffee districts from various quarters. Of these manures lime is one of the most important, and as three samples of soil from my property were all found to be very deficient in lime, it is probable that applications of lime are as desirable in Mysore generally as they are in the case of plantations on the Nilgiri slopes. Limestone can be procured from the interior of Mysore, and also from the port of Mangalore. It should always be burnt on the estate. It is a cheaper plan than having it burnt before importing it, and we get, besides, the ashes of the wood used for burning the lime. Lime is as valuable ground as burnt, and when it is ground is not so liable to suffer from rain as burnt lime is. It must not be mixed with bonedust, oil-cake, or potash salts, but should be put down some weeks before these manures. Lime should only be used in small quantities of half a ton or a ton an acre (it is usually used at the latter rate in Ceylon), as a free use of it would favour the escape of ammonia from the soil by too rapidly converting inert into active nitrogen, and, as a neighbour of mine once found, the result would probably be a heavy crop of coffee followed by exhaustion of the tree. Lime might be advantageously used more often where the land is liable to be soured, or where much vegetable matter has accumulated. It should be remembered that, as ashes contain about 30 per cent. of lime, we should diminish the quantity of lime when we have applied ashes. I have said that lime should be used at the rate of half a ton to a ton an acre, but I may remind the reader that Mr. Reilly had found that 4 or 5 cwt. regularly applied every three years was enough, and as to the quantity that should be used, the planter must be largely guided by the local experience. As lime is easily washed out of the soil, it seems to me that more should be applied in the case of a heavy, and less with a light rainfall.

Bonedust has been largely, and I think, as the reader will see from my previous remarks, very wastefully used in manuring coffee. It varies much in quality, and the purchaser would do well to obtain a guarantee as regards its genuineness. Bonedust should be mixed with fine top soil, and then applied to the land, or it may be mixed with cattle manure, or applied as a surface dressing, but either of the two first-named methods of application is to be preferred. In 500 lbs. of bones there are, in round numbers, about 250 lbs. of phosphate of lime, which consists of 125 lbs. of phosphoric acid and as many of lime. I may remind the reader that 5 cwt. of parchment takes from the soil 1 lb. of lime and 1½ lb. of phosphoric acid.

Fish manure is of great value, especially in bringing rapidly on backward or sticky coffee. A sample I have had analyzed contained 7⅓ per cent. of ammonia and nearly

$9\frac{1}{2}$ per cent. of phosphate of lime. The whole fish can be imported from the coast, and they should be broken up and mixed with top soil. This is not only advantageous for distributing the manure throughout the land when it is applied, but it is particularly necessary in the case of fish, as I have found by practical experience that, if applied whole and covered with soil, crows, kites, jackals and pigs dig them up and carry them off.

Oil-cakes of various kinds have always been a favourite manure, and it is a particularly desirable one, because the nitrogen in it is in a slowly convertible form. Of all the cakes castor is said to be of the highest manurial value (though an analysis I have had made of ground nut cakes gives a better result in nitrogen), and besides nitrogen it contains phosphate of lime, magnesia, and potash. In an analysis I had made of brown castor oil-cake, *i.e.*, cake made after crushing the entire seeds, there was over 4 per cent. of phosphate of lime, or about equal to 5 per cent. had the cake been white castor, which is made after the seeds have been decorticated. But another sample of brown castor which was analyzed for me, only gave a little more than $2\frac{3}{4}$ per cent. of phosphate of lime. From this difference, and from the general consideration of the differences of all seeds in particular seasons, and also in some degree from various soils, it seems to me there must often be, from natural causes, a considerable difference in the value of cakes. The attention of purchasers should be directed to these differences; they should obtain, if possible, a guarantee as to the composition of the cakes they buy, and occasionally test the manure.

From what I have said as to the composition of castor cake, it is probable that white castor contains from 4 to 5 per cent. of phosphate of lime, and I desire to call particular attention to this, because oil-cake is usually regarded purely as a nitrogenous source of manure, whereas one of the oil-cakes commonly used—*i.e.*, castor cake—contains an appreciable quantity of that phosphate of lime of which bones are generally considered to be the sole suppliers by the planter. But it is evident that if we annually used 300 lbs. per acre of white castor, we should, even if it contained only 4 per cent. of phosphate of lime, be supplying six times the amount of lime and more than three times the amount of phosphoric acid removed by an average crop of coffee, and though the lime is liable to loss from waste, it must be remembered that the phosphoric acid is firmly retained by the soil. It is important to remember that castor cake should, like bones, be mixed with a considerable quantity of fine top soil, so that the manure may be widely distributed through the soil.

Nitrate of potash, or saltpetre, is an extremely expensive manure, and not a desirable one, because the nitrogen in it is in a too quickly assimilable form, and is very liable to be lost in drainage. But it might be used with effect, and in small quantities, for bringing forward supplies, and I am informed that for this purpose it has been used with advantage in Coorg. I have used the nitrate of potash on my property—an experimental amount only—and it caused the trees to throw out strong and numerous shoots. It should be bought in the form of pure nitre.

Nitrate of soda is also liable to the objection that the nitrogen in it is in a too quickly available form, and liable to be lost. I have never used it on my property, but from observing its effect on an estate in Coorg, and the effect it had in causing the trees to throw out a fine supply of young wood, can see that it might be used with great effect in rapidly forcing forward worn-out coffee growing on an exhausted soil. But if used for this purpose it should be backed up with a liberal supply of bones and castor cake, or of bones and farmyard manure, or bones and top soil, as, if not so backed up, the result would be unsatisfactory, if not disastrous, seeing that the nitrate of soda, if applied alone, would cause the plant to wring out everything that was available in the soil. The application of nitrate of soda on the estate alluded to was at the rate of 2 cwt. an acre, and cost 21 rupees an acre, inclusive of the cost of application. I saw the estate at the end of October, and the nitrate had been put down in March previous. The wood it had been the means of producing was very good and strong, dark green, and abundant, and the effect of the nitrate was by no means confined to one season, for the effect of the nitrate put down the year previous was still apparent. The land here evidently was short of nitrogen, and hence the good effect of the nitrate, but as I mentioned previously, an application of nitrate had produced no perceptible effect on another estate belonging to the same proprietor, which had been regularly well manured with bones and cattle manure and composts, and because, of course, the land was so well supplied with nitrogen that the coffee required no more. In concluding my remarks on the effects of nitrate of soda, I may observe that by using this manure, unremunerative coffee might be turned into a paying estate in less than two years, while without the aid of it, from three to four years would be required.

Potash is a manure as to which I can give no distinct information, or, at least, only information of a negative kind. I once sent out a small quantity of the muriate of potash, but my manager could perceive no effects from it whatever, and I have been informed of an instance of its having been applied to an estate in Coorg at the rate of one quarter of a pound a tree, or at the rate of between 3 and 4 cwt. an acre, without any perceptible effect having been produced from the application.

Then it must be remembered that the quantity of potash

removed by an average crop of coffee is only $7\frac{1}{2}$ lbs. an acre, that potash is firmly held by the soil, and that it is constantly being supplied in small quantities by the fallen leaves (these contain $\frac{3}{4}$ per cent. of potash) of the shade trees and the decomposition of stones in the soil, and in applications of farmyard manure. And with reference to the demands for potash by the tree, I may mention that I, in conjunction with a friend, endeavoured to estimate the consumption of potash by the crop, and we sent to Professor Anderson, of Glasgow, a carefully drawn sample of soil taken from between four coffee trees from which twelve crops of coffee had been removed without any manure being supplied, and also a sample of virgin soil adjacent to the coffee (soil similar in every respect except that it had not been cropped), and asked him to spare no expense in analysis. The result was remarkable, for the soil from which the twelve crops had been taken was found to be very little deteriorated in anything except the quantity of lime it held, which was less than in the virgin soil. The explanation evidently was that the leaves from the shade trees, and perhaps decomposing stones, had supplied all the potash removed by the crops. "Why, then," asked my friend, who had called on the Professor to hear the result of the investigation, "can young coffee easily be grown on the virgin soil, while it would come on very slowly and poorly in the soil from which the twelve crops of coffee had been taken?" "Simply," was the answer, "because the untouched virgin soil is in a beautiful physical condition, while the soil in the plantation has been rained upon and walked upon, and thus had its physical condition impaired." I need hardly add that what I have just written is highly instructive, as it corroborates what Sir John Lawes has said, and which I have previously quoted, as to the physical condition of the soil being of more importance than its, strictly speaking, chemical composition, and it shows us the importance of maintaining a perfect physical condition of the soil, partly by cultivation and partly by additions of bulk manure—farmyard manure—top soil, and composts.

To grow young plants in old soil requires great attention to manuring and preparing the soil, so as to supply the physical and chemical requirements necessary for the vigorous growth of the young plants. Now we know that the plants thrive well in virgin soil, and we cannot do better than fill the holes with it, if it can possibly be procured within any reasonable distance. If it cannot, then the soil should be mixed with some thoroughly decayed and dried cattle manure, mixed with bonedust, and if it is desired to rush the plant forward, a slight dressing of nitrate of potash might subsequently be applied.

Coprolites, the supposed fossilized remains of animals, which would probably contain about 40 to 50 per cent. of phosphate of lime, have been discovered in Mysore, and I am informed by an executive Engineer officer in the Mysore offices that they are to be found over an area of about two square miles, and at about a distance of seven miles from the Maddur Railway Station on the Bangalore Mysore line. This is a highly important discovery, and, when developed, ought to be the means of furnishing the planter with cheap supplies of the mineral phosphate of lime. I may mention that as one find of coprolites has been made in the province, it is highly probable that further discoveries of this valuable manure may be made. A discovery of phosphatic nodules has also been made near Trichinopoly, in the Madras Presidency, and though not of quality sufficiently good for export to England, has been reported on by Dr. Voelcker as being good enough for use amongst the plantations of Southern India. A deposit has also been discovered in the Cuddapah district.

We have now glanced at all the local manurial resources at the command of the planters, and also the manures which may be purchased at a distance from the plantations, and as to the latter the question now naturally arises as to how the planter can best lay out his money when manuring his coffee. Now I know of no planter in India who has knowledge enough to decide as to how he should lay out his money. The planter knows in a general way that he wants nitrogen, phosphoric acid, lime, and perhaps some potash, but as to the most desirable and economical sources from which to obtain them he is unable to decide, and it is not a question, even if he called in an agricultural chemist, to be decided once for all, for the prices of the various manures are constantly liable to change. Here, then, is a matter that should be taken up by the Government, which in this respect should follow the example of the Sussex Agricultural Association, the chemist of which publishes every spring the most economical manurial mixture which the farmer can use for his various purposes. In this thinly populated country the well-to-do planters are too few, and the humble native planters too poor, to do what is done by the rich agricultural societies of Great Britain in the way of aiding the farmer. The societies at home are mainly composed of landlords and the richer tenants. The Government in India is the one great landlord over two-thirds of British India, and should perform the duties of one.

In concluding my remarks on manures, I need hardly say that it is of the greatest importance to keep a careful record of all the manures put down, and a special manure book should be kept for this purpose, in which notes should be kept of the effects observed. But for ready reference I have found it most convenient to have a plan made of each field on the estate, and on one side of it a space should be left in order to enter the manures applied.

The date on which the field was planted might also be entered on the plan.

Finally, I may remind the reader of the Tamul proverb which declares that "With plenty of manure even an idiot may be a successful agriculturist," and may add to it the English adage, which says to the farmer, "Never get into debt, but if you do, let it be for manure."

The work of bringing round an old and neglected plantation is by no means an easy one. The first thing to be done is to see to the physical condition of the land. This is sure to be hardened and deficient in vegetable matter, and this condition of things can only be remedied by applying large quantities of cattle manure or jungle top soil, or both. Now it will generally be found impossible to obtain enough cattle manure to fully manure even fifty acres in the year, nor, if it could be obtained in large quantities, would cattle manure have nearly such lasting effects in ameliorating the condition of the land as would applications of jungle top soil, and besides, the latter, if procurable (which it often is), can at once be applied in large quantities, and at about one-half the cost of cattle manure, in the case, as has been previously shown, of the best top soil, and at about the same cost in the case of the most inferior quality of top soil. It is evident, then, that great efforts should be made to procure a supply of jungle top soil, and the best top soil could of course be carried from a considerable distance without exceeding the cost of cattle manure. With the cattle manure or top soil, bonedust and white castor cake should be applied at the rate of 8 cwt. an acre, and 5 cwt. of the former to 3 cwt. of the latter; and, if the planter is in a hurry for immediate results, he might put down a small dressing of nitrate of soda—say 112 lbs. an acre. With the addition of the nitrate I feel confident, after observing the results of it on one of Mr. Mangles' estates in Coorg, that a remunerative crop would be picked in about two years after the application of the above suggested manures. I would particularly point out that, though the land, of course, must be well dug, the planter must not look to that alone for ameliorating the hardened condition of the soil, for however well dug, it will, unless cattle manure or jungle top soil should be applied, speedily run together again into as hardened a condition as ever. After the soil has been thoroughly manured and ameliorated in the manner suggested, moderate annual manuring will be quite sufficient for the future, for, as I have pointed out, coffee is not an exhaustive crop, though it is essential that a considerable supply of fertilizing matter should always be present in the soil. Where top soil is not available, red soil (kemmannu), if procurable, might be used with advantage, and the results of the experiments previously given seem to show that it might be even preferable to top soil.

After such an application of manure as I have above advised, the planter must be on his guard against producing such a heavy crop as will lead to an exhaustion of the tree, and a failure of the following crop. And should there be reason to apprehend an over heavy crop, it must be reduced by free handling and pruning.

In the case of a neglected plantation the trees are sure to be covered with moss and rough dead bark, and it is of great importance to remove this at once, and rub the trees down thoroughly.

When manuring, always leave here and there, and at some convenient point or edge of a road, a short block of coffee un-manured, perhaps about twelve trees, and next to that a similar block with double the dose of manure applied to the field, and note the results. In order to have the effects of the different systems of manuring under constant observation experiments with different manurial mixtures can be best conducted at places where four roads meet. I need hardly say that in the observation of results, nothing should be left to memory, but the planter, the moment he has observed any result, should on the spot write it in his note book. The experiments of most importance are the following:—(1) As to the manure best calculated to bring on vacancy plants rapidly in old and worn soil. (2) To determine the value of potash as manure. (3) To determine the best time of year for manuring. (4) To determine how far it pays to manure little and often, as compared with manuring seldom but in large quantities. (5) How far the value of bones is due to their lime, and how far to the phosphoric acid they contain; and (6) how far it would pay to top dress old soil with earth taken from the adjacent grass lands. Such are some of the many experiments that might usefully be tried. It would also be useful to experiment as regards native manurial practices. For instance, the growers of Areca nut palms, and pepper vines, make a mixture of Kemmannu, or red, or rather pink hued soil, which looks like recently-decomposed rock, black earth, and sheep dung, and apply the compost to their palms and pepper-vines, and it would be interesting to try such composts in the case of coffee. It would also be interesting to experiment with ordinary good soil taken from the grass lands. I am informed by a native farmer that the terraces on which ragi is grown, are occasionally dressed with such soil, and that the manurial effect of it lasts for two years, but no doubt the effect is much increased by the physical effect caused by the addition of the soil. The more I have studied these subjects the more am I convinced that the most economical way of keeping up coffee land from a physical and chemical point of view is one of the many secrets yet to be discovered, and I would strongly urge planters to experiment. There is a common saying amongst farmers and planters that they cannot afford to make experiments. This is merely the refuge of the indolent and the ignorant. Experiments may, of course, be made on such a scale as to be hazardous or even ruinous, but they can be made in such a way as to be neither the one nor the other.

CHAPTER XIII.

NURSERIES.

SINCE the introduction of the Coorg plant, it has been customary for Mysore planters to send annually to Coorg for seed, and they have always endeavoured to obtain it from the best coffee grown on the best land, and, as the results from this practice have been very satisfactory, it may seem that no better course could be suggested. But till all courses are tried it is certainly open to doubt whether this is the best, and I am now experimenting with seeds produced not from the richest, but from the poorest and most exposed portion of a Coorg estate (but of course neither so poor nor exposed as to be incapable of producing strong, healthy trees and sound seed), and I think it probable that seed from such trees will produce hardier plants than can be produced from seed gathered in rich and sheltered situations. As regards the climate from which the seed should be produced, one well-known planter, Mr. Edwin Hunt, writing in the "Madras Mail," Feb. 27th, 1891, says that he attaches the greatest importance to change of seed irrespective of the poorness or richness of the soil on which it has been raised, and thinks change of climate does as much as change of soil, and has for some years found it advantageous to procure seed from the wettest climate for the driest climate, and *vice versa.* I have had no experience on this point as regards coffee, but it may be interesting and useful from a shade-planting point of view, to note here that I have found that seeds of the jack tree from the dry plains of the interior produce plants which grow much more rapidly in the wet coffee districts than plants do which have been raised from local seed, and this naturally raises a question, I am now experimenting on, *i.e.*, as to whether we should not procure coffee-seed from trees grown in the dry plains of the interior where the rainfall is less than half of that of our driest coffee districts. I may here note that coffee can be grown in low-lying sheltered land as far east as Bangalore if the coffee is irrigated. I was shown in 1891 coffee that looked well, and had borne well, in Mr. Meenakshia's gardens, some miles from Bangalore. One hundred and seventy trees planted 6 × 6 ft. in 1885 gave an appreciable crop in 1889, and in 1890 3 cwt. of clean coffee, or at the rate of upwards of a ton an acre. When I saw the trees in July, 1891, they were looking well, and had a fair crop on them. There was no shade except a bushy tree here and there. The proprietor, encouraged by his success, had been extending his cultivation. In the same garden I also saw cardamom plants about seven feet high and in blossom ; these had been planted eighteen months previously. There were also some vines, grown from plants imported from Caubul, which produced large fine white grapes.

It is of course very important to select a good site for the nursery, and a ready command of water is essential, as it is both costly and unsatisfactory to carry to the beds even a short distance, and the aspect should, if possible, be northerly, as in that case very little shading is required if the ground is on a slope, as, if a line of trees is left at the head of the slope, a large amount of lateral shade will be thrown on to the beds. Next to a northern an eastern aspect, if the land is low-lying, with a hill or sloping land rising rather abruptly behind it, is by no means a bad situation, as the sun will be entirely off the land early in the afternoon. Should the planter unfortunately have to fall back on a southern aspect, this may be aided by leaving forest trees rather thickly on the western side of the nurseries so as to shield it from the afternoon sun, or a line of casuarinas may be planted on the west, and also on the southern side, so as to cast lateral shade on the nursery. A western aspect is to be deprecated, in consequence of the scorching heat of the afternoon sun.

There is a common idea, which I myself once shared, that it is always best to have your nursery on new land, but this is really not at all necessary if you renew your land by carting on to it top soil from the jungle, or even a mixture of any fresh soil that has not been trampled upon, and which has been mixed with cattle manure and some bone-meal. I consider it most important to retain the same site for the nursery, because, by growing casuarinas to cast lateral shade on it, you can ultimately dispense with shading the nursery, as these trees run up quickly, and attain a great height. The light, too, comes readily through them, so that their lateral shade is most desirable, and lateral shade, it must be remembered, allows the plants to benefit by the dew fall. I may add that the height to which the trees grow enables the planter to grow them at such a distance from the beds as to be practically unable to reach them with their roots.

As regards the best time for putting down the seed, opinions and practice have varied considerably, but it is now generally admitted that seed put down at Christmas, which will give plants with ten leaves on them in June (the planting season) are the most suitable for new clearings. Seed put down in September or October will give fine sturdy plants with one or two pairs of branches, and these are considered to be the most suitable for vacancies in old land. In order to do full justice to the last-named plants, they should, three months before planting out, be transplanted into small circular baskets, about the size of a small flower pot, and with wide spaces between the wickerwork. These baskets should be filled with a mixture of dried cattle dung and good soil; they should then be placed on the surface of the bed and touching each other, and, when the plants are put out, they should be put down with the basket, which will then be quite filled with a mass of fibrous roots all ready to extend themselves into the surrounding land. When this course is pursued the plant receives no check, and its rapid growth is insured. If this method is not adopted in the case of replanting old land, or filling up vacancies amongst old coffee, many plants are sure to perish, and the survivors will make but poor progress. But in the case of virgin soil this course, though obviously a safe one, and freeing the planters from all anxiety as to a failure in the rains, may be dispensed with. Where baskets are expensive, or difficult to procure, pieces of worn out gunny bags answer the purpose fairly well, and I have seen them used on the Nilgiri hills.

The pits for vacancy plants should be dug shortly after the monsoon, and filled in soon after being dug, when the soil is quite dry, with a mixture of jungle top soil, bone-meal, and ordinary soil, or old, well dried cattle manure mixed with some fine bone-meal and ordinary soil. I have never used the nitrate of potash for manuring vacancy plants, but it has been used in Coorg with good effect, as may be readily understood by anyone who has had any experience of that valuable manure.

In conclusion, I may say that if the planter is not prepared to take all the steps necessary to insure the growth of vacancy plants in old land, he had far better not put down any at all, as he will find it to be a mere waste of money and labour, which is often more precious than money.

As regards the important point of topping, there are

considerable differences of opinion. I am in favour of short topping, because the coffee thus more quickly and completely covers the ground, and the trees are more easily pruned and handled, and some planters top at from three to three and a half feet. Others again prefer four feet, and some four feet and a half, while I know of a planter who prefers a greater height, and cuts off the lower branches of his trees so as to turn them into an umbrella shape. The last practice I thought a very strange one once, but taking rot and leaf disease into consideration, I am by no means sure that, for our shade coffee, it is not the best, and at any rate feel quite sure that, as the lower branches in the case of highly topped trees soon become poor and thin, the practice of high topping, and removing some of the lower branches, is one to be decidedly recommended, and I am now adopting it on my estate. For, in the case of our shade plantation, if the coffee is short and thickly planted, so as to closely cover the ground, there is necessarily a great want of ventilation, and, when this is the case, rot must, from the great dampness of the ground, have a tendency to increase in the monsoon, while from there being no room for the passage of air underneath the trees, the spores of the leaf disease will be preserved from being dried up and killed during the season of strong and parching winds. But quite independently of these reasons, it seems to me that the souring of the land owing to excessive saturation would be much lessened were there free ventilation under the coffee trees. And, taking all these points into consideration, I am now letting up all my short topped trees, which is easily done by letting a sucker grow from the head of the tree, and topping it when it reaches the required height. In places which are exposed, or fairly exposed, to wind, short topping would not be attended with such disadvantages, as in the case of the land in more sheltered situations, but for all sheltered situations it certainly seems to me that, with reference to the limitation of rot, leaf disease and the souring of the land, the trees should be topped at not less than four feet and a half.

The trees should not be topped until after the blossom comes out, as the result of topping at an earlier period would be to cause the trees to throw out a heavy crop on the primary branches, and more suckers, and so cause more trouble and expense in handling. It should be remembered, too, that in the case of all young plants if, before the first blossom, you cut the top, you check the growth of the roots. When topping, remove one of the topmost pair of branches as, if both are left, a split in the top of the stem is liable to occur. Should waiting until after the bursting of the blossom cause the tree to grow so high as to be affected by wind, the top may be pinched off by hand, and the tree afterwards topped at the proper height. This is often necessary in the case of shaded coffee, which is, of course, liable to be drawn up.

I have said that the evil of topping before blossom is, that a heavy crop is thereby thrown out on the primary branches, and I know of nothing more injurious to the young tree, or more certain to throw it out of shape, as the branch shrinks, and the tendency then is for the strongest secondary branch to take the lead. A judicious and full-pursed planter, it is true, would either remove the whole of the maiden crop, or at least from the three upper pairs of primaries, but the crop of the fourth year is apt to find a young planter with empty pockets, and he may not be able to afford the sacrifice; but he should in any case remove the immature berries, or blossom buds, from the greenwood of the primary branches, and if he refrains from topping before blossom, his trees may stand their maiden crop fairly well. But if the maiden crop threatens to be a heavy one it should certainly be lessened, as the following year there would be little crop, and much growth of superfluous wood, and an over heavy crop the succeeding year, and so on continuously. The trees would thus be thrown into the habit of giving heavy alternate crops, which is most injurious to the plant which, like all other fruit-yielding plants, should be worked so as to give even, moderate crops every year. But is it not evident that a heavy crop followed by a small crop and much superfluous growth must be extremely bad? for the trees thus produce an over heavy crop of berries one year, and an exhaustive crop of shoots and suckers during the next, and thus call for an extra expenditure of labour.

It is very important, by what is called handling, to keep the tree clear of shoots within six inches of the stem, and to remove all cross shoots and suckers and thin out superfluous wood as soon as possible. For we must constantly keep in mind that a given weight of leaves is as exhaustive to the tree as a given weight of berries. Prompt handling, and the removal of suckers, is also very necessary for the free ventilation of the tree, and especially during the monsoon months. I would call particular attention to the bearing that judicious and timely handling has on rot and leaf disease, as these are both much encouraged if the tree, at the beginning of the monsoon, has much immature foliage. We should handle them (and prune too, as is subsequently pointed out) so as to meet the monsoon as much as possible with well ripened leaves, and this can obviously be best done by preserving all the September and October shoots we can, and removing all the February shoots that the tree can spare. In connection with this subject I would strongly advise planters to study Mr. Marshall Ward's third Report on leaf disease in Ceylon, to which I have elsewhere referred, and would particularly call attention to what he urges as to the advisability of giving every leaf that is to be preserved as long a life as possible, in order that it may feed the tree for the greatest possible length of time.

In our climate, anything approaching to heavy pruning is regarded as an abomination, and the general opinion is now in favour of shortening back long drooping primaries, removing cross shoots and wood that is not likely to bear anything more, and thinning out overgrowths of new wood. The most luxuriantly wooded part of the plantation should be pruned first, and the sticky coffee last, because, in the first place, it is important to stop the growth of superfluous wood as soon as possible, and in the second case, time will be given to the sticky coffee to throw out new shoots, so that the pruner can see exactly where to apply the knife, which is often a matter of difficulty, if he is dealing with trees quite exhausted from bearing a heavy crop, or from the land being insufficiently manured. It is very important to pare closely off the spikes left after cutting off a secondary branch, so that the bark may heal over the junction of the branch with the parent branch, as, if this is not done, the free circulation of the sap is checked. It runs up the branches, and, of course, cannot readily get on when it meets with a spike of wood sticking out of the branch. This spike or stump may be green or half or quite dead, but whatever state it is in the free circulation of the sap will be checked, and the quantity of sap in circulation for the benefit of the main branch will be lessened.

The time for pruning trees is obviously of great importance. Our present practice is to prune as soon after the crop as possible, and no doubt this follows the rule as regards all fruit tree culture, which is, that the trees, from the time of blossoming till up to the picking of the crop, should not be interfered with. But pruning at that time causes the tree to throw out much young wood which in the beginning of the monsoon is in an immature state, and, as Mr. Ward has pointed out (*vide* p. 389), this succulent foliage is a good breeding ground for leaf disease. Mr. Brooke Mockett, too (*vide* p. 401), has pointed out that leaf disease is worst in the case of trees which have been heavily pruned, and obviously because the heavier the pruning the greater the supply of succulent foliage. Such succulent foliage, too, is liable to be rotted away in the drenching rains of the south-west monsoon. So that, taking all the points into consideration, it is obvious that pruning should be so managed as to increase mature foliage, and, as much as possible, limit the amount of succulent foliage, at the beginning of the monsoon. How this object is to be attained it is difficult to see, but we can certainly do something towards attaining it by very light pruning; and I would suggest here that planters should make experiments both in pruning and manuring, with the view of growing the young wood earlier in the season. And I would suggest that planters might set aside say an acre, and leave the trees untouched at the usual pruning season, and confine their pruning to removing useless wood at the end of the monsoon. This, I surmise, would have the effect of throwing out new wood then, which would be mature at the beginning of the monsoon. Such experimental plots should not be manured after crop, but should be manured immediately after the monsoon. It certainly seems to me that, if we could both manure and prune at the end of the monsoon, we should attain, as far as it can be attained, the production of mature wood and leaves at the beginning of the monsoon.

Some planters, when pruning, remove moss and rub down the trees at the same time, but this, I am sure, can be done more cheaply and effectually as a separate work.

The removal of moss and rough bark, and generally cleaning and rubbing down the trees is a work of very great importance, and should be carried out once every two or three years. The injury arising from moss is too well known to call for any remark, but the reason why the removal of rough bark, and especially rough bark at the head of the tree, and at the junction of the topmost branches with the stem is of such importance is, that it is in the crevices of the rough bark that the Borer fly lays its eggs. When thus removing the moss and rough bark, the eggs may often be destroyed, and in the absence of rough bark to shelter them, it is probable that the insect would probably not lay the eggs at all, or that, if it did, they would either become addled, or fall to the ground. I may add here that we have found a piece of square tin the best thing for scraping down the trees, and that the hair-like fibre of the sago palm is an excellent thing for rubbing down the stems.

Though moss thrives best in damp situations, and on northern aspects, it sometimes exists on open and eastern aspects, and, when the latter is the case, the moss is certainly due to poverty of soil, and in such cases, in addition to scraping the trees thoroughly, an application of top soil mixed with lime, or bonedust, should be applied to the land. I may add that I have seen trees on a dry knoll, and with no shade over head, covered with moss, and this was no doubt owing to poverty of soil, which caused the bark to be in an unhealthy condition, and therefore a suitable home for the growth and spread of moss.

Digging and working the soil in order to keep it in an open condition is of great importance, because, to use for the second or third time the words of Sir John Lawes, "it is the physical condition of the soil, its permeability to roots, its capacity for absorbing and radiating heat, and for absorbing and retaining water, that is more important than its strictly speaking chemical condition." In other words, a moderately fertile soil, if maintained in fine physical condition, will give better results than a rich one which is in a hardened state. But to keep the soil in good condition, and yet comply with the fruit cultivators' chief axiom that, "from the time of blossom till the crop is ripe the roots should not be disturbed," is a matter of great difficulty—I might almost indeed say an impossibility. For, from the trampling of the people in their passage up and down the lines, and the dash of the rain, the soil becomes exceedingly hard immediately after, or at least very shortly after the rain. Here, then, the planter finds himself between the devil and the deep sea. Is he to leave his soil in a hardened state from the beginning of November to the end of January, or perhaps the middle of February, or is he to violate the axiom which tells him not to disturb the roots till after the crop is ripened? And here I think the condition of things is such that he should come to a compromise, and dig up at the end of the monsoon a space of about 2 to 2½ feet up the centre of the lines, which, being the part always walked upon, is necessarily liable to be puddled and hardened, and then, after crop-picking is finished, lightly dig, or pick over and stir, the remainder of the soil, breaking, of course, all clods at the same time. By such a process we should prevent the central portion drying up and cracking, and aerate laterally the rest of the soil, and at the same time do as little damage as possible to the roots. I need hardly say that it is of great importance to begin with all those places where the soil is most hardened, as, should the planter not be able, from shortness of labour, to complete his digging before crop, he will at least have dug those places most urgently in need of cultivation. If the soil of the estate is pretty even in character, the hottest aspects will of course harden soonest, and should be dug first, but it may so happen that a hot aspect may have a soil of a loose and open character, while a north aspect might have a soil of stiff character, and here the planter must alter the rule so as to suit his particular case.

For digging, or rather loosening the soil at the end of the monsoon, my experience is that the four-pronged Assam fork is the best tool, and that for the light picking over of the whole of the soil after crop a light two-pronged digger is best. This last tool is shaped like a mamoty, but with two prongs rather widely set apart instead of the broad blade of the mamoty. It being very light, it can easily be turned in the hand, so that clods may be broken with the back of the tool, and it can be used by women, which of course is of great advantage for pushing forward the work.

Renovation pits, as they are called, were once regarded as an excellent means of deeply stirring the soil, but, of recent years, have fallen out of favour with many planters, and I think justly so. These pits, or rather trenches, are dug in the spaces between four trees, and are generally about fifteen inches in depth, as many in width, and about ten feet long. Weeds and rubbish were thrown into them, and when they were filled with these, and soil washed into them, the pits were abandoned and another set opened. I am now satisfied that these pits did much damage by the sub-soil—which is often of an undesirable quality, and always, of course, more liable to run together and harden than the original top soil—being thrown on to the surface of the land. In fact, they did the same damage that the steam plough has often done at home in unskilful hands, *i.e.*, turned a fine loose surface soil into one of an inferior character. Then the sides and edges of the pits harden and crack, and this of course adds to the heat of the plantation. But renovation pits may be put to an excellent use if employed in their character of water-holes, as they are called by the natives, and whenever land is liable to wash, they are of great service, and, though but small portions of our shaded plantations are ever liable to wash, a line of renovation pits should always be put on the lower sides of roads to catch the water that runs off them, and thus cause it to soak gradually into the soil. When renovation pits are used as water-holes no new ones should be opened, but the old pit should be cleaned out and its contents scattered on the surface of the land, not between the rows of coffee, as the soil would at once run into the renovation pits below, but around the stems of the coffee trees and in the lines. I have found that renovation pits, or water-holes, are of great value as water conservators, and wherever it is necessary to increase the supply of water for a tank, deep water-holes—say from 3 to 4 feet in depth and width—should be dug around the upper sides of the tank, and the rain water conducted into them by small channels. We have found, on my property, such an appreciable effect from even a moderate amount of such holes, that I am now largely increasing their number. A friend of mine has also found a similar effect in connection with his tank, though, I may mention, he had made the pits in connection with his coffee, and not with the view of increasing the water supply in his tank. I believe that this method of increasing the water supply would be well worth the attention of Government in connection with its numerous tanks.

The reader will remember that I have recommended applications of jungle top soil and other soil, and it should be remembered that such applications will, by rendering the soil more open, much lighten the work of digging, and this is a point that should be carefully estimated when calculating the expense of dressing the land with fresh soil.

CHAPTER XIV.

THE DISEASES OF COFFEE.

THOUGH coffee in Mysore is liable to two diseases, and to the attack of one insect, these, when the cultivation is good, and the shade suitable in kind and degree, are not likely to cause any uneasiness in the minds of the planters. But it is, of course, necessary to go carefully into the whole subject of these diseases and the insect attack, in order to bring out fully the steps that should be taken so to cultivate and shade the coffee as to render these evils as innocuous as possible, and I have therefore, in addition to my own knowledge, taken pains specially to procure from two planters of long practical experience their views. The views, I may say, of Mr. Graham Anderson as regards leaf disease are particularly valuable, as he has paid much attention to the subject.

Leaf disease is the common name given to the attack of *Hemeleïa Vastatrix*, a fungoid plant which distributes its spores in the form of a yellow powder. These alight on the leaves of coffee, and in weather favourable to the fungus, will germinate in about a day, and the fungoid plant then roots itself between the walls of the leaves. After the plant has completed its growth, which it generally does in about three weeks, more spores are produced to fly away with the wind, or be scattered by the movements of the coolies amongst the coffee, and thus the disease spreads. A great deal, of course, has been written about it, and those who desire more particular information may refer to Mr. Marshall Ward's report on coffee leaf disease in Ceylon. It is sufficient to say here that when the attack is severe the tree is deprived of its leaves, or of a large number of them; that much injury to the crop results; and that both the tree and the soil are heavily taxed in replacing the foliage that has been destroyed.

Leaf disease has probably existed[1] in Mysore as long as coffee has, but was, from the small amount of it, so entirely unnoticed, that, when I wrote my chapter on coffee in the "Experiences of a Planter," more than twenty-two years ago, I had never heard of it, nor, I am sure, had any of my neighbours. A trick, however, I once played on Mr. Graham Anderson's cousin about thirty years ago, enables me to trace it backwards so far with certainty. On coming through his plantation on one occasion, I picked off a very large yellow coffee leaf, and placed it below the first of several plates with the aid of which he was helping his visitors. When the servant lifted the first plate, there was the leaf, and I said to my friend, "There are your golden prospects." Many years afterwards Mr. Graham Anderson recalled the incident to my memory, and said, "That was the leaf disease." But it was not till leaf disease appeared in Ceylon in a severe form that our attention was called to the subject, and since then leaf disease has undoubtedly increased, and, in the opinion of one of the two experienced planters I have consulted, has caused much loss directly and indirectly, while the other informs me it has caused much loss on some estates. But I confess my own observation causes

[1] Mr. Reilly, of Hillgrove Estate, Coonoor, told me that he had first noticed leaf disease about twenty-six years ago. It commenced low down on the coffee on the Coonoor Ghaut, and then came gradually up the Ghaut.

great doubts in my own mind as to whether the losses of leaves which planters attribute to leaf disease are entirely owing to that cause, and I was much struck with what Mr. Reilly, of Hillgrove Estate, Coonoor, said to me on the subject; and when we were discussing leaf disease in general, he observed that it was often said to be the cause of leaves falling off, when their doing so was really owing to an over heavy crop of coffee. Then with our dry east winds many leaves become yellow and fall off, and some become so because they have been injured by the pickers, others from rot, and others from old age, and all these leaf losses are commonly put down to leaf disease, so that, taking all these points into consideration, I find myself quite unable to determine, even approximately, the amount of loss arising from *Hemeleïa Vastatrix.*

But of one thing, however, I do feel absolutely certain, and that is, that when the land is well cultivated, manured, and judiciously shaded with good caste trees, leaf disease may be reduced to such a degree that we need not trouble ourselves about it, and I feel equally sure that the most important of all the agents for controlling and limiting the disease is the shade of good caste trees. And as to the effect of shade upon *Hemeleïa Vastatrix*, I made particular inquiries when visiting estates in 1891 on the slopes of the Nilgiris, and conversing with planters on the subject. One manager went so far as to say that there was no leaf disease under the shade trees. Mr. Reilly, of Hillgrove Estate, said there was much less leaf disease under the shade trees. Another planter of great experience told me that leaf disease begins on the coffee in the open, and then spreads into even the finest trees under shade, but that these are affected in less degree. "In the end," he said, "You see the estate all yellow, but with green patches of coffee under the shade trees." In short, I found that all the planters I consulted were agreed in saying that there was but a small amount of leaf disease under the shade trees. The estates on the Nilgiri slopes have been originally all in the open, but latterly shade has been encouraged on some estates, but not to a degree which in Mysore would be called shade. However, the shade was quite sufficient, as we have seen, to illustrate the important fact that shade can control leaf disease. And as shade can control leaf disease, I need hardly say that it is of the utmost importance (just as it is as regards Borer), to carefully fill up at once all spots where shade is deficient, because this deficiency encourages leaf disease, and forms a breeding ground for spores to fly into the surrounding coffee. Open spots here and there may not strike one at first sight as being of much importance, but if they are all added together, the planter will see that they will amount to a considerable area of land, and quite sufficient, at any rate, to inoculate his plantation with leaf disease.

The reader will observe that I have said that leaf disease may be reduced within practically speaking harmless limits if the coffee is judiciously shaded with good caste shade trees, and I would call particular attention to the term good caste trees, because bad caste shade trees will not control leaf disease. On the contrary, Mr. Graham Anderson informs me that he has seen worse leaf disease under a dense covering of bad shade trees than he has in the open, and he also informs me that, though shade is the backbone of our success in Mysore, he has had more misfortune from all causes when his estate was under the heavy shade of bad caste trees than he has ever had since, though many places are not yet properly covered with the good kind of shade trees which he had planted to take the place of the bad ones he had removed. I am much indebted to Mr. Graham Anderson for information on the subject of leaf disease, and he has been kind enough to enumerate the following conditions under which leaf disease is liable to occur in the cases of good soils under good shade:

"In the case of good soils under good shade trees," writes Mr. Graham Anderson, "leaf disease is liable to occur under the following circumstances, or at the following times:

"1. From the soil being saturated at some critical period of growth, particularly just when secondary growth commences in September.

"2. During the time when the plants are maturing a heavy crop.

"3. After the plants have been exhausted by ripening a heavy crop.

"4. After heavy weeds—particularly if late in the season.

"5. After a heavy digging where roots have been cut.

"6. After pruning without manure having been applied, or from want of digging.[1]

"7. Even after manuring when the trees have large succulent roots in an immature condition—generally a sign that fibrous surface roots are deficient, and that large, deep-feeding roots are present in excess.

"8. After large quantities of green or rotting weeds have been deeply buried, or large quantities of acid, unrotted, or forcing manures have been applied.

"Leaf disease is also liable to occur:

"1. In poor gravelly soils, and on land which has caked in the hot weather, or become unmanageable during rain.

"2. On land where ill-balanced manurial preparations have been used.

"3. In soils suffering from a deficiency of the available supply of phosphates and alkalies.

[1] A planter on the slopes of the Nilgiris gave me a well marked instance of leaf disease being increased from want of digging, when there was a good opportunity of contrasting the dug with the undug soil.

"4. Under unsuitable shade trees."

Now it is to be observed that these are preventable causes, or aggravations of leaf disease, and, if carefully attended to, the planter will have little to apprehend from leaf disease. Mr. Anderson, in his communication to me, lays, and very rightly, particular stress on the maintenance of the physical condition of the land and its state of fertility. And it is satisfactory to find that he is exactly confirmed by Mr. H. Marshall Ward in his third report (dated 1881) on coffee leaf disease in Ceylon, and he points out (p. 3) that "Leaf disease appears to affect different estates in different degrees on account of varieties in soil, climate, and other physical peculiarities."

"But," he continues, "I would draw particular attention to this. Careful cultivation and natural advantages of soil, climate, etc., enable certain estates to stand forth prominently, as though leaf disease did not affect them, or only to a slight extent, while poor nutrition, the ravages of insects, etc., have in other cases their effects as well as leaf disease." Or, in other words, he states that, as was suggested to me by Mr. Reilly—a planter of long experience near Coonoor on the Nilgiris—that much loss of leaves, which has been attributed to leaf disease, is often due to other causes.

Mr. Brooke Mockett—one of the planters previously alluded to—informs me that "Leaf disease is certainly worst (1) on trees that are cropping heavily, (2) on trees that have been severely pruned (heavy pruning being ruination in my opinion), (3) on plants under bad caste shade trees (these plants it seems to cripple), and (4) on plants in the open."

It is worthy of note that the Coorg plant is not nearly so liable to attacks of leaf disease as the original Mysore Chick plant. I have seen a tall plant of the latter variety heavily attacked, while a Coorg plant partly under it was only slightly attacked on the side next the Chick plant, and hardly at all on the side not under the Chick plant. I observe, too, from the Planting Correspondent's Notes in the "Madras Mail" of January 30th, 1892, that the same thing has been observed in Coorg, and that occasional Mysore plants, which had by some accident found their way into the Coorg coffee, got the disease first, and that it then spread into the surrounding coffee.

It should be borne in mind that leaf disease does not kill the tree, but only injures it, and diminishes its powers by depriving it of much of its foliage, so that there is nothing alarming in leaf disease when it is controlled by good management of the tree, and good shade, cultivation of the soil, and manuring; and the only case I can hear of where anything like permanent injury has occurred, is where the disease has existed under the shade of bad caste trees. But it is far otherwise with the justly dreaded Borer insect, which, however, can, as we shall see, be effectively controlled by good shade. To the attacks of this insect I now propose to direct the attention of the reader.

The too well-known coffee Borer is a beetle, about as large as a horsefly, which lays its eggs in any convenient crevice, and generally, it is supposed, near the head of the tree, in the bark, or wood of the coffee tree. After the larvæ are hatched they at once burrow their way into the tree, where they live on the dead matter of the inner or heart-wood of the stem, and there they reside from, it is supposed, three to five months, till their transformation into winged beetles. Then they bore their way out of the tree, and fly away to carry on their mischievous work. This insect has been declared to be, by Mr. John Keast Lord, "a beetle of the second family of the Coleoptera Cerambycidæ, and to be closely allied to a somewhat common species known as the wasp-beetle (*Clytus avietis*), which usually undergoes its changes in old dry palings." And in a collection made by M. Chevrolat in Southern India, and now in the British Museum (at least it was so in 1867, when Mr. Lord investigated the point), a specimen was found, to which the name of *Xylotrechus quadrupes* was attached. This Borer, like the leaf disease, has probably always attacked coffee, but the earliest probable notice of it is to be found in Mr. Stokes's Report on the Nuggur Division of Mysore, in about 1835, where he observes that coffee trees in dry seasons often wither and snap off suddenly at the root. The cause, or probable cause of this he does not state, but there can be little doubt that the Borer had attacked the trees alluded to. Since then the Borer seems to have attracted little or no attention till towards the end of 1866, but about that time, and during the three following years, an alarming attack of Borer took place, and inflicted immense injury on plantations, and there can be no doubt that this was in a great measure owing partly to insufficient shade, and partly to bad caste shade trees, accompanied by dry, hot seasons, which were favourable to the hatching of the eggs of this destructive insect. But since then much attention has been paid to shade, both as to quantity and kind, and the Borer may now be regarded as an insect which can with certainty be held in check if the land is properly shaded with good caste trees. And I say good caste trees, because bad caste trees encourage Borers, and Mr. Graham Anderson, who has had a very large and disagreeable experience of the effects of bad caste trees, informs me that he has "seen worse Borer under dense *bad* caste shade than in open places in good soil on northern slopes." "Some bad shade trees," he continues, in his communication to me on the subject, "keep the coffee in a debilitated state. They allow it to be parched up in the dry weather, and they smother it in the monsoon. They rob it of moisture and manure with their myriads of surface-feeding roots, and prevent dew and light showers benefiting the plant. I do not fear Borer under well-regulated shade of approved descriptions. Renovation pits left open in the hot weather, large clod-digging in a light soil even under fair shade, weeds left standing in dry weather; all these, by increasing evaporation, tend to cause increase of damage from Borer. A hard caked surface, or a compact, undug soil is equally bad. Rubbing and cleaning the stems is a valuable operation, because it removes rough bark in which eggs may be deposited, and contributes to the health of the tree. The prompt removal and burning of all affected trees, properly arranged shade of selected varieties, frequent light stirring of the surface soil, having well arranged shoots distributed all over the coffee trees, not opening the centre of the trees too much, and keeping the trees succulent and vigorous by culture and manure, may be at present classed among the best remedies for the Borer pest." In other words, he would say that the Borer loves dry wood. Keep your coffee tree green and succulent and well shaded, and you have little to fear from it.

I have also obtained the opinion of Mr. Brooke Mockett, who informs me that "Borer is certainly as destructive under bad caste trees as in the open." "Borer," he continues, in his communication to me on the subject, "is always much worse in land where there has been a burn than in unburnt land. It is also bad in rocky and stony places. In good soil, where there has been no burn, I have never had Borer severely, even though for a time there has been no shade whatever. I do not fear Borer now that such an excellent system of shade raising has been discovered. Rubbing stems once in about three years I look upon as of great use."

I too have had great experience of Borer, and agree with what my friends have written on the subject, with the exception of what Mr. Graham Anderson has said as to the advisability of promptly removing and burning all bored trees. This I am aware is the common practice, but I have never carried it out on my property, and yet, though the trees were riddled with Borer in the great Borer years, and I have had since then a fair proportion of it on some part of my property, I believe that no estate has less Borer now. Instead of removing the bored trees I removed the Borer itself with the aid of the shade of good caste trees, and especially, I believe, by paying strict attention to what I have particularly enforced in my shade section—the prompt filling up of every spot in the plantation that called for more shade. For it is in such spots that the Borer first locates itself, and then it spreads to other dried up trees in the plantation. There is little use, I think, in removing the affected trees. You must remove the cause of their being affected, because, if you do not, the *sound* trees that are insufficiently shaded will in time be affected: and then it must be remembered that the Borer is a winged insect which, as long as you leave suitable ground for it, will be sure to make its appearance. Out of curiosity I lately cut down and carefully examined a coffee tree which I could see, from the appearance of the bark, had once been heavily bored, but which I felt certain had no Borer now, nor any recent attack of it. The tree I found, after a careful dissection, had not a sign of Borer present in it, nor any sign of a recent attack, and yet in years gone by it had been heavily attacked and bored literally from end to end of the stem. The explanation was that the land had formerly not been sufficiently shaded, while now the shade is ample. The Borers had then left the trees, and their descendants had either not thought it worth while to lay any eggs on them, or the eggs had, from the lowered temperature caused by the shade, become addled. Many years ago I remember cutting down a fine coffee tree, when the round gimlet-made looking hole through which the insect makes its escape was plainly to be seen, when I found that a single Borer had drilled a hole down a part of the centre of the tree, then passed into the fly state and left the tree. It was a fine succulent and flourishing tree, and would, in all probability, have not again been attacked. To remove, then, all attacked trees, as some planters do, seems to me to be a great waste. To do so will not prevent other Borers arriving from some quarter or other to continue the deadly work; but shade, if it does not prevent their arrival, either prevents the insect from laying its eggs, from instinctively feeling that the ground is unsuitable for their being hatched, or causes the eggs to become addled. But whatever the cause may be, it is certain that succulent trees in well shaded land will not suffer from Borer, while it is equally certain that coffee trees in a dried up state, and with either insufficient shade, or shade of bad caste trees over them, are certain to be attacked by Borer again and again, and will eventually be killed.

I turn, lastly, to the consideration of a disease in coffee which is popularly known by the name of rot, and scientifically as *pellicularia koleroga,* a fungoid plant which crawls over the leaves and seals up their breathing pores, till at last the leaf dies, as man does, from want of breath. On one of my estates we have had a considerable experience of it, and, whatever may cause rot, I feel sure that what aggravates it, and causes it to be very injurious, is the want of free circulation of air over the land, and through the coffee trees; and I am the more convinced of this because we have found rot worse in the open, and where there was little undecayed vegetable matter present in the soil, than in rather thick shade with abundance of undecayed vegetable matter on the surface. But in the latter case the land is on a rather high ridge exposed to the constant winds of the south-west monsoon, while in the former case the land was in a hollow under a hill which lies between it and the west—a hollow completely sheltered from the wind. And it is in such sheltered spots that we find rot worse, and quite independently of the presence or absence of shade or of vegetable matter lying on the land. To check rot, then, the free circulation of air is necessary both over the land and through the plant. Much may be done in the first case by judiciously opening channels for air through the shade trees so as to admit a free circulation of air into hollows, and much in the latter by freely handling out the centres of the trees which, in the monsoon, and especially in hollows, are apt to grow a superabundance of young wood, which chokes up the centre of the tree and thus hinders the free circulation of air. The soil, too, is often excessively saturated in these hollows, and, where this is the case, the land should be surface drained. Though I have not as yet adopted the plan of sweeping up and putting into the manure heap, or burying with a little lime added, the numerous dead leaves that are apt to drift into hollows, I feel sure that either of these plans would be attended with advantage, by lessening damp, and allowing a free circulation of air over the land. I am confident, I may add here, that the removal of the lower branches of the coffee trees, branches which in any case bear hardly anything in well-shaded land, would be of great advantage in lessening the damp in the plantation, and so diminishing the causes that promote rot.

With reference to rot, it is of great importance to thin out young wood as early as possible, so that, when the rot season arrives, the trees may have a moderate amount of well-matured young wood, with fully-developed hardened leaves, instead of a large number of small succulent shoots covered with succulent leaves, which are very apt to be rotted bodily away. And the importance of this is equally great with reference to leaf disease, and Mr. Ward, in his "Report" (p. 15), points out that pruning and manuring should be so timed that the tree may have, at the beginning of the wet weather, mature wood and leaves, and the whole of his observations on this head point to the conclusion that manuring ought to be carried out at the close of the monsoon, and that pruning, which encourages the growth of much young wood, should be limited as much as possible to the removal of utterly useless, worn-out wood. Under the head of pruning and handling, the reader will find some remarks with reference to the important subject of the best time for pruning so as to limit rot and leaf disease.

I am glad to say that I have no other pests to chronicle as regard Mysore estates, but as estates on the Nilgiris sometimes suffer from green-bugs, I give the following treatment, which was discovered, and has been effectually used by Mr. Reilly of Hill Grove Estate, Coonoor, who has kindly permitted me to publish the recipe.

For every 30 or 35 gallons of water take a bundle of wild merang (*Leucas zeylanica* or (Kanarese) Thumba Soppu) plants about two feet in diameter, and, after removing the roots, boil it for about four or five hours, and let it cool all night, and in the morning apply the decoction to the coffee trees affected, with the aid of a garden syringe. The trees should be well syringed, and it is advisable to give the tree a second application. The refuse of the boiled plant should be scattered on the ground around the stem of the tree.

This prescription might probably be useful in the case of garden plants or shrubs which have been attacked by insects.

CHAPTER XV.

THE SELECTION OF LAND FOR PLANTATIONS, AND THE VALUATION OF COFFEE PROPERTY.

THE selection of land for the planting of coffee requires great judgment, and the consideration of many circumstances besides the question as to whether the land is or is not capable of growing good coffee. For, in addition to questions of the age of the forest land, climate, the steepness of the gradients, aspect, and soil, we have to consider the healthiness of the climate, the water supply, the facilities for procuring labour, and the proximity of the land to good means of communication. Then as to the valuing of coffee plantations we have, of course, to consider all these points, as well as many others, to which I shall presently allude when I come to treat of that branch of my subject.

In Mysore, notwithstanding the enormous quantity of forest land stretching along the Western Ghauts, there is, compared to the total area of forest, but comparatively little land, suitable for coffee, to be cleared. In the southern part of the province there is none, that I am aware of, worthy of the attention of Europeans, but one of the planters in the northern part of Mysore tells me that in that part of the country there is still much uncleared land, partly in the hands of the State, and partly the property of individuals. Such uncleared lands (and it is important when valuing a plantation to remember the following classification) may be divided into three classes, (1) the original forest, or, as the natives call it, mother jungle, that has never been touched by man; (2) the forest of secondary growth which has sprung up after the mother forest land has been cleared for grain growing, and abandoned after a crop or two has been taken from the soil; and (3) land on which young forest is growing, and which has never previously had any other forest on it. These three classes of lands are easily recognized by experienced persons, and even at a considerable distance. In the first there are large numbers of trees of great size, and often of timber of good quality. In the second there are no large trees, or perhaps only one or two samples of the original forest—generally mangoe, as they are often used as worshipping places—towering from fifty to sixty feet above the present level of the forest. In the case of the third, or young forest: this class of land may readily be recognized by the number of young Nundy and other deciduous trees. The first-named class of forest is of course by far the most valuable; the second will be more or less valuable according to the time that has elapsed since the mother jungle was felled—in some cases this may be only 40 or 50 years ago, in others from 50 to 100, and perhaps in some instances upwards of 150 years ago. In the last case, of course, the land will approximate in value to the mother jungle, but in the first there is an enormous difference in the value of the land, which will easily be understood when we consider what takes place when forest is cleared, burnt off and cropped. For in the tremendous conflagration that ensues, much of the accumulated wealth of ages is destroyed; and I may remind the reader that an iron peg driven firmly down till its head was level with the ground of a newly-cleared piece of forest, was found to be projecting no less than six inches from the surface after the fire was over. Then a crop is sown which indeed is not an exhaustive one, but it must be remembered that the land is exposed to heavy tropical rains, and perhaps for two years, after which it is abandoned, and allowed to grow up again into forest. So that the injury to the land from the burning of the forest, the removal of one or two crops of grain, and especially the loss from wash, bring about a state of exhaustion which a very long time is required to repair. The value of the land, then, in which this secondary growth of forest has sprung up, will entirely depend upon the time when the forest was cleared and burnt off, and as this is more or less conjectural, it is difficult to give on paper any guide as to the probable time, and the valuer can only form an opinion from the practice he has had in examining forest lands. As regards the third class, *i.e.*, young forest on land that has never had any previous forest growth, the valuer can have little doubt. Such lands are not desirable, and are as inferior to lands of the second class as these generally are to those of the first, or mother jungles.

I have said that a vast quantity of forest along the Western Ghauts is unsuitable for coffee; and it is so because of the excessive and continuous rainfall, and the estates, fortunately very few in number, which were started in the wet mountain regions which fringe the Mysore table-land, have all been abandoned. But on the eastern side of the passes the rainfall gradually diminishes, and at a distance of about six or seven miles from the crests of the Ghauts the coffee zone commences, and stretches inland to varying distances from the Ghauts till the forest region gradually dies away into the wide-spreading plains of the interior of the province. Of the rainfall in this coffee region we have no reliable accounts, and it varies much even within short distances, but it is generally believed to range from 50 inches on the most easterly side of the coffee districts[1] to about 120 on the

[1] My friend Mr. Graham Anderson presented to the Durbar, at the meeting of the Representative Assembly in 1892, an interesting

west. Opinions vary much as to the most desirable site for plantations, but I think that most planters are inclined to think that a rainfall of about 70 inches is the most desirable. As regards elevation above sea level, plantations vary from 2,800 feet to upwards of 4,000, and it is generally supposed that the highest elevations yield the best coffee, but it is very difficult to form any precise conclusion on the subject. Cannon's coffee, which is mostly grown at about 4,000 feet, always fetched a high price, but this was owing, I believe, to its long-established good name, for, when I grew coffee at elevations of from, I believe, 3,200 to nearly 3,500 feet, and of the same variety

memorandum on rainfall in Mysore, and the influence of trees on the condition of climate, and in this he has given a return of the rainfall for a section of the Manjarabad Talook, stretching inland from the crest of the Ghauts to about the termination of the forest tract—a parallelogram of fifteen miles in length from west to east, and about four miles from north to south. This section shows, from April to end of August, a rainfall of 291·53 inches on the extreme west, as compared with 44·21 inches on the extreme east. But it is remarkable that this variation of no less than 247·32 inches occurred on the northern side of the tract, the variation on the southern side being only from 232·46 inches to 72·42 inches, or a difference of only 160·04 inches. This shows an extraordinary, and at present unaccountable, deflecting of the South-West Monsoon current. Mr. Anderson remarks that, though in heavy weather and with favourable winds, the Monsoon rain is often carried to a considerable distance to the east of the termination of the forest tract, it is of common occurrence to find an almost total cessation of continuous rain a few miles beyond the forest zone.

In the memorandum in question Mr. Anderson also remarks on the well known and interesting fact that the clearing away of certain descriptions of trees, and the substitution of others improves the supply of water in the springs. But the whole memorandum is both interesting and practical, and its presentation at the meeting of the Representative Assembly is an additional illustration of the value of that institution in pressing matters of importance on the attention of the Government. The returns of the rainfall were obtained from various planters on the section of country investigated by Mr. Anderson.

of plant, a large wholesale and retail dealer told me that whether they bought my coffee, Cannon's, or Santawerry (an estate of the best reputation) it was all the same. After looking over many lists of sales in recent years, I am struck with the small differences in the prices obtained for Mysore coffees, with the exception of Cannon's and a few estates which still grow the old original plant of Mysore. But all the estates which grow the Coorg plant obtain prices very similar, though there is a considerable difference in the elevation of the estates, and therefore, so far as the price of the coffee is concerned, I should not, in valuing land for planting, attach much importance to mere elevation, as long as it does not go below 2,000 to 3,000 feet, for below that we have no experience to go by, and are, therefore, unable to say what effect a lower elevation would have on the character of the coffee. We have now considered both climate and elevation, and the values of the various kinds of forest land, and have next to look at, and if possible value, the effects of aspect.

The more I have seen and studied coffee the more am I struck with the value of aspect, and this is of enormous importance in such a climate as Mysore, which is liable to suffer so often from prolonged droughts, and as it is quite a common thing to have five months without a drop of rain, and also during part of that time to have either dry winds or hot desiccating blasts of air coming in from the heated plains of the interior, it can easily be understood that in valuing lands, much consequence should be attached to forest which contains a large proportion of north and north-western aspects. As to the relative value of the various aspects I have fully treated the subject in my remarks on shade, and I must leave it to the personal experience of planters to determine how much more value they would attach to land mainly facing north and north-west as compared with land facing mainly south and south-west. For myself I should consider that the former was at least ten per cent. more valuable than the latter; and that the relative value of the other aspects should be carefully weighed before coming to an opinion as to the price that should be given for forest land.

In the valuation of land the next thing we have to consider is the steepness of the gradients on it. Now after having had much experience of steep land, land on moderate slopes, and land which might almost be called flat, I have no hesitation in giving a decided preference to the moderately sloping land. I object to the steep land, because it is troublesome to work and manure, and because the ridges on it are sure to be poor; and to the flat land, because the soil is apt to become sodden in our heavy monsoons, and because it is soon apt to harden, and thus is troublesome to work. In my opinion, the highest value ought to be attached to the moderately sloping lands, less value to the flat, or nearly flat lands, and less still to steep lands.

As regards the kinds of soil suitable for coffee, there are points on which some difference of opinion exists. All however are, I think, agreed in thinking that the most desirable soils are those of dark chocolate colour, considerable depth, and of easily workable character—what would be described in England as a rather heavy loamy soil. Then, and sometimes touching these soils, there are soils of decidedly whitish appearance, against which a general prejudice exists; but though some of these soils are light and of inferior character, others are capable of growing coffee quite as well as the best of the chocolate soils. Occasionally there are small sections to be found in good coffee lands of soil of a light character and pinkish hue, which few people not familiar with it could suppose to be a good soil, but in this I have found that coffee flourishes remarkably well. There are other classes of soil which are generally considered to be inferior to those above mentioned, lightish, bright red soils, black soils (though I have seen very good coffee in such), and soils of a whitish and rather sandy character; but it may be laid down as a general rule that all the soils we have, and I think I have soil of almost every class, are capable of growing good coffee if the climate is suitable, and if the forest in it is of undoubted primæval character; and I have much reason to think that, where soils have been found to be unfavourable, it is owing to the original jungle, say 50 or over 100 years ago, having been felled, burnt off, and cropped with grain for a season, and then abandoned. In from thirty to forty years very fair forest can be grown, but I should say that it would take at least 150 years to restore the land to anything approaching its chemical and physical condition when the primæval forest was first felled.

We have, lastly, to consider the healthiness of the climate, the water supply, the facilities for procuring labour, and the proximity of the land to good roads.

As regards the climate of the coffee districts in Mysore, I have no evidence before me to show that there is much difference as regards health in any of the climates, though some, from elevation and nearness to the Ghauts and the source of the sea-breezes, are decidedly more agreeable than others which are lower, hotter, and more distant from the western passes. Manjarabad, however, is generally considered to be the healthiest district, and some are of opinion that certain parts of the northern coffee district are rather below the average as to healthiness. A good water supply for drinking, and for pulping and nurseries, is, of course, of great importance, and a careful account should be taken of this in valuing land for planting. Then the facilities as to the supply of labour require to be carefully taken into consideration. They vary very much, as, in some cases, the whole labour has to be imported, while in other cases a considerable supply can be drawn from villages in the immediate proximity of the land. At one time it was always considered that it was a great advantage to have local labour, but the local labourers have now become so well off and independent that many planters much prefer the imported labourers, because the former are so uncertain in their attendance, while the latter, when once on the estates, have nothing to take them away from their work till the season arrives for their departing to their homes, either below the Ghauts, or in the interior of the province, from both of which sources the planters of Mysore draw so much of their labour. But in the picking season there can be no doubt that the vicinity of villages is a great advantage, as this generally occurs before the rice harvest, and before that takes place, many people are glad to work for a month or two months on the plantations. So that, in valuing land, proximity to villages ought certainly to be taken into favourable account. Finally, in valuing land, the proximity to good roads and easy access to them is of great importance—and I say easy access to them because it sometimes happens that land is situated on the wrong side of an unbridged river which is sure to be in flood for many months of the year. I now turn to the important subject of valuing plantations of various ages.

I may commence here by observing that all the points enumerated as regards the valuation of land suitable for coffee apply equally to plantations, but it is hardly necessary to say that there are many additional points to be considered when valuing a plantation that is for sale, or for which a valuation may be required for any other purpose. The first point that a valuator should inquire into, is the age of the forest land on which a plantation has been formed. This may not be very easily determined, as the whole of the original forest may have been removed, but there are nearly certain to be corners left, and the valuator should remember that the surest sign of very old forest is an occasional very old and partly decayed Nandi tree, or large and aged Marragudtha trees. The next point to be considered is as to whether the forest was all felled at once and burnt off with a running fire, or whether it was cleared by degrees—*i.e.*, in the first year cleared of underwood and a few of the large trees, and the wood piled and burned in separate heaps, and the large trees gradually removed in subsequent years. This may be regarded as a very important point, for in the latter case the physical condition of the soil will be sure to have been better maintained, and, in the opinion of one of our most experienced planters, the coffee will be much less liable to attacks of the Borer. The age of the plantation should next be inquired into, but mere age, it must be remembered, though it may be of great importance, is by no means always so. At first sight it would appear that a young plantation, with its virgin soil, must be more valuable than an old one, but I have in my mind's eye a plantation in Manjarabad, belonging to friends of mine, and the planting of which was begun as far back as 1857. Last year one of my friends took me over it, and a finer plantation it would be impossible to find, and at the end of our walk he said to me, "The place is better than you ever saw it." And so it most undoubtedly was: and, as another planting friend once wrote to me, "All the old established estates in Mysore are to the front still, and many of them better than they ever were," and better because manuring and cultivation have improved pieces of inferior land and ridges to such a degree as to make them superior to what they were before the land was first cleared and planted. One of the estates in question was opened about ninety-five years ago, and yet contains as fine coffee as one could wish to see. All depends upon the care with which the estate has been kept up, and into that the valuator must specially inquire, and he must also specially inquire into the age of the coffee trees, which, always supposing that the soil has been well kept up, is of far more importance than the mere age of the estate. My friends' estate, for instance, above alluded to, was an old estate, but it was, comparatively speaking, a fresh plantation, for all the old trees had been removed, and the whole property replanted with the Coorg plant. So that, though the estate was old, the coffee was by no means so.

From what I have hitherto said, it is evident that in many cases the valuing of an estate presents to the mind an extremely complicated problem, and there are so many exceptions and limitations, and so many points of doubtful nature—the question of the age, for instance, at which the coffee tree declines—that I cannot attempt to do more than indicate those to which the valuator should turn his attention. There are, however, points on which I can express a more decided opinion—the shade on an estate, its kind, or kinds, and regulation.

After what has been previously written as to shade, its weight in determining the value of a plantation must obviously be very great; so much so, that planters, when going round an estate in Mysore, are generally more taken up with observing the shade than the coffee underneath it. And I cannot, perhaps, better illustrate the effects of bad caste trees than by mentioning what a neighbour said to me when I was going round his plantation. He pointed to the coffee under a bad caste tree and said, "The coffee there gave a good crop this year, but the trees are suffering now, and will give a poor crop next year; while the coffee under the good caste trees there gave a good crop this year, are looking well now, and will give a good crop next year." Such, then, is the difference, and sometimes it is much more, between bad and good caste shade trees. And when the reader remembers that Mr. Graham Anderson has said that he has experienced more misfortune of every kind owing to the presence of bad caste shade trees, it is evident that a valuator should attach a much higher value to a plantation shaded entirely with good caste shade trees than to one with bad or indifferent kinds of shade trees. For the latter mean diminished crops, and more Borer and leaf disease, while the former lead to the very opposite effects.

Manurial facilities have next to be taken into consideration, and here we shall find a very great difference between estates. Some, but I am afraid very few, have spare, odd bits of jungle land which the proprietors have acquired for the purpose, or angles of the original forest which they have left uncleared, from which valuable top soil may be procured, while others are in parts of the country where the grazing for cattle is good, and where cattle manure can sometimes be bought from the natives. But many estates have no top soil resources, and but poor facilities of making bulk manure, and all these points require to be carefully considered when valuing an estate.

But besides all the previously mentioned points, there are the labour facilities, the water supply, and lastly, but by no means leastly, the concentration of all the points of most importance in one central point to be taken into consideration. It often happens on estates that the nursery is in one place, the pulping-house half a mile from that, and the bungalow half a mile from either. But is it not obvious that an estate is more valuable when the bungalow, drying-ground, pulper, and nursery are all within a stone's throw of each other?

Lastly, we come to the most difficult question of all. How many years' purchase is a coffee property worth? To this question I can give no answer at all, nor is it likely that any answer can ever be given till all the facts connected with the industry become widely known. And of all these determining facts, the execution of the projected railway line through the southern coffee district to Mangalore will certainly be the most important. This line, in fact (which will probably be opened in three years' time), will alter the entire position of coffee, as it will not only provide for the carriage of coffee to the coast and the importation of manure, but will bring the planters within ready touch of the finest sanatorium in the world—the Nilgiri Hills.

CHAPTER XVI.

HOW TO MAKE AN ESTATE PAY, AND THE ORDER OF THE WORK.

THE first step towards making a plantation pay is to eliminate all sources of loss, and the first point claiming attention relates to the advisability of abandoning all the spots on an estate which are difficult to keep up, sometimes from defects of soil, sometimes of aspect, and more often of both. At present you often find, just as you do in the case of farmers in Scotland, that planters often make money on the good land to throw much of it away on the bad, and the people who thus act simply do so from want of strength of mind; for everyone knows that it costs more to keep up inferior coffee than it does to keep up the best, and that the latter yields good and certain crops, while the former yields poor and uncertain crops. And it is equally well known that highly manured and well situated coffee on good land can always be relied on to give a paying crop, even in the very worst season, while coffee on poor land with a bad aspect is simply at the mercy of the season. And one of the oldest planters in Mysore told me that, some thirty years ago, when his land was, comparatively speaking, unexhausted, if the blossom showers were favourable he got a good crop all over the estate, but that if they were unfavourable, the best situated coffee on the best land still gave a fair crop, while the rest of the plantation produced very little.

The maximum of high and safe profits, then, will be obtained where the land kept up is all good, well situated, and well manured. There are, of course, occasional spots of half an acre or so in the very best lands which must by no means be abandoned. On the contrary, they should be kept up at any cost, as they would be the means of spreading weeds into the surrounding land, and the places that should be abandoned are continuous pieces or blocks on the outside of the coffee to be kept up. I may remind the reader here that where an outside block can, as it were, be sliced off one side of the estate, an application can be made to the Government to have it measured and classed in future as land thrown out of cultivation, which is liable to a reduced rate of taxation, but the Government will make no reduction in the case of pieces of land, which are in the plantation, being thrown out of cultivation. I have said that the pieces of inferior land which may be occasionally found in the good coffee should certainly be kept up; but there are, in the case of steep lands, sometimes pieces of land at the heads of slopes, and next to the fence, where, from injudicious management, the soil has gradually worked down the hill, and in such cases a strip of the barest land near the head of the slope may with advantage be thrown out of cultivation, and the abandoned land should be thickly planted with trees, the leaves of which will be shed downwards amongst the coffee. And in planting such abandoned strips with trees an addition will be made to the value of the estate, as wood, as elsewhere pointed out, soon becomes scarce in any country that is taken up for coffee.

The next source of loss which calls for observation is that arising from the system of giving advances to labourers and to maistries—the name for a class of men who take large sums to advance to coolies, and are paid a commission on the number they bring in. The planters have lost large sums from this pernicious and troublesome system, and in the remarks previously made on planters' grievances, the reader will find allusions to the existing legislation on the subject, and the need for fresh legislation to grapple with the evils arising out of giving advances for labour. Sometimes the coolies die, and the money is lost altogether; sometimes, and not unfrequently, they abscond, and in the latter case it is such a difficult matter to trace them that the planter simply resigns himself to the loss of the money. Then as regards money advanced to maistries to bring coolies, somewhat similar difficulties occur. The maistry may die, he may abscond, and sometimes he advances to coolies who decamp and take advances from another planter or his maistry. In short, whether the planter advances directly to coolies, or to maistries to bring coolies, he finds himself involved in a mixture of losses and worries and uncertainty as to getting through his various works at the proper time.

Now nearly every human system is calculated to serve some purpose, and arises out of a greater or lesser degree of necessity. But it sometimes happens that the original causes for the system have either disappeared or very largely vanished, and that the system goes on by the force of custom—very strong in all countries, and especially so in the East. And thus it is with the advance system. When labour was as low as 2 rupees 4 annas a month (which was the rate I paid at first), it was quite impossible that a man could, within any reasonable time, save enough money to pay the expenses of a marriage; thus borrowing became a necessity, and the labourer therefore mortgaged his future labour, the sole security he had to offer. The lender was, of course, always a man who wanted work done, and by lending the required money obtained a certain command over the labourer. In the early days of planting the local labourers were always in debt to some native employer, and when they wanted to come to a European plantation the owner of it had to pay off the sum owed by the labourers, and when these labourers' sons wanted to marry it was customary to advance enough for the purpose, and sums of from 20 to 40 rupees a head were thus advanced, and, in the end, many thousands of rupees were thus lent to the labourers, and led to the losses I have described. But in these days, when labour has risen to 7 rupees a month, and the labourer can live on about 2 rupees a month, he can save in a single year nearly enough for his marriage, and therefore the old necessity for his getting into debt no longer exists, and some years ago I began to give up making advances for marriages, and find that I am still well supplied with local labour; and I feel sure that if other planters would only follow my example, the advance system would gradually be reduced within small limits, and thus one great source of loss on a plantation would be either abolished or reduced to a minimum.

But besides the advances made directly to local labourers by the planter, there are the advances made by him to maistries to bring in coolies from a distance. In former days the sums advanced were very small, and amounted to little more than a retaining fee of a few rupees a head. But from the competition for labour, or from planters weakly yielding to the demands made on them, the sums so advanced gradually rose to as much as ten rupees ahead, and, of course, the risks of the planter increased in proportion. Now this, of course, is a state of things very difficult to contend against, but I see no reason why some attempt might not be made to reduce these advances to about one-half of their present amount; and I feel sure that if the planters would only agree amongst themselves not to advance more than five rupees a head, they would obtain as many coolies as they do now.

I may remark, finally, that the evils connected with this system, and the great temptation to fraud held out by it, certainly call for the legislation which I have elsewhere alluded to when treating of planters' grievances.

The losses arising from not closely supervising the people employed in minor works; from not having tools sharpened over night; and from delay in setting the people to work, I do not touch on here, as I have alluded to them in my hints to managers: and the mention of tools reminds me that much loss is often incurred from their careless use, and from neglect in seeing after them, the result of which, of course, is that they are often lost or stolen. Then losses often occur from want of attention to the order in which the various works should be carried out, and which should be influenced by the aspect and the kinds of soil on the plantation. Even if all the work of the plantation could be finished with ease and certainty, it is important to observe the proper order, as to do so is most beneficial to the coffee, and then it should be considered that, should labour from some accident run short, it will at least be certain that the most important parts of the plantation will have been attended to.

Removing moss or rough bark and cleaning the trees should be begun on all northern aspects. Then attend to the low-lying eastern aspects which have the sun off them all the afternoon. Do next the north-western aspects, then the southern, and lastly the due western and south-western aspects, which are so much exposed to the sun that the trees there have little moss on them. The mossing party, it is hardly necessary to mention, should follow the pruners.

Pruning should be begun in the most luxuriantly wooded part of the estate first, and the same order as to aspect should be followed as when removing moss, as it is important to let light as soon as possible into the trees which are on the darkest aspect, and this order will, of course, suit the mossing party, which is, as I have said, always to follow the pruners.

Shade should be thinned in the same order as to aspect as that laid down for the removal of moss, and as soon after crop as possible. The shade cutters should precede the pruners, as, after pruning, the coffee is of course more liable to be injured by falling branches.

Dig all the hottest aspects first, as the soil on these hardens soonest and more severely. Begin with the southern and south-western aspects, then dig the western aspects, then the eastern, and lastly the northern aspects. When all the soil is of much the same degree of stiffness, this order should be followed, but the rule may require to be modified on some estates, where the soil may be of loose character on a southern slope, and of stiffer character on another aspect, in which case the stiff soil aspect should be dug first.

Removing parasites should be done immediately after crop, and at the same time as removing shade, or at any rate before pruning, as the branches with the parasites on them would otherwise injure the coffee. It is important to remove these parasites before they seed, which is about the beginning of the rains.

Young jack fruit removal should be begun about the last week in February. Do not remove the fruit when very small, as the tree will in that case at once blossom again, and the work will then have to be repeated.

Fences should all be in order, and every gap filled up by the time the rice harvest is over, when the natives either never herd their cattle at all, or so carelessly that they are liable to be frequently in the plantation.

As regards weeding, wherever an estate is liable to rot, all the places that are most liable to it should be weeded first, as it is very important to keep the ground quite clean, so that there may be a complete circulation of air across it. Should it be found that any part of an estate is more liable to leaf disease than other parts, then the weeding should be carried out first on the portion of the estate most liable to the disease.

CHAPTER XVII.

THE MANAGEMENT OF ABSENTEE ESTATES.

AS many of my readers are no doubt aware, elephants are employed to pile timber in the Government yards, in other words, to arrange the logs one above another, and at equal distances from each other. This they are soon trained to carry out with mathematical accuracy, and all that the mahout requires to do is to rest himself comfortably on some adjacent log and look on, cheering the elephant with his presence, and perhaps throwing in an occasional remark. But sometimes the mahout goes to his dinner, or absents himself for some other reason, and, before he leaves, addresses a few parting injunctions to the elephant to continue his exertions. And at first the animal does so, but not for long does he proceed with his work at the same pace as he did when the mahout was present. He soon begins sensibly to relax. Presently, finding or imagining that there is no prospect of the mahout returning, he stops altogether, and stands for a moment in doubt. Then all doubts seem to vanish, and finally he takes a bunch of foliage and begins to fan himself. Such is the nature of the elephant, and the human animal does not greatly differ from him. Exceptional men there may be, and no doubt also exceptional elephants, but, as the late Sir Charles Trevelyan good-naturedly said to an official in the Madras Presidency, "The fact is, we all require a little looking after." And hence it is that, when the proprietor cannot look after his own property, he finds it always advisable to give the manager an interest in the concern, or some interest which will induce the manager to fan himself in moderation. In the case of tea plantations in India, sometimes a share is sold to the manager, and then he is given time to pay for this out of the profits of the concern. In coffee, sometimes, a salary is given, and a bonus of one rupee a hundredweight on the coffee produced. Then on some estates belonging to a firm, as it was found that this worked unevenly, a bonus of a rupee a head was given on each coolie, which was done to encourage managers to make their estate as attractive to coolies as possible. In one case I know of, the manager is allowed to invest capital of his own in the concern to even as small an amount as 1,000 rupees, and for the sum invested he receives a share in the profits of the estate. The 1,000 rupees are treated as part of the capital of the estate, and whatever the profits may be, the owner of the capital gets his share. If he leaves, his capital is returned to him, or, in the event of death, paid to his heirs. Another plan, and I think the best, is to give a share of the profits in lieu of salary; or, should the manager not like the risk, a salary enough for the manager to live on and a share of the profits besides. But I do not think it wise ever to part with a share in the ownership of the land, as, in the event of the death of a manager, who has been turned into a working partner, a very unsatisfactory state of things is liable to arise. And the original proprietor might, and probably would, have trouble as to the management of the estate, as he would then have to deal with the heirs of the deceased.

It seems hardly necessary to say that a proprietor should exercise great care in the selection of a manager, but the circumstances of the estates in Mysore, which are always surrounded by a native population, and sometimes a very considerable population, are such that unusual care is required when appointing a manager. For in dealing with the people around him, he requires to exercise much tact, and careful circumspection, and great control over his temper, which is often sorely tried. And he needs it all the more for the first few years, because anything new is sure to be attacked and worried. When alluding to the fact that the new comer is exposed to many annoyances, while the old planter seldom is, a native official once said to me, "The new man must submit to being worried and annoyed, and," he added with a laugh, "even to be kicked for four years, and then he may do anything." Any planter, then, settling in a new district requires to act with great care and tact till he passes the four years period, when he may do anything in reason. But unless he has a full control of himself, he will be sure to be involved in squabbles and disputes of a more or less troublesome character, which are injurious to the interests of the estate. And hence there is the greater need for the proprietor being careful in his selection of a manager.

It is very important that, at the outset, a clear understanding should be come to between the absentee proprietor and his manager, so as to prevent disputes and confusion. To avoid these it should be laid down either that the manager is to have full power to act on his responsibility, or that he is to act entirely under the instructions of the proprietor. When the latter understanding is come to, the manager must adhere strictly to the orders of the proprietor, even though the agent may think that he would serve the proprietor's interests better by neglecting the orders, and because, obviously, the proprietor may have reasons for his orders which are not apparent, or only partially apparent, to the manager. In the event of a manager not being disposed to carry out orders to the letter, he should at once resign his situation, as he has no right to receive his pay on the understanding that he is to carry out his employer's wishes, and then fail to do so.

Powers of attorney to managers should be carefully and fully drawn, as it is often of great importance that a manager should have full power to act in the courts as to buying and selling land, and other matters. If the full power of acting on his own responsibility is to rest with the manager, it should be distinctly so stated in the power of attorney. If the power of direction lies with the principal solely, it should be remembered (a fact that is not always remembered, by the way, as I know from my own experience) that, though the manager has the power of acting for the proprietor, he cannot do so in any degree at variance with the instructions received. If, for instance, the proprietor orders that, in the case of a dispute between him and another party, the manager is to call in arbitrators to decide on certain points in a dispute, the manager would have no right to put other points connected with the dispute to the decision of the arbitrators, because he, the manager, might think it would be of advantage to his principal to do so, or for any other reason whatsoever.

The proprietor of an absentee estate is necessarily entirely in the power of his manager; and whatever the number of accounts, reports, and returns may be is of little consequence, as the proprietor cannot get behind them, *i.e.*, he cannot count the coolies that enter the estate in the morning, and that being the case, he is wholly dependent on the honesty of the manager. But the proprietor, it might be urged, can call for the check-roll of people. So he can, but there is nothing to prevent the manager keeping two check-rolls, one to pay the people with and the other to send to the proprietor, and I have heard of this being done. Nor is there anything to prevent a manager representing himself to be present on the estate and attending to his duties, while in reality he may be amusing himself fifty miles away. It is, if a little amusing, certainly very instructive to read in "Balfour's Cyclopædia"[1] that "coffee is liable to fail from leaf disease, Bug, Borer, and the absence of the eye of the owner," and the statement would have been quite complete had the writer added that it is the absence of the eye of the owner which, in Mysore at least, I may certainly say, is responsible for much of the leaf disease and nearly all the Borer. But the reader will readily understand that money is very easily frittered away in employing large bodies of labourers unless an active personal interest is taken in seeing that full value is obtained from them, and that their efforts are rightly directed. It is no wonder, then, that Dr. Balfour treats the absence of the eye of the owner as an equivalent for the presence of Borer or leaf disease. I know of two estates in Mysore, of about similar size, one of which gave a clear profit of over £5,000 one year, while a neighbouring estate as well situated, and with better soil, yielded a small loss. Both estates were started in the same year. But in the case of the first, the eye of the owner was always present, while in the case of the second, the owner was totally absent for many years, and afterwards only visited his property at long intervals, sufficiently long to enable him NOT to estimate its steady decadence.

Every estate should have an information book,[2] so complete that, in the event of a new manager being appointed, he should hardly have to ask the proprietor a single question. The book should either be type written, or written in a hand as clear as type, should of course be paged, and have a well drawn up table of contents, and a blank page

[1] "The Cyclopædia of India, and of Eastern and Southern Asia," by Surgeon-General Edward Balfour. Third edition. London: Bernard Quaritch, 15, Piccadilly, 1885.

[2] And so should every estate in England, and every business, too.

opposite every written page, for the insertion of notes and observations. The book should give, firstly, a history of the estate, then a list of the various fields, the dates on which they were planted, a description of the soil of each field, and an account of the manures put down in it, with notes on the results observed from the various manures applied. A list should be given of the native staff, and of the character and capabilities of the individuals comprising it, their pay and length of service, and also of those amongst the work people who would be likely to make good duffadars. The experience of the estate as to the order and way in which the various works should be done should be carefully recorded. A section should be devoted to observations made when visiting neighbouring estates, as it is of the greatest importance to record all the local experience and opinions. Remarks should be made as to the best means of obtaining transport either for the estate or carrying coffee to the coast, and as to how and where anything and everything the estate may require can be procured. The dates of feasts and holidays should be entered, and a section should be devoted to financing the estate, accounts and rates of pay, and the advances given by the estate to coolies, or maistries. Another section should be devoted to giving a complete inventory of all the tools, sawn timber, machines, carts, cattle, bungalow furniture, in short, everything on the property. And a section should be devoted to lines, or coolie houses, and sanitary precautions regarding them. Careful record should also be entered of all the coffee sold, and the prices obtained for it, and remarks as to the changes, if any, in the quality of the produce, as such changes would perhaps throw light on the treatment of the property, and the manurial system most advisable.

The dates on which vegetables should be put down, and the kinds most suitable to the locality, and the best method of growing them should also be noted, as well as the most suitable kinds of fruit, and the most desirable kinds of ornamental trees. The rainfall register should also be given, as well as any other information of interest, as for instance, a list of game shot from the estate.

Much of the above kind of information exists on estates, but it is either buried in diaries or accounts, and, in short, is not in a readily available form. When preparing my own information books I was especially struck with their value as books of reference, and found my first one of use even before I had completed it. Notes soon accumulate, and in the course of about three or four years it will generally be found that a new edition is required. The book is especially valuable when you wish to hear the opinions of any planter whose experience you would like to compare with your own. In that case, instead of much talk ending perhaps in no very clear result, you can ask that the information book should be glanced over and a note made opposite any point as to which the experience of the person you wish to consult may differ from your own. I was particularly struck with the advantage of my information book when an eminent agricultural chemist once paid a visit to my estate. I handed it to him and asked him to be kind enough to look over the section relating to manures, and make any notes he thought fit on the conclusions arrived at. He presently came to me with the book marked here and there with brief yes, no, or, perhaps, memo.'s. I then took my note-book, and in a very short time wrote down his opinions as to the conclusions I had come to.

An absentee proprietor should have the information book written in duplicate and keep one copy with him, and in this he should write his opinion as to how it would be advisable to deal with the property in the event of his death. The book, I need hardly add, would be of the greatest value to the proprietor's heir, as with it he would be the master of the manager, while without it the manager would be the master of the new proprietor.

Another great advantage arising from the information book is that it does away with all possibility of misunderstanding. There can be no "Oh, I understood this, or thought you wanted the other," or, "Oh, I was not informed, and now that I know what you want." In short, there can be no room either for disputes or excuses with a well-kept, written up to date, information book.

The following hints may prove useful to young planters, or managers, but, as it will be more convenient, I shall use the word manager solely, and the reader will understand that in the term manager I include planters who are their own managers, or who, in other words, do not employ a manager.

When the Duke of Wellington was asked by Lord Mahon (afterwards the Earl Stanhope) to what he attributed the success of his campaigns, the Duke replied, "The real reason why I succeeded in my own campaigns is because I was always on the spot. I saw everything and did everything for myself." Managers should remember this secret of success, and remember that, when they give orders they must always go and see that they are carried out, and if they do not do so, they may certainly rely on their orders being imperfectly, or inefficiently executed. And here I am reminded of a case to the point which happened one morning. My manager had ordered some top soil to be laid on one of the roads in the plantation, and on this bone-dust was scattered, the intention being that each basketful of top soil should contain a certain proportion of the bone-dust. On passing the spot on the way to look at some other work my manager dismounted, and said, "if you will remain here for a moment I will rejoin you." Then he went down into the coffee to look at the application of the manure. During his absence I overheard a woman say to the man who was filling her basket, "You have put no bones in my basket." This called my attention to the subject, and I then observed that the bonedust had not been scattered right up to the edges of the top soil, which overlapped the deposit of bonedust by about a foot, and hence her basket, which was being filled from the edge of the heap (which was a flattened one), contained no bonedust, or but a very little of it, and the result of this, of course, would be injurious to all those trees which had been deprived of the proper share of bones, or got none at all. This may seem a trifling matter, but it will illustrate and enforce my suggestion as to the necessity of being always on the spot, and it is the attention to, or neglect of, all these apparently trifling matters which, in the total, makes estate management either a success or the reverse. What I have said will also illustrate the fact that coolies, who to those who do not understand them, appear so lifeless and uninteresting, do take an interest in what is going on, and this poor woman, as the reader will have observed, was defending my interests, and remonstrating with the duffadar (native overseer) as to the way in which the manuring was being carried out, at least so far as her share in the work was concerned at the moment. I do not think I could add anything further as to the necessity of being always on the spot, though I may as well mention that one planter of long experience once said to me, "Every day that a man is off his estate is a loss to him."

Managers are apt to neglect seeing to the execution of the minor works of an estate, and it is there that there is often a great leakage of money, and, what is often of more importance, waste of labour which is required for pushing forward other works. I will take, for instance, the people sent off to gather leaves for littering the cattle sheds. I have found by personal inspection that, unless closely looked after, much of this labour will be lost, and the same is sure to be the case with the people employed in other minor works. To keep the people employed in minor works up to the mark the manager should always visit them daily, and, besides, pay them a surprise visit three times a week.

Another source of leakage on an estate, and not an inconsiderable one, arises from tools not being sharpened over night, or by some one before the arrival of the people, and nothing is more common than to see a group of coolies hanging round the grindstone in the morning waiting to have their axes or knives sharpened. Ten minutes may here easily be lost, and on six men this leads to the loss of one hour's work. Then time by a slow manager is often lost in getting his gangs under weigh and setting them to work. Where the work can be done by contract, or task work, this does not of course matter, but such work as pruning, shade tree thinning, etc., cannot be tasked, and delay in setting to work is then a serious loss, partly in direct money, and partly from work delayed which it may be very important to push on.

Managers should always carry note-books and take down at once anything they may wish to remember. They should afterwards take out the principal points, enter them on a slip of paper and put it on the writing table, for, as the native saying goes, "A good memory is not equal to bad ink" for recording a fact. Points or facts of more especial interest should be at once entered on the blank leaves of the information book to which I shall presently allude. When visiting other estates managers should always note down any points of interest, and especially as regards manuring and the effects of shade trees on the coffee.

Managers, in the case of a large estate, should never walk along the roads, unless of course for a very short distance, but only amongst the coolies at work, or when inspecting work done, or laying out fresh work. For these purposes all the strength and freshness of the managers are required, and it seems superfluous to observe that a tired man is seldom a good observer, or rather in a good state for observing. On a steep estate the manager should dismount on the upper road and walk downhill to his coolies, and send his horse down to the lower road so as to avoid climbing the hill.

Managers should be careful of their health, make it a rule always to change at once the moment they come in, and see that their food, however plain, is of good quality and well cooked. They should take remedies immediately at the first indication of disorder, and should be very careful to attend to the directions in the preceding section, and avoid all unnecessary fatigue, as it is when over fatigued that a man is most liable to the inroads of disease.

It is very important to, as soon as possible, make a beginning, however small, as regards any work, even if it should have to be discontinued for a time on account of other works coming in the way. For the beginning stands there as a reminder that the work has to be done, and the proverbial first step has been taken.

It is also important so to arrange work that parties may be within easy reach of each other, as this of course lightens the work of supervision.

When visiting a working party the manager should not trouble himself so much about the work being then done, but should occupy most of his time in examining the work of the previous day, and he should see that the duffadars are not merely staring at the coolies as they work, but that they are examining the work that has been done. When pruning, for instance, the duffadar should move from one end of the line to the other examining as he goes the trees just finished by the people. It is hardly necessary to say that a fluent command of the vernacular is of the utmost, or I may say, of the most indispensable importance, for, as an old planter once said to me, "A native thinks that a European who can't speak the language is a perfect fool." The reader will find a chapter in the "Experiences of a Planter" on learning languages by ear, and I regret that I cannot, from want of space, insert it in this volume.

CHAPTER XVIII.

THE PLANTER'S BUNGALOW, AND THE AMENITIES OF AN ESTATE.

THE best form of bungalow is, in my opinion, one with the rooms in a row and an open veranda ten feet wide running around three sides of the house. The veranda at the back should also be ten feet, but there it would require to be partially inclosed, partly for bath-rooms, and partly for a store-room for household supplies. The advantage of this form of bungalow is that the wide veranda is a pleasant place to sit in, and walk up and down in the rainy season, and besides, if an additional room is required, a temporary partition may be put up, and should a permanent addition to the accommodation be necessary, a portion of the veranda at the end of the bungalow may be built up. Such a form of bungalow, too, can easily be added to in length.

Willesden paper should be put under the tiles, as it prevents leaks, keeps the wood of the roof largely free from the influence of damp, and the bungalow, too, in the monsoon months. For bedrooms I should recommend glazed tiles, and for the dining-rooms and verandas, unglazed square red tiles, fringed at the edges of the room with two or three rows of glazed tiles. I do not recommend the latter for any place where there are many people moving about, as I have found that the glazing soon becomes injured.

It is generally the custom to have the kitchen at some little distance from the bungalow, but I do not think that this is a good arrangement, partly because it is inconvenient in the rainy season, and partly because the kitchen is apt to be turned into a resort for horsekeepers and loungers. The plan I have adopted is to have the kitchen and the go downs in a wing running at right angles to the west end of the bungalow, and with the kitchen door facing the back veranda. This arrangement is most convenient for the servants, and enables the master of the house to have the kitchen under easy observation, so as to see to its cleanliness, and prevent its being made a place of common resort. The dirt and disorder usual in an Indian cook room is well known, but there is no reason why it should not be kept as neat and clean as an English kitchen. The floor should be paved with square tiles, and I believe it would pay well, for economy of fuel, and ready supply of hot water, to have a small Wilson range (227, High Holborn—range No. 11 is a convenient size). Owing to the shape of the ground it may not be convenient to have the kitchen and go downs built as a wing of the bungalow, and in that case they should be opposite the back of the bungalow, and connected with it by a covered way. No drain should be made out of the kitchen or scullery. I have found it cheaper, and safer, from a sanitary point of view, to have all the dirty water used for watering purposes. I have a group of orange trees on a slope near the kitchen, and above each tree a hole is made. Into this the dirty water is poured for several days. Then the pit is closed with earth, and others are used in succession. I thus get rid of a nuisance in a wholesome way, and at the same time water the orange trees.

The aspect of the bungalow is of great importance. It should front due north, as the declination of the sun is southerly during the cloudless season, and the sun is thus entirely off the front veranda, and if the situation should not be naturally well sheltered from the east, a solid block of casuarinas should at once be planted on the eastern side, as the easterly wind is disagreeable, and liable to create drafts, and consequently cause chills. A line of casuarinas should be planted on the south and west side of the bungalow, and at such a distance as to cast a shadow on to the southern and western walls, and also on to the roof, as this will keep the house much cooler than it would otherwise be. Other trees might be suggested for this purpose, and trees affording more coolness, but I have suggested the casuarina as it is a quick grower, very ornamental, and not at all liable to be blown down. No carriage drive should be made up to the front of the bungalow, as it is obviously much pleasanter to look out of the veranda on to a pretty garden without a road intervening, and carriages should either drive up to the back of the bungalow, or to one end of it where a wide space may be left for turning. I have said that a line of casuarinas should be planted on the southern and western sides of the bungalow so as to shade it from the sun, and I would suggest that, in order to keep the ground on these aspects cool, orange trees should be thickly planted, and I may mention that I have done this with excellent effect on the southern side of my bungalow. When orange trees are planted for this purpose they should either not be allowed to bear fruit, or but a very small number of oranges, as the object of course is to have, for ornamental reasons, fresh looking trees, and full of foliage, so as to keep the ground near the bungalow as cool as possible.

The bungalows in Mysore are usually built on the grass land outside of the plantation, and where this is practicable it should always be done, as, from the value of the coffee land, much of it cannot be spared for planting, whereas in the open, as the land is of little value the planter can, by planting clumps of casuarinas and other trees, make his residence so much more agreeable and cheerful. But sometimes it is advisable or even necessary to have the bungalow in the plantation, and in that case the most must be made of the situation, and vistas cut here and there through the shade trees so as to let in the best available views. It should be remembered, a fact too often forgotten, that, what are called in Scotland the amenities, are not only agreeable in themselves, but have an important marketable value, and when people discover that the winter on a Mysore plantation is one of the pleasantest climates in the world, and have practically realized the ease with which the journey may now be made, a plantation will be often regarded (as I regard mine) as a pleasant winter home. And, whatever it may be regarded as, it is certain that an intending purchaser of coffee property on which he proposed to reside would naturally, and perhaps unknown to himself, be influenced by the amenities of the estate.

As regards the garden in front of the bungalow, it should of course be limited to such an amount as may be within easy command of the water available. Roses should be freely used, and violets, mignonette, geraniums, and phlox, while the edges of the veranda should have some crotons and ferns in pots. I have given this limited list because it contains all that is necessary to make a place reasonably presentable, but many additions may of course be advantageously made.

I need hardly say that it is very desirable to place the bungalow as close as possible to the points where the near presence of the planter is advantageous. These are the pulping-house, store, drying-ground, nursery, vegetable garden, and orchard. I have two estates where this desirable combination exists, and by the exercise of a little care and time to study the situation, it may often be carried out; but the best site for the bungalow cannot sometimes be discovered without a residence of some duration on the estate, and it is of great advantage in making a new plantation to defer for some time building a permanent bungalow. For all practical purposes a house with sun-dried brick walls, and a roof of rough jungle wood, will answer very well for some years, and during that time a careful study of the land will generally disclose a much better site than one might at first be disposed to select. And I speak with personal experience on this point, as, had I built a permanent house on the site I at first selected on my head estate, I should certainly have had cause for regret. At first sight it may seem that the proximity of the bungalow to the drying-ground is not desirable, but the drying-ground, estate office, store, and other buildings may, by planting, be completely and quickly screened off from the dwelling-house. The permanent bungalow should be built of brick, but all steps should be made of stone, and not of brick, as is so commonly done, as the stone is so much more suitable in a climate which is wet for so many months of the year. It is very advisable to keep a bungalow cool at night, so that you may be able to have a cool house in the day, and in order to effect this a free admission of air is necessary, and the doors of the dining-room certainly should have wire gauze doors as well. The wooden doors may then be left open at night. The bedroom doors that open into the verandas should have the same too, for, though this is not quite so necessary, it is a great comfort to have plenty of air, and yet be able to exclude cats, rats, or snakes.

Building materials should be constantly collected—stones, stone-posts, the wood-work of native houses which is sometimes for sale; and a careful eye should also be kept on all the felled wood left in the plantation, as this is often overlooked till it partially decays, and it is very apt to be stolen. Trees with a central dark wood, like Jack, may be left unsawn for some years, but trees which have not, like Neeral or Mango, should be sawn up as soon as they are dry. Sawn wood should be brought home at once and stored in a house sheltered from the east wind which dries up the wood extremely, and a careful list should be kept of it. Wood for rafters is the better for being put into a tank and left there for four or five months. I may explain that stone posts (we use the literal translation from the Kanarese) are blocks of from 8 to 12 feet in length, which are raised by fire by an ingenious process. The natives first light fires on the slab of sheet rock they desire to operate on, and then cut small holes along the segment they wish to split off. They then drive wedges into the side of the rock, and the segment splits off, giving a stone post of the length required (they may be raised as long as 20 feet) and about 18 inches wide and 5 inches thick. There are no more useful things to have a supply of on an estate, and we use short ones for the posts of wire fences and for stiles. They are particularly useful for supporting verandas.

To prevent white ants attacking the roofs of buildings I have successfully used the following mixture. Tar, one pailful; asphalte, 2 lbs.; and castor oil, one seer. Mix and boil these ingredients. Afterwards add sand. Then plaster the mixture on the top of the walls to the depth of about two inches, and on this place the wall plates. This plan was adopted when one of my bungalows was re-roofed many years ago, and we have not a sign of white ants, though they are numerous all around the house.

If posts, when put in the ground, are buried in sand, and surrounded with it up to the level of the floor, white ants will not attack the wood, as they cannot apparently work in sand. This is important to remember, as wooden posts are often used for cattle, and other sheds.

Toddy trees past yielding toddy should be cut down, split into convenient sizes for reapers and other purposes, and should then be smoked to preserve the wood. As I previously pointed out, the toddy tree (*Caryota Urens* palm) is a most useful tree, and the seeds of it should be freely sown in the fences, waste jungle, and the bottoms of deep ravines, but it is not a desirable tree to have in the plantation.

Wood for handles should be kept in store, as it is of great importance to use well seasoned wood. Jack roots are valuable for all short handles.

Lines, or rows of houses for labourers should be made of sun-dried bricks, and roofed with corrugated iron. For sanitary reasons they should, if possible, be divided over several sites. The manager should occasionally visit the lines, and a duffadar be appointed to see after them, and that no dirty water is thrown down in front of the doors. The houses should be numbered, and a list of the occupants kept. New arrivals should be at once reported, as bad characters are often harboured in the lines. A pensioned sepoy might be advantageously employed to look after the lines, and report on new arrivals, and also keep an eye on persons who may be suspected of stealing coffee. The advantage of employing a stranger for such purposes is obvious, as natives residing permanently in the locality are much afraid of making enemies, whereas a fresh pensioned sepoy might be got in from time to time, and he should be changed before he had time to make any friends on the estate. An application for a sepoy should be made to the officer in charge of pensioned sepoys in Bangalore. These pensioned sepoys might also be employed with advantage in the crop season, with the special object of preventing coffee robbery from the plantations, which are often surrounded with villages.

As regards coolie lines, it is important to consider aspect, and a slight slope towards the east, or slightly south, is a good one, as it catches the first rays of the sun, and so reminds the people of their duties in coming early to work, and enables them to warm themselves when the mornings are chilly. Such an aspect is also sheltered from the south-west monsoon blasts, and, in the hot weather, from the heat of the westering sun.

When I look at a magnificent row of Casuarinas (*Casuarina Equisetifolia,* the Tinian pine or Beefwood) which I planted on my property about the year 1859, and which are now about 150 feet high, and consider the value of this tree, both for timber and firewood, I stand astounded at my own stupidity in not having planted them on a considerable scale. But it is thus in all new countries where you are surrounded by trees, and it is difficult to believe that, under such circumstances, timber and wood can ever become dear and scarce, and the Englishman rarely plants trees for timber or fuel,—in fact, I am the only one who has done so as far as I am aware—and perhaps they do not realize, being born in a land of slow timber growth, how rapidly some trees shoot up in Mysore. It may encourage planting if I mention that I took careful measurement by line of one of the row alluded to. In January, 1882, the height of the tree was 153 feet, in girth near the ground, 5 feet 8 inches; at 50 feet, 3 feet 8 inches; and 1 foot 6 inches at 100 feet. In February, 1884, the same tree was in girth at 4 feet from the ground, 5 feet 3 inches; at 50 feet, 4 feet 5 inches; and at 100 feet, 2 feet 3 inches. In March, 1886, this tree, at 6 feet from the ground, was 5 feet 4 inches in girth; at 77 feet, 3 feet 2 inches; and at 100 feet, 2 feet 3 inches. This tree was again measured in February, 1893, when its dimensions were found to be as follows. Height, 154 feet. Girth at 3 feet from ground, 6 feet 3 inches; at 6 feet, 5 feet 10 inches; at 77 feet from ground, 2 feet 9 inches; and at about 20 feet from the top of the tree, 1 foot 2 inches.

The wood is very strong, and may be used for rafters.

It makes excellent fuel, giving much heat, and little ash.

The *Grevillea Robusta*—Silver Oak—should also be planted, as it affords excellent firewood.

And *Poinciana Regia*—the gold Mohur, which is also good for making Charcoal. *Pithecolobium saman*, the rain tree, should also be planted, as I find that (Report of Government Gardens, Bangalore, for 1888-89) "In good open soil it grows more rapidly than any introduced trees." I have an *Eucalyptus Globulus* (the blue gum) growing fairly well on my property, and about eight or nine years old, but, as it is unfavourably reported on for Mysore in the Report previously mentioned, I do not recommend it.

Casuarinas should be planted in holes four feet deep, and certainly not less than that depth if a safe and rapid growth is desired. I have been particularly struck with the great difference in the rapidity of growth where the holes have not been deeply dug. The plants will require a little water during the dry weather of the first year.

As the most important part of a planter's capital is his health, it is obvious that great pains should be taken to conserve it, for, though Mysore will be found to be a very healthy country if ordinary precautions are taken, the extremes of temperature are very great—often cold in the morning—very hot in the sun in the middle of the day, and often turning suddenly cold again at sunset. In England the lowest Mysore temperature would not be called cold, but relatively to the heat of the day it is so. Then the east winds, if you get heated to the extent of perspiration, are apt to produce that chill which is the starting point of illness in most countries. For a great many years past I have, as a matter of curiosity, which has since become a matter of habit, always asked when told of the death of anyone, "Did he not get a chill?" And I have almost invariably found the answer to be in the affirmative.

When, then, a planter comes in, he should make it a rule always to change his things from head to foot, and he should avoid sitting in drafts when the wind is from the east. When he goes out shooting he should take a spare flannel shirt with him, change his shirt when suitable opportunities occur, and, of course, dry the one he has taken off in the sun. He should always take a cover coat with him to put on, when, after a hot day in the sun, he may have to ride home in the chilled evening air. As a protection against the sun there is nothing better than a coat padded with cotton all down the back and front, and with a stand up padded collar. Some people prefer large solar topees. I dislike them, as they heat and oppress the head, and always prefer a light topee and an umbrella. It is well known that the head is affected more through the eyes than in any other way, and smoked glasses should always be used when going along unshaded roads, and especially across dried grass lands. Over fatigue should be avoided as much as possible, and the effects of it done away with immediately. When tired do not call for brandy or whisky and soda-water, but if you feel that you require anything to keep up the system, a plateful of soup, made with one of Brand's beef preparations, will be found to be far preferable. Then a bath, and an hour in bed will turn you out a fresh man fit for anything, mentally or bodily, and you will be able to eat a good meal with appetite and advantage. The best kind of clothing is light tweeds, such as might be used in England in warm summer weather. Cholera belts, or cummerbunds, are often recommended, but I much prefer thick, short flannel drawers coming rather high up over the middle of the body. You thus admit free ventilation, and at the same time avoid risk of chill about the loins.

Next to protecting the body from without, or perhaps of equal importance, is fortifying it from within. Here the first point of importance is to get a good cook who is a good baker, and supply him with American flour. Toddy from the sago-palm is an excellent substitute for yeast, and I imagine it must be better, for I never get better, and very seldom as good, bread anywhere in the world as I do in my Indian home in the jungle. The flour usually to be bought in India, made from wheat grown in the country, is either bad or adulterated, and often has sand in it, and the bread made from it is of poor quality. As regards food, there is no difficulty in Mysore, and at a moderate cost as good a table can be kept as could be desired for purposes of health and comfort. Attention should, of course, be paid to having a good vegetable garden, in which a good supply of lettuces and tomatoes should form a principal feature, and during the wet weather months, when vegetables cannot be procured on the spot, tinned vegetables should be used. I have found the French tinned vegetables to be the best. There are now many excellent preparations of herrings preserved in tins, and these should be used occasionally. Ghee is commonly used in India for cooking, but for all dishes for which it is suitable, oil is much cheaper and better. Gingelly oil (*Sesamum Orientale*) is the best, or, I think, the only oil which is good for this purpose. It is, I find, by the article on oils in the "Encyclopædia Britannica," the finest culinary oil in the world, and superior to olive oil, for which, indeed, it is commonly sold, and large quantities of the seed go to Southern Europe. The seed should be procured and washed in cold water to remove the red epidermis, and then a native oil-maker may be got in to prepare the oil. When ghee, or clarified butter, is required, never buy that article in the bazaar, but buy the best native butter and have it made into ghee. Boil the butter, and add to it a small quantity of sugar and salt, and skim off floatage. If to the clarified butter some fresh milk is added, it may be used for the table instead of butter, but it is better, I find now, to use tinned butter.

Cleanliness in the kitchen, and vessels in good order, are points easily talked about, but cannot be attained without some inspection, and the kitchen and its utensils should be examined from time to time. People who are particular have all the pots and pans ranged out ready for inspection daily, and such inspections are most necessary for health, as the dirty habits of the native servants are such that persistent vigilance is requisite. And I may here add that there is no use in telling the servants a thing once—they must be told again, again, and again. At last they give in to your persistence, and being, like most people in the world, a good deal creatures of habit, go on fairly well. It is only fair to the native servants to mention that, if they do keep things in a dirty state, it is often because they have not the means that servants have at home. The water supply at their command is commonly very deficient, and often not over clean, and they are generally ill supplied with places to wash up in, and with dusters and glass cloths, and then they are rated, and often abused, because plates are badly washed and things in general dirty.

Under the heading of health requisites, I, of course, include literature. This, for a planter of moderate means, is generally a matter of great difficulty, and must continue to be so till the railway system is extended to the planting districts. At present novels that cannot be read more than once are quite out of the question on the score of cost, and, under the circumstances, the planter should content himself with buying Scott's and Bulwer's and George Eliot's novels. He should, of course, have a good Atlas, an Encyclopædia —Chambers' is good and moderate in price, and Balfour's "Cyclopædia of India," which contains much valuable and interesting information. He might also buy Lecky's Works, and Sir John Strachey's "India," and Buckle's

"History of Civilization," for, whatever the faults of the last may be, the writer's style is admirable, and the book stirs up thought and inquiry in the mind. Addison's "Spectator," as it is commonly called, Amiel's "Journal," and Locke's "Conduct of the Understanding," might also be bought. Ville's "Artificial Manures" should be procured and studied. Then for newspapers, I may certainly recommend "The Spectator," "The Mail," or tri-weekly edition of the "Times," and "The Illustrated London News"—not the thin paper edition of it, which is most unsatisfactory in every way. One of the best, if not the very best of Indian papers is the "Madras Mail," and that should certainly be taken, more especially as there is much planting intelligence in it. A note should be kept of the various books reviewed in "The Spectator," and of any books the reader might fancy to buy, and Smith's lists of second-hand books, and also the lists of Messrs. Mudie and Co., should be procured, and from these booksellers books may often be bought at a very moderate price. Do not buy cheap editions of novels, but buy the original three volume editions, which have good paper and print, and which may be bought second-hand at most moderate prices.

It is of great importance that a planter should have some pursuit which may be both useful and interesting, such as botany, natural history, or geology, and drawing, too, would be most valuable. In the old days sport filled up our leisure hours, but that, in these days, is not always to be had without going far a-field, as, from the number of guns in the hands of the natives, the game within their reach has been mostly destroyed. It is of great value, then, to have some pursuit to fill up time when there is not enough of it to spare to go to a distance from home for sport. Attending to, and taking an interest in a garden is a great resource, and indirectly a source of great pleasure, which I am reminded of as I write these lines, and at the same time listen to the warbling of the Bulbuls in the flower garden in front of my bungalow. These charming little birds are very active, and are now (February 28th), collecting materials for building their nests. There are, too, many charming warblers which are attracted by a garden so arranged as to attract birds. The beds in the foreground should consist of a mixture of flowers and standard roses, and those at the back of various flowering shrubs, and low trees which are suitable for the birds to nest in. I have no carriage road in front of the bungalow, and with this arrangement can have the beds quite close to the foot of the steps of the inclosed veranda. I am much struck with the persistent loquacity of these Indian birds, and at no time of day—not even for a minute—is the sound of birds absent, and their notes are to be heard all through the fine weather.

It is very advisable to take up waste paddy fields, *i.e.*, abandoned rice terraces, for cattle grazing, and I may point out that this is also of advantage to the amenities of an estate, by providing snipe shooting close at hand. It will also be found of advantage for feeding ducks and geese. I have a stretch of such land on one of my properties, and find it most useful. The water, I may add, should be carefully conducted to the various terraces, just as if they were to be cultivated with rice, this, as I need hardly say, being necessary for the snipe. Amongst these scraps of hints, which may be useful, I may mention the fact that tealeries were once common in India. I am told that they are easily established, though I have, myself, no experience of them. It is sometimes possible to add to the amenities of an estate by reserving pieces of land for tigers to lie up in, and this is very important, now that every scrap of land is being taken up for planting either coffee or cardamoms, and that cover for game is becoming proportionately scarce. There are two such pieces that I have reserved on my estate for tigers, but care must be taken beforehand to see that such reserves are on the exact route by which tigers cross from one part of the country to another. For instance, the pieces I have reserved are about three miles apart, and I have never known or heard of a tiger being between them excepting on one occasion last year, when a royal tiger inspected a cattle shed of mine about five minutes' walk from the house. At first sight it seems singular that these animals, like hares, should have their runs, and still more that the runs should be so regularly adhered to, though they may be several miles apart.

In concluding this chapter, and my remarks on planting, I have only to observe that, if a planter chooses to take an interest in everything that is going on around him, and learns to make himself at home in the country, he will find the life both interesting and agreeable. In former times there was, no doubt, a sense of remoteness in the situation, but that, as we have seen, has been considerably removed by the railway extensions of recent years; and when the proposed lines, to which I have alluded in my introductory chapter, are carried out, planters, during the unimportant seasons of the year, may reside either at Bangalore or on the Nilgiri hills (the climate of the latter, taking it all the year round, is the finest in the world), and yet be in full touch with their affairs.

Finally, I may observe that in Mysore we have the great advantage of being out of reach of the faddists of the House of Commons, who, for the sake of their votes, have to be humoured, whether the interests of India suffer or not. There is no chance, for instance, of the opium faddists thrusting a Commission on the Mysoreans, and then making them pay for part of the expenses of the inquiry. The progress of India may be checked by the ignorant or unprincipled action of a party in the House of Commons (and certainly will be checked if the opium faddists are allowed to have their way), but Mysore is free from the only danger that threatens India—the sacrifice of its interests in order to serve party ends in the House of Commons.

CHAPTER XIX.

THE INDIAN SILVER QUESTION.

SINCE the preceding chapters were written a great and most momentous step has been taken by the Indian Government. On the 26th of June, 1893, the Finance Minister in India announced that a gold standard was to be established, and that the mints were to be closed to the free coinage of silver. This measure, which so profoundly affects the prospects of the producers and manufacturers of India, I am compelled to notice. To do so, however, in an exhaustive manner would be quite beyond the scope of this book, and I shall confine my remarks as much as possible to the points of the subject which bear upon the welfare of those who produce or manufacture anything in India. The reports[1] and papers enumerated at the foot of the page supply me with a large amount of information and opinion, but I must warn those interested in the subject that a complete view of the whole situation, as far as India is concerned, cannot be obtained from them. For some, and in my opinion the most important, points connected with the question, have either not been alluded to at all, or quite inadequately investigated. These defects I hope in some

[1] "Minutes of Evidence taken before the Committee appointed to inquire into the Indian Currency, 1893." "Report of Committee appointed to inquire into the Indian Currency, 1893." "Indian Currency Correspondence between the Government of India and the Secretary of State, 1893." "Abstract of the Proceedings of the Council of the Governor-General of India, the Viceregal Lodge, Simla, Monday, June 26th, 1893."

degree to be able to supply from my long experience of the effects of the expenditure of capital in developing the resources of India—and I say in some degree, because I feel sure that a much fuller investigation is required before all the far-reaching effects of this momentous measure can be adequately weighed. I trust, however, that, even in the short space I am devoting to the subject, I shall be able sufficiently to elucidate those points which dominate the situation, and a consideration of which will show that if the Government succeeds in forcing up the gold value of the rupee in the manner proposed, the prosperity of the people, the popularity of our rule, and the state of our trade in the East will be most seriously prejudiced. And now let me begin at the beginning, so that the uninformed reader may have a clear view of the whole subject as far as India is concerned.

The origin of the movement in India with reference to the introduction of a gold standard and forcing up the gold value of the rupee is shortly, and I believe very accurately, stated by Sir Frank Forbes Adam in his evidence given before the Currency Committee; and on November 26th, 1892, he told the Committee that "Though there is undoubtedly dissatisfaction existing among a certain number of those carrying on foreign trade, really the origin of the movement and its true force proceed from the servants of Government." Of this, I think, there can be no doubt whatever; and it is important to remember that this movement did not originate with the people, or planters, or merchants, or manufacturers, or from any section of the producers and traders of India. The servants of the Government had a great and legitimate grievance, because they found that, though rupee prices in India were not to be complained of, they experienced a grievous loss on their home remittances, and it was their persistent agitation which created and maintained the true force of the movement. The agitation they thus originated was joined in by some of the merchants of India, though to what extent does not appear, and I can only say generally that the merchants who did join the movement were small in number. Bombay and Karachi were clearly against any interference with the currency; and from the expression of disappointment which fell from the Hon. Mr. Mackay—President of the Currency Association, Calcutta—with reference to the small number of his supporters, I am led to the conclusion that, with the exception of a certain proportion of Calcutta merchants, occasional individuals in other parts of India, and the servants of the State, all India was, and is, dead against the monetary policy of the Government. Of the twenty-two witnesses examined before the Currency Committee, thirteen were against the Government measure, six in favour of it (four of the latter being Government servants), two doubtful, and one presumably against the measure.

The main features of the measure I take from the statement of the Finance Minister, who, on the 26th of June, 1893, announced the introduction of a Bill "with the object of altering the Indian monetary standard from silver to gold," and who in his next sentence declared that "It is not intended to do more at present than stop the free coinage of silver at the Indian mints, and as a provisional arrangement to provide for the issue of rupees at these mints in exchange for gold at the ratio of 1*s.* 4*d.* per rupee.[1] In a subsequent part of his speech Sir David Barbour states "that an arrangement for the receipt of gold at the mints at a ratio of 1*s.* 4*d.* per rupee will be made by executive order, and so will the arrangements for the receipt of sovereigns in payment of sums due to Government at the rate of fifteen rupees a sovereign." The

[1] I may mention that formerly anyone could take bullion or ornaments in silver to the mints and change them for rupees.

current rate of exchange then, and still existing, is about 1*s.* 3*d.*, and the Government thus proposed, by creating an artificial scarcity of rupees, to force up the gold value of the rupee by one rupee per sovereign. Let us now glance at the cash effects of the measure on the finances of the Government and the prosperity of the people; and in doing so I shall, to aid the comprehension of the English reader who knows nothing of lakhs, or crores, or Rs. ×, state the figure in pounds sterling, treating the rupee at its old value of 2*s.* To do this will not materially affect my statements, for, though some articles have risen in price, others have fallen, and, on the average, the rupee (excepting as regards labourers' wages, which have much risen in many parts of India in recent years) goes nearly as far in India as it ever did, a fact which is fully corroborated by several very competent witnesses examined by the Currency Committee, though one witness maintained that silver prices in India had risen.[1] It may be interesting to note in this connection that the purchasing price of silver in China has remained

[1] It is very difficult to form an accurate opinion on this point. Returns seem at first sight very conclusive, but you require a knowledge of facts which the returns do not disclose. For instance, in the Government return quoted in the "Economist" of September 30th, 1893, it would appear that, compared with 1873, there had been an enormous rise in the price of ragi—a millet which is the staple food of the people of Mysore. In the table, the prices of 1873 being taken as equal to 100, the rise from 1876 to 1880 is 209, from 1881 to 1885 the ratio falls to 103, and remains at that till 1890. Then, in 1891, it rises to 138, and in 1892 to 177. From this return the writer in the "Economist" concludes that the purchasing power of the rupee is now about 30 per cent. lower than it was in 1873. But to my mind the rupee price of ragi, judging by the returns and omitting periods of famine and scarcity, has probably only risen 3 per cent. The high price of the 1876-80 period was caused by the great famine, and the price in 1891 is to be accounted for by the partial failure of the ragi crop in that year—the country being on the brink of a famine—and this circumstance of course affected prices in the year following.

unchanged for many years past, and that for the last thirty years there has been little change in the purchasing power of the rupee in Ceylon. Both these statements I make on the authority of witnesses examined before the Currency Committee.

What then would be the cash effect (1) on the finances, and (2) on the people, were the Government successful in forcing up the gold value of the rupee by one rupee a sovereign? The saving that the Government would effect in remitting money to England to pay home charges would amount to about £1,570,000,[1] but as the amount is liable to loss by exchange we must make a deduction, and, in round numbers, the sum that the Government would save is about a million and a half sterling. Now as to the people of India. What the Government gains, *i.e.*, a rupee a sovereign, the seller of produce must lose, as exporters could afford to give them just so much less than they now do. Now, taking the exports of India at one hundred millions,[2] the currency measure of the Government would cause a loss to producers of 7 per cent., which is equivalent to a tax on the exported

[1] The amount that the Government would save is about 1,570,000 Rs. ×.

[2] The reader will see that, for the sake of making even figures, I have taken the value of the exports at upwards of eleven millions less than they really are. The return of the trade of British India for 1891-92 is as follows:

		Rs. ×
Private imports		81,310,119
Private exports		111,179,196
Government imports		2,844,926
Government exports		281,082
Total trade	Rs. ×	195,615,323

The above figures show that—

The export trade is	Rs. ×	111,179,196
The import trade is	Rs. ×	84,155,045
Net excess exports of total trade	Rs. ×	27,305,233

productions of India of seven millions. The result of course is, that to get little more than one million and a half into the Treasury, the Government proposes to take seven millions out of the pockets of the people. Now I have no wish to pose as what is commonly called an expert, and I naturally shrink from any idea of criticising that long chain of financial luminaries which, beginning at the Council Chamber at Calcutta, stretches through the rooms of the Currency Committee which recently sat in London, right up to that Cabinet over which the greatest of financial luminaries presides, but I trust I may be allowed to go as far as to say that the arrangement made by Mr. Gladstone's Government—which is the body ultimately responsible—does not seem to be of a very alluring character, as it entails on India, viewed as a whole, a loss of £5,500,000. And this cheering result has apparently been viewed with such satisfaction by the financial experts, that it is to be regarded as merely a small instalment of the blessings they have in store for the happy toilers whose destinies they have been empowered to influence. For if the policy of taking five and a half millions sterling out of the pockets of the people in order to put about one million and a half into the financial till is a good one, the extension of the process, up to certain limits, must be equally so. For such an extension the Indian Finance Minister is evidently prepared, as one may see by looking again at the sentence I have quoted from the speech, in which he declares that "it is not intended to do more *at present* (the italics are mine) than aim at a rate of 1*s*. 4*d*." This, coupled with statements subsequently made, and by what the Currency Committee has suggested as to a further increase if it should seem necessary, shows that the Government evidently contemplates a rise to 1*s*. 6*d*.; and indeed this must obviously be the case, as the anticipated gain from a rise to 1*s*. 4*d*., when put against the probable loss on opium, and the allowances to be made to Government servants to compensate them for the loss they sustain on home remittances, would go far to swallow up the gain to the State from a 1*s.* 4*d.* rate. Supposing, then, that the Government should be able to carry out its project of a 1*s.* 6*d.* rate, the blessings previously showered on the producers will be trebled; so, of course, will be the gain to the Exchequer; and the account will then in round figures stand thus:—gain to the Exchequer on home remittances, £4,500,000; loss to the producers, £21,000,000; or, in other words, the levy of an export tax of 21 per cent. on all the productions of India,[1] and a total annual loss to India considered as a whole of £16,500,000 sterling. This seems pretty well for a beginning, but it is really a very small part of the results that may with certainty be anticipated from the measure, which, as Sir David Barbour says, will have far-reaching effects. Of this, as we shall see, there can be no doubt whatever. Of the direct loss we can form a rough calculation; the indirect losses are indeed incalculable. But let me proceed.

We have seen that, at the least, the Government proposes to impose, and will impose if it can force up the exchange, an export tax (or what is practically an export tax) of 7 per cent., which is to be ultimately raised to 21 per cent. And we have now to follow out the effects of this on the producers, the people generally, and the financial prospects of the State.

The producers in India of articles for foreign export either, as the planters generally do, send their produce for

[1] I observe that one of the witnesses calculates the export tax thus proposed to be levied by forcing up the exchange to 1*s.* 6*d.* at 20 per cent., but I have obtained my figures from a highly competent authority, and I have no doubt they are substantially correct. I may add that the "Times" correspondent, telegraphing from Calcutta on October 23rd, says, "Exports cannot be profitably financed. The currency legislation alone is equivalent to 20 per cent. tax upon them."

sale to London, or, as the main body of producers do, sell them to merchants who export the goods. Both these classes of producers are of course much benefited by a low rate of exchange—the former when they sell in gold and remit money to India to pay for the up-keep of their estates, and the latter when they find that the merchant can afford to pay more rupees than they could when exchange was higher. If then, to put the case in a more precise way, the Government succeeds in forcing up the gold value of the rupee, and the merchant is thereby compelled to turn his sovereign into 15 rupees instead of 16 rupees, it is obvious that to make the same profit as before he must give the seller of produce one rupee less. Now let me take the business with which, as a planter, I am most familiar. I have roughly estimated the total value of the coffee annually produced in Mysore at £870,000, and if, for the sake of even numbers, we knock off £70,000, a 7 per cent. export duty on this will amount to £56,000, and if the Government could raise, as it proposes, the rupee to 1*s.* 6*d.*, £168,000 a year would be the price that the measure would entail on a portion of the inhabitants of the native state of Mysore on this single article of export. But this direct cash loss is far from being all; and if the reader will turn back to the Introductory Chapter, and to that on Coffee Planting in Coorg, he will there find an explanation of the extraordinary effect produced by the introduction of capital into the rural districts of India, and of the remarkable effects it produces on the prosperity of the people, the development of the agricultural resources of the country, and the finances of the Government. But, for the convenience of the reader, I may briefly repeat here what I have pointed out in greater detail in the chapters alluded to.

From the estimate given of the profits of well-managed European plantations which have been formed on the best land (*vide* chapters on Coffee Planting in Coorg, and in Mysore), it is evident that, though these would be greatly injured by the exchange being forced up, they could still make fair profits; and, indeed, it is conceivable that, from the losses that the Government measure would entail, they might ultimately be in as good a position as they are now; for there are large amounts of poor lands which, if the Government policy is pursued, would be thrown out of cultivation, either partially or entirely, and the diminished production and demand for labour would, of course, be of great advantage to the estates which survived. And what would largely accelerate the decrease of cultivation would be the fact that if the exchange is forced up all confidence in the Government will naturally be shaken. For how can producers have any confidence in a Government which, instead of levying on the country as a whole the increased taxes it requires, seeks to attain its financial ends by manipulating the currency in such a way as to reduce to the producers the prices of the commodities they grow for export? And if the gold value of silver is to be forced up to 1*s.* 4*d.*, and with the declared possibility of its being forced up to 1*s.* 6*d.*, what is more likely than that the Government may persevere with this disastrous policy whenever it again finds itself in financial straits? And is it not evident that the present financial policy of the Government, and the possibility of its being further pursued, must give that shock to confidence which will at once repel capital and injure credit? And is it not equally evident that if the gold value of the rupee can be forced up in the manner proposed, the first effect of this will be shown in a large decline in the demand for labour? Now, as pointed out in the chapters previously alluded to, the results of an increased employment of labour are quite different from what they would be in England, where an increase of employment given to labourers merely means an increase of comfort amongst the working classes, and of the profits of the shopkeepers with whom they deal. For in India, the introduction of capital to be spent in labour in the rural districts means a social revolution, as large numbers of the labourers set up as cultivators the moment they have saved enough capital to do so. In some cases they give up working for Europeans, in others they combine agriculture with occasional months of work on the plantations, or other sources of employment; the whole lower classes of the people are thus elevated, and this tells at once on the finances, enabling (1) rents to be more easily paid, and (2) because the finances improve as more land is brought under cultivation. Now, not only would a large diminution of employment take place in connection with coffee-planting were exchange forced up, but the same cause would act on the growers of pepper, cardamoms, and other products, and the prosperity of the province would be thrown back, and the same kind of result would obviously occur in any part of India which grows articles for export.

But there is yet another result from this truly far-reaching measure, as Sir David Barbour justly calls it, which to my mind is the most important of all—the bearing of it on famines; for we all know that the population is rapidly increasing, and that of all apprehensions which haunt the minds of those responsible for the safety of India, those as regard famines are by far the greatest. And here I must ask the reader to turn back to my Introductory Chapter, and consider the facts relating to famines—facts which show how constantly the fear of famine lies before the Indian administrator, both from a financial and humane point of view. I ask him carefully to survey these facts, and then consider what effect the forcing up of the gold value of the rupee is likely to have on famine-producing causes. And is it not evident that the effect of the measure in diminishing the demand for labour must be enormous; that if less money is spent on labour, less will be spent in improving and developing the agricultural resources of India, in digging wells and other famine-preventing works; and that if the labourers fail to find the amount of employment they can now readily obtain, the greater will be the financial burden thrown on the hands of the State in times of famine and scarcity? And must it not be equally evident to anyone possessed of the humblest form of human reason that the Government had far better exhaust every taxational resource before embarking on a course which, if the anticipations of Government are realized as to silver, will be ruinous to the country, and which, at a vast direct and indirect cost to the people, will only, as I have shown, afford a comparatively speaking trifling financial relief to the State? But it is time now to pass to other points connected with the measure. And first of all let us glance at the evident political results that must arise from it.

From what has been previously said, it is evident that the Government has arrayed against itself every class in India excepting its own civilian and military servants, and to these we have only to add, not another class, but only a small proportion of the mercantile class. With the exception of some just complaints they had to make as regards charges[1] that had been unjustly thrust on the Indian Exchequer, and which I myself made in the "Times" and elsewhere long before the Congress was even thought of, the agitators of the Congress had no serious grounds to go upon. But who can say that now? Up till lately there was no cause for discontent. India has never

[1] As a set-off against the charges complained of, it should be remembered—a point which I did not take into account when formerly writing on the subject—that England bears the cost of the naval protection of India.

been more prosperous, and has never shown greater, or nearly as great signs of progress, as she has within the last twenty years. Not only has the demand for labour been abundant, but in many instances it has exceeded the supply. The rates of wages had largely increased, and were producing, as I have previously shown, an accelerated quickening of attention to the development of the resources of the soil. All that the country wanted was to be let alone, and if the financial conditions required increased taxation, no agitator could have successfully complained of this, seeing that it could only have been imposed on account of that cheapening of silver which has been one of the great causes (railways were the other) of the increased prosperity which all classes have enjoyed in recent years. But, if the Government measure raises the gold value of the rupee, the agitator will be able to point out that, at an enormous cost to the producers of India, the Government has only obtained a most trifling financial relief, and be able to complain with justice that the Government has lessened the profits of the agriculturist and diminished the employment for labour. What an admirable advantage has the monetary measure of the Government conferred on the popularity of British Rule in India!

I have alluded to the losses that the measure must inflict on the planters of Southern India, and my remarks on that head apply equally to the tea-planters of India; but the latter have, besides, a special grievance which they share in common with the tea-planters of Ceylon, and this grievance is also shared in by the coffee-planters, though, as far as I can see, hardly to the same extent. This well-founded grievance lies in the fact that if no international agreement (and there seems no probability whatever of such an agreement ever being come to within any time to be even guessed at) is come to between the silver-using countries in the East, the tea-planters of India and Ceylon will be brought into unequal competition with their rivals in China, and the coffee-planters of India and Ceylon will in like manner be unfairly weighted in their competition with the coffee producers of Brazil. With reference to the tea-planters of India and Ceylon the case is very clear, and it is perfectly obvious that if in India you have silver artificially raised in value relatively to gold, and that in China silver remains unprotected, the Chinese will be able to accept a smaller gold value for their tea than the Indian producers, and the difference in the exchange may be such that China may regain her former position in the tea market, and that Indian teas may be partially driven from the field; and if we add to that that the Indian tea-planter will, in consequence of exchange being forced up, have fewer rupees to pay his coolies than he has now, it is evident that the result of the Government measure will be most serious to this industry. The evidence (Currency Committee) that relates to Ceylon is very decisive on this point, and the witnesses examined with reference to tea expressed extremely depressed views as to the ruinous results that must arise if the monetary policy of the Indian Government can be carried into effect. From the correspondence that has passed between the Government of India and the Secretary of State for the Colonies, it would seem that India has no objection to Ceylon establishing its own mint for the coinage of silver (the silver coins at present in use in Ceylon are rupees) and the island would then be in the same position as other silver-using countries. But if Ceylon starts its own mint, and is thus able to prevent the evils of the artificial scarcity of silver to be created in India with the view of forcing up the gold value of the rupee, then it is plain that Ceylon tea-planters would retain their present advantages, which arise from a low rate of exchange, and thus be able to carry on their business on far more advantageous conditions than their Indian rivals.

To estimate the effect on the Indian coffee-planters with reference to the effect of the monetary policy of the Government in placing the Indian at a disadvantage as regards his competition with the Brazilian planter would be difficult, and I am not in a position to form a decisive opinion on the subject; but I may mention that the manager of the London and Brazilian Bank informed the Currency Committee that the production of coffee in Brazil has largely increased, and will still further largely increase, owing to the greater facilities of communication, and also the direct influence of a low rate of exchange. The last-mentioned fact gives, I may observe, one more instance of the direct effect of a low rate of exchange in stimulating production, and so swelling the volume of exports. If, then, the Brazilians are to retain, and we are to lose, the benefits of the cheapness of silver relatively to gold, it is evident that the coffee-planters of India must be handicapped in their competition with those of Brazil; but I do not hazard a decisive opinion as to the exact weight of the competition, as I am uncertain as to how far our quality of coffee comes into competition [1] with the quality produced in Brazil.

I must now at least allude to the effects of the measure on the trade, manufactures, and railways of India. I regret that I am unable to go more fully at present into a consideration of the effects on them of this ill-starred

[1] I have since ascertained, on good authority, that, though the coffee of Brazil has not as yet come into competition with Indian coffee (as people used to the latter do not care for the former, and would not use it unless there was a very great difference in the value), the coffee from Costa Rica, Columbia, Guatemala, and Mexico (all silver-using countries) does so to a very considerable extent.

measure, but all that the general reader requires to know is, to use the words of Sir Frank Adam (one of the most important witnesses examined by the Currency Committee), that if the Government succeeds in forcing up the gold value of the rupee, China would be able to undersell India in tea and rice; the Bombay manufacturers would receive fewer rupees for their wares, and, as in the case of opium, the advantage would go to the Chinese and Japanese; the railways would have little to carry from the interior if the rupee prices went down. Finally, I may observe that the gold industry of India would be largely injured, and that, especially, mines struggling towards a successful issue would be seriously hampered if the gold value of the rupee were forced up.

Brief though my survey of this great subject may be, I trust I have said enough to expose the harmonious rottenness of the monetary policy of the Government, and by this I mean a rottenness so complete that it is impossible to find a single redeeming feature in the measure that has been adopted. It is rotten economically, it is rotten financially, and it is, if possible, still more rotten from a political point of view. Those who have knowledge enough to understand the bearing and ultimate evil effects of the measure are angrily arrayed against the Government now, and when the ryots and labouring classes of all kinds experience the fall in prices and dearth of employment that will assuredly follow if the Government should be able to force up the gold value of the rupee, and are able to trace this to the action of their rulers, widespread and serious will be the abiding discontent which will take possession of the people.

I cannot conclude this short notice of a great subject without commenting on what, at first sight, seems the remarkable fact, that the Government in India, as represented by the Viceroy, and those merchants who are represented by

Mr. Mackay, President of the Currency Association, have admitted that a low exchange has been a stimulus to the progress of India, and that producers have gained by it. It is true that the Viceroy declared in his speech in Council of June 26th, 1893, that "to leave matters as they were meant for the country as a whole a fatal and stunting arrestation [*sic*, probably a misprint for arrestment] of its development."[1] But the cat escapes later on

[1] It might be imagined from this statement that a low rate of exchange had been already setting back, or at least arresting, the hand of progress, and I therefore quote the following passage from p. 40 of the "Report of the Currency Committee."

"The following facts relating to the recent progress of India are taken from a paper read by Sir W. Hunter (one of the greatest existing authorities on the subject) at the Society of Arts, on the 16th of February, 1892.

"Between 1881 and 1891 the whole number of the Army had been raised from 170,000 to 220,000, and the number of British soldiers in it from 60,000 to 71,000, or, including reserves, volunteers, etc., to very much more. Many large and costly defensive works had been constructed, both on the north-west frontier and on the coast. In recent years almost all the public buildings have been reconstructed on a large scale.

"Railways, both military and commercial, have been greatly extended. Notwithstanding these extraordinary expenses, there were, during the twenty-five years which followed 1862, fourteen years of surplus and eleven years of deficit, yielding a net surplus of Rs. × 4,000,000. In 1889 the public debt of India, exclusive of capital invested in railways, showed a reduction since the mutiny period of Rs. × 26,000,000. The rate at which India can borrow has been reduced from 4 or 5 per cent. to a little over 3 per cent. The revenue of India, exclusive of railways and municipal funds, has grown between 1856-57 and 1886-87 from Rs. × 33,378,000 to Rs. × 62,859,000, and in 1891 it had increased to Rs. × 64,000,000, or, including railway and irrigation receipts, to Rs. × 85,750,000; and this increase is due to the growth of old revenue rather than to new taxation. Further, whilst the rent or land tax paid by the people has increased by one-third, the produce of their fields has more than doubled, in consequence partly of higher prices and partly of increase in cultivation. Further, in 1891 there were nearly 18,000 miles of railway open, carrying 121,000,000 of pasin the speech when a hope is expressed that one of the effects of the measure will be "that capital will flow more freely into the country without the adventitious stimulus which we have hitherto been unable to refuse." The Viceroy thus admits, what everyone knows, that a low exchange has acted as a stimulus to the progress of India, and in doing so has given away the whole case for the Government. But no one has ever denied the admission in question except Mr. Mackay; and his absolute denial, when questioned on the subject, that the producers of India would be affected by the measure, was subsequently eaten up by himself in cross-examination towards the close of his evidence given before the Currency Committee. But it is of course the rule, to which there are few exceptions, that those who are engaged in the unfortunate business of bolstering up an indefensible case, invariably let out something which is absolutely destructive to the cause they are advocating; and we find another instance of this at p. 191, Appendix I. of the "Report of the Currency Committee." And if Mr. Mackay has given away the whole case in London, one of his followers equally did so in Calcutta when a deputation, headed by Mr. Mackay, was received by the Viceroy. And on this occasion Mr. W. O. Bell Irving, as representing over 3,300 square miles of land in Lower Bengal, stated that he "was not prepared to contend that in certain respects the ryots and zemindars have not benefited from the depreciation of the rupee." We thus see that both the Government, as

sengers and 26,000,000 tons of goods, and adding a benefit to the people of India calculated as far back as 1886 at Rs. × 60,000,000. Further, the Indian exports and imports at sea, which in 1858 were about Rs. × 40,000,000, amounted in 1891 to about Rs. × 200,000,000, and the produce thus exported has increased in quality and variety no less than in amount."

What evidences of "a fatal and stunting arrestation of development"!

represented by the Viceroy, and the most active supporters of the present monetary policy, have admitted that the measure would have injurious effects on the producers of India—in other words, on those on whom the financial stability of the empire entirely rests.

And the producers of India have as little reason to be satisfied with the action of the Currency Committee which was presided over by Lord Herschell as they have with the Government in our Eastern Empire. A glance at the first page of the Report, and at the professions of the witnesses examined, will show that this is the case. The Committee was requested by Mr. Gladstone's Government to form, *inter alia*, "a just estimate of the effect of a varying, and possibly much lower exchange, upon the commerce and people of India." Now, the people of India almost entirely live either directly (and I think about ninety per cent. do so directly) or indirectly on the land; and yet, though in England there are to be found persons who, like myself, are Indian landowners, and who, from having lived amongst the people in the rural districts, are well able to testify to the effects of the measure on the welfare of the people, not a single Indian landed proprietor was called before the Committee. If a Parliamentary Committee were called upon here to consider any proposed measure that would widely effect the people of England as a whole, and the landed classes in particular, would it not be scandalously unjust if not a single landed proprietor, or any person directly or indirectly connected with land, were requested to give evidence before it? But notwithstanding that a certain proportion of the witnesses were Indian officials, and that the examination of representatives of the classes chiefly concerned (the producers) was carefully left out, the weight of the evidence was entirely against the monetary policy of the Government. And yet the committee supported the Indian Government.

So that this measure has been passed after a partial investigation, during which the most important points that ought to have been minutely examined were never even touched upon, and even then in the teeth of the majority of the witnesses examined, and whose opinions, from their character and position, were of great value. Were it not that the Committee was composed of English gentlemen, who would not wittingly do anything but examine into matters to the best of their ability, it would really seem, after a careful survey of the whole situation, as if this Committee was a mere sham got up as a shield to protect a foregone conclusion.

There can be little doubt that the Indian Government and the Currency Committee were acting under the idea that (1) India had been pushed into a financial corner, and (2) in fear of the result of the probable repeal of the Sherman Act in the United States; and so, urged on by a panic-stricken feeling to rush somewhere, the Government began in haste to burn the whole house down in order to roast its financial pig. As to the first point, the state of the finances in India no doubt requires all the care and economy that can be exercised; but to imagine, as many people seem to do, that it has exhausted its taxational resources, is ridiculous. The salt tax, taking the price all over India, is lower than it was fifteen years ago, and this could be raised without hardship to the people. Import duties might be imposed to the amount of several millions. Then, considerable charges now defrayed from current revenues might be passed to capital account, as they would be in England. And if the worst came to the worst an export duty of three per cent. might be imposed, for though is would not be good policy to do so, it would still be better than the seven per cent. export duty the Government would practically levy were exchange forced up to 1*s.* 4*d.*, and obviously very much better than the twenty-one per cent. export tax which the Government evidently look forward to, for, as we have seen, it is aiming at a 1*s.* 6*d.* rate. A large saving, too, might be effected by going back to the old system of having a local European force in India. Let anyone consider these points, and weigh the remarkable and interesting statement quoted from Sir William Hunter, and he will at once see that the condition of India generally is full of hope (or at least was so till the monetary policy was announced), and that its taxational resources are by no means exhausted. It should also be considered that as the Government has not only spent large sums in recent years in defensive works and public buildings, and at the same time paid off debt to the amount of twenty-three millions, it would be perfectly justified in borrowing, if it were necessary, in order to meet temporary difficulties.

Now let me turn to what is the dominant cause of the monetary policy of the Government—the dread that if the Sherman Act were repealed exchange might sink even as low as a shilling per rupee.[1] What if it did? Let us examine the consequences of that to India considered as a whole. The apprehension in question was proclaimed in the Viceroy's speech of June, 26th, 1893, and in considering the consequences of a 1*s.* rate of exchange, he pointed out that this would entail an increase of Rs. × 7,748,000

[1] This extraordinary assumption must evidently have been founded on another, if possible still more wonderful; namely that the American Government was composed of individuals so short-sighted that they would fail to take the precautions which men of ordinary common sense would be sure to adopt with the view of preventing, as far as possible, a sudden fall in the value of silver. But the American Government, as we know, naturally diminished its purchases of silver, and as no one supposes (except perhaps the Indian Government) that it can be so silly as at once to lose money and create a gratuitous disturbance by suddenly flooding the market with the silver accumulated, we see that, since the repeal of the Sherman Act, the price of silver, so far from having gone down, as anticipated by the Viceroy, has even slightly gone up.

in the remittances required to be made for the home charges of the Government, being, curiously enough, almost the exact sum which the people of India would lose on their exports were exchange forced up to 1*s.* 4*d.* by the monetary policy of the Government. But as the producers of India would gain largely by the 1*s.* rate of exchange, the total account would stand thus:—loss to the Government say, for the sake of round figures, seven millions; gain to the producers, twenty-one millions; total gain to India, considered as a whole, fourteen millions. So that if the very worst anticipations of the Government were realized India would be a large gainer by the fall to a 1*s.* rate of exchange, and the finances could be squared by increased taxation, which, if levied considerably on imports, would be distinctly a popular measure. And, in any case, the agitators could have no ground to go upon, as I have shown, as the increased taxation could be amply justified.

One word more. I cannot refrain from calling attention to the remarkable circumstance that Mr. Gladstone's Government has in a single year adopted two measures which are highly objectionable from political, economical, and financial points of view—the Home Rule Bill for Ireland and the Currency Measure for India; and that both were forced on by arbitrary and tyrannical action. For just as the Home Rule Bill was forced through the House of Commons with inadequate examination and discussion, so was the Currency Measure forced through, not only without adequate investigation, but in the teeth of the majority of those whose opinions were laid before the Viceroy, and in the teeth of the majority of the witnesses examined before the Currency Committee. But arbitrary and tyrannical action seems to be the order of the day with the Gladstonian Government; and it is worthy of notice in this connection that it forced an Opium Commission on India merely to buy a few votes in the House of Commons, and, with the grossest injustice, provided that India should pay for a part of the cost. The outcry raised has, indeed, brought about a reduction of the charge that was to have been made, but, from a statement made in the "Times," I observe that the Government has clung to the travelling expenses of the members of the Commission, which are to be charged to India, and probably with the view of proving that extreme meanness is not one of the national failings.

As the English reader might imagine that the Indian Government was solely responsible for this measure being passed into law, I may point ont that the decision of the Cabinet was required and obtained in connection with the Currency Measure. From such a Government the producers of India, while they have everything to fear, can have nothing to hope. Our sole hope depends upon its being tnrned out, and replaced by an Unionist administration which will either annul the suicidal policy that has been adopted, or at least suspend its action till a full and searching investigation has been made into all the immediate and all the consequential results that must arise from the measure in question, should the Government be able to force up the gold value of the rupee. If the facts adduced in this chapter are substantially correct, the verdict cannot be doubtful, for these facts prove that the Government proposes to levy what is practically a heavy export tax on the products of India, and in a form, too, most injurious to its best interests, and ultimately to the finances of the State. And I say in a form most injurious, because the Gladstonian Government (for the Cabinet is distinctly responsible for the policy proposed to be carried into execution) has practically adopted a policy of protection, not for the benefit of the productions and industries of India, but for the protection and encouragement of the productions and industries of those silver-using countries which now compete with India. Of all the grotesquely ludicrous policies that have ever been adopted by perverted human reason this surely is by far the most absurd. By one and the same measure to stamp down the progress of India and promote the progress of other silver-using countries; to diminish the traffic on Indian railways, and correspondingly increase the traffic in such countries; to diminish the volume of India's trade and increase that of other Eastern countries; to raise a comparatively small sum for the Indian Exchequer at a vast cost to the producers of India; to diminish the amount of capital that would otherwise flow into the hands of the people, and to, at the same time, sacrifice all its consequential effects; to diminish employment for labour and increase the causes that aggravate famines and scarcities; to ultimately diminish the financial resources of our Indian Empire; to create a serious cause of dispeace (a useful Scotch word) between us and the people we govern;—such are some of the effects that must be produced should the Government be successful in carrying out that monetary policy which it has forced on India in the most arbitrary and tyrannical manner. Can we wonder then that Sir David Barbour, the Indian Finance Minister, said that the measure would have "far-reaching effects, and ought not to be attempted unless under the pressure of necessity?" No such necessity, as I have completely shown, has arisen. Out of its own mouth, then, does the Government stand condemned.

In this connection it may be interesting to quote the opinion of the great Duke of Wellington, who, speaking in the House of Lords in 1833 (July 5), said, "My lords, I wish the noble lords opposite had taken the advice of Sir John Malcolm upon the subject of forming an independent body in London, representing the interests and carrying on the concerns of India. My lords, it is persons of this description who interpose an efficient check upon the

Government." Unfortunately for India there is no such body, and the final decision on this great question has rested with a Cabinet composed of men who know nothing of Indian interests, and who, indeed, have no time to attend to them, seeing that their thoughts require to be almost exclusively devoted to a consideration of those vote-catching, parochial politics with the aid of which alone the Government can hope to maintain its balance on the political tight-rope.

I may observe, in conclusion, that, as regards the effects of the depreciation of silver on a silver-using country, we have, in the case of Mexico, circumstances exactly parallel to those in India, and in the "Times" of October 21st, 1893, a most interesting analysis is given of the report of our consul at Mexico—Mr. Lionel Carden—as regards the effects on that country of a further serious depreciation of silver. Mr. Carden sums up his conclusions on the hypothesis that the present value of the dollar, which is 3*s*. 1*d*., falls to 2*s*. 6*d*., and proceeds then to examine into the effects of such a fall on the country considered as a whole. He estimates the losses to the Government and the railways which would arise from the sums they have to pay in gold, and then puts against them the advantages that the fall in silver would confer on miners, agriculturists, and manufacturers. His final conclusions are as follows:

"In striking a balance between the advantages and disadvantages arising to different interests in Mexico from a depreciation of silver, it must be borne in mind that the losses which would be sustained by the Government and the railway companies are essentially limited in their amount, whereas the benefits that would accrue to certain of the productive industries are susceptible of indefinite extension. Moreover, an increase in the productiveness of the country would make itself felt at once in an increase of the revenue of the Government, as well as of the railways. The only conclusion, then, at which it is possible to arrive is that a low price of silver, if permanent, would not only not be prejudicial to Mexico as a whole, but would conduce to its ultimate benefit by the stimulus it would afford to the development of its immense agricultural resources."

Yes. The losses from the payments that have to be made in gold are a comparatively speaking fixed quantity, while the gain to the people from cheap silver will yield wide-spreading consequential benefits far beyond the reach of calculation. This, too, is the case as regards India; we require for it a Government which can appreciate, and act up to, this view of the situation.

MYSORE

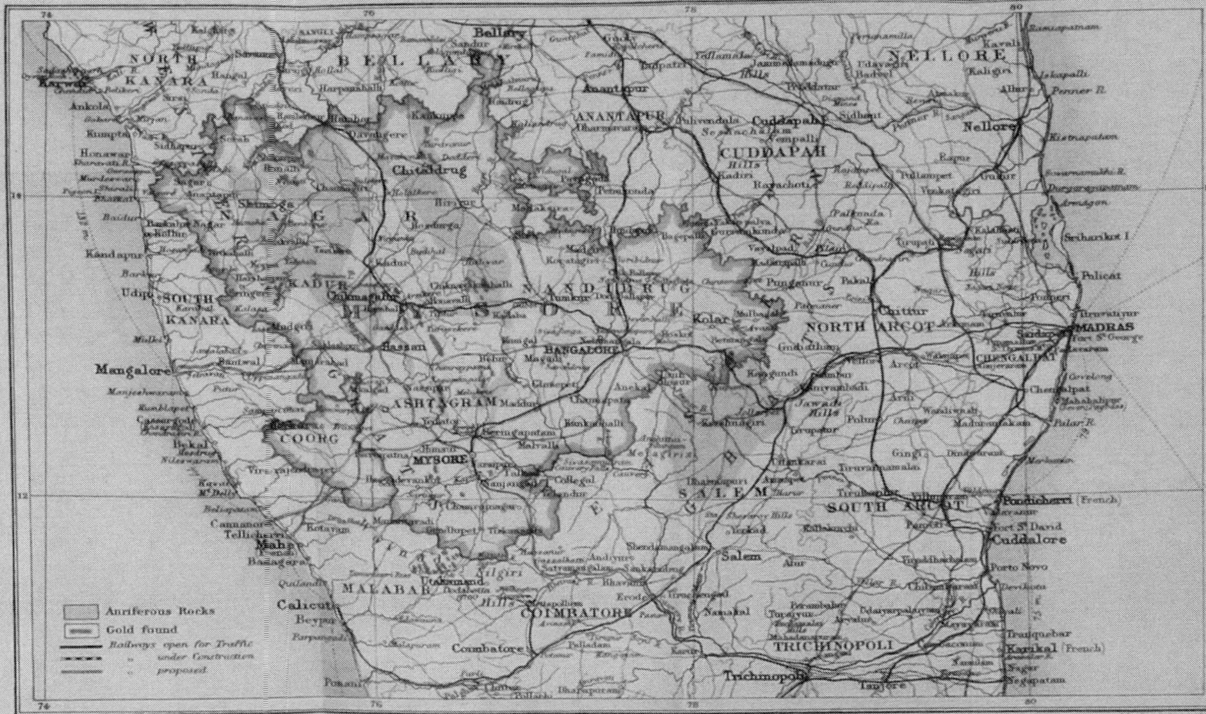

NORTH KANARA
BELLARY
NELLORE
Bellary
Anantapur
ANANTAPUR
Cuddapah
CUDDAPAH
Nellore
Chitaldrug
Shimoga
NAGAR
KADUR
NANDIDRUG
SOUTH KANARA
Mangalore
Hassan
BANGALORE
Kolar
NORTH ARCOT
Chittur
MADRAS
CHENGALPAT
ASHTAGRAM
COORG
MYSORE
SALEM
Salem
SOUTH ARCOT
Pondicherri (French)
Cuddalore
MALABAR
Calicut
COIMBATORE
Coimbatore
TRICHINOPOLI
Trichinopoli
Tanjore
Karikal (French)
Auriferous Rocks
Gold found
Railways open for Traffic
" under Construction
" proposed